D1552013

JEFFERSON AND WINE
Model of Moderation

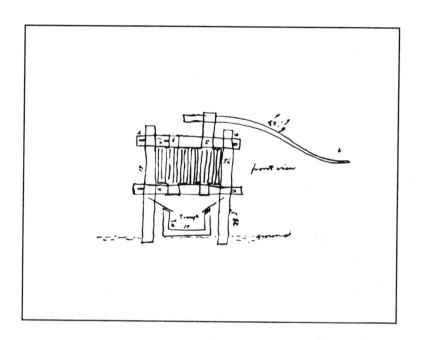

Edited by
R. de Treville Lawrence III
Second Edition
Revised and Enlarged

JEFFERSON AND WINE: Model of Moderation; published by The Vinifera Wine Growers Association, Inc., P.O. Box P, The Plains, Virginia. 22171. Tel. 703/754-8564.

Printed in the United States of America.

ISBN 0-922893-00-3

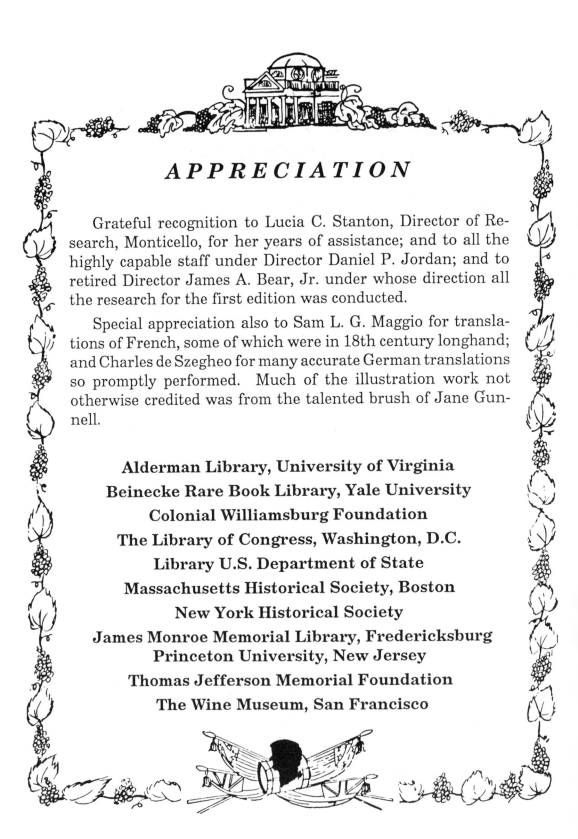

APPRECIATION

Grateful recognition to Lucia C. Stanton, Director of Research, Monticello, for her years of assistance; and to all the highly capable staff under Director Daniel P. Jordan; and to retired Director James A. Bear, Jr. under whose direction all the research for the first edition was conducted.

Special appreciation also to Sam L. G. Maggio for translations of French, some of which were in 18th century longhand; and Charles de Szegheo for many accurate German translations so promptly performed. Much of the illustration work not otherwise credited was from the talented brush of Jane Gunnell.

Alderman Library, University of Virginia

Beinecke Rare Book Library, Yale University

Colonial Williamsburg Foundation

The Library of Congress, Washington, D.C.

Library U.S. Department of State

Massachusetts Historical Society, Boston

New York Historical Society

James Monroe Memorial Library, Fredericksburg
Princeton University, New Jersey

Thomas Jefferson Memorial Foundation

The Wine Museum, San Francisco

PREFACE

When Thomas Jefferson was nominated to be the third President of the United States, he gave his profession as "farmer". He built on a farm, and during his absences from Monticello, he regularly longed to be there where he could supervise experiments in premium wine growing with the goal of making his own wine. Who better than he, could write the Preface:

"Wine from long habit has become an indispensable for my health. . .

"No occupation is so delightful to me as the cultivation of the earth. . .

"I rejoice, as a moralist, at the prospect of a reduction of the duties on wine. . .It is an error to view a tax on that. . .as merely a tax on the rich. . .

"No nation is drunken where wine is cheap; and none sober, where the dearness of wine substitutes ardent spirits as the common beverage. . ."

Th Jefferson

CONTENTS

ILLUSTRATIONS

INTRODUCTION

This volume is an enlarged version of the very successful Jefferson And Wine *(192p; 1976). Both were assembled and edited by the indefatigable Vinifera Wine Growers Association of The Plains, Virginia, whose contributions to the renaissance of grape culture in the old Dominion compare favorably with those of the subject of this study, Thomas Jefferson of Monticello, an early and active participant.*

Historically Jefferson's niche as one of America's first distinguished viticulturists remains unchallenged, despite the fact that he was never able to bottle a varietal wine using his own grapes — an accomplishment of the Editor's in 1970.

Jefferson most probably met his first wine at the Communion Rail; at the family table, or at a roadside tavern. His early preferences varied little from those of his peers whose choices ranged no farther than the heavily fortified Maderias, Sherries, Ports (which he later detested as detrimental to ones health), or perhaps undistinguished clarets.

It was the peripatetic Philip Mazzei, the ambivalent Florentine viticulturist, wine merchant, and neighbor at nearby Colle, who introduced Jefferson to the nuances of fine wine and methods of grape culture. His palate was honed to sharpness in the Parisian salons and particularly during his extensive tour in 1787 of the outstanding French vineyards. By 1790 Jefferson was an acknowledged connoiseur who readily dispensed advice to all who sought his counsel. He was so emersed in the subject that all but six lines in his lengthy congratulatory letter to James Monroe on his elevation to the presidency dealt with those wines most suitable for public entertaining. Eight years of presidential levees and soirees supplied from the President's House cellar played a large role in Jefferson's advice to Monroe and told him a great deal about his countrymen's preferences for strong drink, a fact that disturbed him.

No president ever assembled a finer or more diverse cellar. In addition to a copious flow of champagne (mousseux, non-mousseux; red and white) his guests were treated to unlimited *servings of Sherry, Madeira, Port, superior growths of Bordeaux and Burgundy, Sauterne, White Hermitage, and Portuguese and Italian varieties. Only the German Hock seems to have been absent. Over a period of eight years the cellar cost the chief executive about $16,000 of his salary of $200,000.*

This collection did not necessarily reflect Jefferson's personal tastes. After four years in France and twelve years in public office he still preferred the lighter French and Italian varieties which he loosely described as "silky" – dry wines "with a little sweetness." As he aged, less expensive and sweeter wines such as Clairette de Limoux, Ledanon, Frontignan, Lunel dominated, probably because of considered "restorative qualities."

No matter the content of his glass, Jefferson by an admission never took more than three glasses (small in those days) cut with water at a sitting. He followed the English custom of taking his wine after dinner, a practice not favored by his mentors the French. The only account of Jefferson's consumption took place at a Charlottesville reception for Lafayette where he drank two glasses after a particularly stirring toast.

As a viticulturist Jefferson was enthusiastic if not successful. After learning from Mazzei, then the French, then the printed page, and finally by corresponding with others of like interests such as Peter Legaux and Major John Adlum; however little that was done in the Monticello vineyards, where numerous varieties of grapes were planted, ever rewarded him with success.

The conclusion is that Thomas Jefferson was a better oenologist than a viticulturist. The following pages will render sufficient grounds for each gentle reader to reach his or her own conclusions on this yet another of the great man's many facets.

James A. Bear, Jr.
Director, Monticello, Retired
Ivy, Virginia

Copy of an original drawing inscribed, "Albert Rosenthal after Terra-Cotta by Houdon", Thomas Jefferson Memorial Foundation, Monticello, Charlottesville, Virginia.

Photograph by Edwin S. Roseberry

CHRONOLOGY
of THOMAS JEFFERSON

1743, April 13	(New Style Calendar) born at Shadwell, Goochland (now Albemarle) County, Virginia.
1760-1762	Student at William & Mary College.
1762-1767	Studied law under George Wythe.
1767	Admitted to the bar.
1769	Building at Monticello begun.
1769-1776	Member of the Virginia House of Burgesses.
1770	Shadwell burned; November 26 moved to Monticello.
1772, January 1	Married the widow Martha Wayles Skelton.
1774	Became owner of the Natural Bridge.
1775	Attended the Continental Congress.
1776	Drafted the Declaration of Independence.
1776-1779	Member of the Virginia House of Burgesses. Act for Religious Freedom drafted.
1778	Bill outlawing importation of slaves to Virginia enacted; a measure long advocated by Jefferson.
1779-1781	Governor of Virginia
1782, Sept. 6	His wife died.
1784-1789	In France as minister and commercial representative.
1785	Notes on Virginia printed. Revised Code of Virginia, on which Jefferson worked, enacted.
1790-1793	Secretary of State under Washington.
1797-1801	Vice-President of United States under John Adams.
1801-1809	President of the United States.
1803	Louisiana Territory purchased.
1819	University of Virginia chartered.
1825	University of Virginia opened; Jefferson as first Rector.
1826, July 4	Died at Monticello.

Replica of desk on which the Declaration of Independence was written.

Monticello   212745

Jefferson's Key To His Cellar,
His Own Wine Glass, And Slider

The huge key to the cellar's heavy, reinforced door must have been closely guarded. His own wheel-engraved wine glass holds little more than three ounces, and the "slider" bottle coaster of silver and fruitwood bears his engraved signature. On display at the Thomas Jefferson Visitors Center, Monticello.

Courtesy T.J. Memorial Foundation
Photo H. Andrew Johnson

THE OENOLOGIST OF MONTICELLO
Music, Art, Architecture, Poetry, Agriculture And Wine

By William S. Howland[1]

Thomas Jefferson is one of the most splendored men of American history. All of us have studied in school about his achievements in playing a major role in bringing our nation from wistful thinking to factual existence and in making the principles of democracy work in the early years of the republic.

Many of us who live in the Southern states have heard demagogs seeking public office shout for seemingly endless hours about what they called "Jeffersonian Democracy"—and which often had little or no community with Jefferson's political thinking and action. And I feel reasonably certain he would have been as bored by and disgusted with this ranting rhetoric as we have been.

Jefferson is recognized around the world as one of the prime movers of the American revolution. He is famed as the author of the Declaration of Independence which the tall, red headed Virginian wrote at the age of 33. He is acclaimed for his outstanding diplomacy as Minister to France, 1785-89...from which he went on to serve with distinction as Secretary of State. Then his political career climaxed when he became our third President for two terms, 1801-1809.

Politically, Jefferson stands high among our Presidents. Perhaps the greatest of his efforts in the Presidency was the Louisiana Purchase which brought to our young country a vast quantity of land beyond estimable value and opened the door to our expansion westward — an expansion he sparked with the Lewis and Clarke expedition.

What kind of man was Jefferson and how did he attain so much?

Perhaps here is the answer — in his common place book, Jefferson included a favorite quotation from Euripides (as reported in "Time" magazine's Bicentennial issue): "For with slight efforts how should one obtain great results? It is foolish even to desire it."

Those few words aptly characterize Jefferson himself. He never did anything lightly or half heartedly, and all his life the young author of the Declaration made great efforts to obtain great results.

Another well known Jefferson splendor is his architecture of buildings. He helped design Washington as the Capital of the U.S., and was the first President to be inaugurated there. He was one of the founders of the University of Virginia and designed its campus which is one of the most beautiful, probably the most beautiful in America. He was the architect of his home, Monticello, which continues to delight the eyes of all who see it.

The list of Jefferson's political, architectural and philosophical splendors could continue almost endlessly.

But we are centering on a Jefferson splendor that is not so well known as the others —

This splendor is his leadersip as an oenologist and viticulturist — in which he was one of our nation's pioneers, if not the first.

How did this angle of his thought and action come about? Probably the foundation for his pioneering and eminence in these arts lay in the kind of life he lived as a young man. Again to quote "Time" magazine's Bicentennial edition: "A native Virginian, Jefferson, 33, shares with other wealthy tobacco planters a love of good food, good wine and fast horses." Then adds "Time", "unlike most of his neighbors in the Piedmont or Tidewater, however, Jefferson has been a lifelong student of natural philosophy and the arts, a man who reads easily in Greek, Latin, French and Italian, and who, when he can, still practices three hours a day on the violin."

A student of the Latin and Greek classics, he must have read many paeans in praise of wine, of its benefits to health and pleasure. He may have read the many lyrical lauds to wine in the "Rubaiyat of Omar Khayyam," such as:

"Come, fill the Cup and in the Fire of spring
The Winter Garment of Repentance fling
The Bird of Time has but a little way
To fly - and Lo! the bird is on the Wing."

or

"You know, my friends, how long since in my
House
For a new Marriage did I make Carouse;
Divorced old barren reason from my Bed
And took the daughter of the Vine to Spouse."

Jefferson would not go the way of Omar, because, never, so far as can be learned in his enjoyment and culture of wine did he reject Reason.

But it is a safe bet that Jefferson would go along with the following (and probably did many times with his lovely family at Monticello):

"A Book of verses underneath the Bough
A jug of Wine, A Loaf of Bread — and Thou
Beside me singing in the Wilderness
Oh, Wilderness were Paradise enow."

And with his love of gardens and vineyards, he doubtless would have been pleased with the following epitapth from Omar:

"Ah with the Grape my fading life provide
And wash the body whence the life has died
And lay me, shrouded in the Living Leaf
By some not unfrequented garden side."

To use a current expression, we do not know what turned Jefferson on in his ardent commendation and study of wine, but whatever did, also did a very good turn for the appreciation and production of wine in the early years of our nation.

It is no exaggeration to say that along with being author of the document which proclaimed our independence politically, Jefferson was a leading originator of viticulture in America and laid the foundations for the modern independence of our great and growing production of wines of distinction. Jefferson would be pleased to see that we no longer have to bow our heads in submission to the "first quality" of European wines. We can now enjoy the fruits of our home grown grapes.

That is an achievement of no mean horticultural and industrial stature.

Whenever Jefferson travelled, especially during the years when he was Minister to France, he was a keen observer of the production and merchandising of wines.

Probably his most philisophical observation was expressed in a letter to Monsieur de Neuville, Dec. 13, 1818 (Appendix A):

"No nation is drunken where wine is cheap; and none sober, where the dearness of wine substitutes ardent spirits as the common beverage. It is, in truth, the only antidote to the bane of whiskey. Fix the duty at the rate of other merchandise, and we can drink wine here as cheap as we do grog, and who will not prefer it? It's extended use will carry health and comfort to a much enlarged circle."

EQUAL TARIFFS FOR WINES

In order to achieve his objectives, Jefferson would not shy away from going to any pains and detail to accomplish the task. He clearly saw that high duties were pricing wine beyond the reach of the average wage earner who was turning to rum and hard spirits to the detriment of many. He firmly believed in wine as a natural medicine for health, and in order to make it more readily available on the open market he often, while President, advised his Secretary of the Treasury, Albert Gallatin, on more reasonable tariffs. After what must have been a personal exhaustive study of all the wines imported into the United Sates, their quality, their prices, and undoubtedly compiled by himself, he proposed to Secretary Gallatin[2], June 3, 1807:

"I gave you some time ago, a project of a more equal tariff on wines than that which now exists. But in that I yielded considerably to the faulty classification of them in our law. I have now formed one with attention, according to the best information I possess, classing them more rigorously. I am persuaded that were the duty on cheap wines put on the same ratio with the dear, it would wonderfully enlarge the field of those who use wine, to the expulsion of whiskey. The introduction of a very cheap wine (St. George) into my neighborhood, within two years past, has quadrupled in that time the number of those who keep wine, and will ere long increase them tenfold. This would be a great gain to the treasury, and to the sobriety of our country. I will here add my tariff wherein you will be able to choose any rate of duty you please and to decide whether it will or not, on a fit occasion, be proper for legislative action. Affectionate salutations." (See following page for chart of Jefferson's proposed wine tariffs).

ADVICE TO TRAVELERS

Jefferson was loyal to his friends and went to extra trouble to assist them on occasions. As anyone might do today for an acquaintance visiting a country for the first time, he wrote travelling notes for two young men, Rutledge and Shippen, on their way through Europe, June 3, 1788, whose fathers were Governor of South Carolina and a prominent Philadelphia surgeon respectively:

"...When one calls in the taverns for the *vin du pays* (local wines), they give what is natural and unadulterated and cheap: when *vin étrangere* (foreign wine) is called for, it only gives a pretext for charging an extravagant price for an unwholesome stuff, very often of their own brewery. The people you will naturally see the most of will be tavern keepers, *valets de place*, and postilions. These are the hackneyed rascals of every country. Of course they must never be considered when we calculate the national character..."[3]

Although he studied, observed, and himself experimented with many growing things that produced food, Jefferson sometimes made errors in judging what plants and trees might do well in new habitats. In a letter to Monsieur Lasteyrie[4], Jefferson wrote from Washington while he was President, his belief that the sugar maple tree would do well in France, that

Jefferson's Tariffs*

	Cost per gallon	15%	20%	25% being the average of present duties	30%	35%		Present Duty
Tokay, Cape, Malmesey, Hock	$4.00	$0.60	$0.80	$1.00	$1.20	$1.40	Tokay, Malmesay, Hock,	45 cents which is 11⅓% 58 cents which is 14½% 35 cents which is 25%
Champagne, Burgundy, Claret (1), Hermitage	2.75	41½	.55	.68¾	.82½	.96⅓	Champagne, Burgundy Claret, Hermitage	$0.45 which is 16½% 35 cents which is 12½%
London particular Maderia	2.20	.33	.44	.55	.66	.77		58 cents which is 26½%
All other Maderia	1.80	.27	.36	.45	.54	.63		50 cents which is 27½%
Pacharetti, Sherry	1.50	22½	.30	37½	.45	52½	Pacharetti Sherry	23 cents which is 15% 40 cents which is 26½%
The wines of Modoc and Grave not before mentioned, those of Palus, Coterotie, Condrieu, Moselle (2)	1.25	18¾	25	31¼	37½	43¾		35 cents which is 28%
St Lucar and all of Portugal	.80	.12	.16	.20	.24	.28	St. Lucar Other Spanish	40 cents which is 50% 23 cents which is 28¾%
Sicily, Teneriffe, Fayal, Malaga, St. George and other western islands	.67	.10	.13	.16¾	.20	.23	Sicily Teneriffe, etc.	23 cents which is 34% 28 cents which is 41%
All other wines							in bottles in casks	35 cents, often 400% 23 cents, often 400%

"(1) The term Claret should be abolished, because unknown in the country where it is made, and because indefinite here. The four crops should be enumerated here instead of Claret, and all other wines to which that appellation has been applied, should fall into the ad valorem class. The four crops are Lafitte, Latour and Margauz, in Medoc, and Hautbrion, in Grave."

"(2) Blanquefort, Calon, Leoville, Cantenac, etc. are wines of Medoc, Barsac, Sauterne, Beaume, Preignac, St. Bris, Carbonien, Langon, Podensac, etc. are of Grave. All these are of the second order, being next after the four crops."

*"Writings of Thomas Jefferson," 1907, Bergh, Washington, D.C.

sugar cane would not grow anywhere in the United States, and expressed doubt about the wine vine doing well here. He was wrong on all three,

"Sir,—I have duly received your favor of March 28th, and with it your treatises on the culture of sugar cane and cotton plant in France. The introduction of new cultures, and especially of objects of leading importance to our comfort is certainly worth the attention of every government, and nothing short of actual experiment should discourage an essay of which any hope can be entertained. Till that is made, the result is open to conjecture; and I should certainly conjecture that the sugar cane could never become an article of profitable culture in France. We have within the ancient limits of the United States, a great extent of country which brings the orange to advantage, but not a foot in which sugar cane can be matured. France, within its former limits, has but two small spots, (Olivreles and Hieres) which brings the orange in open air, and a *jortiori*, therefore, none proper for the cane. I should think the maple-sugar more worthy of experiment. There is no part of France of which the climate would not admit this tree. I have never seen a reason why every farmer should not have a sugar orchard, as well as an apple orchard. The supply of sugar for his family would require as little ground, and the process of making it as easy as that of cider. Mr. Micheaux, your botanist here could send you plants as well as seeds, in any quantity from the United States. I have no doubt the cotton plant will succeed in some of the southern parts of France. Whether its culture will be as advantageous as those they are now engaged in, remains to be tried. We could, in the United States, make as great a variety of wines as are made in Europe, not exactly of the same kinds, but doubtless as good. Yet I have ever observed to my countrymen, who think its introduction important, that a laborer cultivating wheat, rice, tobacco, or cotton here, will be able with the proceeds, to purchase double the quantity of wine he could make. Possibly the same quantity of land and labor in France employed on the rich produce of your Southern counties, would purchase double the quantity of the cotton they would yield there. This however may prove otherwise on trial and, and therefore it is worthy the trial. In general, it is a truth that if every nation will employ itself in what it is fittest to produce, a greater quantity will be raised of the things contributing to human happiness..."

CORRECT MANNER

One of the fascinating facets of reading the vast amount of Jeffersonia, is the amusing and correct manner that always came through in his writings. Few Colonial writers ever expressed themselves so well, and so accurately, and in such informative detail. An example of this relating to a lost order for wines to the long-time U.S. Consul Stephen Cathalan at Marseilles was written by Jefferson at Monticello February 1, 1816;[5]

"My dear Sir and Friend,—I received yesterday your favor of Nov. 29, from which I learn with much mortification of (the palate at least) that my letter of the third of July has never got to your hands. It was confided to the Secretary of State's office. Regrets are now useless, and the proper object to supply its place. It related generally to things friendly, to things political, etc., but the material part was a request of some particular wines which were therein specified.

"1. White Hermitage of the growth of M. Jourdan; not of the dry kind, but what we call silky, which in your letter just received you say are called doux. But by our term *silky* we do not mean *sweet,* but sweetish in the smallest degree only. My taste in this is the reverse of Mr. Butler's who you say likes the dry and sparkling, I the *non mousseux* and *un peu doucereux.*

"2. Vin de Nice, as nearly as possible of the quality of that sent me by Mr. Sasserno formerly, whose death, by the bye, I had not heard of and much regret.

"3. Vin de Roussillon. I used to meet with this at the best tables of Paris, where it was drunk after the repast, as *vin de liqueur.* It was a little higher colored than Madeira, near as strong and dry, and of fine flavor. I am not certain of the particular name, but that of Rivesalte runs in my head. If, from what you know of the Rivesalte it should answer this description nearly, then we may be sure this was the wine; if it does not, you will probably be able to know what wine of Roussillon corresponds with the qualities I describe.

"I requested that after paying the 50 lbs. of macaroni out of the 200 dollars, and reserving what would pay all charges till shipped, about a fifth of the residue should be laid out in Hermitage, and the remaining four-fifths in *Vins de Nice* (and?) Roussillon equally. Send to any port from Boston to the Chesapeake inclusive, but to Norfolk or Richmond of preference, if the conveyance occurs. If addressed to the Collector of the Port, he will receive and forward them to Richmond, which is at the head of the tidewater of James River on which I live, and from whence it comes by boat navigation. I suppose you can never be long without vessels at Marseilles bound to some of our ports above described. Were it to be otherwise the wines might come through the canal of Langeudoc to Mr. Lee, our consul at Bordeaux, but this would increase risk and expense, and is only mentioned as a *pis-aller,* and left entirely to your judgment.

"The political speculations of my letter of July 3 are not worth repeating because the events on which they were hazarded have changed backwards..."

A realist as well as a romanticist, philosophical but practical, Jefferson near the end of his days was in debt. The firm, businesslike attitude he could assume however, was expressed in a letter to a Philadelphia merchant, May 18, 1783, written from Monticello. The letter[6] to Simon Nathan also reveals the unbelievable fiscal problems of the day concerned with bartering tobacco for wine, extremely slow transportation during which rampant inflation was driving up costs, and the prices had to be translated from Continental pounds to American dollars,

"Sir,—On my arrival at home I turned my attention to the transaction between us for wine, which was the subject of your letter of Jan. 16. I was to pay for the two quarter casks by our original agreement 3000 lb. of tobacco or it's price. The current

price of tobo. in Philadelphia at the date of your draft on me
was 60 continental or 200 Doll. the hundred. So that the 3000
lb. of tobo. was then worth 6000 Dollars. For this sum precisely
you drew in favor of Mr. Rose (as indeed there could be no
reason for your drawing less than your whole demand) and I
paid the draught on sight. No time intervened between the
date of your draught and my paiment, but while it was on the
road from Philadelphia to Richmond, and if, during that, another month happened to enter, it is not sufficient ground for
opening the account again. The difference of exchange in
Virginia from July to Aug. 1781. was that of 65. and 70. for
one. So that on the whole the balance appearing due your
account is the result of a double error; first the charging me
3000 Continental instead of 1800 for the wine; and secondly
the extending the debit at one exchange and the credit at
another. I hope that on revising the matter you will find the
state of it contained in this and my letter on Jan. 18. to be
satisfactory, and that at the time of furnishing the wine you
drew for the whole sum; which was paid. I am sir Your very
humble servt.,"

Jefferson loved his family, and after the loss of his wife after
ten years of happy marriage, he exerted his interests to educate
and make the most comfortable home possible for his two
daughters Martha and Maria. This warm letter[7] expressing
his fatherly feelings, relates also to a shipment of 500 bottles
of wine and attempts to coordinate horse, mule and carriage
travel when communicaitons were very primitive,

                              " Philadelphia Aug. 18.93.

"My Dear Martha,

Maria & I are scoring off the weeks which seperate us from
you, they wear off slowly, but time is sure tho' slow. Mr. D.
Randolph left us three days ago, he went by the way of
Presquisle & consequently, will not enrapture Mrs. Randolph
till the latter end of the month. I wrote to Mr. Randolph
sometime ago to desire he would sent off Tom Shackleford or
Jupiter or anybody else on the 1st of September with the horse
he has been so kind as to procure for me to meet at Georgetown

(at Shuter's tavern) a servant whom I shall send from hence on the same day with Tarquin, to exchange them, Tarquin to go to Monticello & the other come here to aid me in my journey. the messenger to ride a mule & lead the horse. I mention these things now, lest my letter should have miscarried. I received information yesterday of 500 bottles of wine arrived for me at Baltimore. I desired them sent to Richmond to Colo. Gamble to be forwarded to Monticello, they will be followed the next week with some things from hence. Should any waggons of the neighborhood be going down they might enquire for them, with the things sent from hence will go clothes for the servants to replace those sent last winter, which I did not conclude to be inrecoverably lost till Mr. Randolph's last letter. my blessings to your little one, love to you all, and friendly how dy'es to my good neighbors. Adieu.

Yours affectionately

Th : Jefferson"

Moving the wine scene from 1786 to 1988, we can see that Jefferson all through his very active life in politics, in diplomacy, in education, in architecture, in music, in agriculture, as he met with kings and commoners, always was interested in everything pertaining to the production, merchandising and enjoyment of wine.

Assayed in modern terms, he was clearly the greatest public relationist during the Colonial period for wine. Along with his other many splendors he richly deserves meriting the title of Oenologist of Monticello. And as historians during the next century study his papers, they will smile at his list of baggage shipped from France in September 1789, where, next to "...19. box. Harpsichord" is "20. Hamper, 12 Sauterne. 12 Rochegude. 12 Frontig. 12 Monrach. 12 Champ...."

References:

1. Deceased, Mr. Howland was founder and chief for 17 years, Southern News Bureau, "Time & Life", Atlanta.

2. "Writings of Thomas Jefferson", A. E. Bergh, 1903, Vol. 11, p. 216.

3. "Papers of Thomas Jefferson", Boyd, Princeton University.

4. Bergh, op cit, V. 12, p. 90.

5. Bergh, V. 18, p. 292.

6. Boyd, op cit, V. 6, p. 270.

7. Alderman Library, University of Virginia.

"QUALITY NO MATTER THE WINE"[1]

By James A. Bear, Jr.[2]

From the early years of his manhood, Jefferson, like his peers, drank the British-supplied standbys of Port and Maderia– wines perhaps more heavily fortified then than now.

Philip Mazzei's arrival in Albemarle county in 1773 was the direct result of Jefferson's persuasive powers and his very generous offices. The latter consisted of a gift of 193 acres of prime farm land.

Jefferson valued highly his association with the enterprising Italian and its influence was particularly strong in at least three ways. First it sparked his interest in grape culture to a degree not before exhibited. Second it turned his preferences for table wine away from the old standbys to the more sophisticated and unfortified varieties. And third, it was the first step in the revolution of his tastes and knowledge.

This is the revolution that reached its peak in 1789, after four years of apprenticeship in France. Once in Paris he quickly adapted his bucolic tastes to those of the Parisian aristocrats and Philosophers with whom he associated. It was here that he became *en rapport* with the spectrum of great French table wines, with her finest dessert wines, and the light after dinner *vin de liqueurs* from the south of France. His revolution was incomplete until he visited in 1787 the vineyards of Burgundy and Bordeaux where he tasted in their natural locales their famous vintages. No American of his time could match his experience or the resulting expertise.

As long as he could afford them, Jefferson drank only the finest wines which were always procured from the producing vineyards, most of which he knew first hand. Quality no matter the wine, rather than alcoholic content, was always an object in stocking his cellars, and every effort was made to introduce his countrymen to the lighter and better wines of France and Italy in place of the stronger ones of the Iberian Peninsula.

Retirement from the presidency in 1809 marked the end of more than half a century of public service. It also meant that he no longer received $25,000 a year salary and could not continue to import the best wines. It would now be the more modestly priced varieties, but still through agents abroad. It was not until late in life when in very straitened circumstances that he called on American merchants for some of his wine.

Jefferson never succeeded in the "Great Desideratum" of making a good wine at Monticello and for a number of reasons. 1. Once Antonio Giannini and the other Italian workmen inherited from Mazzei departed there was no one capable of overseeing the vineyard. 2. There were never a sufficient number of varietal grapes of a single species. This was certainly the case in 1807 when the first seven terraces of the Southwest Vineyard, an area of approximately 130 feet by 100 feet, were planted with at least six different grape varieties. The same held true for the Northeast Vineyard, an area of approximately 90 feet by 100 feet in whose seventeen terraces there were fifteen different varieties. Jefferson was not at home enough before 1809 to oversee the culture of the grapes.

It is my considered opinion that following Giannini's departure not a single bottle of varietal wine was made at Monticello, if indeed he ever made any, and secondly Monticello's best grapes were yet another table delicacy

"FADDIST" WITH WINE

It is the opinion of Mrs. Lucia Stanton, Monticello's very able Research Director, and mine, that Jefferson was essentially a faddist with wine in the same way he was a faddist about other things, namely inventions, agricultural crops, etc. For example, in 1813, a particularly pale unfortified sherry pleased him so much that he drank nothing else and clearly avowed that he could not face the prospects of being deprived of his daily dose.

He was certainly ambivalent about wines. In 1804 it was a Montipulciano, a light red Tuscan wine, that caught his fancy and caused him to write that "no wine pleases me more." later the same year he was attracted to a "white Hermitage virgin" which he classified as the "most excellent wine." In 1807 it was a red Bellet, referred to by Jefferson as *"vin de Nice"*, which he praised as "the most elegant everyday wine in the world." Eleven years later his ardor for the Bellet had not cooled when he wrote of it as "the most delicious wine I ever tasted and still little known outside France."

In 1806 he was very complimentary of an Italian Nebiolo, a sparkling wine of the Italian Piedmont, which was described as "superlatively fine" and "entirely admired here [Washington]." One last allusion, this time to a North Carolina scuppernong, labeled it as "exquisite," but just so long as it was preserved from the "barbarous practice "of adulteration with brandy.

"SILKY" PREFERRED

We might summarize his personal preferences as generally for a dry "non-mosseaux wine with a little sweetness," or as he phrased it, "silky, or sweetish, in the smallest degree only."

A hurried review of the contents of his last cellar is indicative of the final turn of his palate, which began, as you will recall, with the well-fortified Madeiras and Ports, then to the more sophisticated table wines of France, then to the lesser Italian and French varieties, and finally to those wines indigenous to southern France.

Jefferson very definitely credited wine with medicinal properties and this is evident in a number of situations. For example when ordering a cask of Lisbon Termo he opined that "wine from long habit has become indespensible for my health, which is now suffering from its disuse." Again in 1823 he wrote a neighbor; "Th: Jefferson with his friendly respects to Mrs. Lewis asks her acceptance of some wine which he hopes may be serviceable for her stomach. The Muscat is thought remarkably so, but not knowing whether she would prefer that or Madeira he has sent both."

An inventory of his cellar (he kept no cellar book) taken in 1824 and recorded in his Memorandum Book, and before its depletion by the lavish entertainment during Lafayette's visit, is strong evidence of his preferences at eighty-one years of age.

The wines included a

Lednanon. A port-like wine from the Pont du Gard area of southern France. 187 bottles.

Claret. A red wine supplied by M. Bergasse, whose *chaix* Jefferson had visited in Marseilles in 1787, and who produced this claret by mixing inexpensive imitations of expensive Bordeaux wines that Jefferson swore by. 142 bottles.

Blanquette de Limoux. A light white sparkling wine. 49 bottles.

Claret. From Richmond, Va.; no further description. 22 bottles. Muscat de Rivesalte. A dry *vin de liqueur.* or the superior Roussillon of Rivesalte, or both. 186 bottles.

Total bottles 586.

WINE AFTER DINNER

Before concluding here are some personal notes about Jefferson's serving and consumption of wine: After his retirement to Monticello no wine was served at dinner until after the cloth had been removed. Cider and malt beverages were drunk during the meal.

By his own admission, Jefferson limited himself to three or four glasses at dinner and "not a drop at any other time." A granddaughter stated he halved each glass with water.

The only account of his actually seen drinking wine that I am aware of is that by a visitor, Benjamin Richardson, who attended the banquet in Charlottesville honoring Lafayette. He reported the fervor of the gathering was so great that the Presbyterian minister got a little high and during one toast Jefferson drank two glasses.

I will conclude with these statements.

Jefferson was firmly convinced that wine was a superior beverage. This is evident in a number of observations but none more than this made in 1823: "In countries which use ardent spirits drunkeness is the mortal vice; but those which make wine for common use you never see a drunkard."

This last statement concerns his prediction on the future of making wine in America and which is surely of interest here. This was voiced in 1822, "That as good wines will be made in America as in Europe, the scuppernon of North Carolina furnishes sufficient proof. The vine is congenial to every climate in Europe from Hungary to the Mediterranean, and will be found in the same temperatures here, wherever tried by intelligent vigerons [sic]. The culture, however, is more desirable for domestic use than profitable as an occupation for market."

References:

[1]**Paper read at the 13th Annual wine Growing Seminar, Highbury Vineyard, August 25, 1984, The Plains, Virginia 22171, tel. (703) 754-8564.**

[2]**Retired Director, Thomas Jefferson Memorial Foundation, preserving as a National Memorial Monticello, the home and burial place of Thomas Jefferson, P. O. Box 316, Charlottesville, Virginia 22902.**

JEFFERSON'S ITALIAN VIGNERON:
Philip Mazzei, Revolutionary Patriot

By H. Christopher Martin[1]

"Mazzei...fixed on these South West mountains [central Virginia], having a South East aspect, and abundance of lean and meagre spots of stony and red soil, without sand, resembling extremely the Cote of Burgundy from Chambertin to Montrachet where the famous wines of Burgundy are made..." Jefferson.

While Thomas Jefferson and his colleagues of the House of Burgesses in Williamsburg were winding up the 1773 legislative session on a day in November, a ship bearing a small band of Italians was entering the Chesapeake Bay. Their leader, Philip Mazzei, was questioning the pilot about the Burgesses. This group of vignerons (wine growers), for such they were, was headed for Augusta County in the Valley of Virginia, or so they believed, to begin the planting of grape vines and olive trees which they had brought with them in accordance with plans Mazzei had worked out in London. They came almost midway in the long stream of vignerons from Europe which began with Frenchmen at Jamestown in 1610 and which continues to this day.

Mazzei was not the sort of man one would expect to lead a group of peasants to the new world. By the age of forty-three he had already been a physician in Turkey, a merchant in London, and a horticulturist who traveled extensively in Europe. He showed great versatility even for those days of men of wide talents. Before twenty years were to elapse, Mazzei would also have become a political activist, a linguist, a diplomatic agent, a historian and a royal adviser as well as a naturalized citizen of Virginia and of Poland. Mazzei's natural talents and liberal political views coupled with charm, wit and intelligence were bound to assure his acceptance among that remarkable group of men in Virginia then beginning to take steps which would lead to the American Revolution.

FLORENCE WINE MERCHANT FAMILY

Philip Mazzei was born on Christmas Day in 1730 at Poggioa-Caiano, near Florence Italy, into a family of merchants and brandy distillers. He went off to medical school at the age of sixteen but withdrew before graduation at the request of school authorities for failure to attend religious services. This event naturally rankled Mazzei and doubtless led to his warm embrace of Thomas Jefferson, with his love of religious freedom. Mazzei's failure to finish medical school did not, however, prevent his journeying to Smyrna (now Izmir), Turkey, at the age of twenty-two as a physician associated with a European who had an established practice there. Mazzei remained in Smyrna for about two and a half years, when he gave up the practice permanently and left for London to embark upon a career of nearly twenty years as a wine merchant and an importer of olive oil, cheese, lemon tree shoots, candied fruits and silks.

As a merchant in London, Mazzei met Benjamin Franklin in 1767, who introduced him to Thomas Adams, a businessman there. Adams, in turn, introduced Mazzei to many of the Virginians then living in London, and Mazzei began selling them goods for shipment to the wealthy Virginia planters. Franklin and Adams urged Mazzei to go to Virginia, where he would find a "well governed colony." Adams believed Virginia was a fertile field for many Mediterranean types of plants and urged Mazzei to draw up plans for their culture there.

By 1771, Mazzei had developed a plan for Adams and a group of Virginians, including Thomas Jefferson, under which Mazzei was to import 10,000 grape vines from Champagne, Burgundy, Languedoc, Nice, Tuscany, Naples and Sicily as well as from Spain and Portugal. Of these, about 1,000 vines were to be selected for shipment to Virginia. Also envisaged were the selection of 4,000 olive trees, 1,000 fruit trees and the recruitment of 50 farmers skilled in these cultures. Of the farmers, five or six were to be particularly skilled in grafting and in making champagne. A few more were to be skilled in silk making. Terms of their engagement were to be four years, as was the custom in the Colony. The Plantation was to encompass 4,000 acres of new land "in the back part of Virginia where hills and risen ground favor the cultivation of the vine and olive trees,"

MAZZEI MEETS JEFFERSON AND WASHINGTON

Efforts to form a company in London to finance and carry out this grandiose plan were not successful, and by 1773 Mazzei had scaled down his plan to cover only ten vignerons and lesser amounts of plant material. Finding funds for this more modest venture, and with the permission of the Grand Duke Leopold of Tuscany, Mazzei selected his ten vignerons, collected spades, pruning knives, sickles, trees, cuttings and other necessities. On September 2, 1773 the group sailed from Leghorn. Mr. Adams, Mazzei's adviser in all matters, had earlier procured a grant of 5,000 acres from the Colony of Virginia for the scheme but Mazzei had wisely rejected the grant because it consisted of many small, scattered tracts.

Upon landing in Virginia after two months at sea, by pre-arrangement Mazzei went to the home of Francis Eppes, who lived near Williamsburg and was the brother-in-law of Thomas Jefferson. There Mazzei demonstrated his ability to meet easily with people and by the end of the first day in America had met George Washington, Thomas Jefferson, George Wythe and other important political figures. Thomas Adams had preceded Mazzei to Virginia from London and saw him in Williamsburg, where the two men arranged to set off for Augusta County to investigate the possibility of buying land adjacent to Adams' holdings for Mazzei's project. The journey to the Valley began only after Mazzei had fulfilled some commitments to ship grain and tobacco to Leghorn and to send a gift to Grand Duke Leopold of Tuscany — three deer and a live rattlesnake, fifteen years old and packed in sawdust. En route to Augusta County, Mazzei and Adams stopped off at Monticello for a rest.

COLLE CHOSEN AS VINEYARD SITE

The next morning, before the others were awake at Monticello, Jefferson took Mazzei out in the morning frost and showed him a 50-acre piece of cleared land adjoining his which contained a cottage judged adequate for Mazzei's vignerons.

Jefferson said the land could be bought and offered to assist Mazzei in his negotiations with the owner for its purchase. Jefferson also offered to make Mazzei a present of about 2,000 adjacent uncleared acres. As Mazzei recalled the event many years later in writing his memoirs[2], "when we returned, all the others had risen, and Mr. Adams, seeing Mr. Jefferson, said, 'I see in your face that you have taken him from me, and I expected it.' Jefferson without paying any attention to him, looked at the table and said 'Let's take breakfast, and later we'll arrange everything.' After breakfast he sent a letter to his brother-in-law, Mr. Eppes, in which he told him to send my men from the ship together with some things described in the note..."

When the vignerons arrived from Williamsburg a few days later, Jefferson was apparently intrigued with them and their *accoutrements*. He used his home-grown Italian on them with happy results. He had his blacksmith at Monticello copy their spades and other gardening implements. He also had the vigneron who was a tailor copy for him their Italian hunting coat. Soon after, Mr. Jefferson appeared in the coat, it was all the rage among Albemarle County's landed gentry, and the Italian tailor was a busy man indeed.

Mazzei soon put his men to work preparing land for his plantings and clearing additional land for plantings and for the construction of his house, to be called Colle. The house was situated atop a hill, thus accounting for its name. Mazzei wrote that Jefferson "burdened himself with the execution of this work," although there is no evidence that Jefferson designed Colle. Judging by descriptions of the house, it was simple and by no means in a class with the homes of wealthy planters like Jefferson. While the house was under construction Mazzei and his future wife, and step-daughter-to-be stayed at Monticello with Jefferson. Mazzei was not to marry for about another year. It was during their stay at Monticello that Jefferson began making entries in his *Garden Book* in Italian.

Colle, original house on the estate just north of Charlottesville, now owned by Ambassador and Mrs. Stanley Woodward. From an old watercolor sketch.

MAY FROST KILLS VINES

An unusually heavy and late frost the following May 5-6 froze all vines and young trees and caused many in the Charlottesville area to be leafless all summer. Mazzei wrote in his memoirs many years later that "the grapes were rather small and frost-bitten, and the joints of the new branches suffered; but the vine grew out again and produced about half the quality of grapes of the preceding year, and ripened at the same time." Since this great frost struck only six months after Mazzei's arrival in Virginia, he must have been writing about native vines or vines planted by others in previous years, unless Mazzei had brought vines of sufficient age to be in at least their second year of production. The fact of the frost is confirmed in Jefferson's *Garden Book.*

In spite of the frost, Mazzei said he found the Virginia soil and climate superior to that of Italy, and in a letter to George Washington later wrote that "...this country is better calculated than any other I am acquainted with for the produce of wine; but I cannot say the same in regard to oil and lemons." Moving ahead Mazzei brought over an additional six Tuscan vignerons in the spring of 1774, and in the fall drew up another proposal to form a company to raise grapes, make wine, and produce oil and silk. A subscription of 2,000 pounds sterling was raised among about a dozen men, including George Washington and Thomas Jefferson.

NATIVE VINES AND WINE

Being a horticulturist as well as a winemaker, Mazzei did not neglect investigating the growth of the native grapevines. He later reported that he "had learned from his men, who had explored the woods, that they had observed two hundred varieties of wild grapes. I myself had observed thirty-six on my own property — good, fair and bad. I chose six of the best to make two barrels of wine, one of which I saved for myself and the other I gave to my men. They did not drink the wine but sold it for a shilling a bottle."

The production of those two barrels of wine made Mazzei believe he had fallen upon a veritable Garden of Eden, for a year later he was writing the following, "In my opinion, when the country is populated in proportion to its extent, the best wine in the world will be made here. It must be remembered that the grapes from which I made the two barrels of wine were picked from the top of a tree in a very dense woods, and the vine had a tremendous number of branches. When I pulled the cork three months later, it was like the sparkling wine of Champagne. I do not believe that nature is so favorable to growing vines in any country as this. I measured two which were more than a foot and a half in circumference. The shoots of the lugliola grape produced vines of such size that my men wanted me to make wine. The first year they produced branches of such length that my good Vicenzo Rossi told me, 'Master, don't write of this to our village, because they won't believe it, and you'll pass for a liar...' "

POLITICS OVER VITICULTURE

During the time that Mazzei's men were preparing and planting the vineyard at Colle, he became increasingly concerned with political matters and began to absent himself frequently for visits to Williamsburg. He later wrote, "I have not said much about my agriculture, for I did not attend to it as I should have, because the great public issue occupied almost all of my time...(although) from time to time I went home to see how my orders were being carried out, and to issue new ones..." It was by then obvious that Mazzei had become more intoxicated by the revolutionary spirit than by his own alcoholic products. Thus, when news that British troops had landed at Hampton reached Albemarle County, it was not surprising that Mazzei and Jefferson joined a militia unit called the Independent Company and marched eastward, as privates, to meet the enemy. An Italian friend visiting at Colle and one of the vignerons also joined the small unit, which met a similar unit from neighboring Orange County containing young James Madison and his brother. These units never met the British troops in combat for they had reimbarked and sailed away. This the volunteers learned from Patrick Henry, the leader of a third group whom they had met *en route*. Henry then delivered an impromptu speech of gratitude, specifically mentioning the three Tuscan volunteers, which caused the vigneron to weep.

Although Mazzei returned to Colle after his abortive military venture, it was obvious that, as he himself wrote, he "was more occupied with national affairs than with [his] own." We therefore learn little of Mazzei's viticultural efforts during the early days of the American Revolution. Mazzei continued his political work, which seems to have been largely in support of others, especially Thomas Jefferson, with whom he began publishing a patriotic propaganda sheet. For this Mazzei was well remembered because immediately after the Declaration of Independence was adopted, Jefferson sat down at his desk in his lodgings in Philadelphia and made five copies of the Declaration for five close friends. Mazzei received one of those copies, which he later presented to Countess Noaille de Tess, whom Jefferson met in France and with whom he exchanged seeds over a span of 26 years. The Countess was an avid horticulturist and an aunt of Lafayette. That copy of the Declaration has disappeared.

As the war progressed, the need for money to finance it increased. Late in 1778, Thomas Jefferson, Patrick Henry, George Mason and others decided to send Mazzei over to Italy to borrow money from the Grand Duke of Tuscany, the friend of Mazzei's to whom he had earlier presented the deer and rattlesnake from Virginia. Early in 1779 Mazzei began making arrangements for his trip, including the rental of Colle. The place was easy to rent because of the presence in the area of a number of British and Hessian officers who were seeking quarters.

HESSIANS AT COLLE

About 4,000 British and Hessian troops who had surrendered at Saratoga had been sent first to Boston and then to the Charlottesville area as prisoners of war; they remained from January 1779 until October 1780. Among them was Baron von Riedesel, commanding general of the Hessian troops. In those days of more "civilized" warfare, von Riedesel was allowed to rent Colle from Mazzei and there to ensconce himself, his wife and daughters, adjutants, aides, chickens, pigs and horses. A contemporary observer wrote that the place resembled the home of a peasant more than the residence of a general. Von Riedesel's horses "in one week" trampled out the vines, and the "considerable vineyard" ceased to exist five years after Mazzei and his vignerons landed in America. Mazzei never mentioned this sad event in his memoirs.

Mazzei remained in Europe for four years, traveling as an agent for the State of Virginia and returning in November 1783. He had some difficulty in receiving compensation for his services in Europe but eventually received a settlement. Mazzei's step-daughter and her French husband arrived in Virginia early in 1784 and were given the use of Colle as well as a loan by Mazzei.

After visiting George Mason at Gunston Hall and George Washington at Mount Vernon in May 1785, Mazzei left Virginia for a sojourn in Europe, apparently to get away from his shrewish wife whose behavior Mazzei decribed in a memorandum as being "obstinate and indecent." Madame Mazzei, who seems to have been French, died some years later and is buried in the Jefferson family graveyard at Monticello. In quitting Virginia, Mazzei left behind Colle, with verbal instructions to rent it for twenty guineas or sell it for five hundred guineas, and to dispose of a house and lot in Richmond, and some bonds of the State of Virginia.

MAZZEI IN POLAND

After arrival in Europe, Mazzei began to roam about the continent, principally in France and Holland. He was frequently in dire financial straits and called for assistance from his friend, Jefferson, then American minister to France. To help ease his financial situation, Mazzei wrote the first history of the United States in the French language. He later became the "Intelligencer" in Paris for the King of Poland; his duties were those of an unofficial political reporter since Poland did not then have a diplomatic mission in Paris. Apparently pleased with Mazzei's performance, the King brought him to Warsaw as a royal adviser, a capacity in which he served until political developments in Poland caused Mazzei to recommend that the King abdicate the throne and take up residence in Italy. Mazzei, who believed rightly or wrongly that he had convinced the King to quit the throne, departed for Pisa to prepare the way for the King's retreat. The King never followed. After that last fling at political affairs, Mazzei remained permanently in Pisa, marrying a younger woman who bore him a daughter, his only child.

Mazzei never lost touch with his American friends nor flagged in his desire to serve the country he had so enthusiastically embraced and in the creation of which he participated after becoming a naturalized citizen of Virginia the year after his arrival. Mazzei continued to be a source of plant material and horticultural information for a host of Americans. Department of State archives in Washington contain many references to shipments Mazzei made to the United States through the American Consul in Leghorn. In 1805 he recruited for Benjamin Latrobe, architect of the Capitol in Washington, two sculptors to carve statuary for the Capitol. Latrobe wrote a grateful letter to Mazzei for this service. Mazzei continued to correspond with Jefferson, who wrote him in 1813 that he had sold Mazzei's house and lot in Richmond for $6,342.21. Colle had already been sold for 375 pounds sterling in 1795 to "a Mr. Catlet, a farmer, whom I do not know," as Jefferson wrote to James Monroe. Jefferson later became involved in litigation over Mazzei's estate, which continued after Jefferson's own death.

JEFFERSON PLANTS WINE VINES

But neither Jefferson's nor Mazzei's real interest was finances, and Jefferson's *Garden Book* is replete with references to their mutual involvement in horticulture. The *Garden Book* reveals that Mazzei gave Jefferson many seeds and plants for spring planting soon after Mazzei's arrival in Virginia and that on April 6, Jefferson planted 30 vines, the planting of which he described as follows: "Planted 30. vines just below where the new garden wall will run, towards the Westermost end of the row were Spanish Raisins from Colo. Bland's, next to them were 16. native vines from Winslow's in New Kent, and at the Eastermost end were 6. native vines of Monticello. They were planted by some Tuscan Vignerons who came over with mr Mazzei. the manner was as follows. "A trench 4.f deep and 4.f wide was dug. at the bottom were put green bushes, and on them a thin coat of dung and earth mixed, which raised the bed to within 2 1/2 feet of the surface. the cuttings which were from 3 1/2 to 6.f. long, and which has been hitherto buried in the earth, were then produced, about 18.I. of their butts were dipt into a thick paste made of cowdung and water and then planted in the bottom, the Raisins 3.f. apart the best about 2.f. having a stick stuck by each to which it was bound with bear grass in order to support it while the earth should be drawn in. the earth was then thrown in, the mould first, and afterwards the other earth in the same order in which it was dug, leaving the bottom clay for the last. the earth was thrown in very loose & care was taken to avoid trampling in it. the trench was not quite filled, but left somewhat hollowing to receive & retain the water, & the superfluous earth was left on each side without the trench. then the supporting sticks were drawn out and would have served for the other rows had the plantation been to be continued. in such as case, the rows are to be 4.f. apart, so that in fact the whole surface is taken up to the dept of 4.f. the best way of doing it is to dig every other trench, and leave the earth which is thrown out exposed for a twelve month. then the vines may be planted at any time from the middle of November to the first week in April. afterwards dig the other alternate trenches, and leave the earth of those also exposed for a twelve month. When the latter trenches are planted, leave the superfluous earth in ridges between the rows of vines till by the subsidence of the earth it becomes neccessary to pull it into the trenches. if any of your grapes turn out illy, cut off the vine & ingraft another on the stock. an acre in vines where they are 2 1/2 f apart in the row will admit 4316. in all."

The *Garden Book* also records that Jefferson hired Antonio Gianini, one of Mazzei's vignerons, in 1778 and that Gianini apparently stayed with Jefferson until at least 1793. It shows too, that Jefferson planted peach stones sent from Pisa by Mazzei in 1802 and that the American consul in Leghorn in 1805 put aboard ship a case of plants from Mazzei. "Put a few seeds in every letter you may write me," Jefferson wrote Mazzei in 1796.

JEFFERSON PRAISES MAZZEI'S EXPERIMENT

That Jefferson valued Mazzei's viticulture skill is proved by a letter which he wrote in 1811, thirty-two years after the end of Mazzei's experiment. Jefferson wrote: "...the Italian Mazzei, who came here to make wine, fixed on these South West mountains, having a South East aspect, and abundance of lean and meagre spots of stony and red soil, without sand, resembling extremely the Cote of Burgundy from Chambertin to Montrachet where the famous wines of Burgundy are made. I am inclined to believe he was right in preferring the South Eastern face of this ridge of mountains."

Philip Mazzei died in Pisa on March 19, 1816 at the age of 85 and was buried there. Jefferson, in a letter of 1793 to Albert Gallatin, had recalled the viticultural experiment which Mazzei had launched, as follows: "Mr. legaux called on me this morning to ask a statement of the experiment which was made in Virginia by a Mr. Mazzei, for the raising vines and making wines, and desired I would address it to you. Mr. Mazzei was an Italian, and brought over with him about a dozen laborers of his own country, bound to serve him for four or five years... We made up a subscription for him of 2000 pounds sterling, and he began his experiment on a piece of land adjoining to mine. His intention was before the time of his people should expire, to import more from Italy. He planted a considerable vineyard, and attended it with great diligence for three years. The war then came on, the time of his people soon expired, some of them enlisted, others chose to settle on other lands and labor for themselves; some were taken by the gentlemen of the country for gardeners, so that there did not remain a single one with him, and the interruption of navigation prevented his importing others. In this state of things, he was himself employed by the State of Virginia to go to Europe as their agent to do some particular business. He rented his place to General Riedesel, whose horses in one week destroyed the whole labor of three or four years; and thus ended an experiment which, from every appearance, would in a year or two have established the practicality of that branch of culture in America. This is the sum of the experiment as exactly as I am able to state from memory, after such an interval of time..."

Colle was torn down in 1933 and a new house built on the site but faced in a different direction. Parts of the old house were incorporated in the relocation of and additions to nearby historic Michie Tavern. Today, the only visible sign of Mazzei's viticultural experiment, his partriotic efforts in America, and his seven and a half years' residence in Virginia is a Virginia state historical marker about four miles east of Charlottesville on the old road to Richmond, near Shadwell. It marks the area as the site of Colle and states that "Mazzei, an Italian, lived here for some years adapting grape culture to Virginia." But perhaps Mazzei's real tribute came in a letter to him from Benjamin Latrobe in 1805. The letter read, prematurely but perhaps prophetically: "The time is already approaching when our vines...will spread your name and gratitude over a great portion of our country."

COLLE VINEYARDS REBORN

Just 207 years after Philip Mazzei planted the first vineyard in the Colony in an area known as Simeon, another Italian has repeated history there. In 1981 Gabriele Rausse, a native of northern Italy who managed the establishment of Barboursville Vineyards for the Zonin company of Italy five years earlier, moved 20 miles down the road and began planting on the farm still called Colle. Under the direction of the proprietors, retired Ambassador and Mrs. Stanley Woodward, he put in five acres of Vinifera in 1984. With plans to expand to 12 acres, the noble varietals of Chardonnay, Cabernet Sauvignon, Pinot Noir, Zinfandel, and Barbera, went into the same red soil in which Mazzei had planted his vineyard for Jefferson.

It took a very long time, but the soil and climate are ideally suited to the cultivation of the vine as both Jefferson and Mazzei had predicted, because excellent vintages are now being grown, pressed and bottled at Simeon Vineyards Winery. They would both be happy to know their dream has at last been fulfilled.

References:

[1]Retired State Department Foreign Service Officer, Mr. and Mrs. Martin built a brick Colonial style home overlooking the Rapidan River and planted an all–Vinifera "Halcyon" home vineyard near Barboursville, Orange County, Virginia.

[2]Marchione, "Philip Mazzei: Jefferson's Zealous Whig", 1975, American Institute of Italian Studies, 8 E. 69th Street, N. Y., N. Y. 10021. It is believed that Jefferson gave Mazzei the original draft of the Declaration of independence.

THE GARDEN BOOK[1]
Notes On Wines & Vines

The original *Garden Book* is in memorandum form with handwritten entries by Thomas Jefferson covering a period from 1766 to 1824. Measuring 20.3 cm. by 16.2 cm., it has leather-strip board covers, contains 158 leaves of which the majority are blank and is in possession of the Massachusetts Historical Society.

In 1944, The American Philosophical Society, using the data contained in the above, published *Thomas Jefferson's Garden Book*, 704 pages, annotated by Edwin M. Betts and containing many extracts from Jefferson's other writings. This chapter is derived from this extensive publication.

He was untiring in his efforts, for example, in introducing olive trees and upland rice in Georgia and South Carolina for the purpose of improving the lives of all people, and "He was equally interested in cultivating a grape that would produce a wine comparable to those of Europe."

In a letter to M. Giroud expressing his thanks for a new species of flora from another country, Jefferson wrote, "One service of this kind rendered to a nation is worth more to them than all the victories of the most splendid pages of their history, and becomes a source of exalted pleasure to those who have been instrumental in it."

Entries in the *Garden Book* indicate the wide scope of Jefferson's interests as Mr. Betts points out, "The entries range from contracts with overseers, plans for building roads and fish ponds, and observations on the greatest flood in Albemarle [county], to comments on Mrs. Wythe's wine and figures on the number of strawberries in a pint measure."

FIRST MENTION OF WINE

His first notation about wine was made March 30, 1766 at the age of 21, at the home of his father "Shadwell" near Charlottesville, where he was born April 13, 1743. He studied in Williamsburg from 1760-1767, two years attending the College of William and Mary and five years in the study of law under his friend, George Wythe. It was during this period that he first developed his interest in wine. He later spent much time attending to law duties in Williamsburg where he enjoyed the playhouse, musicals, and other gayeties of the capital city.

His earliest mention of Monticello was August 1, 1767 (Italian, meaning Little Mountain). In his *Account Book*, 1767-1770, he wrote, "four good fellows, a lad and two girls of abt. 16. each in 8 1/2 hours dug in my cellar of mountain clay a place 3 f. deep, 8 ft. wide and 16 1/2 f. long-14 2/3 cubical yds. under these disadvantages, to wit; a very cold snowy day which obliged them to be very often warming..." This cellar was under the South Pavillon.

In 1770, when Shadwell burned and Jefferson moved to Monticello, he attended sessions of the House of Burgesses in Williamsburg . In the early spring of that year, he sent William Beck there to pick up plants. George Wythe, March 9, wrote, "I send you some nectarines and apricot graffs and grape vines, the best I had; and have directed your messenger to call upon Major Taliaferro for some of his." This is the first mention of viticulture.

1771, March 28, Monticello, Jefferson noted, "planted 5. grapes from N. Lewis's on S. E. edge of garden."

1772, January 1, he was married to Mrs. Martha Skelton, widow of Mr. Bathurst Skelton, and daughter of John Wayles of The Forest, Charles City County.

1773 (before March 12). "mrs. Wythe puts 1/10 very rich superfine Malmesey to a dry Medeira and makes a fine wine." His first mention of oenology. He was in Williamsburg in January and February and no doubt drank this wine.

April 2, "planted 50. vines of various kinds from the Forest."

May 28, Mrs. Jefferson's father died, leaving her about 40,000 acres of land and 135 slaves. The land included Poplar Forest in Bedford County, where Jefferson later built a house which he loved almost as well as Monticello.

1774, April 6, "Planted 30. vines just below where the new garden wall (separated the vegetable garden from the terraced

Orchard below) will run, towards the Westermost end. 8 of
them at the Westermost end of the row were Spanish Raisins
[first mention of *Vitis Viniferas*] from Colo Bland's, next to
them were 16. native vines from Winslow's in New Kent [un-
identified], and at the Eastermost end were 6. native vines of
Monticello, they were planted by some Tuscan Vignerons who
came over with mr Mazzei [Philip Mazzei brought over with
him from Italy ten vignerons. They landed in Virginia late in
1773 and in the summer of 1774 six others arrived from Luca,
Italy] the manner was as follows."

Mr. Mazzei, born Dec. 25, 1730 in Tuscany, died March 19,
1816 at Pisa, Italy, came to Virginia in 1773 to raise grapes and
other plants. While searching for land, he stopped off at
Monticello and Jefferson gave him about 2000 acres adjoining
Monticello on the east. *The Virginia Gazette*, July 28, 1774
noted, "The Triumph, captain Rogers, arrived in James river
near 3 weeks ago, from Leghorn, addressed to Mr. Mazzei: By
this vessel, we understand, Mr. Mazzei has received sundry
seeds, vine cuttings, plants, &c. together with several Italian
emigrants, consisting of husbandmen and mechanics; and by
her we also learn that the presents of birds, seeds, and plants,
sent by Mr. Mazzei, to the grand Duke of Tuscany, were
graciously received, and that his highness was pleased to order
his thanks to be given Mr. Mazzei for his attention and kindness, and to assure him of his royal favour and protection, on
all occasions, that may contribute to his advantage and success."
(see preceding chapter on Mazzei).

FATAL FROST IN MAY 1774

May 5, "a frost which destroyed almost every thing. it killed
the wheat, rye, corn, many tobacco plants, and even large
saplings. the leaves of the trees were entirely killed. all the
shoots of vines. at Monticello near half the fruit of every kind
was killed; and before this no instance had ever occurred of
any fruit killed here by the frost. in all other places in the
neighborhood the destruction of fruit was total. this frost was
general & equally destructive thro the whole country and the
neighboring colonies." (The frost was so severe, it killed all of

the grapes in the public vineyard at Williamsburg).

1775. Jefferson recorded only one planting in the garden.

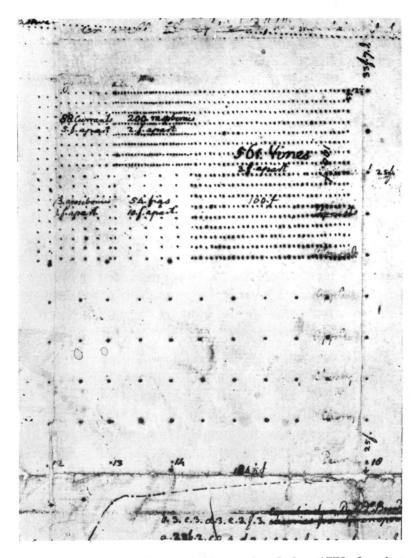

Vineyard detail of Jefferson's first orchard plan, 1778, showing 561 vines planted three feet apart in an area 100 x 100 feet. Cleared, outside were 25 ft. and 33ft. 7 in.
(Massachusetts Historical Society, Boston)

1776. No entries. His mother died this year and he had the responsibility of settling her estate. He was in Philadelphia from May to September where he had been elected to the

Continental Congress. It has been said that he wrote the Declaration of Independence in a tavern, and if so, he probably enjoyed a glass of wine that evening.

1777. Few entries. He was at Williamsburg three times attending the Assembly for many weeks where he held posts on many important committees. The birth of his only son May 28, and his death on June 14, was a sad burden for him.

1778. Of several men who were hired this year, one of the most important was Anthony Giannini, a vigneron, brought from Italy by Mazzei to work at his farm Colle. Jefferson's *Account Book* 1776-1778 states, "agreed with Anthony Giannini that he shall serve me one year from the 27th Inst. I am to give him (pounds) 50. & find him 15 bushels of wheat & 480 lb. meat. i.e. bacon when we have it. If Mazzei undertakes in writing to pay the expenses of his passage to Italy hereafter, I am to stand security for it so long as he is in my service." Reference is made by Betts to, "These orange trees were probably brought back to Virginia in the ship under Captain Woodford, which Mazzei had sent to Leghorn, Italy to bring back plants and vignerons."

1779. The election of Jefferson as Governor of Virginia made it necessary for him to move to the capital, Williamsburg, with his family. He probably took an active interest in the gardens there, the vineyard, and in the wine cellars of the Palace. No entries were made about plants this year, but reference was made to the gardeners at the Governor's Palace. [See chapter on Governor's Palace.]

1780. No entries. However, George Mason of Gunston Hall, Fairfax County, wrote him October 6, 1780, "As my very ill Health, at present, makes my attendance at the next Session of the Assembly rather uncertain, I take this opportunity, by my son, of sending you a pint of the Portugal, and best kind of rare-ripe peach stones..."

1781. Only a mention of orchard terraces. While at Monticello he barely escaped capture by the British. In June he fell from his horse,. and while confined for several weeks he wrote the greater part of the only book he ever published, "*Notes On The State of Virginia.*"

MRS. JEFFERSON DIES

1782, October 22, "seventeen bushels of winter grapes — the stems first excluded — made 40 gallons of vinegar of the first running... 20 bushels of peaches will make 75 gall. of mobby i.e., 5/12 of it's bulk." Mrs. Jefferson died September 6, leaving him with three daughters. It was the tragedy of his life. He never remarried.

1783, September 2-3, "White frosts which killed vines in this neighborhood, kiled tobo in the N. Garden, fodder & Latter corn in Augusta [county], & forward corn in Greenbriar." He was elected to Congress on June 6 and took his seat there in Trenton, N. J.

1784. No entries. Appointed our Minister Plenipotentiary to France, to serve in Europe with his old friends Benjamin Franklin and John Adams.

1785. No entries. He was now in position to enjoy the great wines of Europe and to study the vines that made them. From Fontainbleau, Oct. 28 of this year he wrote to James Madison, "...I am tomorrow to get [to] M. Malsherbes [an uncle of the Chevalier Luzerne's] about seven leagues from hence, who is the most curious man in France as to his trees. He is making for me a collection of the vines from which the Burgundy, Champagne, Bordeaux, Frontignac, and other of the most valuable wines of this country are made. Another gentleman is collecting for me the best eating grapes, including what we call the raisin."

1786. No entries. John Adams, then Minister Plenipotentiary to Great Britain, urged Jefferson to come to London to help negotiate a treaty with Portugal and attend to other important matters.

Feb. 5, he wrote to his manager at Monticello, Anthony Giannini, " ...how does my vineyard come on? Have there been grapes enough to make a trial of wine? If there should be, I should be glad to receive here a few bottles of the wine..."

Dec. 28, in a letter from Paris to Ferdinand Grand about seeds for Benjamin Franklin, Jefferson wrote, "P.S. I must add that tho' we have some grapes as good as in France, yet we have by no means such a variety, nor so perfect a succession of them."

VINEYARD TOUR OF 1787

1787. No entries. His oldest daughter joined them in Paris. He lived for his family, and this event together with a tour of southern France and northern Italy gave him great pleasure. His notes on this trip about the wines and vineyards are so extensive that they read almost like a travel story from a modern day wine magazine. (See chapter on 1787 tour.)

July 30, writing to William Drayton, chairman of the Committee of the South Carolina Society for promoting & improving Agriculture, Charleston, Jefferson observed, "Wine, too, is so cheap in these countries, that a laborer with us, employed in the culture of any other article, may exchange it for wine, more and better than he could raise himself. It is a resource for a country, the whole of whose good soil is otherwise employed, and which still has some barren spots, and surplus of population to employ on them. There the vine is good, because it is something in the place of nothing. It may become a resource to us at a still earlier period; when the increase of population shall increase our productions beyond the demand for them, both at home and abroad. Instead of going on to make an useless surplus of them, we may employ our supernumerary hands on the vine. But that period is not yet arrived..."

1788. No entries. Jefferson left Paris March 4 for an official trip to Amsterdam, but on the return to the French capital he took a tour of the Rhine to Strasburg and through the French vineyards on the way through Nancy and the Champagne region of Epernay. Again, his interests were centered more on viticulture and wines than any other subject, and his observations "Memorandum on a Tour from Paris to Amsterdam, Strasburg, and back to Paris," are noted in another chapter.

1789. No entries. Jefferson departed Paris with his daughters September 26, and arrived at Monticello December 24. They had been absent from their Albermarle County home for nearly seven years.

May 7, Jefferson wrote William Drayton, that he had sent by Mr. Cathalan, his agent in Bordeaux, among other plants, "43 pieces de vigne (I ordered the Muscat of which the dried raisens are made.)"

1790. He made only two entries this year, neither referring to wine. He accepted President Washington's invitation to become Secretary of State and left Monticello for New York March 1, seat of the government then, to assume that post. Martha married her second cousin Thomas Mann Randolph who became an outstanding manager and farmer whom Jefferson greatly admired and relied on in later years.

JEFFERSON SHUNS WHISKEY

1791. He continued in office as Secretary of State and it is said that his agricultural work on the side was responsible for the present day U. S. Department of Agriculture. He wrote to Randolph May 1 about horticultural matters and expressed his true interest, "...I long to be free for pursuits of this kind instead of the detestable ones in which I am now labouring without pleasure to myself or profit to others., In short I long to be with you at Monticello."

Jefferson shunned hard spirits, much preferring wine. However, spirits made from the grain crops of the farm were given to workers and overseers on a ration basis primarily during the harvests. In this connection, he wrote George Washington May 1 of this year, "...A Mr. Noble has been here, from the country where they are busied with the Sugar maple tree...He informs me of another very satisfactory fact, that less profit is made by converting the juice into a spirit than into sugar. He gave me speciments of the spirit, which is exactly whiskey." Jefferson planted many sugar maple trees at Monticello.

1792. No entries. He continued as Secretary of State to oblige and support his friend, President Washington, but wrote him May 23 expressing his wish to return to his farm work at Monticello. Earlier, Jan. 1, he wrote his son-in-law Randolph, "I feel with redoubled ardor my desire to return home to the pursuit of them [farming, horticulture], & to the bosom of my family, in whose love alone I live or wish to live, & in that of my neighbors. — But I must yet a little while bear up against my weariness of public office..." And on Feb. 26 to his daughter Martha Randolph, "...The season is now coming on when I shall envy you your occupations in the fields and garden, while I am shut up drudging within four walls..." And again to her, March 22, "...The ensuing year will be the longest of my life, and the last of such hateful labors; the next we will sow our cabbages to-gether.

1793. One entry only in the *Garden Book* this year. He consented to President Washington's wishes that he remain Secretary of State until Dec. 31. To James Madison in June he confided his real love, "...The motion of my blood no longer keeps time with the tumult of the world. It leads me to seek happiness in the lap and love of my family...in an interest or affection in every bud that opens, in every breath that blows around me, in an entire freedom of rest, of motion, or thought..."

1794 and 1795. Activities increased in gardening but no entries about viticulture.

1796. No entries. Jefferson was elected Vice President of the United States, a beginning in national political affairs to last until March, 1809.

March 22, Benjamin Hawkins wrote from Warrenton, North Carolina to Jefferson, "The vines you were so kind as to send me by Mr. Chiles were delivered to me alive. every one budded after it was planted. yet every one died immediately after. it was certainly not for want of care. yours is unquestionably the most valuable collection in America, and I must keep it in view, & I pray you to do the same, to have a complete assortment of them, by the first opportunity which may occur...I have also a grape from Italy, of a brick dust color, coming about a fortnight later than the (sweet water) & lasting till frost, the most valuable I ever knew..."

1797, 1798, 1799 & 1780, not represented in the *Garden Book.*

1801. No entries. Jefferson was elected the third President of the United States February 17 and inaugurated March 4.

March 24, Jefferson wrote Peter Legaux thanking him for his offer to send him some grape vines, and adding, "...It is too late this season but will want them for next."

1802, May 11, "planted grape vines recieved from Legaux in the S. W. vineyard. in vacant spaces of rows in the upper or 1st row very large white eating grapes. 2d 3d row 30. plants of vines from Burgundy and Champagne with roots. 4th 5th row 30.plants of vines of Bordeaux with roots. 6th row 10. plants of vines from Cape of good hope with roots." Jefferson during a visit to Monticello this month directed Anthony Giannini to plant these vines. His *Account Book* notes, "May 11. pd Anthony Giannini for planting grape vines from Legaux 1. D."

L. H. Bailey, *"The Evolution of Our Native Fruits,"* New York, 1911, p. 19, says that Legaux lived at Spring Mills, Pa., thirteen miles from Philadelphia and that he, "...appears to have been the most intelligent and public-spirited grape-grower which the country had known; and he was the person who introduced–though unknowingly–the grape which ushered in the distinctive American viticulture."

1803 and 1804, no viticulture entries.

1805. No entries. Jefferson began his second term as President.

May 29, he wrote Patrick Gibeon, "There was lately shipped for me from Philadelphia 1. box of grape vines, and 4. open boxes of monthly strawberries from Italy. altho' from the account I receive of the latter they seem irrecoverable yet if there be any hope of life I would ask the favor of you to give them to any careful gardener in Richmond who will hereafter furnish me with some roots from them if they live...the other box to be forwarded to Monticello by the first post..."

Sept. 20, he wrote to W. A. Burwell, "...I thank you for the vines & seeds which are all new and acceptable..."

1806. No viticulture entries. His interest was very active in this field however as indicated by his diagrams of the vineyards. For some unaccountable reason he noted in his *Weather Memorandum Book 1776-1820.*

"Note the order of the terrasses below the garden wall is as follows. the fig terras next to the wall. then, the wall terras, the strawberry terras, 1st terras of the vineyard & so on to the 17th, the 18th terras of the vineyard is occupied chiefly by trees, the l9th is Bailey's ally.

Mar. 25, S. W. vineyard. at S. W. end of 1st. terras planted 2.

Malaga grape vines.   Maine. at N. E. end. 1st. terras   12 black Hamburg grape vines

2d.......12. red do

3d.......10. white Frontignac.

4th.....20. Chasselas.

5th........3. Muscadine.

6th......11. Brick coloured grapes

7th......10. Black cluster grapes.

N. E. vineyard. Beginning at S. W. end of it, & planting only in vacancies

1st. terras. 6. plants of Seralamanna grapes 11. cuttings from them.

2d.......15 cuttings of the same, or Piedmt Malmsy

3d.......13 Piedmont Malmesy. or Seralamana

4th........1. Smyrna without seeds

5th........7. Galetlas.

6th.......7. Queen's grapes.

7th.......5. Great July grapes

8th.......6 Tokay

9th......13 Tokay.

10th....13. Trebbiano

11th......17. Lachrima Christi.

12th........6. San Giovetto.

13th......15. Abrostine white

14th......21. do...red or Aleaticos

15th......15. Aleatico. or Abrostine red.

16th......13. Margiano.

17th......15. Mamsnole.

S.W. vineyard N. E. end. 9th terras 4. Tokays, same as 9th. of N. E. Vineyard.

10th...... 6. Trebbianos. same as 10th. of N. E.

11th...... 3. Lachrima Christi, same as 11th. of N. E.

1807, April 21, "6. plants of Purple Syrian grape from Twickenham. upper row of S. W. vineyard at the N. E. end." Timothy Matlock, Lancaster, Penn. Feb. 25, had sent him, "...The Purple Syrian Grape form Twitman..."

May 13, Jefferson wrote to Edmund Bacon at Monticello, "Wormly must be directed to weed the flower beds about the house, the nursery, the vineyards, & raspberry, when they need it ..."

October 19, Jefferson to Timothy Matlack, "...I will not trouble you with a new request until I go home myself to remain, which will be on the 4th of March after next. but if in the February preceeding that (say Feb. 1809) you should have any plants to spare of what you deem excellent pears, peaches, or grapes, they will then be most acceptable indeed, and I shall be able to carry & plant them myself at Monticello..."

1808. No entries. July 15, in a letter to C. P. de Lasteyrie in France expressed his confidence in premium wine growing in America, "...We could, in the United States, make as great a variety of wines as are made in Europe, not exactly of the same kinds, but doubtless as good. Yet I have ever observed to my countrymen, who think its introduction important, that a laborer cultivating wheat, rice, tobacco, or cotton here, will be able with the proceeds, to purchase double the quantity of the wine he could make..."

FOREIGN VARIETALS FAIL?

1809. His notes imply extensive plantings of grapes when he refers to the upper terrace of the Northeast vineyard, West vineyard, and 7th terrace of the East vineyard.

October 7, he wrote John Adlum, "...I think it would be well to push the culture of that grape (Fox Grape), without losing our time & efforts in search of foreign vines, which it will take centuries to adapt to our soil & climate. the object of the present letter is so far to trespass on your kindness, & your disposition to promote a culture so useful, as to request you at the proper season to send some cuttings of that vine. they should be taken off in February, with 5 buds to each cutting, and if done up first in strong linen & then covered with paper & addressed to me at Monticello near Milton, and committed to the post, they will come safely & so speedily as to render their success probable.   Praying your pardon to a brother—amateur in these things..."

1810, April 20, "...planted in the 11. uppermost terrasses of the E. vineyard 165. cuttings of a native winegrape recd. from Major Adlum of Maryland. this grape was first discovered by a gardener of Governor John Penn's & transplanted into his garden in or near Philadephia. I have drank of the wine. it resembles the Comartin Burgandy." Major Adlum of Maryland, wrote perhaps the first book of its kind in America in 1823, "*A Memoir on the Cultivation of the Vine in America and the Best Mode of Making Wine*", Davis & Force, Washington, D. C., 142 pages, copy in V.W.G.A. library.

March 13, John Adlum wrote to Jefferaon, "With this day's mail I send you a number of cuttings of the vines which I made the wine..."

April 20, Jefferson to Adlum, "...On the 15th inst. I received yours of the 10th. & concluding the bundle of cuttings had been rejected at some post office as too large to pass thro' that line, I had yesterday, in despair, written my acknowlegements to you for the kind service you had endeavored to render me but before I had sent off the letter, I received from the stage office of Milton the bundle of cuttings & bottle of wine safe, yesterday was employed in preparing ground for the cuttings, 165. in number, & this morning they will be planted. their long passage gives them a dry appearance, tho I hope that out of so many some will live and enable me to fill my ground. their chance will be lessened because living on the top of a mountain I have not yet the command of water, which I hope to obtain this year by cisterns, already prepared for saving rain water..."

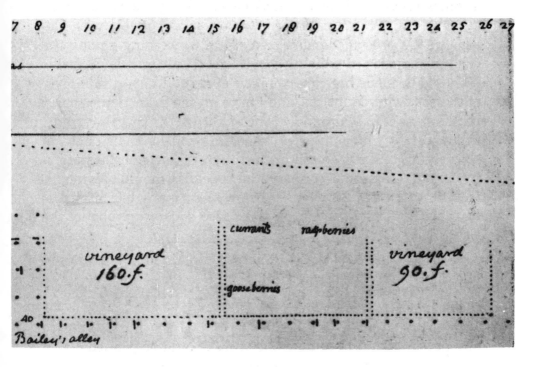

Vineyard detail of Jefferson's orchard and garden plan, about 1811, showing one vineyard 90 feet long and another 160 feet. (Massachusetts Historical Society, Boston)

1811. No viticulture entries. Jefferson's financial worries of the prior year were lessening and he was pleased this year at the birth of a son to his grand-daughter, Mrs. Anne Cary Bankhead, making him a great-grandfather. He was grief-stricken however over the death of his sister, Mrs. Dabney Carr who had been a member of the Monticello household for years.

OLD MAN, BUT YOUNG GARDENER

August 20, he wrote to Charles W. Peals, "Under a total want of demand except for our family table, I am still devoted to the garden. But though an old man, I am but a young gardener...But Sundays and rainy days are always days of writing for the farmer..."

October 1, Jefferson wrote to John Dortie, "...I am come over therefore to your opinion that, abandoning to a certain degree those agriculture pursuits, which best suited our situation, we must endeavor to make every thing, we want within ourselves, and have as littler intercourse as possible with Europe in it's present demoralised state. wine being among the earliest luxuries in which we indulge ourselves, it is desirable it should be made here and we have every soil, aspect & climate of the best wine countries, and I have myself drank wines made in this state & in Maryland, of the quality of the best Burgundy, in answer to your enquiries respecting soils & their depth of soil required may be found in the different parts of the state...I live in a mountainous country, the vegetable mould of which is from 6. to 12. inches deep, & below that, many feet of fertile loam without any sand in it, but these soils are probably too rich to make fine wine..."

Feb. 27, his *Account Book* noted, "...planted...11. grapes of one kind, 21 grapes of another..."

SOUTH AFRICAN VINES PLANTED

1812. June 25, Jefferson mentioned the East Vineyard and noted that in December the vines should be pruned.

March 12, "also planted...8. Cape grapes for wine in the 2d terras or 1st. terras of E. Vineyard S. W. end 6. Cape grapes for wine or eating 2d terras of (above) S. E. end all the above from Mc.Mahon [born in Ireland about 1775, Bernard McMahon settled in Philadephia and was one of the first successful gardeners in America. In 1806 he published *"The American Gardener's Calendar"* and he corresponded and did business with Jefferson frequently.]

Jefferson and John Adams were reconciled this year, and

their old close friendship returned. They died on the same day July 4, 1826. Madison was elected President and war was declared against England. Jefferson supported the declaration. The blockade that had been going on for some time made it necessary that he be more self-supporting at Monticello.

February 28, McMahon wrote Jefferson, "...This morning I done myself the pleasure of sending you by Mr. Gilmer a box containing the following articles...No. 4 Cape of Good hope Grape Vine, according to Mr. Peter Legaux, who says he received it originally from thence. This I am confident. from several years observation, is the variety of grape most to be depended on for giving wine to the United States, but particularly to be cultivated for that purpose in the middle and eastern states. No. 5 An improved variety of the Cape grape, somewhat earlier and better for the table, and equally good for making wine...Excuse the confused manner in which I write, as there are several people in my store asking me questions every moment..."

March 19, Jefferson noted in his *Account Book*, "pd. Giovanini for work in vineyard 1. D."

1813. December 24, among notes on general gardening, he mentioned the East and West Vinyards.

The War of 1812 with England was hurting his finances and he wrote President Madison suggestions to hasten the victory for the United States. His close friend Dr. Benjamin Rush died in April, the avenue through which friendship with Adams had been renewed.

1814. No entries relating to viticulture. The war was terminated this year but not until the British had burned the Capitol. The books for a library were destroyed and on September 21 Jefferson wrote to Samuel H. Smith offering to sell his extensive library to the Government.

1815. No entries relating to viticulture. Jefferson must have been saddened to see his library go to Congress this year, but the income from its sale of $23,950 was badly needed for his home and farm expenses.

March 2, in a letter to Jean Baptiste Say who was apparently planning to move from France to Virginia, Jefferson wrote about northern Virginia, "...It is a portion of the country which certainly possesses great advantages...it is red and hilly, very like much of the country of Champagne and Burgundy, in the route of Sens, Vermanton, Vitteaux, Dijon, and along the Cote to Chagny...there is navigation for boats of six tons from Charlottesville to Richmond, the nearest tidewater, and principal market for our produce..."

December 25, Jefferson wrote to John David, "...must apologize for the delay in acknowleging the receipt of your letter of Nov. 26. on the subject of the vine & wine. in the earlier part of my life I have been ardent for the introduction of new objects of culture suited to our climate. but at the age of 72. it is too late. I must leave it to younger persons who have enough of life to pursue the object and enjoy its attainment...There is in our woods a native grape which of my own knolege produces a wine so nearly of the quality of the Caumartin of Burgundy, that I have seen at my own table a large company acknolege they could not distinguish between them. I do not know myself how this particular grape could be known in our woods, altho' I believe it abounds: but there is a gentleman on Potomak who cultivates it. this may be worth your attention should you think it worth while to examine the aptitude of this part of the country for the wine, I shall be very happy to receive you at Monticello..."

PHILIP MAZZEI DIES

1816. No entries about viticulture, but his correspondence was very active in this regard. His old and devoted friend Philip Mazzei died March 19. He began sharing the expense of his grandson's education, Francis Eppes, who looked after Jefferson's affairs until his death. Writing on horticulture matters August 24 to John Campbell White, Jefferson again expressed his abiding phylosophy in this research, "...it is by multiplying the good things of life that the mass of human happiness is increased, and the greatest of consolations to have contributed to it..."

Jefferson wrote John David Jan. 13, 1816,

"Your favor of Jan. 1 is received. you intimate in that a thought of going to the Potomac to examine the vines I mentioned to you. it was a majr. Adlam [Adlum] near the mouth of that river who sent me the wine, made from his own vineyard. but this was 7. or 8. years ago, and whether he still pursues the culture or is even still living I do not know. I should be sorry you should take such a journey on such an uncertainty. I will write to him by the next mail, and will even ask him to send me some cuttings of the vines.

"I have heard with great pleasure that you have had somne conversation with Genl. Cocke of the county adjoining this on the subject of his undertaking a vineyard under your direction. there is no person in the U.S. in whose success I should have so much confidence. he is rich, liberal, patriotic, judicious, & persevering. I understand however that all his arrangements for the present year being made, he cannot begin on the vineyard till the next . . . . Colo. Monroe, our Secretary of State, whose seat is within 2 or 3 miles of me, has a fine collection of vines which he had selected & brought with him from France with a view to the making wine. perhaps that might furnish something for you . You will here too be within a few hours ride of Genl. Cocke, should any communications with him be desired. . . ."

1817, April 4, "planted 15 Scuppernon vines in lowest terras Vineyards." His neighbor and close friend, James Monroe, with whom he had worked closely in viticulture experimentation, was elected President of the United States.

April 8, Account Book) "gave Colo Monroe's gardener for vine 1. D."

May 13 (Account Book) "pd. postage box of vines 1."

1818. No viticulture entries. Jefferson wrote the Marquis de Lafayette complaining of age and failing health. His finances had deteriorated. He was extremely busy with plans for establishing the University of Virginia.

1819. No viticulture entries. The North Pavilion of Monticello burned. He was busy with the University building program.

1823. No viticulture entries. Jefferson was eighty years old, both arms were crippled, but he maintained his spirit and his granddaughters wrote many letters for him. In October he made visits to his friend James Barbour at Barboursville whose beautiful mansion he had designed. It is interesting to note that in the Bicentennial year of 1976, this 800 acre farm was purchased for a commerical winery and vineyards to make the European (Vinifera) wines that Jefferson loved so much. The new owners, Barboursville Vineyard & Winery, are preserving the elegant ruins of the house.

1824. Only the vegetable garden calendar noted, the last year of the *Garden Book*. Lafayette visited him at Monticello. Building the University occupied much of his time, but he maintained his interest in viticulture. Bernard Peyton, March 22, wrote him from Richmond, "... By a waggon a few days prior to the one above referred to, sent you a Box of Grape cuttings, sent to my Counting House, by Dr. Norton of this City..."

LAST WINE ENTRY

1826. Three months before he died on July 4, he wrote one of the last known references to wine and indirectly his preference for it in a letter to Ellen Randoph College, March 19, "...They are called the Taliaferro apple, being from a seedling tree discovered by a gentleman of that name near Williamsburg, and yield unquestionably the finest cyder we have ever known, and more like wine than any liquor I have ever tasted which was not wine..."

The author and signer of the Declaration of Independence never gave up his quest for scientific progress in grape culture, nor of his fondness for the moderate beverage. He knew that *Vitis Vinifera* made the finest wines, but he did not know how to combat the fungi and root louse Phylloxera that destroyed it in America. Undoubtedly he would be pleased to know that these obstacles have been overcome, just in recent years, and that the noble wine vines are flourishing in his beloved Virginia, and other eastern states. The memory of Thomas Jefferson can still loom as an inspiration of advancement in this increasingly popular field of horticulture. He should be remembered as the father of viniculture science in the United States.

References:

[1]"Thomas Jefferson's Garden Book", annotated by Edwin Morris Betts, The American Philosophical Society, Philadelphia, 1944.

RESTORING THE VINEYARDS

By Peter Hatch[1]

"I expect to be gratified with the great desideratum of making at home a good wine."[2]

A pattern of renewal and failure marked the vine-growing efforts of Thomas Jefferson at Monticello, and it seems most appropriate to perceive his viticultural pursuits as experimental, his approach optimistically scientific, his vineyard a vital part of the Monticello garden laboratory. Although these vineyards were cultivated with, at best, mixed success between 1770 and 1826, and while most scholars would concur that wine was never made at Monticello, it was the sincerity and urgency of his efforts, the eclectic collection of varieties, and the enthusiastic experimental approach that inspired the restoration of the Northeast vineyard in 1985.

Jefferson's appreciation and knowledge of the world's finest wines has been often documented, yet his continual re-planting of the Monticello vineyards suggests a perennial difficulty with grape cultivation. In the 1770's, inspired by his relationship with Philip Mazzei and aided by Italian vignerons such as Anthony Giannini, the vineyard probably flourished with mostly native vines planted three feet apart in a 10,000 square foot plot. The vineyard was revived in the 1790's following Jefferson's tour of European wine country and the planting of the most-esteemed French and German cultivars. In 1807 he recorded the most concise notes on a planting of the Southwest and Northeast vineyards that included a varied collection of European table and wine grapes. An 1812 drawing delineates the boundaries of these vineyards, which has again been replanted in 1811 with 165 cuttings of a hybridized Fox grape, the Alexander.

VINIFERA CHALLENGE

Jefferson's lack of success in vine cultivation can be attributed to his long absences from Monticello, the inevitable attacks of insects and especially disease, and probably, simple neglect. His failure resulted in a continual wavering between the de-

sirability of the easier-grown native grapes and the more difficult Vinifera species, whose superior wine-making properties
he would certainly acknowledge. In 1816, Jefferson would
state that Americans should not be "losing...time & effort in
search of foreign vines," yet in the same year he was purchasing
a collection of European varieties from James Monroe for still
another Monticello planting. By 1817 he was again planting
native grapes, the Scuppernong from North Carolina.

A study of viticulture of Monticello is a study of the ambi-
guities, contradictions, and even the elusiveness of Thomas
Jefferson. Although Benjamin Hawkins of North Carolina
would write him in 1796 that "yours is unquestionably the most
valuable collection in America," Jefferson himself would write
John Adlum in 1823; "of your book on the culture of the vine
it would be presumptuous in me to give any opinion, because
it is a culture of which I have no knowledge whether from
practice or reading."

The 1807 planting was restored by the Thomas Jefferson
Memorial Foundation because the 1807 date corresponds to
the years to which the gardens have been restored, the wide
spectrum of varieties reflects the experimental and scientific
function of all of Jefferson's horticultural efforts, and this
planting is the most completely documented scheme we have
of the vineyard. The Northeast, rather than the Southwest,
vineyard was chosen because archaeological excavations of the
area had been completed in 1984. They confirmed the existence
of terraces and suggested the use of posts upon which to
construct an espalier system.

WOODEN TRELLISING

Although Jefferson wrote instructions in 1799 for one of
his workers, John, to "espalier" the vines, the training methods
and possible espalier structure used at Monticello are a matter
of speculation. The Tuscan vignerons employed in the earlier
vineyard certainly would have adapted Italian techniques,
while most early American viticultural writers suggested the
use of a helter-skelter system involving the strategic placement
of numerous thin stakes to each vine. Although known by

Jefferson, metal wire was too precious to use for horticultural purposes. After much study and deliberation, a method and structure was adapted from the writings of Edward Antill, who wrote a discourse on vine culture in the 1769 edition of the *Transactions of the American Philosophical Society*. Antill's system essentially involved the construction of a four-rail fence, the posts four feet apart, the horizontal rails at three-four, five, and six feet above the ground. Although we were uncertain of Jefferson's exact 1807 spacing, practical considerations dictated that both the posts and vines would be spaced six feet apart.

Jefferson's 1807 planting included 23 varieties of European table [eating] and wine grapes from three sources. Eight varieties of wine grapes were purchased from Thomas Main, a Georgetown, [D. C.] nurseryman, seven varieties of table grapes were sent from Italy by Philip Mazzei, and eight varieties of dry wine vines were relayed from the Florence Botanical Garden by Thomas Appleton, the local American Consul. The diversity of varieties—there were no more than 20 vines of each cultivar—and the fact that the Northeast Vineyard consisted of more table grapes than wine varietals, suggests again the experimental function of the vineyard and the low priority given to the possibility of a genuine Monticello-grown wine. Despite being a keen grafter of fruit trees, it is indeed unfortunate that Jefferson never realized the potential of grafting the European grape onto native stock. Jean David, a French vigneron looking for employment opportunities in the New World, had even suggested the possibility (and perhaps was one of the first to do so) in a letter to Jefferson in 1816. All Vinifera varieties restored to the vineyard have been grafted, mostly onto SO-4 rootstock.

NOMENCLATURE PROBLEMS

Just as archaeologists probed the vineyard site for evidence of earlier terracing and posts, so have we investigated the viticultural literature to uncover the character of the grape varieties. Most Vinifera cultivars are of ancient origin and have retained a stability in their characteristics, unlike for

Note, the order of the terraces below the garden wall is as follows.
the fig terras next to the wall. then
the walk terras.
the strawberry terras.
1st terras of the vineyard & so on to the 17th
the 18th terras of the vineyard is occupied chiefly by trees.
the 19th is Barley's alley.

Mar. 25. S.W. vineyard. at SW. end of 1st terras planted 2. Melaga grape vines. Maine.
at N.E. end. 1st terras   12. black Hamburg grape vines.
   2d ....   12. red do.
   3d ... - 10. white Frontignac.
   4th ...   20. Chasselas
   5th .... 3. Muscadine
   6th .... 11. Brick coloured grapes.
   7th .... 10. Black cluster grapes

} from Main
planted only in
vacancies.

N.E. vineyard. beginning at S.W. end of it, & planting only in vacancies.
   1st terras. 6. plants of Seralamanna grapes & 11 cuttings from them.
   2d ..... 15. cuttings of the same, or Piedmt malmsey
   3d .... - 13. Piedmont Malmsey. or Seralamanna
   4th ---- 1. Smyrna. without seeds.
   5th ---- 7. Galettas.
   6th ---- 7. Queen's grapes.
   7th --- 5. Great July grapes
   8th --- 6. Tokay.
   9th ---- 13. Tokay.
   10th - 13 Trebbiano.
   11th .. 17 Lachrima Christi.
   12th ... 6. San Giovetto.
   13th -- 15. Abrostine white
   14th .... 21. do . . . red or Aleaticos
   15th ..... 15. Aliatico. or abrostine red.
   16th ---- 13. Marziano.
   17th .... 15. Mammole. - - -

S.W. vineyard. N.E. end. 9th terras 6. Tokays, same as 9th of N.E. Vineyard.
   10th ... 6. Trebbiano: same as 10th of N.E.
   11th - - 3. Lachrima Christi. same as 11th of N.E.

Apr. 11. Nursery. begun in bed next the pales, on the lower side, where Genl Jackson's peaches end
to wit within 2.f. of the 4th post from the S.E. corner.
   No 1. Quercus coccifera. Prickly Kermes oak. 3. cross rows.
   2. Vitex Agnus castus. Chaste-tree. faux Poivrier. 9. rows
   3. Cedrus Libani. Cedar of Lebanon. 2. rows.
   4. Citisus Laburnum of the Alps. 2. rows.
   5. Lavathera Albia. the shrub Marshmallow. 2. rows.

} seeds recd from
Doct Gouan
at Montpelier

Jefferson's notes on the 1807 vineyard planting now restored.
Dreer Collection, Letters and Papers of Thomas Jefferson

example, peach or tomato varieties which have been altered dramatically by plants breeders over the last 200 years. The problem lies in the nomenclature; to find modern synonyms for what Jefferson called the "Queen's grape" or the "Great July," or what was sold to Jefferson as the "Black cluster" or "Brickcoloured" type. The nature of the Italian varieties was traced by using Viala'a *Ampelographie* (1910) and Giorgio Galesio's *Pomona Italiana* (1817) while Dr. John McGrew's utilization of French works by Molon and Galet was an indispensable aid. The early American terminology for grape varieties was deciphered with the help of William R. Prince's *A Treatise on the Vine* (1830) and by using works by Bernard McMahon, John Adlum, and A.J. Downing. The ampelographical skills of Lucy Morton were also very helpful. While it is difficult for us to prove decisively that the "Black cluster" grape sent by Thomas Main to Thomas Jefferson was indeed the Cabernet Sauvignon, it is not easy to disprove it. Although our decisions on synonymity were occasionally arbitrary and based on the variety's current availability, the evolution of varietal names is an extremely complex and controversial field.

The following 21 varieties were planted in the Northeast vineyard at Monticello in the Spring of 1985. The variety name as it appears in *The Garden Book* is in parentheses.

Varieties sent by Thomas Main from his Georgetown nursery:

Cabernet Sauvignon ("Black cluster")

Chasselas Dore ("Chasselas")

Chasselas Rose ("Brickcoloured")

Malaga Rosada (possibly "Malaga")

Muscat Blanc ("white Frontignac")

Muscat Hamburg ("Black Hamburg")

Table grapes sent by Philip Mazzei from Tuscany:

Chasselas Rose (possibly "Toccai")

Kishmishi (possibly "Smyrna without seeds")

Luglienga ("Great July")

Malvasia Bianca (possibly "Malvagia di Piemonte")

Muscat of Alexandria ("Seralamanna")

Olivette Blanche ("Galletta")

Regina ("Queen's grape")

Dry wine grapes from the Florence Botanical Garden:

Aleatico ("Aleatico")

Mammolo Toscano ("Mammole")

Sangiovese ("San Giovetto")

Trebbiano ("Trebbiano")

Wine varieties brought from France:

Chardonnay

Pinot Blanc

Pinot Noir

Native American Grapes

Alexander ("Cape," "Cape of Good Hope grape," "native grape from Major Adlum")

Scuppernong

OTHER TYPES SOUGHT

There were other varieties planted by Jefferson in 1807 which we have been unable to locate, but which are possibly still available in Italy. All the Vinifera cultivars, except the Malvasia which came from Barboursville, [Barboursville Vineyards were owned by Dr. Gianni Zonin of Vicencia, Italy.] were sent to us as graft-sticks by the Foundation Plant Materials Service at the University of California, Davis. We have been unable to ascertain the genuine identity of the so-called Alexander, which made a wine "as good as the best Burgundy and resembling it," according to Jefferson in 1816. John McGrew hopefully rediscovered this lost variety on the Carroll estate in Maryland. The Scuppernong, which we are in the process of propagating, came from an extant vine on the former estate of John Hartwell Cocke, Bremo, which was probably the source of the Jefferson planting in 1816.

MONTICELLO GROUNDS
Drawing by Lucia C. Stanton

In many ways, the vineyard site at Monticello is ideal for vine culture; protected and warmed by its southeastern exposure below the garden wall and elevated enough to avoid late spring frost. Jefferson would regularly gloat over a late frost's destruction of his neighbor's fruit while his own remained unscathed. Just as Anthony Giannini of Colle once nourished Jefferson's vines, so has Gabriele Rausse of Colle/Simeon provided us with expert advice and grafting skill.

Although we are optimistic about the fruition of our planting, we will not count our grapes before they are bearing. Half of the vineyard is in table grapes, which will probably be distributed to Monticello employees as are the fruits from the orchard and the vegetables from the garden. Perhaps we will sell the wine grapes, or perhaps concoct a unique Monticello vintage of 17 varieties. We'll see.

An uneasy relationship exists between horticulture and history, between landscape restoration and historical fact. Jefferson's 1807 vineyard planting probably failed. However, to re-create the original effort requires the use of native rootstock, sophisticated grafting techniques, and pesticides. Still, the historic vineyard at Monticello should serve as a model for its emphasis on the use of both documentary evidence and archaeology to preserve an important varietal collection and to interpret Thomas Jefferson as an experimental horticulturist. It will not be so much a salute to his accomplishments as a testament to his vision and the urgent ambition of his great experiment.

References:

[1]Superintendent of Grounds & Gardens, Monticello, P. O. Box 316, Charlottesville, Va. 22902, in charge of vineyard restoration. Paper read at the VWGA 14th Annual Wine Growing Seminar, 10th Annual Festival, Valley View Vineyard. August 31, 1985, Middleburg, Va.

[2]Thomas Jefferson to Levin Gale, May 7, 1816.

BORDEAUX WINE SELECTIONS
Jefferson's Agents And Orders

On May 7, 1784 Thomas Jefferson was appointed Minister Plenipotentiary (Ambassador) to France to replace the venerable and ageing Dr. Benjamin Franklin and to work with him and John Adams, who became Ambassador to London later, on commercial treaties. He was in France until October 1789.

"Jefferson proved a diligent and skillful diplomat," according to Dr. Dumas Malone[1] "He and his colleagues succeeded in negotiating in 1785, a treaty of commerce with Prussia. Early in 1786 he joined Adams in London, but their efforts to negotiate a treaty were futile. He made careful note of English domestic gardening and mechanical appliances, but of their architecture and manners had few kind words to say. He supported Thomas Barclay in the negotiation of a treaty with Morocco in 1787, but was convinced that the Barbary pirates could be restrained only by force and worked out a scheme for concerted action on the part of a league of nations...Though he could not hope to make much of a breach in the wall of commercial exclusiveness, he gained some relaxation of French duties on American products..."

"Though greatly impressed with French manners, he was strongly opposed to any aping of them by Americans. He was attracted by the cuisine and wines and found the French a temperate people, but thought their life lacking in domestic happiness and on the whole rather futile [prior to the French Revolution]. Life for him was empty when not purposeful. He thought little of French science, but was enthusiastic about their arts—architecture, painting, and, most of all, music, which he valued the more perhaps because a fractured wrist had ended his days as a violinist. Distressed by the inequality of conditions, he came to think less than ever of royalty, nobility, and priests...From his stay in France he gained, not new doctrines, but an emotional stimulus, returning to America strenghtened in his civic faith...in his ripe old age, he declared that every traveled man would prefer France as a place of residence to any country but his own."

On July 5, 1784 Jefferson sailed from Boston on the ship *Ceres* with the oldest of his three surviving children (all daughters) Martha. The other two, Lucy Elizabeth, the youngest (died in November of that year), and Maria were left in Virginia with Mr. and Mrs. Francis Eppes, Eppington, Chesterfield County. Mrs. Eppes was the daughter of John Wayles, The Forest, Charles City County, and the sister of Jefferson's wife. The Eppes were close friends of the Jeffersons for many years. Francis Eppes assisted in the management of Monticello while Jefferson was in Europe. On August 6th, Jefferson and Martha were in Paris, and "Patsy" as he affectionately called her was soon in School at the Abbaie de Panthemont. In April 1785 his address was given as Hotel d'Orleans, rue des Augustins.

WINE CHOICES, TRANSPORT PROBLEMS

The records indicate that throughout the years Jefferson favored Bordeaux wines more than any other type. He not only had a high regard for their taste and general quality, but the location of the extensive vineyards near a large port made transportation—always a problem in those days, with goods of a perishable nature—to Paris, England and especially America possible. Communications were primitive which complicated payment for the wines.

The letters and other data included here cover the period December 19, 1784 to February 24, 1789. They do not include all the communications relating to wine at this time, a number of which are found in other chapters.

Some data not directly related to wine is provided to bring in the context of events of the day, and to show Jefferson's moods at the time and his warm feelings for his family and friends.

Thoughout the extensive research on Jefferson and wine, one has been impressed with the frequency that he discussed matters of his favorite beverage first in his letters, while matters of considerable political importance were often mentioned afterwards. This was also noted in letters written *to* Jefferson.

When we consider the time frame of 200 years ago, and the vast difficulties of sailing ship transport over seas threatened by storms and pirates, it is fascinating to follow a series of connecting events like in the correspondence with his friend Alexander Donald in Richmond. Although the letters exchanged took more than a year to and fro, the liveliness of their mutual interest in good wine can be easily felt as they discussed quality, prices, orders, delivery in Virginia, tasting, enjoyment and appreciation. Time, trouble and expense were all forgotten in the pleasureable sharing of their wine experiences.

Wine was not as important to editors and writers of Jeffersonia as other subjects, in many instances we see merely summaries of letters instead of full texts that would be important to wine historians and their readers.

The letters and extracts quoted here in chronological order, unless otherwise noted, came from *The Papers of Thomas Jefferson*, Julian P. Boyd, Editor.[2]

TO JOHN BONDFIELD
(U.S. Consul, Bordeaux)

Paris, December 19, 1784

Boyd notes entry in SJL (Jefferson's *Summary Journal of Letters*, written and received), "Mr. Bonfeild. Bourdeaux. Advice as to his land warrants–send me 1. gross such wine as he drank at Dr. F's [Benjamin Franklin] and another gross to Mr. Eppes by some ship going above Bermuda hund. to be delivered him before May."

FROM JOHN BONDFIELD

Sir: Bordeaux, 19th. April 1785

I have to acknowledge the honor of your favors of 19th. Decr. and 10 Instt. I deferd replying sooner to your favor of the 19 Decr. hoping a change of weather would have admitted my forwarding the wine you Commissiond. Within this four Days the weather is become moderate. I have in consequence forward[ed] to you four Cases containing thirty six Bottles each of our first Growth per the messagerie. I have also shipt on board the Brig fanny Capt. Smith, who will sail the 23 Inst. for Falmouth in Virginia recomended to the particular care of a Young Man who goes passenger in the said Brig to be forwarded to Mr. Eppes at his arrival four Cases of the said wine. I shall write Mr. Eppes by the said conveyance and inclose him a Bill of Loading for the same. Inclosed you have the Invoice for the said eight Cases for which I shall draw on you at my convenience.

I am much obliged to you for your information regarding Land Warrants. I propose to let mine lay dormant till occation serves either to sell or Improve.

There are two Vessels bound to Virginia that will sail in this week. We have not any other at present loading for the American States. It is probable some will offer in the month of May. If any I shall advise you..

TO FRANCIS EPPES

Paris, 11 May 1785

Entry in SJL reads: "F. Eppes. Receipt of his and Mrs. E's of Oct. 13 and 14. My appointment will keep me somewhatlonger. I must have Polly. As would not have her at sea but between 1st. of Apr. and Sep. this will allow time for decision—is there any woman in Virga. could be hired to come. I sometimes think to send one. Pray his advice and Mr.s E's—his wine shipped for Falnath.

TO JOHN BONDFIELD

Paris, 20 May 1785

Entry in SJL reads: "Jno., Bonfield. Receipt of his of Apr. 19. and 25. and of wine in good order. Will answer his bill. Wine good." TJ must have erred either in the present entry or in that of 5 May in which he recorded the receipt of "Bondfeild's Bordeaux Apr. 28, 1785, "for if there had been two letters he doubtless would have acknowledged them in the present; at any rate, neither a letter dated the 25th or 28th nor the present acknowlegement has been found.

TO JOHN BONDFIELD

Sir: Paris Jan. 24, 1786

On the departure of Mr. Barclay I was so hurried that in a letter I was writing to him, I could only ask him to be the bearer to you of a wish that you would be so good as to send me 6. dozen bottles of red Bourdeaux and 6 dozen of white, of fine quality. I now repeat this prayer to yourself, only desiring a gross of each instead of half a gross, mentioned to Mr. Barclay. You are the best judge whether it will come best in bottles or in casks. I will also pray you to send by the first vessel which shall go from Bourdeaux to James river in Virginia, the following articles. Anchovies, dried figs, raisins, brugnols and almonds, of each 20.pounds weight, 12. pint bottles of best Provence oil and 3. doz. pint bottles of Frontignac wine English measure, each article being separately packed. Be so good as to have all the separate packages put into one box and directed to Francis Eppes esqu. Chesterfield to be delivered to the care of Charles Carter esquire at Shirley hundred, James river Virginia. These articles being intended for a particular friend, I will pray you to have them chosen of the best quality. Be so good as to inform Mr. Eppes, and also myself, by letters, of the conveyance by which they are sent. My own wine I would wish to receive as soon as convenient. Your draughts on me for these objects shall be duly honoured, and many thanks to you for the kindness by Sir your most obedient and most humble servant,   Th:Jefferson

TO FRANCIS EPPES

Dear Sir: Paris Jan. 24. 1786

Since my letters by the Mr. Fitzhughs, I wrote you the 11th. of December and 7th. of January. Both went by the way of London. About a week ago your favor and Mrs. Eppes's of Sep. 14 and my dear Polly's came to hand. The latest of your letters before this, which have reached me, were of 15 months ago, that is, of Octob. 1784. That which you mention to have written in May last by a confidential person, I have never heard of. I wish you would be so good as to let me know by whom you sent it, that I may hunt it up. The one now before, of Sep. 14. is very comfortable as it contains the first account of my private affairs which I have received since I have been in Europe. You will perceive by my former letters that your disposal of the money given me by the assembly met my perfect approbation; as whatever you do, assuredly will. The motives which induce you to take this trouble have my full confidence, and you can better judge on the spot what should be done, than I can here. My last letters were intended chiefly as cautions about the sending my dear Polly to me. Lest they should have miscarried I will repeat my desire that she be sent in no vessel but a French or English one having a *Mediterranean* pass. However small the probability is by the capture of the Algerines of any vessel passing from America to France, yet the stake is too enormous to be risked in any other bottom...

In December 1784 I desired Mr. Bonfeild at Bourdeaux to send you a cask of fine claret. This he did by a brig called the Fanny, Capt. Smith, which sailed Apr. 26, 1785. from that port for Falmouth. It was put under the care of a young gentleman who went passenger. I have never heard what was it's fate.

FROM THOMAS BARCLAY
(U.S. Diplomat)

Dear Sir   Bayonne 24 Feby 1786

I had the pleasure of receiving your note addressed to me at Bordeaux and delivered your Inclosure agreeable to your directions. Tomorrow we shall set forward, and I expect in about Twelve days to get to Madrid from whence I shall write to you, as at present there is nothing better to offer than a Detail of Bad roads and Interruptions.

I Received a letter yesterday from Mr. Carmichael who wishes to see us, a pleasure I have, by this days post, given him reason to expect as soon as possible. Mr. Bondfield bought 2 hhds. of Haut Briers wine for you, and Fined it before I reach's Bourdeaux, so he has Robbed me of any share in the merit of that Purchase. I hope there is not any occasion for me to assure you of the Respect and Esteen wherewith I am, Dear Sir, Your Obliged and Obedient Hum. Serv.,   Thos. Barclay

FROM JOHN BONDFIELD

Sir   Bordeaux 27 May 1786

I am honor'd with your favor of the 17 Instant also with the Observations of Monsieur St. Victouer, to the Contents of both I shall pay every attention. If the Cases arrive the next month they will be in time to go by the Ship Comte d' Artois bound to portsmouth and will be a perfect good safe conveyance.

I have to Acknowledge the receipt of your favor of the 24 January, buissness having soon after called me up the Country. At my return learning you was in England I postponed forwarding the wine to your return of which I was uncertain. It shall be forwarded by the first Rouliers that leave this for Paris. The little articles you Commissioned for Virginia shall be shipt Pr. the Comte d'Artois...

FROM JOHN BONDFIELD

Sir   Bordeaux 24 June 1786

...I have forwarded by the publick Roullier who will arrive in Paris 13 or 14 July, Twelve Doz. Claret and twelve Doz. Vin de grave in eight Cases of three Doz. bottles each which I hope will get safe to your hand.

The Articles for Mr. Eppes are all packt up and shall be shipt on board the Comte d'Artois...

TO ACHARD FRERES

Gentlemen   Paris August 7. 1876.

I have been duly honored with your favor of the 2d. instant, and thank you for your attention to the wine forwarded for me by Messrs. le freres Roussac. I expect every moment to receive a proper order to the Douane of Rouen to permit these wines to pass on to Paris free of duty, which order shall accompany this letter, or be sent directly to the officers of the Douane at Rouen. I will beg the favour of you to forward the wine by water, addressed to me at Paris at the grille des champs elysees, notifying me of any expense you may incur which shall be paid to your order. I have the honour to be with sentiments of much esteem Gentlemen your most obedient humble servt.,

Th: Jefferson

TO JOHN BONDFIELD

Sir   Paris August 8. 1786.

I have now before me your several favors of May 27. June 10. 24. and July 15. I know of no appointments of agents in the ports of Rochfort, Rochelle or Bayonne, made by Mr. Barclay, nor, till the receipt of your letter did I know that you had been so kind as to extend your cares to those ports. In consequence of this, I had inclosed a copy of the order of Council of Berny to a Mr. Louis Alexander, with whom I had had a correspondence on another occasion. I am sensible of the inconveniences which attend the want of arrangement in the department of our commerce here. This is owing to the load of business before Congress which prevents their concluding a system of consular establishment which they have under contemplation. We expect this daily, which is the reason Mr. Barclay has not made arrangements finally. Your bill for the disbursements on account of arms was paid on sight. I have not applied for a license to export arms, because I am solliciting a general regulation on that subject. The wine is come to hand, and the cost of it shall be paid when you please. We find the red wine excellent. The Grave is a little hard. I am much obliged by your attention to the several objects public and private with which I have troubled you, and am with great respect & esteem, Sir, Your most obedient humble servt.

Th: Jefferson

FROM DE CALONNE [IN FRENCH]

Oct. 22, 1786

[Postscript at end of letter]   Fontainbeau
...Your nation, Sir, will see no doubt with pleasure, the assistance that the King is going to give for the export of the wines of Bordeaux, of Guyenne and of Touraine, and the suppression of the rights accorded to this effort by different decrees of the Council about which M. Le

Mis de la Fayette will give you the information.

TO ACHARD FRERES

Gentlemen   Paris, Nov 22, 1786

I have now the honor to inclose you the acquit a caution for the two cases of wine. They arrived only two days ago which has occasioned the delay of returning you this paper. I return you many thanks for your services and have the honor to be gentlemen your most obedient & most humble servant,

Th: Jefferson

TO WILSON MILES CARY

(Close friend, Carysbrook, Fluvanna County near Monticello)

Dear Sir   Paris Aug. 12. 1787.

Your favor of Mar. 28. has been duly received and I thank you for the kind enquiries after my health and that of my daughter, still more for the information that the several members of your family are well. The distance to which I am removed renders that kind of intelligence more interesting, more welcome, as it seens to have given a keener edge to all the friendly affections of the mind. Time, absence, and comparison render my own country much dearer, and give a lustre to all it contains which I did not before know that it merited. Fortunatus's wishing cap was always the object of my desire, but never so much as lately. With it I should soon be seated at your fireside to enjoy the society of yourself and family. I congratulate you on the additions to it which my neice is making; but tell her she has chosen a bad model for their heads. Neither the outside nor the in is worth her copying. I am in hopes therefore to hear that the hair of the next will indicate a better taste in the choice of the original form which she copies. You ask if we know a merchant in Bourdeaux who may be recommended for a consignment of tobacco. My acquaintance there is not extensive. There is a Mr. John Bondfeild of whom I have a good opinion. He is an American, and is Agent there for the United states . If wine is your object, he is a good judge of that. He supplies me, as he had before done Doctr. Franklin, with very good. They cost now 30 sous a bottle, and

2 livres when 3. years old, which is the age before which they should not be drank. If you like white wines, ask for Sauterne which is the best in that country, and indeed is excellent. Mrs. Oster is arrived here, and is gone to settle herself among her friends in Lorraine. My younger daughter is arrived also, tho by a different route, and is in good health as well as her sister. It is difficult to say which of them is most anxious to get back to their own country.We are here in a crisis of unknown issue. All the indications are of war, yet the desperate state of finances in the two principal parties, England and France, renders it so impossible for them to furnish supplies for a war, that we still presume they will come to an arrangement. They are endeavouring to do it, this country heartily, England thro' compulsion from the voice of the nation and the wisest part of her ministry. A war between those two powers would, at the first blush, promise advantage to us. But it might perhaps do us more injury on the whole by diverting us from agriculture, our wisest pursuit, by turning us to privateering, plunging us into the vortex of speculation, engaging us to overtrade ourselves, and injuring our morals and in the end our fortunes. A steady application to agriculture with just trade enough to take off it's superfluities is our wisest course. I beg leave to be presented to Mrs. Cary, the elder and younger, to Mr. Cary, and the young ladies in the most affectionate terms, and that you will be yourself assured of the sentiments of esteem and respect with which I have the honour to be Dear Sir your most obedient humble servant,

Th: Jefferson

TO ALEXANDER DONALD
(Merchant friend in Richmond)

Paris, 17 Sept. 1787

...Judge now if you acted wisely in offering me your services, or whether you can contrive to indemnify yourself by entrusting me with the execution of any commissions on your part, which I chearfully offer, and will faithfully execute. Particularly I can undertake to procure for you in the cellars of the persons who make it, any wines of (this country) which you may desire. I have visited all the most celebrated wine cantons, have informed myself of the best vignobles [vineyards, wine regions] and can assure you that it is from them alone that genuine wine is to be got, and not from any wine merchant whatever; for this or any other purpose make what use of me you please, being with sentiments of real esteem and attachment Dear Sir your most obedient friend and servant,   Th: Jefferson

Editor's Note:

"Chateau d'Yquem...The incomparable *Grand Premier Cru* of Sauternes; the one wine, red or white, to be accorded this exalted rank in 1855, a higher classification even then the great Clarets. It is probably the most famous as well as the most valuable vineyard estate in the world, and its superb 15th century chateau dominates its vine–covered hillsides like a queen. For nearly two hundred years it has been the property of the Lur–Saluces family...the Grand Duke Constantine of Russia (brother of the Czar) paid the staggering price of 20,000 gold francs for four barrels of the 1847 vintage...with the lowest yield per acre–an average of about 120 gallons, as compared with nearly three times as much for Chateau Lafite...some 200 acres under vine..."[3]

TO MONSIEUR D'YQUEM
(In French)

Monsieur   Paris, 18 Dec. 1787

Not having the honor of making your aquaintance, I trust in your good faith to excuse me the liberty of writing you directly. I will have need for some small provisions of white Sauterne wine for my own use during my residence in France, and the same after my return to America, whenever this will take place. I know that yours is of the best crus of Sauterne, and I would prefer to receive it directly from your hands, because I would be sure that it is genuine, good and sound. Permit me then Sir, to ask if you still have some of the Sauterne, first quality, of the year 1784, and if you would kindly let me have 250 bottles. In the event you can do me this favor, I would hope that you could supply and package them under the inspection of your manager. Your draught on me at Paris will be paid on sight: and Mr. John Bondfeild, American Consul at Bordeaux will receive the cases and boxes and send on to me. Let me then, if you please, have your kind permission of addressing you directly in the future when I have need of the white Sauterne wine for my own use, and agree to my assurances of sentiment and consideration with which I have the honor to be Sir, your very humble and very obedient servant,

Th: Jefferson

TO JOHN BONDFIELD

Sir   Paris Dec. 18. 1787

I have deferred acknolegeing the receipt of your favor Nov. 30. in daily hope of accompanying it with the ultimate decision on our commerce. But it seems to walk before us like our shadows, always in reach, yet never overtaken. I am disappointed in the proportion of returns of country produce from your port to America. I had received a statement from l'Orient by which I found they had made two fifths of their returns in commodities. And I expected the proportion was greater from Bordeaux on account of the article of wine. I see then we must have patience till our countrymen can clear away their debts and their prejudices.

Having in the course of my journey the last spring examined into the details relative to the most celebrated wines of France, and decided within my own mind which of them I would wish to have always for my own use, I have established correspondences directly with owners of the best vineyards. It remains for me to do this at Sauterne. I have therefore written the inclosed letter to M. Diquem who makes the best of that name, to begin a correspondence on this object, and to ask him for the present 250. bottles of Sauterne of the vintage of 1784. I have taken the liberty to tell him you would receive the package and forward them to me by waggon; and I have assured him that his draught on me shall be paid at sight. But he does not know either my name or character public or private, and may have doubt. Will you be so good as to remove them both for the present and future, and even for the supply now asked for to offer to pay him, assured that your draught on me for reimbursement shall be honoured at sight. I must ask you also to add on the letter the address of M. Diquem with which I am unacquainted, and to inform me of it for my future government. Perhaps I should have addressed myself to Monsr. Salus his son in law, as I am not certain whether he is not either jointly or solely interested at present in the vineyards. I am with very great esteem and respect Sir Your most obedient and most humble servant,

Th: Jefferson

FROM LUR–SALUCE

(In French)

Chateau d'Yquem, 7 Jan. 1788

As Mr. d'Yquem's son–in–law, Sir, and the owner of all his assets, I have the honor to reply to your letter to him.

I have drawn and bottled with the greatest care, the wine you ordered. I hope that it will be satisfactory. Any time you need, I will be happy to handle your orders directly, with utmost attention so that you shall be served with all possible perfection. I am mailing this letter to Mr. John Bondfield so it reaches you more certainly.

I ask you to kindly agree to the assurances with which I have the honor to be most sincerely, Sir, your very humble and very obedient servant,

Count of Lur–Saluces

[Enclosure: Lur–Saluces to TJ, 7 Jan. 1788, q.v. Bondfield may also have enclosed the bill of lading signed by Captain A. Doudet of *L'Actif* for "Cinq Caisses de vin de Cinquante Bouteilles" consigned to TJ and an acquit from Doudet for duty and carriage costs; these are dated 10 and 18 Jan. 1788 and are in DLC: TJ Papers, 38;6504–5]

FROM JOHN BONDFIELD

Bordeaux 15 Jany 1788

Since mine of the 28 nov. I am honor'd with your favors of

the 18 and 31 Decr., the first covering a Letter to M. D'Yquem, that estate at present belongs to the Count de Lur his son in Law to whom I inclosed your letter, to which you have inclosed his answer.

I have received from him five Cases of his wine and have shipt them on board the Actif for Rouen. They goe addrest to the care of Mr. Elie Lefevre with orders to forward them to you so soon as at hand, it is preferable to send bottled wine by water Carriage which is equaly expeditious, less subject to breakage and considerable less charge. I shall pay the amount to Le Comte when he shall apply.

The Vin de frontignan which you Commissioned Mons. Lambert to forward is not yet come to hand.

By your favor of the 31 Xbre. I reveived the arret du Conseil of the 29 Xbre. and Monsr. Lambert's Letter both which I communicate as occasion offers to all interested in Trade with the United States...

FROM MAUPIN

(In French)

paris le 18 Jan. 1788
rue du pont aux choux, no. 43

Sir

One can actually do, although scientifically, great achievements for the welfare of nations, and in general all the societies, and not only receive no prize nor recognition, but still get a little something back. I am an example of this. However, Sir, I would like, among other things, to prefect the vine in the places where it is established, and establish it in a great number of countries where until now, it does not exist.

This double project, Sir, does not interest in the least, no doubt, the United States of America, but only for the most part the states of Europe, and this is why I have the honor of announcing to Your Excellency the new discovery I have made on this subject, and I am notifying the public and all the ministers from the foreign countries to the Court.

Instead of limiting myself, Sir, to giving you advice of this discovery, I shall have been able to give you actual facts about it since it is printed, but according to the terms as I know them, I would only have been able to communicate it to Your Excellency on one condition, I have thought about inviting Your Excellency to procure [buy] them, as well as my patriotic and universal project, I should limit myself to telling you about them.

TO ELIE LEFEBVRE FRERES

Sir   Paris Jan. 31, 1788.

Mr. Bondfeild of Bordeaux having informed me that he has sent to your address five boxes of wine for me, I take the liberty of inclosing you an order for it's free passage at the Douane, clear of duty. Any disbursements you will be so good as to make for freight, transportation &c. shall be paid on your draught. I suppose it will be best to send it on from Rouen to Paris by a roulier or waggon, which trouble I must ask you to take. I am with sentiments of perfect esteem, Sir your most obedient humble servt.,

Th: Jefferson

Note by Boyd

FROM ELIE LEFEBVRE FRERES

Rouen, 4 Feb. 1788. Acknowledge TJ's letter of 31 Jan.; have not yet received from Bondfield the bill of lading for the 5 cases of wine and do not know name of ship, or its captain, by which the wine was shipped; ask TJ to send the bill of lading if he has it; recommended sending the wine on by water.

TO CALLOW FRERES, CARMICHAEL & CO[4]

Gentlemen   *Paris Feb. 15, 1788*

I am honoured with your letter of the 5th. instant covering one from my friend Mr. Donald. The packet of newspapers came also safely to hand. Mr. Doanld's order for wine not leaving me time to have it brought from Bordeaux, I send him two hampers from my own stock, containing 124. bottles, for which I shall charge him only what I paid in Bordeaux. This indeed is dear, being three livres a bottle, but it is Chateau

Margau, of the year 1784, bought by myself on the spot and therefore genuine; and Mr. Donald observed to me he would not limit any price. These go off by water, and therefore will probably not be in time but for the Portsmouth. I send by the same boat a package for the Governor of Virginia containing the bust of the Marquis de la Fayette. It is addressed to Mr. Limozin and I have desired him to ask the favor of you to send it with the wine of Mr. Donald. I inclose to you the late regulations relative to our commerce, by which you will perceive that I am promised there shall be no more such contracts as that with Mr. Morris: nor indeed any purchases of tobacco made but in a port in France.

I have the honour to be with much esteem, Gentlemen, Your most obedient & most humble servant,   Th: Jefferson

TO ALEXANDER DONALD[5]

Dear Sir   *Paris Feb. 15.*
1788

I received your favor of Dec. 15. two days after I had written my letter of the 7th. inst. and at the same time with one from Callow Carmichael & co. informing me that your vessel would sail from Havre about the 19th. instant. The shortness of warning not admitting time to order claret for you from Bordeaux early enough to go either by the Bowman or by your next ship, I send two hampers from my own cellar, containing 124 bottles. I am afraid it will not get to Havre in time for the Bowman. You say you had tasted at Mr.Eppes's some wine I had sent him, which was good, but not equal to what you have seen. I have sent to him twice; and what you say would correspond to the first batch. The second was of Chateau Margau of the year 1784. bought by myself on the spot, and a part of the very purchase from which I now send you. It is of the very best vintage which has happened in nine years, and is of one of the four vineyards which are admitted to possess exclusively the first reputation. I may safely assure you therefore that, according to the taste of this country and of England there cannot be a bottle of better Bordeaux produced in France. It cost me at Bordeaux three livres a bottle, ready bottled and packed. This is very dear; but you say you do not limit me in price. I send you a note [has not been found, but it must have been based upon the notes compiled by TJ during his tour of Southern France and must have been similar to the more extended notes compiled after his journey through the vine-yards of the Moselle and the Rhine in 1788–notes drawn from the travel journals of 1787–1788 and which formed the basic list from which TJ supplied information about European wines to many persons from 1788 onward (DCL: TJ Papers, 234;41990–6; to be printed in Second Series by Boyd.)]of the principal wines of this country, their prices &c. and shall be happy to have you furnished with any of them which you may wish for your own use, only giving me notice enough before hand to have them provided and lodged at Havre or Bordeaux. Notice for the latter need be very short when you have a vessel coming to Bordeaux. Notice for Hermitage must be very long...

TO PRESIDENT PICHARD

Mr. President: Paris, Feb 22, 1788

As I passed through Bordeaux in May of last year, I did myself the honor of introducing myself to you to pay my respects and to thank you for the kindness you extended to Mr. Barclay our consul, in the very unpleasant business he was involved in in Bordeaux. I hasten to renew my thanks and I take the liberty of asking for a favor. The excellent wines called La Fite are produced by your people. If you have some of the 1784 vinntage, and if you could accommodate me with 250 bottles, I would be infinitely grateful. If it is possible to have them bottled at your place, this would be a guarantee that the wine is natural and well drawn. Otherwise, Mr. Bondfield shall be kind enough to attend to this and in any case to accept them and to forward them to Paris. He will also be kind enough to pay you the bill in Bordeaux, or I can draw it to your order in Paris, if this is more convenient to you. Will you then allow me Sir, during my stay in this country, and perhaps even after my return in America, to call on you directly any time I need wines produced by your house? This would be a very valuable obliga-tion and from time to time would make it possible for me to renew the assurance of my respect and attachment.

TO JOHN BONDFIELD
[Wine first, politics second!]

Sir   Paris Feb. 22, 1788.

Your favor of the 15th January came safely to hand. I immediately sent a passport for the wine to Monsieur Elie la Fevre at Rouen. He had not then received the wine or any other notification of it; but, I doubt not, it is on it's way. Your draught for the amount has not yet been presented, but shall be honoured whenever it is. I must ask of you a second favor of the same nature. The inclosed letter to the President Pichard is to ask of him 250. bottles of his wine de la Fite of 1784, and to begin a correspondence for receiving my supplies regularly from him. Will you be so good as to supply any defect in the address of the letter before you deliver it? I have taken the liberty therein to tell him you will be so good as to pay him the amount if he should prefer the receiving it there to the drawing on me for it in Paris. I must also trouble you with the forwarding the wine by water to Paris.

Some opposition has been excited here to the late arret. It is quieted by another arret declaring that the right of entrepot shall not be extended to our cod–fish. The Emperor has declared war against the Turks. There is every appearance however that this country will remain in peace. I am with much esteem, Sir, your most obedt. & most humble servt.,   Th: Jefferson

FROM MONFORT

Rouen, 10 Mch. 1788. At the request of Mr. Bondfield, has forwarded to TJ at Paris, by water, 5 cases of wine containing 50 bottles each; in spite of the rising of the waters of the Seine the boat should not be late; encloses statement of his disbursements at Rouen in the amout of 60.5; the bargeman will receive payment for this in addition to his own charges of 3 per case. [Boyd]

TO JOHN BONDFIELD

Sir   Paris May 17. 1788.

On my return from Amsterdam, I found here your favors of March 7. and April 19. of which I have now the honor to acknolege the receipt. The vin de Sauterne was also safely arrived. I had left directions for paiment of the bill for it, expecting you would have been so kind as to draw on me immediately for the amount. Whenever you shall do this, it shall be duly honoured; only be so good as to draw paible at some days sight, to guard against the inconvenience of my being out of the house when the bill is first presented, which in the case of the bill from Lorient in one instance subjected me to a protest. I will also ask the favor of you to purchase for me from Monsieur le Comte de Fumelle 125 bottles of his vin d'Hautbrion of 1784, of which you say he has some hogsheads still, and to forward it by the way of Havre to the care of M. Limozin, or Rouen to the care either of Mr. Garvey or M. Montfort. Your bill for the amount of that also shall be duly honoured.

FROM JOHN BONDFIELD

Sir,   Bordeaux June 28, 1788

The 125 Bottles of Haut Brion shall be shipt by the first Ship that sails from hence for Rouen or Havre. Inclosed is a Bill of Loading for two Cases of Muscat forwarded to the care of Geo. Clymer of Philadelphia to whom I have wrote to dispose of them agreable to orders he may receive from Le Cte. Moustier.

This part of the Kingdom ferments but has not committed any Act, restrained by respect for the Cheifs.

I have the Honor to be Sir Your most Obedient Humble Servt.

John Bondfield

TO JOHN BONDFIELD

Sir   Paris Nov. 3.1788

It is long since I have done myself the honor of acknoleging the receipt of any of your favors. In the mean time those of

June 28. July 25. Aug.9. and 20. have been received. The reason of my delay was a constant expectation of hearing that the wine of Haut brion was on it's way, and that you would draw on me for it's cost; which shall be paid whenever you please to draw. If the wine has been forwarded, I will thank you for information of the conveiance by which it came. The Sauterne sent me by the Marquis de Saluces turns out very fine. I shall be glad to receive your draught for both these objects. The king of Prussia is marching an army towards Holstein. This may produce either peace or war, as he pleases. In fact, Prussia and England give law to all Europe at present. An alliance is pretty certainly entered into between England, Prussian and Sweden; to be joined by Holland. The particulars not known. An arret is lately passed here on the subject of whale oil which must give great alarm to those trading in that article from America. I hope however to get it set to rights. The moment I can obtain a determination the one or the other, it shall be communicated to you. I am with very great esteem Dr. Sir Your most obedt. humble servt, Th: Jefferson

FROM ALEXANDER DONALD

Dear Sir, Richmond 24 Nov, 1789

The wine you were so kind as spare me from your own stock, is very excellent. It is universally admired, and whenever it is produced (which is only on particular occasions) I am prompted either by my gratitude or vanity to declare whence it came, and give me leave to add, that we never fail to take a toast to your health. Don't I pray you misunderstand me, which you will exceedingly, if you conclude that you are only remembered at my Table, when your wine is produced on it. By the way, I do not believe that you have yet been paid for it. Do me the favour to send me the amount of it, which shall instantly be paid to any person here, or I will order payment of it in London, as is most agreeable to you...

FROM JOHN BONDFIELD

[1784 A Great Year]

Sir Bordeaux 6 xber 1788

A shipment I made in August is the cause of your not having receiv'd the two Cases of hautBrion. My Coopers thro inattention Shipt them with a considerable number I then sent off to the Isl of france and which I did not discover of some Days after, too late to have them landed. The Vintage and a Wedding we have had in our family Capivatived me most of this fall In the Country that in truth I had lost sight of the Comte. The Comte has only four hhds of 1784 on hand. I offer'd him Six hundred Livres for one of them which he refused. I am to have two cases of the first hhd he draws off. It is urging and too much to pay three Livres in Bordeaux for a Bottle of Bordeaux Wine, but so great has been the demand for that Vintage that the holders obtain that exorbitant price...

TO JOHN BONDFIELD

Sir   Paris Dec. 14. 1788.

Your favor of the 6th. has been duly received. The accident of the wine of Haut–brion is of no consequence; and if you should not already have received or engaged for more to replace it, I can do without it, because I have asked leave to take a trip to America which will occasion my absence from hence during the next summer. My hope is to sail in April and return in November. You will therefore be so good as to send me the bill for the Sauterne. This proves a most execllent wine, and seems to have the palate of the Americans more than any wine I have ever seen in France...

FROM JOHN BONDFIELD

Dear Sir,   Bordeaux Jan. 14, 1789

Inclosed I transmit you the Comte De Lur accompt of the five Cases Sauterne, which I request the favor of you to pay to Mr.William Vernon, from whom I receivd a few days past a Letter...

[The enclosed statement of account was probably Bondfield's acknowlegement of receipt of the five cases of wine, dated 11 June 1788, on the face of which Bondfield noted the cost of the 250 bottles and expenses for packing, transportation,&c., and on the verso of which the agent of

Lur–Saluces acknowleged payment of these charges, which totaled 340. 10s. (DCL"TJ Papers, 40: 6818). According to an entry in TJ's Account Book, this amount was repaid on 2 Feb. 1789 to Grand & Cie., through whom Bondfield had drawn on TJ]

FROM ELIE LEFEBVRE FRERES
Rouen, 24 Feb. 1789

Since their letter to TJ of 4 Feb/1789 they have heard nothing concerning the five cases of wine that were to have been sent from Bordeaux for TJ's account by Bondfield. Hence they are returning herewith the "passport" TJ had sent them to obtain exemption to duties along the route. They presume the plans were changed; if not, TJ can return it. [Boyd]

JEFFERSON LEAVES FROM FRANCE

By the year 1789 Jefferson had been abroad over four years, and counting the time just previous to this tour in France when he was engaged in political duties in Trenton, Philadelphia and Baltimore, he had been away from Monticello for about six years.

In 1788 he had requested Congress to allow him to return to the United States on leave. When it took no action after an extended period, he appealed to President Washington who granted his request in June. By September 28th he and his two daughters had arrived at the port of Havre where they boarded the packet boat for Cowes, England. They arrived at Norfolk, Virginia November 23rd on the Clermont and began visiting friends on the way to Monticello. He had lived there only a few months after the untimely death of his wife and so his return the day before Christmas must have been mingled with sadness as well as joy.

Jefferson never returned to France. He became Secretary of State under President Washington from 1790 to 1793. And after serving as Vice President under another close friend John Adams, 1797 to 1801, he was elected President of the United States and served in that high office from 1801 to 1809.

Prior to living in France, Jefferson had mainly enjoyed

fortified wines such as Port, Sherry, Maderia, probably because they were the ones that would keep best over long voyages in sailing ships due to the extra sugar content and higher alcohol. But in Europe it was a different story. He was able to visit

Payment of duties, carting, storage and shipping of wines from Bordeaux to New York by President Jefferson to tax collector, David Gelston, Port of New York.

Courtesy Alderman Library, University of Virginia

many vineyards, taste new as well as the old wines, and enjoy them at their peak at a reasonable price. This he did and enjoyed to the fullest, especially the Bordeaux vintage. He was recognized in America as the leading wine connoisseur of the day.

References:

[1]*Thomas Jefferson 1743-1826*, D. Malone, Charles Scribner's Sons.
[2]*The Papers of Thomas Jefferson*, Julian P. Boyd.
[3]Schoonmaker.
[4]Boyd, op cit, p. 593.
[5]Boyd, op cit, p.594-595.

A 1987 BICENTENNIAL TASTING SEQUEL
Carrying U.S. "Bordeaux" To Bordeaux

By Lewis Parker[1]

A French paper commented on this salute to Jefferson's visit 200 years before, "There is no doubt the great man would have relished this fabulous tasting. But he would have probably still preferred the Bordeaux."

"Carrying coals to Newcastle" simply won't describe the situation. After all, the folks in Newcastle don't claim to have invented coal. But Bordeaux, Ah, that's different!

On June 22, 1987, 71 American wineries provided their government with 140 different wines to be carried to Bordeaux for a tasting at the United States Consulate General in honor of the 200th anniversary of Thomas Jefferson's visit to the area's famous wine country. Many varieties of wine were served, including some of America's most prestigious labels of the Cabernet Sauvignon variety.

The event was superbly organized by the United States Consul General, Mr. Edward Lollis, and his staff. The Consulate at 22 Cours du Marechal Foch in Bordeaux was laid out with white wines downstairs and reds upstairs. The wines were further divided into sub categories so that all of the California Chardonnays, for example, were on the same table. A complete brochure describing each wine and winery was distributed to guests at the entrance. Each table was served by a tri-lingual American who spoke French, English, and Wine.

The guest list was *formidable*. Included was not only the owners and managers of the most famous Chateaux of France, but also Professors from Bordeaux's Institute Technologe du Vin, negotiants [agents], representatatives of the diplomatic corps, and the press. The presence in Bordeaux of over 25,000 professionals attending the Biannual Wine Trade Show at the same time made it possible, in addition, to gather guests and their comments from all over the world. By evening, over 600 guests had been served at the Consulate.

Tasting 140 wines is a challenge. No one that I spoke to laid claim to the whole group. Even the most ardent spitters became palate fatigued after a while. But everyone enjoyed the attempt.

What did the French think? Those who came with an open mind seemed impressed with the variety and quality of the American product. At the California table, I overheard a group from Burgundy in heated discussion with a group from Bordeaux about the "correct style of a Chardonnay." In the end, all agreed that the Chardonnays presented were flawless and of excellent quality.

Mr. Lollis and his staff had done an outstanding job of information gathering for their brochure. Included were approximate retail prices for each wine at a store near the winery. The most expensive wine of the group was the Robert Mondavi 1979 Cabernet Sauvignon Reserve priced at $35.00 per bottle. But many of the wines were listed below $10.00 and some below $5.00. "At today's more favorable exchange rates the French are beginning to see excellent quality American wines on Paris restaurant tables," said one American exporter to France.

Some of the wines which attracted the most attention were of types or from regions which were new to the French. Quipped the Bordeaux paper the next day, "Who's ever tasted wine from Missouri?" The Virginia wineries were well represented as befitted the home state of the father of American democracy: Accomack, Barboursville, Ingleside, Meredyth, Montdomaine, Oakencroft, Oasis, Shenandoah, and Willowcroft all sent Virginia wines.

The best summary of the event came in the opening words of the article in Bordeaux's morning paper, *"C'etait fabuleux!"*

Reference:

[1]Proprietor with his family of the premium Willowcroft Farm Vineyard, Rt. 2, Box 174-A, Leesburg, Virginia 22075, tel. 703/777-8161, Mr. Parker took his own "coals to Bordeaux." His wines have won many top awards.

JEFFERSON'S BURGUNDY FAVORITES
Agent Monsr. Parent's Choices

By Samuel L. G. Maggio[1]

What French wines did Jefferson prefer, Bordeaux, Burgundy, or Marseilles? This is difficult to say because to all he placed large orders for himself and friends over a long period of years. Land shipments by wagon and sea voyage by sailing vessels were very slow and presented problems of freezing in the winter and deterioration of delicate wines from the heat in the summer. Therefore orders had to be placed with the distances and seasons in mind. Bordeaux was the more likely source because of its proximity on the Atlantic side, nevertheless, long after Jefferson returned from his tour in France he continued to order the wines of Burgundy and southern France.

A key figure in his Burgundy choices and a man in whom he placed his trust for many years was Monsieur Etienne Parent. His name first appears in a note that Jefferson made prior to his tour of Southern France (March-June 1787) when he listed the names of persons whom he wished to see on his journey, including some to whom he had been given letters of introduction, "Monsr. Parent Maitre Tonnelier [master cooper] a Beaune fxbrgs Bretonniere". In his diary of the tour, there is an entry under March 8th in his rough expense account notes, "Aussy. Paid Parent, guide to this place which is the depot of the wines of Monrachet 6f." His decendants are still there in the wine business.

```
                              o    la baraque
              "Chambertin o        r.
               Vougeau        o    r.
                        r. r.
               Romanie  o o              Veaune
                          r   o          Nuys
               Beaune         o    r.
               Pommard     o       r.
               Voulenaye   o       r.
               Meursault   o       w.
               Montrachet  o       w.
                              o    Chagny"
```

Jefferson had tasted and studied the wines of Burgundy in detail before he made his tour.[2] He drew the preceding diagram showing the villages and the layout of choice vineyards, the vertical lines indicating the main route, villages are marked by "o", and "r" and "w" refer to red and white wines. M. Parent, who lived in a central location, was not only his guide, but in later years became his trusted advisor and agent.

He relied on M. Parent to do the bargaining for him, but he gave instructions that in the course of making a decision *quality* of the wine was the uppermost consideration and the price secondary. If we compare the quality today of the great domaines in Burgundy with the selections he made 200 years ago, we see that Jefferson was indeed a connoisseur who sought the finest—Chambertin, Romanee, Meursault, Montrachet, and others.

Alas, we can only be amused that he cited 1784 as a great year. What a pity that we cannot go out on today's market and buy a bottle of Montrachet 1784 and judge for ourselves what he was really writing about!

The purchase of vine plants *(ceps)* provides an interesting insight, proving that he consistently thought of planting the same varieties in Virginia from which he admired so much the wine they produced. They were no doubt the Chardonnay, Pinot Noir and Gamay that could not survive in America at the time due to phylloxera and fungi. But they thrive today in the Eastern United States thanks to grafting and fungicides, a fact that Jefferson would surely applaud.

William Short, also a native Virginian, was Jefferson's personal secretary. Probably inspired by glowing accounts of the fine wines and beauties of this region from his chief, Short made a journey over the same route later and excerpts from one of his lengthy letters gives an interesting point of view of what he saw, tasted, and his efforts to find M. Parent. He noted some of his overnight stops which indicates how slow carriage travel was over primitive roads. It would be easier to go over the same route today and enjoy wines from the same vineyards.

The traveller today who is familiar with the vast, sprawling, modern city of Paris and its fast transportation by rail and grand boulevards, will be amused to read Jefferson's instructions to Parent to make sure and give advance notice of what gate the wagon with the wine will be entering so the proper arrangements could be made with the customs office.

Monsieur Parent listed the cost of bottles, straw, wax, string, baskets for packing, clarifying the wine, drawing from the casks, and bottling, no doubt well informed by Jefferson to provide all details. A definition of "feuillette" and other terms may be found in Appendix "B".

Except where otherwise noted, the correspondence was taken from Boyd's "Papers of Thomas Jefferson", Princeton University, N. J. All letters are translated from French except Short's.

DESCRIBING THE REGION

March 6 1787, Vougeau is the property of the monks of Citeaux, and produces about 200 pieces. Monrachet contains about 500 arpents, and produces one year with another about 120 peices. It belongs to two proprietors only, Monsr. de Clermount, who leases to some wine merchants, and the Marquis de Sarsnet of Dijon, whose part is farmed to a Monsr. de la Tour whose family, for many generations, have had the farm. The best wines are carried to Paris by land. The transportation costs 36^{tt} the peice. The more indifferent go by water. Bottles cost 4 1/2 sous each.

March 9. *Chalons. Sennecy. Tournus. St. Albin. Macon.*

On the left are the fine plains of the Saone; on the right, the lands, rather waving than hilly, sometimes sloping gently to the plains, sometimes dropping down in precipices, and occasionally broken into beautiful vallies by the streams which run into the Saone. The Plains are a dark rich loam, in pasture and corn; the heights more or less red or reddish, always gritty, of midling quality only; their sides in vines, and their summits in corn. The vineyards are inclosed with dry stone walls, and there are some quickhedges in the corn grounds. The cattle are few and indifferent. There are some good oxen however. They draw by the head. Few sheep, and a small. A good deal of wood lands.

I passed three times the canal called le Charollois, which they are opening from Chalons on the Saone to Digoïn on the Loire. It passes near Chagny, and will be 23. leagues long. They have worked on it 3. years, and will finish it in 4. more. It will reanimate the languishing commerce of Champagne and Burgundy, by furnishing a water transportation for their wines to Nantes, which also will receive new consequence by becoming the emporium of that commerce. At some distance on the right are high mountains, which probably form the separation between the waters of the Saone and Loire.—Met a malfactor in the hands of one of the Marechaussée; perhaps a dove in the talons of a hawk. The people begin now to be in separate establishments, and not in villages. Houses are mostly covered with tile.

Beaujolais. Maison blanche. St. George. Chateau de Laye Epinaye. The face of the country is like that from Chalons to Macon. The plains are dark rich loam, the hills a red loam, of midling quality, mixed generally with more or less course sand and grit, and a great deal of small stone. Very little forest. The vineyards are mostly inclosed with dry stone wall. A few small cattle and sheep. Here, as in Burgundy, the cattle are all white.

This is the richest country I ever beheld. It is about 10. or 12. leagues in length, and 3. 4. or 5. in breadth; at least that part of it which is under the eye of the traveller. It extends from the top of a ridge of mountains running parallel with the Saone, and sloping down to the plains of that river scarcely any where too steep for the plough. The whole is thick sown with farm houses, chateaux, and the Bastides of the inhabitants of Lyons. The people live separately and not in villages. The hillsides are in wine... They have a method of mixing beautifully the culture of vines, trees and corn. Rows of fruit trees are planted about 20. feet apart. Between the trees, in the row, they plant vines 4. feet apart and espalier them. The intervals are sowed alternately in corn, so as to be one year in corn the next in pasture, the 3d. in corn, the 4th in pasture &c. 100. toises of vines in length yeild generally about 4. peices of wine. In Dauphiné, I am told, they plant vines only at the roots of the trees and let them cover the whole trees. But this spoils both the vine and the fruit. Their wine, when distilled, yeilds but one third of its quantity in brandy. The wages of a laboring man here are 5. Louis, of a woman one half. The women do not work with the hough: They only weed the vines, the corn, &c. and spin. They speak a Patois very difficult to understand. I passed some time at the chateau de Laye epinaye. Monsieur de Laye has a seignory of about 15,000 arpens, in pasture, corn, vines, and wood... [For more descriptions of Burgundy vineyards and wines, see chapter, Tour Notes..., and Appendices.]

FROM PARENT

Beaune, June 20, 1787

Sir:

I have received your letter of the 14th instant requesting me to purchase two feuillettes of wine for your account. I did so, one from the *goute d'or* of Mr. Bachey in Meursault in 84 and the other in Red of the best called Comarenné n 85 which I immediately clarified to be bottled in 12 or 14 days to be fine and clear; in regard to the hot days, once they are properly packed in a basket, there is nothing to fear inasmuch as the heat hasn't been bad so far.

For the Latour Montrachet feuillette, I paid 339...by Messrs. Finguerlin and Scherer of Lyons; to wit, 279 per feuillette, 30 for the bottles, 6 for the baskets. for the packing 8, bottling 4, string and corks and straw 3 and to have the bottles shipped to the wine store and returned filled.3...for a grand total of 339 livres. In connection with the vine plants you wantd, I immediately went to Clos Vougeot and Chambertin to get them for you, but all had been out but I am sure I can get some late in October; I was even promised Chevolles which [words missing]

...

Sir the two feuilletts I am going to send you, I believe that you will have reason to be satisfied with them as to quality, for

I selected the best made in our area. All included, the Red will cost 22 sols per bottle and the White only 21. Mr. Bachey still has 4 feuillettes. I received 6 livres per feuillette, so I can send you the vine plants at no cost. [Jefferson probably wanted these vines for planting at Monticello]

Recorded in SJL as received 23 June 1787. At bottom of text, in TJ's hand, there is the following tabulation of costs and estimate of cost-per-bottle:				
"124. bottles Monrachet.			Voiturage á Paris	34—10
en futailles		274ᵗ		373—10
bouteilles	30ᵗ		It costs then by the bottle en futaille	2ᵗ—4 s
panier	6		the bottle, cork,	
emballage	8		bottling, package, &c.	11
tirage	4		transportation to Paris	5
ficelle, bouchons, paille	3			
voiturage á Beaune	3	65		3—."

TO PARENT

Paris, Dec. 17, 1787

Sir;

Your letter of June 20 informed me that Mr. Bachey still had, at the time, four feuillettes of Meursault goutte d'or of the same vintage and grade that the wine you sent me. I found it so good that I will take another 3 feuillettes, if they are still available. If he ran out, be gracious enough to supply me with one single feuillette of the same goutte d'or grade, where you find it best, and ship it to me in bottles as soon as possible. Send also a feuillette of Red Vollenaye wines, also in bottles. Be kind enough to inform me at your convenience of which Paris gate the carrier will enter, on what day, and how much he will have for my account, so that I can give all necessary orders in advance to the Customs, so that he won't have to leave them in bond and can deliver them directly to my house. Draw on me the amount to be duly paid. Kindly let me know if Mr. de L Tour still has any of those 4 feuillettes of 1784

Montrachet I saw in his cellar, one of which I bought,

Thos. Jefferson

FROM PARENT

Beaune, Dec. 24, 1787

Sir:

In reply to yours of the 17 instant in which you indicated that you were buying three quarter–casks of wine (White wine de la goute d'or), I went to see Mr. Bachey who still has three quarter–casks; but he is willing to sell only two and for no less than one hundred livres per feuillette. then I went to see Mr. Latour; he is out of 84 Montrachet but he has some 85 and will not take less than 300 livres per feuillette. Then Farmer Dents de Clermont in Chagny has six feuillettes of 84 but he wants 300 for it; I think his is better than Latour's. I didn't want to buy any without notifying you; so will you please advise me whether you will buy at this price by return mail because he told me yesterday that he sold a feuillette two weeks ago for 120 livres and that a reply was expected for the other three; thus I arranged for him to sell 22 barrels of Vollenay for 340 livres eight days ago and he promised he would let me have these two feuillettes for 100 each, pending your reply. Or if you prefer I will send you a feuillette of Meursault White, for 84 or 86 per feuillette of 1st quality, and which would not be as good because lately—in the past two months—old wines have gone up in our counties. As for the plants of Clos de Vougeot, Romane and Chambertin and Montrachet, I will send you some if you so desire. If I had not been sick since October until the end of November, I would have done as promiced.

Parent

TO PARENT

Sir: Paris, 28 Dec. 1787

I just received the letter you honoured me with on the 24th instant and I take advantage of the first mail to ask to buy for me the two feuillettes of wine of Meursault from Mr. Bachey, for 84, at 100 francs [sic] if his price does not go down. And to also get me one feuillette of Vollenaye 1st quality of the year 1784. Be kind enough to have them bottled etc. as I requested in my letter of the 17th instant.

As for the Montrachet wine, I will not buy any for now. I might order some from you at a later date. I would appreciate your shipping the Meursault and Vollenay wines at your earliest convenience. I would also appreciate your sending me the wine plants you were kind enough to offer to supply, at your convenience.

Th. Jefferson

FROM PARENT

Sir: Beaune, 16 Jan. 1788

I bought the two feuillettes of white wine as well as one of red Vollenay. I just had them bottled and strawed wrapped ready to go to ship them to you, but since the freeze that is hitting us so hard I believe it would not do at all to ship them to you in this very cold weather. It might break the bottles and the wine would be lost. I pray you to please be patient for a few days, maybe it won't last, and as soon as the weather is more lenient I will send them on to you together with the vine plants which are also ready to go. I am very sincerely Sir, your very humble and obedient servant.

Parent

FROM PARENT

Sir: Beaune Feb. 3, 1788

Will you please have received from Sir George Chauveaux, common carrier of Noux, near Chatillion, the six baskets of wine, including two Volleney, marked PS Né. 2 et 2 and four baskets white wine Goute d'Or, also marked in the same way and numbered three, four, five, six; then 62 in each basket; and you will make him pay sixteen and ten sols on each basket and nothing more. And I gave him a small bunch of vine plants, twelve Montrachet, including six from Mr. de Clermont, and 10 from Clos Vougeot, and 9 from Chambertin, and 8 from Romanee that you will receive through the same carrier, who should deliver them gratis. And if he does not turn them over a Beaune ce 16 janvier 1788 [16 January 1788]

Monsieur

J'ay acheté les deux feuillette de vin blanc aussy que de
Rouge Volnay dont je viens de les mettre en bouteille et en suitte
prest a partie pour vous les envoyé, mais comme les gelée se vient
de prendre si rudement je croire que cela ne luy fasse du tort
de vous les envoye pour ce temps la le grand froid peut faire casse
les bouteille et perte le vin, je vous prie de vouloir prendre patience
pendant quelque jours cela ne durera peut estre pas, et aussytost
le premier Doutemps je vous les ferez passé avec les septs d'origne
que sont tout prest aussy, je suis très sincerement

Monsieur

Votre très humble et
très obeissant Serviteur.

Parent

Example of Parent letter written in 18th century French.

to you, you should withhold 24 livres on the carriage. The two feuilletts of white cost 200 on purchase and the feuillette of Vollenay, the best I could find in Vollenay, 90. For the bottles bought, twenty four livres per hundred, there are 375 of them (?) . 90 baskets, and packing seven livres per basket, 42 and for drawing and clarifying and bottling all 3 feuillettes, 12 livres; and for corks, wax, straw and string, seven livres 10 sols. They were shipped on Jan. 30, you should have them by the 12 or 13 of Feb at the latest, and will you please Sir acknowledge their receipt upon arrival.

Parent

Boyds footnote: At foot of text the various charges, amounting to 441. 10s are recapitulated and 16. 10, the cost of transportation per hamper, multiplied by 6; on verso, in hand of TJ's servant, Petit, there is an unsigned acknowledgment of the receipt of 371 bottles of wine (one bottle was broken, see TJ to Parent, 20 Feb.) below Petit's receipt, in TJ's hand: "droits d'entree 75-3 Voiturage du vin 99 des ceps."

TO PARENT

Sir: Paris, Feb. 20, 1788

The wine you were kind enough to send has arrived in good condition. There was only one broken bottle. Your draft on me for the amount shall be paid. i pray you put three of four days on sight to avoid my happening to be away when the bearer calls at my house with the note. I extend my thanks for your attention and with much consideration, I am, Sir, your very humble and very obedient servant.

Thos. Jefferson

P. S. The vine plants have been delivered in good condition; I gave 6 livres to the teamster for the attention he gave them.

FROM PARENT

Sir: Beaune, March 3, 1788

I would appreciate you paying my draft on you for 441 livres and 10 sols, amount for wine shipped to you; it is dated March 1st, payable on 3 days on sight to Mr. Paschal and Sons in our city of Beaune or their order and I would be grateful for your kindness, hoping you will be pleased with the wine. Sir, I would be grateful for your recommending me with some good house...[?] I paid Mr. Bachey for the two feuillettes and I think he may be able to ship the other. I am very sincerely Sir, your very humble and very obedient servant.

Parent

This settles your account.

FROM WILLIAM SHORT

(While Jefferson was on trip to Holland and Germany Mar. 3, 1788 to Apr. 23, 1788)

Paris, 10 March, 1788

...Your wine man Parent has drawn on you for 441 10s. I have given the money to Petit to go and pay the bill, being out when it was sent here.

Mr. Necker's book has put all the minds in a fermentation. I have heard more religion talked and discussed since the appearance of this book than in three years before. I believe it will work a contrary effect from what the author intended, for I may say also that I have heard more atheism avowed within these three days than during my whole life before. Adieu my dear Sir and believe me with sincerity Your friend and servant,

W. Short

P. S. Miss Jefferson has just sent me word by the commissiare the she shall not write by this post, that Polly is much better and indeed well. The Commissare saw her (Miss Polly) and says she was quite gay and cheerful–a good sign of health.

FROM SHORT

(en route to South of France)

24 Sept.1788

...We with difficulty passed the Pont neuf on account of the mob assembled there, and who stopped several carriages and endeavoured to exact of us money to purchase fusees [guns]. We got only as far as Villeneuf that night, because Mrs. Paradise insisted on staying there. We breakfasted the next morning at Fontainebleau, visited the Chateau and Park and slept that

night at Fossard. The next night at Auxerre, the next at
Vitteaux, and the day after we dined and slept at Dijon. I called
for Irish potatoes, which they gave us. They were excellent, but
I have seen much better beyond the blue ridge. We were at the
same hotel with you. Paradise and myself walked over the
principal streets and ramparts. It is certainly much the cleanest
town I have ever seen in France. The next morning we went to
Beaune. I wished to spend that day there. The first thing I did
was go to Parent's. Unfortunately he was gone some distance
from home. A heavy rain was falling, but still his wife insisted
on sending for him. On our return to the tavern we found Mrs.
Paradise in a fever to be gone. We dined and finding that
Parent did not arrive and that her fever increased we ordered
the posthorses, after being assured by two Benedictins, who
were at the tavern and who had come there to superintend the
making their wine, that even if Parent should arrive he would
not be able to shew us what we wished to see, as the vintage
was finished, and there were no considerable cellars in Beaune.
The Benedictins themselves were setting off for Chalons because the business of wine making was finished. After the
posthorses were put to and we in the carriage Parent arrived.
He assured us the contrary and said he should have been able
to have shewn us several cellars where the wine was still
making. It was now too late and we were obliged to go on. I
saw with a great deal of pleasure Volnais, Meursaut and Mon-
traché. I paid with sincerity my tribute of gratitude to the two
last for the many glasses of fine wine they have given me, by
gazing at them as we passed and by never quitting them with
my eyes long as we remained within sight of them. —They
made us pay at the tavern at Beaune three livres for a bottle of
Volnais. I did not however think it equal to a wine we had at
Auxerre for the same price and which I think was made much
newer. I learned with pleasure from Parent that this year
would be still better for wine than that of 84. He begged me to
assure you of his zeal for your service and the fidelity with
which he would continue to furnish you. I ate of the grape of
which the Volnais is made. I was struck with its resemblance
to some of our wild grapes in Virginia and particularly some

that grow in Surry (County) on my fathers estate. The shape of the bunch, the size and color, and still more the taste of the grape, so absolutely the same, that I think it would be impossible to distinguish one from the other. The vine at my fathers grew on an oak tree which stood in an old field quite separate from any other, so that the sun acted on it with its full force. I could wish much to see a fair experiment made on the grapes of that tree. I recollect my father made one year by way of experiment some wine, of what grapes however I know not. The wine was very sweet and very agreeable to my taste, but not at all resembling the Volnais.—We slept that night at Chalons, and the next at Villefranche. We stopped in the evening at the pavillon of M. de l'Aye, where we learned he was at Lyons. Our intention was to go and stop at Villefranche, from whence I was to write to him my arrival there. Luckily we met him as we entered Villefranche on his return from Lyons. He invited the company to his house which was declined. We took leave to meet the next morning. He was obliged to come and dine at Villefranche the next day with the Chancellor of the Duke of Orleans who arrived there. He came to the tavern where we were and it was agreed he should call on me after dinner to bring me to his house in his carriage. Mr. and Mrs. paradise set off about 11 o'clock. Before their departure we settled all accounts. Their expences were twenty eight guineas, mine five. They had therefore remaining on hand twenty two only so that it was determined by both of them to receive the whole of the amount of the letter of credit which was accordingly indorsed to them. The postillions who set out with them from Villefranche returned there before I left it, and told me they had gone on well and safely the first post. I should have not have entered into all these details about myself and my companions with any other than yourself Sir because few would have the goodness to excuse it; but as I know you will I do not make an apology.

William Short

TO PARENT

Sir: Paris, Jan. 22, 1789

For a few weeks, Sir, I have been meaning to ask you for a shipment of Meursault wine. But the season was so rough that I thought it best to wait until it relents. It was long in coming so now I have an urgent need for it. Therefore, I would appreciate dear Sir, you shipping me 250 bottles of wine of goutte d'or de Mersault. I got so used to Mr. Bachey's 1784 that if he still has some, I would prefer it. If he is out of it, be kind enough to supply the best available in this class of wine. I always trust you for quality, and let the price whatever it should be, while still considering quality rather than price.

Be kind enough to inform me of the carriage that will bring it, and also the name of the Paris gate of entry, so that I may leave my passport with the officials of Customs at the gate. Please also instruct the carrier to request free entry for my wines, by virtue of the passport that will be preissued to them. Your bill for the amount shall be settled as is usual with us.

Th: Jefferson

FROM PARENT

Sir: Beaune, 16 Feb. 1789

A shipment of four baskets in bottles, packed in straw and stringed up and marked [marquée, could mean wheel engraving on a bottle, but this refers to a shipping basket which was probably "labelled".] PS No 1 and 3 and 4, one of which contains twenty-five Boncretien pears that I sent you because I believe they must be rather scarce in Paris after the hard frost of last winter. There are 248 or 249 bottles in the four baskets, which left the 14th and should be received late in the month or by the first of March at the latest. Through Mr. Bernier, common carrier from De Trois [Troyes ?] and you will make him pay (pay him ?) 66 livres for the whole shipment, including carriage and custom fees. Mr. Jefferson should send his passport to the Rambouillet barrier [gate] some days ahead. The wine went off in good condition; he sent all of the better wine of 1784. In a few days the price of wine went way up. The growers claim that most of the plants are lost.

He bought two casks as soon as he received Mr. Jefferson's

letter, yet it cost 170 [livres], plus 60 [livres] for the bottles, 28 for the baskets and packing, and 14 for straw and corks in all 272 [livres]. I went to Mr. Bachey's but he is out of Old Goute d'Or—he has only 87 vintage available and they are not very good, red nor white; but he still has 7 pieces of his two feuillettes of 1788 goute d'Or and these are excellent, but he asks for 500 livres for the tailings. At the present, he has already sold half of them this season. If Mr Jefferson wishes any, he should let him know because it is of high grade this year, it will be right at the end of autumn to bottle. He hopes to see Mr. Jefferson in Paris in May on his way to Rouen.

Parent

TO PARENT

Sir: Paris, March 11, 1789

I duly received in good condition the four baskets of Meursault wine you were kind enough to send me, and I stand ready to pay the amount when I get your bill. I even request you do it as soon as possible because I plan to leave next month for America, not to return before fall. At that time, I will have to call on you for Monrachet, Meursault and Voulenaye. The Bachey wine you sent has made me a bit demanding. The shipment I just received from you was not as perfect. I would have thought it was a year other than 1784, if you hadn't told me it was that year. I am told that last year was excellent for wine quality. Therefore I will order this vintage from you next fall. I send you a thousand thanks for the pears you were kind enough to send me. They were really delicious and very rare.

Th: Jefferson

Although Jefferson praised the wines of Burgundy for many years after his stay in Paris, it was more difficult to obtain them from this region because they had to be shipped overland to Paris, thence to Bordeaux. Nevertheless, he continued to praise and evaluate them as he wrote fourteen years later,

May 4, 1803

"...the wines of Burgundy would be very desirable & there

are three kinds of their red wines, Chambertin, Voujeau &
Veaune, & one of their whites, Monrachet, which, under favorable circumstances, will bear transportation, but always with
risk of being spoiled of [?] on the way, to either great heat or
cold, as I have known by experience since I returned to America.
unlefs the Champagnes have risen in price more than I am
informed, there may be something left of my bill, which I should
like to recieve in Chambertin & Monrachet in equal & even so
small, quantities, if you can take the trouble of getting it for
me, merely as an experiment. if it succeeds I may ask a quantity
the next year. it should leave its cellars in Chambertin &
Monrachet about the beginning of October & come through
without delay at either Paris or Havre. there was living at
Beaune, near Chambertin & Monrachet, a tonnelier name
Parent, who being a taster & bottler of wines by trade, was my
conductor through the vineyards & cellars of the Cote, & ever
after my wine-broker & correspondent. If living, he will execute
for me faithfully any order you may be so good as to send him.
The only wines of first quality made at Monrachet were in the
vineyards of M. de Chermont, & of the Marquis de Sarsnet of
Dijon..."

Th: Jefferson

BURGUNDY 200 YEARS LATER

Two hundred years after Jefferson's tour of France, the
American Consulate General in Bordeaux hosted a Bicentennial Celebration which attracted a great deal of attention, not
only to the vineyards of that area, but also to Burgundy.

The Burgundy Regional Council promoted the occasion and
its wines in a leaflet and citation, "Celebrating two centuries of
friendship between the United States of America and Burgundy," A *New York Times* reporter who retraced Jefferson's
route there (NYT, Sept. 20, 1987) found near the village of
Pommard, M. Jacques Parent, a descendant of Etienne. He
reported that the growing and making of wine had changed
very little, but "the vine still needs a lot of work, and the
vendage still has to be done by hand." He showed the American
visitor probably the same cellars that Jefferson had visited with

M. Etienne, some of which are 500 years old, and still producing great wines.

References:

[1]Mr. Maggio, born in France and a wine connoisseur, is a retired French language expert, Department of State, Washington, D. C. He translated the many documents from the French.

[2]The modern spellings of some of the place names given by TJ are inserted here in parentheses: Vaune, Veaune (Vosne); Voulenay (Volnay); Vougeau (Vougeot); Romanie (Romanée); Connault (Connaux); Valignieres (Valliguières); Terrasson (not certainly identifiable, but probably Tarasçon); Vaune River (Huveaune); Gotier (Eygoutier); Geans (Giens); Mantone (Menton); Bezieres (beziers, Argilies (Argeliers); Le Saumal (Le Sommail); Eraut (Herault); Procaraigne (Portiragnes); Chantennay (Chantonnay); Point Boeuf (Paim Bœuf). TJ's reference to Pumice is to *pomice*, the pulp left after the pressing of the grape. The Marquis De Sarsnet of Dijon was evidently the Marquis de Sassenay of Chàlons-sur-Saône, near Dijon. On Monsieur De Bergasse, see TJ to Chastellux, 4 Apr. 1787. The information about the Canal of Languedoc was furnished to TJ by G. Pin (see his letter of 26 May 1787). In N (CSmH0 TJ listed the names of persons whom he wished to see on his journey.

REFORMING HIS NATION'S TASTE[1]

By Lucia C. Stanton[2]

"The taste of this country [was] artificially created by long restraint..." Th. Jeffereon

Jefferson claimed, in 1818, that "in nothing have the habits of the palate more decisive influence than in our own relish of wines." His own habits had been formed over thirty years before— at the tables of Parisian *philosophes* and in the vineyards of Burgundy and Bordeaux. Before his journey to France in 1784, Jefferson, like most of his countrymen, had been a consummer of Madeira and port, with the occasional glass of "red wine." As he recalled in 1817, "The taste of this country [was] artificially created by our long restraint under the English government to the strong wines of Portugal and Spain." The revolution in his own taste in wine followed swiftly on the breaking of the bonds of British colonial government. Thereafter Jefferson rejected the alcoholic wines favored by Englishmen as well as the toasts that customarily accompanied them. He chose to drink and serve the fine lighter wines of France and Italy, and hoped that his countrymen would follow his example.

While it is often difficult to distinguish the wines Jefferson preferred for the sake of his own palate from those he purchased for the comfort of his dinner guests, the quotations that follow should help to identify some of his personal favorites, as well as to illustrate the standards of reference for his taste in wine and his efforts to redeem the taste of his countrymen.

1803. Writing to a correspondent in Spain, Jefferson confessed that a certain pale sherry had "most particularly attracted my taste to it. I now drink nothing else, and am apprehensive that if I should fail in the means of getting it, it will be a privation which I shall feel sensibly once a day."

1806. Jefferson described a recent shipment of Nebbiolo, a sparkling wine of the Italian Piedmont, as "superlatively fine." This importation proceeded from his memory of drinking Nebbiolo in Turin in 1787, when he described it as "about as sweet as the silky Madeira, as astringent on the palate as Bordeaux, and as brisk as Champagne. It is a pleasing wine;"

When paying a bill for three pipes [one pipe equals 110 U. S. gallons] of Termo, a Lisbon wine drier and lighter than ordinary port, Jefferson said that "this provision for my future comfort' had been sent to Monticello to ripen.

1815. By this time, after years of war had prevented importation, Jefferson's stock of aged Lisbon and leftovers from the President's House was exhausted. Writing to a Portuguese wine merchant in Norfolk, he said that "disappointments in procuring supplies have at length left me without a drop of wine. I must therefore request you to send me a quarter cask of the best you have. Termo is what I would prefer; and next to that good port. Besides the exorbitance of price to which Madeira is got, it is a wine which I do not drink, being entirely too powerful. Wine from long habit has become an indispensable for my health, which is now suffering by it's disuse."

"SILKY WINE"

For his major supply he wrote to Stephen Cathalan, the American agent at Marseilles:

"I resume our old correspondence with a declaration of wants. The fine wines of your region of country are not forgotten, nor the friend thro' whom I used to obtain them. And first the white Hermitage having `un peu de la liqueur' as he expressed, which we call silky, soft, smooth, in contradistinction to the dry, hard or rough. What I had from M. Jourdan of this quality was barely a little sweetish, so as to be sensible and no more, and this is exactly the quality I esteem. Next comes the red wine of Nice, such as my friend Mr. Sasserno sent me, which was indeed very fine. That country being now united with France, will render it easier for you I hope to order it to Marseilles. There is a 3d kind of wine which I am less able to specify to you with certainty by it's particular name. I used to meet with it at Paris under the general term of *Vin rouge de Roussillon*; and it was usually drunk after the repast as a *vin de liqueur*, as were the Pacharetti sec, & Madeire sec: and it was in truth as *dry* as they were, but a little higher colored. I remember I then thought it would please the American taste, as being dry and tolerably strong. I suppose there may be many kinds of wine of Roussillon; but I never saw any but of that particular quality used at Paris. I am certain it will be greatly esteemed here, being of high flavor, not quite so strong as Pacharetti or Madeire or Xeres, but yet of very good body, sufficient to bear well our climate."

HERMITAGE BEST

The Hermitage, which he had regularly imported while President, was described by Jefferson in 1791 as "the first wine in the world without a single exception." The Bellet from Nice he called "the most elegant *every day* wine in the world." The Roussillon, which he continued to import, was evidently bought for the sake of his guests as an intermediate stage in the Madeira weaning process.

1816. "For the present I confine myself to the physical want of some good Montepuciano..." this being a very favorite wine, and habit haveing rendered the light and high flavored wines a necessary of life with me." Jefferson had imported this red Tuscan wine as President and had declared an 1805 shipment "most superlatively good."

1817. Jefferson gave the state of North Carolina credit for producing "the first specimen of an exquisite wine," Scuppernong, and praised its "fine aroma, and chrystalline transparence."

Writing to his agent in Marseilles about a recent shipment of Ledanon, a wine produced near the Pont du Gard, Jefferson declared it "excellent" and said it " recalled to my memory what I had drunk at your table 30 years ago, and I am as partial to it now as then." Elsewhere he described this *vin de liqueur* as having " something of the port character but higher flavored, more delicate, less rough."

Speaking of the French wines of Hermitage, Ledanon, Roussillon, and Nice, he stated that he was "anxious to introduce here these fine wines in place of the Alcoholic wines of Spain and Portugal; and the universal approbation of all who taste them at my table will, I am persuaded, turn by degrees the current of demand from this part of our country, and that it will continue to spread *de proche en proche* [step by step]. The delicacy and innocence of these wines will change the habit from the coarse and inebriating kinds hitherto only known here."

He added that he would order the white Hemitage only occasionally, it " being chiefly for a *bonne bouche* [tit-bit].

1819. No single letter provides a better statement of Jefferson's drinking habits, his tasting vocabulary, and his efforts to convert his fellow Americans than one written on May 26 to Stephen Cathalan:

"I will explain to you the terms by which we characterise different qualities of wines. They are 1. *sweet* wines, such as Frontignan & Lunel of France, Pacharetti doux of Spain, Calcavallo of Portugal, *le vin du Cap* &c. 2. Acid wines, such as the vins de Graves, du Rhin, de Hocheim &c. 3. dry wines, having not the least sweetness or acidity in them, as Madere sec, Pachretti sec, vin d'Oporto, &c,. and the Ledanon which I call a dry wine also. 4. *silky* wines, which are in truth a compound in their taste of the dry wine dashed with a little *sweetness*, barely sensible to the palate: the silky Madeira which we sometimes get here, is made so by putting a small portion of Malmsey into dry Madeira."

ASTRINGENT, ROUGH

"There is another quality of wine which we call *rough* or *astringent*, and you also, I believe, call it *astringent*, which is often found in both the dry & silky wines. There is something of this quality for example in the Ledanon, and a great deal of it in the vin d'Oporto, which is not only dry, but astringent approaching almost to bitterness. Our vocabulary of wines being thus explained, I will observe that the wine of Nice sent me by Mr. Spreafico in 1816 was silky and a little astringent and was the most delicious wine I ever tasted, and the most esteemed here generally. That of 1817 was entirely dry, moderately astringent and a very good wine; about on a footing with Ledanon. That of 1818 last received, has it's usual astringency indeed, but is a little acid, so much so as to destroy it's good flavor. Had it come in the summer I should have suspected it's having acquired that acidity by fretting in the hold of the ship, or in our hot warehouses on a summer passage, but it was shipped at Marseilles in October, the true time for shipping delicate wines for this country. I will now say why I go into these details with you. In the first place you are not to conclude that I am become a *buveur* [drinker]. My measure is a perfectly sober one of 3. or 4. glasses at dinner.[3] But as to these 3. or 4. glasses *Je suis bien friand* [a delicacy of which I am fond]. I go however into these details because in the art, by mixing genuine wines, of producing any flavor desired, which Mr. Bergasse possesses so perfectly, I think it probable he has prepared wines of this character also; that is to say of a compound flavor of the rough and silky; or if he has not, I am sure he can. The Ledanon, for example, which is dry and astringent, with a proper proportion of wine which is sweet and astringent, would resemble the wine of Bellet sent me in 1816 by Mr. Spreafico. If he has any wines of this quality, I would thank you to add samples of 2. or 3. bottles of each of those he thinks approaches this description nearest...I have labored long and hard to procure the reduction of duties on the lighter wines, which is now effected to a certain degree. I have labored hard also in persuading others to use those wines. Habit yields with difficulty. Perhaps the late diminution of duties may have a good effect. I have added to my list of wines this year 50 bottles of *vin muscat blanc de Lunel*. I should much prefer a wine which should be *sweet* and *astringent*, but I know of none. If you know of any, not too high priced I would thank you to substitute it instead of the Lunel."

WINE AND FRIENDSHIP

Unfortunately Henri Bergasse, a producer of blended wines, did not make the desired wines and the death of Cathalan prevented a personal response to Jefferson's request for the perfect "rough and silky" wine. Cathalan's successor sent samples of several wines and from these Jefferson selected a *Clairette de Limoux,* which he found "much to our taste" and continues to order, but which does not seem to have satisfied his personal quest for perfection.

1826. With the exception of a "sufficient" quantity of Scuppernong, all the wines on hand in the Monticello cellar at the time of Jefferson's death came from southern France: red Ledanon, white Limoux, Muscat de Rivesalte, and a Bergasse immitation red Bordeaux. This cellar list and the preceding letters seem to confirm evidence of family members and visitors to Monticello that, at least in his last years, Jefferson drank wine at table only after the completion of the meal, in the English manner. His habits still reflected his British heritage but his tastes were international. High in flavor but low in alcohol, the wine of France and Italy was the perfect accompaniment to social pleasure and the "true restorative cordial," as he designated both wine and friendship.

References:

[1] A "Keepsake" program paper read to guests at the Fall Trustees dinner, Thomas Jefferson Memorial Foundation, Monticello, Nov.2, 1984, honoring the retiring Resident Director, Mr. James A Bear, Jr. He inaugurated the beginning of the replanting of the Monticello vineyard— the fruition of an effort to illustrate, in context, Thomas Jefferson's influential association with the noble product of the grape. Mr. Bear's personal quest for bottles for the Monticello wine cellar culminated under his guidance with the renewal of a vineyard whose bounty may one day fill these bottles. The vineyard restoration was completed in 1985. (See chapter on vineyard restoration by Peter J. Hatch).

[2] Director of Research, T. J. Memorial Foundation, and one of the nations most prominent Jefferson scholars.

[3] A wine glass of his time held about two ounces, as compared to the usual glass today of six and eight ounces.

JEFFERSON'S TASTING VOCABULARY
"Taste Cannot Be Controlled By Law"

Over a period of two hundred years that have passed, it is remarkable that we have the detailed, organized, tasting vocabulary for the first time of the greatest authority on wines in early American history--Thomas Jefferson.

Wine connoisseurs today will be intrigued by his many well-studied and sensitive descriptions when they compare them with their own terms. His enjoyment of fine foods is well known, and he liked dishes cooked with wine that are described in another chapter.

"Taste cannot be controlled by law,"[1] he once said. This may, or may not have been stated in regard to wine, but most assuredly, it must have crossed his thoughts on many occasions because these two subjects were often on his mind: moderate laws and moderate use of alcoholic beverages.

His tastes for certain wines varied over the decades of his long life, just as our tastes change today. His first recorded comment referred to a sweet wine, then as he grew older and had lived in France he cultivated an appreciation of dry table wine with food. But his last known wine order list of February 1, 1826[2] shortly before he died, indicated his appreciation of both dry and sweet types.

Fortunately, the fact of his keen and discerning palate was coupled with his outstanding literary ability which enabled him to record in colorful and elegant terms his sensitive reactions to different wines. And even more important was his careful regard for preserving records which we may enjoy and marvel at today.

In a letter from Monticello to Mrs. John Adams, January 11, 1817, Jefferson philosophized:

"Nothing proves more than this that the Being who presides over the world is essentially benevolent. Stealing from us, one by one, the faculties of enjoyment, searing our sensibilities, leading us, like the horse in his mill, round and round the same beaten circle,

> To see what we have seen,
>
> To taste the tasted, and at each return
>
> Less tasteful; o'er our palates to decant
>
> Another vintage—
>
> until satiated and fatigued with this leaden iteration,
>
> we ask our own congé [holiday]."

Jefferson did not intrude or propound his ideas of what wines he liked best or why his tastes dictated to him certain vintages. Instead the records indicate that often his suggestions and ideas were in response to queries. His advice was sought by presidents, cabinet members, military leaders and close friends. For his day, he possessed an extraordinary wide knowledge of many vineyards in a number of countries.

He employed the usual terms, "best", "very best", "best quality" and might even be carried away so much as to say the "best in all the world". Perhaps he even coined a term or two that we might use today, for example, "silky" which has a very pleasant connotation. It would be intriguing to know for example, whether his description of "body" is the same as 20th century connoisseurs. Above all, he has left a record which enables us to feel as he felt about certain wine qualities, which in turn draws us closer to the times of our nation's birth and to the man who took such an important part in that blessed event.

The two most important perhaps of his records on tasting which will be quoted in their entirety here were written to Samuel I. Harrison, September 18, 1817 and to Victor Aldolphus Sasserno, May 26, 1819. Throughout this book, however, are many of his comments about the quality and tastes of wines. The letter to his close friend President James Monroe, April 8, 1817 for example, used such descriptive terms as "rough", "delicate", "higher flavored", "elegant" and "every-day wine".

Spelling, punctuation, and grammar in the documents have

not been edited.[3] Samuel I. Harrison, who Jefferson offered to assist in choosing wines and importing them, was probably a merchant and tavern owner friend. Jefferson used such adjectives in describing them as "strength", "flavor", "higher flavored", "weakness", "color", "dry", "pretty strong", and "light".

To Samuel I. Harrison
Poplar Forest Sep. 18, 1817

Dear Sir

As you expressed a wish to have a note of the wines I mentioned to you yesterday, I make one on the back hereof. I can assure you that they are esteemed on the continent of Europe among the best wines of Europe, and, with Champagne, Burgundy, Tokay are used at the best tables there. I think Roussillon of Rivesalt is that which will be most used in this country, because strength & flavor are qualities which please here, as weakness & flavor do there. a first importation will enable you to judge for yourself, and should you select any on trial & wish to import them hereafter yourself either for the tavern or your own table, I will give you letters to Mr. Cathalan our Consul at Marseilles & Mr. Appleton our Consul at Leghorn, both of them my friends & correspondents of 30. years standing. I salute you with friendship & respect

Th : Jefferson

[reverse side]

Roussillon wine. This resembles Madeira in colour & strength. With age it is higher flavored, it is considered on a footing with Madeira & dry Pacharetti, and is equally used at the best tables of the continent of Europe. There are many kinds of wine made in Roussillon, but that here meant is the Roussillon of Rivesalt. it cost 74. cents a gallon there, & the duty here is 25.cents the gallon if brought in cask as should be.

Hermitage. This is one of the first wines of France. The white is much the best, costs 831/2 cents a bottle there, bottle included. it is a pretty strong wine, & high flavored. duty 15. cents a bottle.

Florence wine.   There are several crops under different names but that of Montepulciano is the only good, and that is equal to the best Burgundy. it must come in strong bottles well cemented. When sent in the flask, much of it spoils. cost there 25 cents a bottle, duty here 15 cents. requires a good cellar, being a very light wine.

Claret of Marseilles.   made there by a Mr. Bergasse by putting together different grapes, so that it is the genuine juice of the grape, and so perfect an imitation of the finest Bordeaux, as not to be distinguishable.   The Bordeaux merchants get it from Bergasse paying one franc a bottle, bottle included, & send it to the US. as of the growth of Bordeaux, charging 4 francs a bottle.

Capt. Bernard Peyton, of the Commission business in Richmond, will import there on commifsion, the cost being advance him here & a reasonable commifsion allowed him. The Florence is imported from Leghorn. the others from Marseilles. I give him letters to my correspondents there which will insure him faithful supplies both as to quality & price

Victor Aldolphus Sasserno was apparently Jefferson's wine buyer in Nice or nearby Marseilles, and whose father in Nice Jefferson had enjoyed wine with during his tour to Southern France about 30 years earlier. Jefferson wanted Sasserno to understand exactly the kinds of wined he perferred by giving him precise terms to follow in future orders.

In addition to the adjectives used in the directions to Harrison, Jefferson provided such terms as, "character", "sweet", "brisk", "doux" (sweet, mild, smooth), "pitchy", "acid", "barely sensible", "astringent", "bitterness", "delicious", "good body", "excellent" and "superlatively good". It is interesting to note that he classified German wines as "acid" which is not a true description today. He also wrote of the "aroma".

Jefferson complained of wines becoming acid due to prolonged heat from "fretting in the hold of the ship." Many loads of fine wines were lost in this way in the days of sailing ships when unfavorable winds off the coast of the United States drove the ships to the tropical West Indies islands where they had to remain for months. This was another of the many dangers that Jefferson had to plan against in transporting the fine Vinifera wines of Europe:

To Victor Aldolphus Sasserno[4]

Monticello in Virginia. May 26. [18]19 Duplicate

[This letter is similar to one to Stephen Cathalan, same day, in the preceeding chapter. Ed.]

Sir

I have to acknolege the reciept of your two favors of Aug. 18 and Oct.. 14 and also of the 300 bottles of wine of Bellet which you were so kind as to forward to me. My taste for the wine of Nice, and for the particular quality of it which I drank at your father's house in Nice, and which M. Spreafico sent me in 1816 will, I fear, become a troublesome circumstance to you; and chiefly perhaps because the expressions characterising subjects of taste & flavor in one language have not always become exactly synonimous in another. To remove this difficulty, I will explain to you the particular terms we use to designate articularly different flavors or characters of wine. These are 1. sweet wines, such as Frontignan & Lunel of France, Pacharetti *doux* of Spain, Calcavalla of Portugal, Vin du Cap Etc. 2. Acid wines, such as the vins de Grave, du Rhin, de Hockheim Etc. 3. dry wines, which have not the least either sweetnefs or of acidity as Madere sec. Pacharetti sec, vin d'Oporto Etc. 4. silky wines, which are in truth a compound in their taste of the dry dashed with a little sweetishness, barely sensible to the palate. The silky Maderia we sometimes get in this country is made so by putting a small quantity of Malmsy into dry Maderia. There is another quality which is so often found in the dry & silky wines, which quality we call rough or astringent, and the French also, I believe, call it astringent. There is something of this in all the wines of Nice which I have seen, & so much of it in those of Oporto as to approach to bitterness while it is also dry. our vocabulary of wines being thus explained, I will observe that the wine of Bellet sent me by M. Spreafico in 1816, was silky and a little astringent, and was the most delicious wine I ever tasted, and the most esteemed here generally. That of 1817, was dry, a little astringent, and an excellent wine. That of 1818, last reveived, has it's usual astringency indeed, but is a little acid; so much so as to destroy it's usual good flavor. Had it come in the summer, I should have suspected it's having acquired it's acidity by fretting in the hold of a ship, or hot warehouse, on a summer passage, but it was shipped at Marseilles in October, the true time for shipping delicate wines for this country. with this explanation of the meaning of our terms, I will now pray you, Sir, to send me thro' Mr. Cathalan, 150 bottles of wine of Bellet of the silky quality sent me in 1816. by Mr. Spreafico, if to be had; and if that was of an accidental *recolte* [harvest], not always to be had, send it of the dry quality, such as was sent in 1817.

I have made remittance to Mr. Cathalan to cover this demand, and the sooner the wine can reach him, the better will be the chance of it's arriving here before winter. The importance of this proceeds from the prevalence of North West wind on our coast, commencing in December, which frequently drive ships, then approaching the coast, to the West Indies, keeping them at sea, and in danger until the winter months are over. I salute you, Sir, with great esteem & respect.

Th: Jefferson

From the foregoing notes and letters, it is obvious that Mr. Jefferson spent a great deal of time indeed, savoring, analyzing, and enjoying his wines. He also took pleasure in advising others in minute detail.

References:

[1]"Paul Masson Reader", p. 13.

[2]James Monroe Memorial Library, Fredericksburg, Va.

[3]University of Virginia Library, Charlottesville, Va

[4]Wine agent in the Nice, Marseilles region.

TOUR NOTES ON WINES AND VINES
In France And Italy 1787[1]
by George Tener [2]

"I would go to Hell for my country!" said Thomas Jefferson when he was appointed one of the Commissioners to monarchical France in 1784, and if Louis XVI had taken that as an ethnic slur he would have probably been right.

There was much that the author of the Declaration of Independence found hellish in autocratic, hierarchical France, but Jefferson was as successful in his diplomacy as in many other pursuits. Following his appointment as Minister to the French court the following year, an office in which he succeeded Benjamin Franklin, his popularity and effectiveness grew side by side. In addition he developed a real expertise in French wines. He imported wine continuously after his return to the United States and, of course, made efforts to develop viticulture in Virginia.

On two occasions, in 1787 and 1788, he made extended springtime travels through the countryside of France to report on farming in general and wine production in particular, and his journals of these trips are filled with the most minute details: a horse's ration compared with a mule's; the composition of a loaf of bread; the daily wages of a farm woman compared to a man's; the weight a donkey can carry. But considering the times, the voids in Jefferson's journals are almost as interesting as the narrative. Although he closely observes and carefully records his impressions of the life of the people in general there is scarcely ever the report of a conversation. In his official position, to say nothing of his personal fame, he must certainly have met many articulate and reflective persons whose spoken views improved his own insights, yet only two are referred to and those obliquely. His notes are almost entirely technical.

To the modern mind perhaps overly awed of the clandestine Jefferson's notes on the age-old agricultural practices of Europe could have been a "cover" for the true purpose of his tour:

political reconnaissance of the provinces. In 1789 the first flowers of the French Revolution were to blossom in the country; what better place to observe the buds?

In 1787 Europe was filled with ferment as seldom before or since. The year before Frederick the Great of Prussia had died and left his kingdom to a son who saw the path to government lying through Rosicrucian mysticism. In Vienna the Emperor Joseph II had virtually despaired of mastering the Austrian Empire left him by his mother, Maria Theresa, or of reconciling the incompatible political forces within it. He had inherited the most powerful state in Europe; the following year he died defeated by it. By 1787 Kant and Beethoven were disclosing their respective revelations , and the Americans, having won their war contrary to all expectations, were forging their Constitution from principles the *ancien regime* found incredible.

The conciseness of Jefferson's notes are remarkable; not a word is wasted. Yet through it all one can see the innumerable searching questions he asked. "how long do the sticks last?" "What is the hook for?"

Yet Jefferson did not like what he saw in the province of Champagne when he set out to cross it on March 3, 1787 at the start of a three-month trip through the south and west of France:

" The face of the country is in large hills, not too steep for the plough, somewhat resembling the Elk hill and Beverdam hills of Virginia. The soil is generally a rich mulatto loam, with a mixture of course sand and some loose stone. The plains of Yonne are of the same colour. The plains are in corn, the hills in vineyards but the wine not good..."

But, Burgundy seemed otherwise, at least at the outset. "The people are well clothed, but it is Sunday. They have the appearance of being well fed. The Chateau de Sevigny, near Cussy-les-Forges is in a charming situation. Between Maison neuve and Vitteaux the road leads through an avenue of trees 8. American miles long in a right [sic] line. It is impossible to paint the ennui of this avenue."

Jefferson tells us nothing as to his means of transportation except on the rare occasions when he is gliding along in a horse-drawn canal boat at two or three miles an hour. From the rate at which he covered the ground, however, we must assume he was on horseback. From Cussy-les-Forge to Dijon is fifty-three American miles and he did it in one day. As he entered the Burgundy wine district on March 9, though, he slowed his pace. These were his comments the end of his first day there.

"The corn lands here rent for about 15^{tt} the arpent [about 0.85 acre]. They are now planting, pruning, and sticking their vines. When a new vineyard is made they plant the vines in gutters about 4. feet apart. As the vines advance they lay them down. They put out new shoots and fill all the intermediate space till all trace of order is lost. They have ultimately about one foot square to each vine. They begin to yield good profit at 5. or 6. years old and last 100. or 150. years. A vigneron at Voulenay carried me into his vineyard, which was of about ten arpents. He told me that some years it produced him 60. pieces of wine, and some not more than 3. pieces. The latter is the most advantageous produce, because the wine is better in quality and higher in price in proportion as less is made; and the expences at the same time diminish in the same proportion. Whereas when much is made, the expenses are increased, while the quality and price become less. In very plentiful years they often give one half the wine for casks to contain the other half. The cask for 250. bottles costs 6^{tt} in scarce years and 10^{tt} in plentiful. The feuillette is of 125 bottles, the piece of 250., and the *queue*, or *botte* of 500. ...A farmer of 10. arpents has about three laborers engaged by the year. He pays 4. Lois to a man, and half as much to a woman, and feeds them. He kills one hog, and salts it, which is all the meat used in the family during the year. Their ordinary food is bread and vegetables. At Pommard and Voulenay I observed them eating good wheat bread; at Meursault, rye. I asked the reason of the difference. They told me that the white wines fail in quality much oftener than the red, and remain on hand. The farmer therefore cannot afford to feed his laborers so well. At Meursault only white wines are made, because there is too much stone for the red. on such slight circumstances depends the condition of man!

"The wines which have given such celebrity to Burgundy grow only on the Cote, an extent of about 5 leagues long, and half a league wide. They begin at Chambertin, and go on through Vougeau, Romanie, Veaune, Nuys, Beaune, Pommard, Voulenay, Meursault, and end at Monrachet. The two last are white; the others are red. Chambertin, Voujeau, and Veaune are strongest, and will bear transportation and keeping. They sell therefore on the spot for 1200^{tt} the Queu, which is 48. sous the bottle. Voulenaye is the best of the other reds, equal in flavor to Chambertin & but being lighter will not keep, and therefore sells for not more than 300^{tt} the Queue, which is 12. sous the bottle. It ripens sooner than they do and consequently is better for those who wish to broach at a year old. In like manner the White wines, and for the same reason, Monrachet sells at 1200^{tt} the Queue...and Mersault of the best quality, viz. the Goutte d'or, at only 150^{tt}. It is remarkable that the best of each kind, that is, of the Red and the White, is made at the extremities of the line, to wit, at Chambertin and Monrachet. It is pretended that the adjoining vineyards produce the same qualities, but that, belonging to obscure individuals, they have not obtained a name, and therefore sell as other wines." [See Burgundy chapter for his later orders for wine, also appendices for more description.]

SEEDS OF THE REVOLUTION

Jefferson does not mention it, but when he crossed the Saone at Macon and passed through from Burgundy into Beaujolais he took a step of some legal and financial significance. In the first place, he moved from that half of France whose jurisprudence was regulated by the gothic feudal law to the area governed by written law derived from the Roman Empire. Secondly, he moved outside the territory where the Cinq Grosses Fermes, a Parisian tax-gathering consortium, collected the salt tax or *gabelle*, into an area where less rapacious tax gatherers sold salt for half, or less, the price of the Parisians.

The *gabelle* had first been imposed lightly enough in 1286 as a temporary expedient, but like many temporary governmental structures it soon gained the dignity of permanent status. By the time the Revolution broke out in 1789 the *gabelle* had become the focus of great hostility not only because of its regressive nature as a tax but also due to the inequity with which it was administered. A virtual consumers' strike which began in July 1789 caused *gabelle* revenues to plummet from two hundred thousand livres in that month to forty thousand livres in December.

One must remember that at the time of Jefferson's travels no parliment or elected assembly had been called by the Crown for one hundred fifty years, and all national legislation was in the hands of the Executive. The opportunities for tax "adjustments" without the consent of the taxpayers had consequently proliferated, and by Jefferson's time the *gabelle* had grown so monstrousthateach person over the age of eight years—in the territory of Cinq Grosses Fermes—was required to purchase a fixed amount of salt at a fixed price each week. The five other regions in which the *gabelle* was collected varied as to price and tax assessed, and in three favored provinces no *gabelle* was collected at all.

"Through all Champagne, Burgundy and the Beaujolais, the husbandry seems good, except that they manure too little. This proceeds from the shortness of their leases." Says Jefferson. "The people of Burgundy and Beaujolais are well clothed, and have the appearance of being well fed. But they experience all the oppressions which result from the nature of the general government, and from that of their particular tenures, and of the Seignorial government to which they are subject. What a cruel reflection that a rich country cannot long be a free one!"

Seignory was an essential feature of feudal law, and it has been defined as that lordship remaining to a grantor after the grant of an estate in fee simple. "There is no land without its seigneur", was the feudal maxim. In the twelfth century, the clergy and territorial seigneurs had a voice in the feudal council, a legislative body. They represented those who had no voice by right of seignory. In France, by the thirteenth century, the clergy and territorial nobles, grouped into two "estates,' had been joined by the Third Estate composed of merchants of the towns and minor landowners. Because the Middle Ages conceived of society as divided into definite orders, the "three estates of the realm" corresponded to the great divisions of legislative authority. It was these three national legislative houses, the "Estates General," which were not convened by the King of France from 1614 until 1788. They met in Paris the following year, and France was never the same again. The crucial moment of the French Revolution was to come when these three Estates abolished the vote by "order," which is to say as separate legislative bodies, and merged to form the National Assembly. Jefferson's America, while retaining a property qualification in the vote, recognized neither seignory nor separate authority in the clergy and Jefferson himself was, of course, as bitterly opposed to the one as the other.

When he came to the city of Lyons Jefferson passed through without remarking on any edifice other than"some feeble remains here of an amphitheatre of 200. feet diameter and of an aqueduct in brick," Evidently he paid no attention to the Cathedral of St. John, considered one of the finest examples of early gothic architecture in France. It becomes increasingly plain in reading these journals that Jefferson the architect was no gothicist. Roman ruins interested him not the medieval. It was the dead hand of the Middle Ages which lay, in his view, like a monkey's paw on the heart of Europe, and he gave it none of his respect. At Lyons he was 250 modern American miles from Sens and he made the trip in eleven days. Swift, purposeful sightseeing indeed.

COTE ROTIE WINES

The almonds were in bloom, Jefferson reports, as he proceeded southward from Lyonnais to Dauphiny and the vineyards of the Cote Rotie and the Cote Rhone on the fifteenth of March, 1787. "Nature never formed a country of more savage aspect than that on both sides of the Rhone," But of the Cote Rotie(roasted hillside)he wrote,

"Those parts of the hills only which look to the sun at Mid-day or the earlier hours of the afternoon produce wines of the first quality. 700 vines of 3 feet apart, yield a feuillette, which is about 2½ pieces to the arpent. The best red wine is produced at the upper end in the neighborhood of Ampuys; the best white next to Condrieux. They sell of the first quality and last vintage at 150^{tt} the Piece, equal to 12s. the bottle. Transportation to Paris is 60^{tt} and the bottle at 20s. When old it cost 10. or 11. Louis the Piece. There is a quality which keeps well, bears transportation, and cannot be drunk under 4. years. Another must be drunk at a year old. They are equal in flavor and price."

"The wine called Hermitage, is made on the hills over the village of Tains....the last hermit died in 1751." Hermitage was to become one of the most popular French wines among the Victorian Englishmen.

In the Cote du Rhone proper, which extends for more than one hundred miles, Jefferson found still another method of planting and handling vines.

"In the neighborhood of Montelimart and below that they plant vines in rows 6. 8. or 10. feet apart, and 2. feet asunder in the row, filling the intervals with corn. Sometimes the vines are in double rows 2. feet apart. I saw single asses in ploughs proportioned to their strength. The plough formed of three pieces, thus...[there follows a diagram]. Asses and mules, working in pairs, are coupled by square yokes...There are few chateaux in this province. The people too are mostly gathered in villages. There are however some scattering farm houses. These are made either of mud or of round stone and mud....Day laborers receive 16s. or 18s. the day, and feed themselves. Those by the year receive, men 3. Louis and women half that, and are fed. They rarely eat meat; a single hog salted being the year's stock for a family. But they have plenty of cheese, eggs, potatoes and other vegetables, and walnut oil with their sallad. It is a trade here to gather dung along the road for their vines. This proves they have few cattle. I have seen neither hares nor partridge since I left Paris, no wild fowl on any of the rivers."

Jefferson left the Rhone, the "river of wine," at Pont St. Esprit and followed the track of the modern Route 86 through Bagnols, Romoulins and Nimes in the royal province of Languedoc. Salt, by the way, now dropped to one sixth the price paid in Champagne.

"PIQUETTE" WINES

"From the summit of the first hill after leaving Pont St Esprit, there is a beautiful view of the bridge at about 2. miles distance, and a fine landscape of the country both ways. From thence an excellent road, judiciously conducted, thro very romantic scenes. In one part, descending the face of a hill, it is laid out in Serpentine, and not zig-zag, to ease the descent. In others it passed thro' a winding meadow, from 50. to 100. yards wide, walled as it were on both sides by hills of rock; and at length issues into plane country....The horse chestnut and mulberry are leaving; apple trees and peas blossoming. The first butterfly I have seen. After the vernal equinox they are often 6. or 8. months without any rain. Many separate farmhouses, numbers of people in rags, and abundance of beggars...Vin ordinaire, good and of a strong body 2.s or 3.2 the bottles..." Languedoc evidently appealed to Jefferson notwithstanding the absence of chateaux and the presence of beggars.

Had he been less taciturn about his encounters with others on this trip we may well have heard of Arthur Young through him. Young, an English agriculturist two years his senior, was touring the French countryside and studying its agricultural practices even more thoroughly than Jefferson in the same year 1787. Young came to the conclusion in his two-volume *Travels in France* that the soil of France was superior to that of England but that it produced less because of its neglect by the educated class. "Banishment from the court alone will force the French nobility to execute what the English do for pleasure—reside upon and adorn their estates," he wrote. "Give a man secure possession of a bleak rock and he will turn it into a garden; give him nine years lease of a garden and he will convert it into a desert." Young and Jefferson seemed to have deplored France equally from different viewpoints. Some of the brightest scenes of contentment and prosperity which surprised Young on the eve of the French Revolution were those of the grape harvests in the vineyards of Languedoc.

March 25, Jefferson noted, "...after quitting the plains of the Rhone, the country seems still to be a plain cut into compartments, by chains of mountains of massive rock running thro it in various directions. From Pontroyal to St. Cannat the land lies rather in basons. The soil is very various. Grey and clay, grey and stony, red and stony; sometimes good, sometimes midling, often barren...Toward Pontroyal the hills begin to be in vines..."

March 25-28, On approaching Aix the valley which opens from thence towards the mouth of the Rhone and the sea is rich and beautiful: a perfect grove of olive trees, mixt among which is corn, lucerne and vines...They drink what is called Piquette. This is made after the grapes are pressed, by pouring hot water on the pumice [pomace]. On Sunday they have meat and wine...(Note it is 20. American miles from Aix to Marseilles, and they call it 5. leagues. There league then is of 4. American miles.)"

SEEDLESS GRAPE AT MARSEILLES

March 29, Marseilles, "The country is hilly, intersected by chains of hills and mountains of massive rock. The soil is reddish, stony and indifferent where best. Whenever there is any soil it is covered with olives. Among these are vines...I met a small dried grape from Smyrna without a seed. There are a few of the plants growing in this neighborhood. The best grape for drying known here is called des Panses. they are very large, with a thick skin and much juice. They are best against a wall of Southern aspect, as their abundance of juice requires a great deal of sun to dry it... Monsieur de Bergasse has a wine cellar 240. pieds long, in which are 120. tons of from 50. to 100 peices each. These tons are 12. pieds diameter; the staves 4. I. thick, the headings 2½ pouces thick. The temperature of his cellar is 9½ (degrees) of Reaumur. The best method of packing wine, when bottled, is to lay the bottles on their side, and cover them with sand... to preserve the raisin, it is first dipped into lye and then dried in the sun."

From Marseilles Jefferson followed eastward along the French Riviera to Toulon, Hyeres and Nice seeing vineyards, but without making notable observations on the wines. At Nice he noted, "The wine made in this neighborhood is good, tho' not of the finest quality." He then went northward to Turin [Italy] capital of the Duchy of Savoy, then a possession of Austria. As he entered the Piedmont Plain south of the city, April 16, he noted a new way of planting vines:

"At intervals of about 8. feet they plant from 2. to 6. plants of vine in a cluster. At each cluster they fix a forked staff, the plane of the prongs of the fork at a right angle with the row of vines. Athwart these prongs they lash another staff, like a handspike, about 8. f. long, horizontally, 7. or 8. feet from the ground. Of course it crosses the rows at right angles. The vines are brought from the foot of the fork up to this cross piece, turned over it, and conducted along over the next, the next, and so on as far as they will extend, the whole formation an arbour 8. f. wide and high, and the whole length of the row, little interrupted by the stems of the vines, which being close round the fork, pass up thro' hoops, so as to occupy a space only of small diameter."

In Truin he relished a "red wine of Nebiule...which is very singular. It is about as sweet as the silky Madeira, as astringent on the palate as Bordeaux, and as brisk as Champagne. It is a pleasing wine."

This Nebiule, or Nebbiolo, is identified in Alexis Lichine's comprehensive *Encyclopedia of Wines and Spirits* (1967) as a grape used in modern Italian red wines and not a wine itself. But we are less partial to sweet wines than our forebears who, like Jefferson, considered Sauterne "the best white wine of France." To the modern palate, wines like Barolo and Barbaresco from the Monferrato district of the Italian Piedmont are among the region's finest; Jefferson found then "thick and strong."

April 19, Jefferson noted, "There is a wine called Gatina made in the neighborhood of Vercelli, both red and white. The latter resembles Calcavallo. There is also a red wine of Salusola which is esteemed. It is very light."

ITALIAN PLANTING METHOD

By April 20, while approaching Milan from the west Jefferson found yet another way of planting vines:

"Along rows of trees they lash poles from tree to tree. Between the trees are set vines which passing over the pole, are carried on the pole of the next row, whose vines are in like manner brought to this, and twined together; thus forming the intervals between the rows of trees alternately into arbors, and open space." He turned to the coast at Genoa, noting vineyards, but without finding any further significant wines or vineyard techniques.

April 28, at Noli, he noted, "The wine they make is white and different..." For a man as purposeful as Jefferson it is pleasant to see that he was not immune to the charms of the villages, (Louano to Albenga) of the Italian Riviera west of Genoa: "If any person wished to retire from their acquaintance, to live absolutely unknown, and yet in the midst of physical enjoyments, it should be in some of the villages of this coast, where the air, earth and water concur to offer what each has most   precious. Here are nightingales, beccaficas, ortolans, pheasants, partridge, quail, a superb climate, and the power of changing it from summer to winter at any moment, by ascending the mountains. The earth furnishes wine, oil, figs, oranges, and every production of the garden in every season. The sea yields lobsters, crabs, oysters, thunny, sardines, anchovies &c."

By May 10 he was back in Languedoc sampling the sweet wine of Lunel: "Lunel is famous for it's *vin de muscat blanc*, thence called Lunel, or vin Muscat de Lunel. It is made from the raisin muscat, without fermenting the grape in the hopper. When fermented it makes a red Muscat, taking that tinge from the dissolution of the skins of the grape, which injures the quality. When a red Muscat is required, they prefer colouring it with a little Alicant wine. But the white is best. The price of 240. bottles, after being properly drawn off from it's lees, and ready for bottling costs from 120^{tt} to 200^{tt} of the 1st quality and last vintage." [This price compares with 150^{tt} for the best quality Mersault in Burgundy, as reported by Jefferson.] "It cannot be bought old, the demand being sufficient to take it all the first year. There are not more than from 50. to 100. pieces a year made of the first quality. A setterie yields about one piece, and my informer supposes there are about two setteries in an arpent. Portage to Paris by land is 15. the quintal. The best recoltes are those of M. Bouquet and M. Tremoulet. The vines are in rows 4. f. apart every way." Nowadays all Muscat de Lunel is sold fortified.

May 11. Montpelier, he wrote, "Snow on the Cevennes, N. W. for hence. With respect to the Muscat grape, of which the wine is made, there are two kinds, the red and the white. The first has a red skin, but white juice. If it be fermented in the cuve, the colouring matter which resides in the skin, is imparted to the wines. If not fermented in the cuve, the wine is white. Of the white grape, only a white wine can be made..."

FRONTIGNAN–CETTE–BEZIERES

May 12, Frontignan [See chapter, "Frontignan..."] Some tolerable good plains in olives, vines...There are but 2. or 3. peices a year, of red Muscat, made, there being but one vineyard of the red grape, which belongs to a baker called Pascal. This sells in bottles at 30.s the bottle included. Rondette, *negociant en vin*, Porte St. Bernard fauxbourg St. Germain a Paris, buys 300. pieces of the 1st. quality, every year. The coteaux yeild about half a piece to the Setterie, the plains a whole piece. The inferior quality is not at all esteemed. It is bought by the merchants of Cette, as is also the wine of Bezieres, and sold by them for Frontignan of 1st. quality. They sell 30,000 pieces a year under that name. The town of Fontignan marks it's casks with a hot iron. An individual of that place, having two casks emptied, was offered 40. for the empty casks by a merchant of Cette. The town of Frontignan contains about 2000 inhabitants. It is almost on the level of the ocean. Transportation to

Paris is 15. the quintal, and is 15 days going. The price of packages is about 8^tt—8 the 100 bottles. A setterie of good vineyard sells for from 350 to 500. and rents for 50. A labouring man hires at 150. the year, and is fed and lodged : a woman at half as much..."

At the town of Cette, Jefferson noted, "There are in this town about10,000 inhabitants. It's principal commerce is wine. It furnishes great quantities of grape pomice for making verdigriese [then used as a medicine]. They have a very growing commerce, but it is kept under by the privileges of Marseille."

May 13, Agde, "On the right of the Etang de Tau are plains of some width, then hills, in olives and vines..."

May 14, Bezieres, "Rich plains in corn, ...some vines..."

May 15, "...From Argilies to Saumal are considerable plantations of vines. Those on the red hills to the right are said to produce good wine...The Canal of Languedoc along which I now travel is 6. toises wide at bottom, and 10 toises at the surface of the water, which is 1. toise deep...the locks are mostly kept by women, but the necessary operations are much too laborious for them. The encroachments by the men on the offices proper for the women is a great derangement in the order of things. Men are shoemakers, tailors, upholsters, staymakers, mantua makers, cooks, door-keepers, housekeepers, housecleaners, bedmakers. They coeffe the ladies, and bring them to bed; the women therefore, to live are obliged to undertake the offices which they abandon. They become porters, carters, reapers, wood cutters, sailors, lock keepers, smiters on the anvil, cultivators of the earth &c. Can we wonder if such of them as have a little beauty prefer easier courses to get their livelihood, as long as that beauty lasts." Ladies who employ men in the offices which should be reserved for their sex, are they not bawds in effect? For every man whom they thus employ, some girl, whose place he has taken, is driven to whoredom..."

BORDEAUX

May 22, "Toulouse. 23. Agen. 24. Castres. Bordeaux. The

Garonne and rivers emptying into it make extensive and rich plains...The hills are in corn, maize, beans and a considerable proportion of vines...When we cross the Garonne at Langon we find the plains entirely of sand and gravel, and they continue so to Bordeaux. Where they are capable of anything they are in vines, which are in rows 4.5.or 6. feet apart, and sometimes more. Near Langon is Sautern, where the best white wines of Bordeaux are made. The waste lands are in farm, furze, shrubbery and dwarf trees..."

By May 24, Jefferson had arrived in Bordeaux, and there he stayed for five days reporting on the viticulture and wines of that famous river mouth. He wrote his impressions as follows [See also Bordeaux chapter for his later orders],

"The cantons in which the most celebrated wines of Bordeaux are made are Medoc down the river, Grave adjoining the city and the parishes next above; all on the same side of the river. In the first is made red wime principally, in the two last, white. In Medoc they plant the vines in cross rows of 3½ pieds. They keep them so low that poles extended along the rows one way, horizontally, about 15. or 18.I above the ground, serve to tye the vines to, and leave the cross row open to the plough. In Grave they set the plants in quincunx, i.e. in equilateral triangles of 3½ pieds every side; and they stick a pole of 6. or 8. feet high to every vine separately. The vine stock is sometimes 3. or 4. f. high. They fine these two methods equal in culture, duration, quantity and quality. The former however admits the alternative of tending by hand or with the plough. The grafting of the vine, tho a critical operation, is practiced with success. When the graft has taken, they bend it into the earth and let it take root above the scar. They begin to yeild an indifferent wine at 3. years old, but not a good one till 25. years, nor after 80, when they begin to yield less, and worse, and must be renewed. They give three or four workings in the year, each worth 70. or 75., the journal, which is of 840. square toises, and contains about 3000 plants. They dung a little in Medoc and Grave, because of the poverty of the soil; but very little; as more would affect the wine. The journal yeilds, *communibus annis*, about 3. pieces of 240. or 250 bottles each. The vineyards of first quality are all worked by their proprietors. Those of the 2d. rent for 300. the journal: those of the 3d. at 200. They employ a kind of overseer at four or five hundred livres the year, finding him lodging and drink; but he feeds himself. He superintends and directs, but is expected to work but little. If the proprietor has a garden the overseer tends that. They never hire labourers by the year. The day wages for a man are 30. sous, a woman's 15.sous, feeding themselves. The women make bundles of sarment, weed, pull off the snails, tie the vines, gather the grapes. During the vintage they are paid high and fed well.

MARGAU-LA FITE-DIQUEM-LATOUR

"Of Red Wines, there are 4. vineyards of first quality, viz. 1. Chateau Margau, belonging to the Marquis d'Agicourt, who makes about 150. tonneaux of 1000 bottles each. He has engaged to Jernon a merchant. 2. La Tour de Segur, en Saint Lambert, belonging to Monsieur Mirosmenil, who makes 125. tonneaux. 3. Houtbrion, belonging ⅔ to M. le comte de Femelle, who has engaged to Barton a merchant, the other third to Comte de Toulouse at Toulouse. The whole is 75 tonneaux. 4. Chateau de la Fite, belonging to the President Pichard at Bordeaux, who makes 175 tonneaux. The wines of the three first are not in perfection till 4 years old. Those [of] de la Fite, being somewhat lighter, are good at 3 years, that is, the crop of 1786 is good in the spring of 1789. These growths of the year 1783 sell now at 2000^{tt}. the tonneau, those of 1784, on account of the superior quality of that vintage, sell at 2400^{tt}, those of 1785 at 1800^{tt}, those of 1786 at 1800^{tt}, tho they sold at first for only 1500^{tt}. Red Wines of the 2d. quality are Rozan belonging to Madame de Rozan, Dabbadie ou Lionville, la Rose, Quirouen, Durfort; in all 800 tonneaux, which sell at 1000^{tt} new. The 3d class are Calons, Mouton, Gassie, Arboete, Pontette, de Terme, Candale; in all, 2000 tonneaux at 8 or 900^{tt}. After these they are reckoned common wines and sell from 500^{tt}. down to 120^{tt} the ton. All red wines decline after a certain age, losing colour, flavor, and body. Those of Bordeaux begin to decline at about

7 years old.

"Of White Wines, those made in the canton of Grave are most esteemed at Bordeaux. The best crops are 1. Pontac, which formerly belonged to M. de Pontac , but now to M. de Lamont. He makes 40. tonneaux which sell at 400^{tt}. new. 2. St Brise, belonging to M. de Pontac, 30 tonneaux at 350^{tt}. 3. De Carbonius, belonging to the Benedictine monks, who make 50 tonneaux, and never selling till 3. or 4. years old, get 800^{tt}. the tonneau. Those made in the three parishes next above Grave, and more esteemed at Paris are 1. Sauterne. The best crop belongs to M. Diquem at Bordeaux, or to M. de Salus his son in law. 150. tonneaux at 300^{tt}. new and 600^{tt}. old. The next best crop is M. de Fillotte's 100 tonneaux sold at the same price. 2. Prignac. The best is the President du Roy's at Bordeaux. He makes 175 tonneaux, which sell at 300^{tt}. new, and 600^{tt}. old. Those of 1784, for their extraordinary quality sell at 800^{tt}. 3. Barsac. The best belongs to the President Pichard, who makes 150 tonneaux at 280^{tt}. new and 600^{tt} old. Sauterne is the pleasantest; next Prignac, and lastly Barsac; but Barsac is the strongest; next Prignac, and lastly Sauterne: and all stronger than Grave. There are other good crops made on the same paroisses of Sauterne, Prignac, and Barsac; but none as good as these. There is a Virgin wine, which tho' made of a red grape, is of a light rose colour [rosé wine], because, being made without pressure the colouring matter of the skin does not mix with the juice. There are other white wines from the preceding prices down to 75^{tt}. In general the white wines keep the longest. They will be in perfection till 15. or 20. years of age. The best vintage now to be bought is 1784, both of red and white. There has been no other good year since 1779.

ENGLISH, FRENCH MERCHANTS

"The celebrated vineyards beforementioned are plains, as is generally the canton of Medoc, and that of Grave. The soil of Hautbrion particularly, which I examined, is a sand, in which is near as much round gravel or small stone, and a very little loam: and this is the general soil of Medoc. That of Pontac, which I examined also, is a little different. It is clayey, with a fourth or fifth of fine rotten stone; and of 2. feet depth it becomes all a rotten stone. M. de Lamont tells me he has a kind of grape without seeds, which I did not formerly suppose to exist, but I saw at Marseilles dried raisins from Smyrna, without seeds. I see in his farm at Pontac some plants of white clover and a good deal of yellow; also some small peach trees in the open ground. The principal English wine merchants at Bordeaux are Jernon, Berton, Johnston, Foster, Skinner, Copinger and M^{C}Cartey. The chief French wine merchants are Feger, Nerac, Brunneau, Jauge, and de Verget. Desgrands, a wine broker, tells me they never mix the wines of the first quality: but that they mix the inferior ones to improve them. The smallest wines make the brandy. They yield a fifth or sixth."

Jefferson visited the city of Bordeaux at a pinnacle of its prosperity. A treaty with Britain concluded the year before, although it ruined the cloth traders of Amiens and Abbeville, brought new prosperity to Bordeaux and the Gironde River. Twelve thousand tons of wine were being shipped to England annually and sixty shipyards there were spawning ships at a rate of more than sixty a month. The city, furthermore, suffered little from labor troubles or class conflict, and when the Estates-General were to convene in Paris two years later the deputies from the Gironde were to have difficulty understanding the class-conscious atmosphere of the capital.

Yet the life of the peasants in the country was otherwise. Discontent with their fees and charges with which they were saddled, as well as their sense of social injustice and discrimination, had been growing for years. There developed a more dangerous condition than class hatred—the isolation of class from class. The burges and peasants knew nothing of each other. Revolution was not expected in the cities, yet in the Spring of '89, while the deputies were travelling toward Versailles, the first peasant outbreaks warned them of what might be in store. For a time the peasant tightened his belt and hoped that the new assembly would give him bread. The disappointment of this hope led to the more serious insurrection of the summer.

LOIRE WINES

The last great wine growing area of France which Jefferson visited before returning to Paris lay in the Duchy of Anjou along the banks of the Loire. The native wines there, principally white, are remarkable today and Anjou is known to us principally for its fine *rosé*. In Jefferson's time, though, the tastes and doubtless the wines themselves were different.

"There is a very good wine on these hills; not equal indeed, to the Bordeaux of best quality, but to that of good quality, and like it. It is a great article of exportation from Anjou and Touraine, and probably is sold abroad under the name Bordeaux...."

In these reports on the French wine and viticulture Jefferson was not describing new processes, nor indeed, any new wines. All had been in place at least since the Crusaders brought the muscat vines back from the Middle East. For the most part the making of the wine was a craft introduced into France by the ancient Romans. So perhaps viticulture's link to classical Rome had something to do with Jefferson's close study of it. The only architecture he found worth noting in the journals were the remains of Roman architecture and that he was blind to the most conspicuous architectural feature of the French countryside: the village church. He was, furthermore, at the forefront of the Neoclassical movement which swept European and American culture at the close of the eighteenth century and whose principles were embodied in Jefferson's own University of Virginia. For whatever reason, though, viticulture was a keen interest of Jefferson's for his lifetime. Now that science has allowed us to overcome some of the difficulties of viticulture which Jefferson found insuperable his opinions on wines are the more valuable to us.

References:

[1]*The Papers of Thomas Jefferson,* Vol. II, p. 415-464, Julian P. Boyd, Editor, Princeton University Press, Princeton, N. J., 1955.

[2]Farmer, Greek scholar, and wine connoisseur of Washington, D. C.

ADAMS TO JEFFERSON ON WINE
"I Shall Be Ruined..."

One of the most amusing stories to come to light from the Jefferson correspondence had been a series of letters in 1785 between John Adams in London and Jefferson in Paris concerning their urgent efforts to stop a large shipment of wine from France to England.

Adams had just arrived from The Hague, Holland, to take up his new post as Ambassador to England in London. His trusted and respected advisor on wines, Jefferson, was Ambassador to France and had ordered a large quantity of wines for him from Bordeaux and other sources.

Following protocol, Adams had paid a formal call on the Minister of Foreign Affairs at His Britannic Majesty's Court promptly upon arrival. One would expect that his first letter to Jefferson would officially report on the important conversation held at a time when relations between the two countries were still strained after the Revolution. This was not the case however, as Adams wrote May 27, 1785, "...received by the Marquis, but of this more hereafter...", the rest of the letter was a distraught plea about a wine problem.

Adams must have used the fastest available mailing service because the letter took only four days to reach Jefferson in Paris, probably some kind of record in those days of postmen on horseback and English Channel crossings by sail or rowboat.

Adams had been shocked when he was told that he would have to pay up to about $1.75 a bottle duty on all the wine he wanted to bring in from the Continent. This would have cost him in duties approximately $1000 or more which was a very large sum in those days.

His letter to Jefferson appealed for help, "...I must stop all that I have in France..., ...beg you to write to Mr. Garvey..., ...beg you to take the wine at any price..., ...accept it as a present..."

Jefferson promptly replied on June 2nd that just the day

before he had cleared all the wine through French Customs at the gates of Paris and then put it on a river boat to go to the port of Rouen for shipment to London.

However, on receiving the SOS from Adams, Jefferson had sent his servant Petit (a faithful employee in France who followed him to the United States and remained many years in (his service there) dashing off to stop the boat. Alas, the boat was just departing when Petit arrived at the docks, and he found it was impossible to reland the wine.

Jefferson informed his dear friend of his failure to stop the boat, expressing his disappointment, but that he would take immediate steps to stop the shipment of wine coming from Bordeaux.

Before learning this however, Adams had rushed off another letter to Jefferson June 7th, stating a little frantically, "For Mercy Sake stop all my Wine but the Bourdeaux and Madeira, and Frontenac...I shall be ruined..."

The letters, written in frustration and urgency, follow:

FROM ADAMS

Dear Sir   London May 27. 1785

I arrived yesterday and have made my visit today, and been very politely received by the Marquis, but of this more hereafter. This is devoted to a smaller subject.

Upon Enquiry I find that I cannot be exempted from paying duties upon my Wines, because no foreign Minister is, except for a less quantity than I have of the best qualities in my Cellar at the Hague, so that I must stop all that I have in France if I can. To pay six or eight Shillings Sterling a Bottle upon the Small Wines I packed at Auteuil would be folly. I must beg you then if possible to stop it all except one Case of Madeira and Frontenac together. Let me beg you too to write to Mr. Garvey and stop the order for five hundred Bottles of Bourdeaux. All my other Things may be sent on to me, as proposed.

Coll. Smith has Letters for you, but waits a private Hand. He Sends his Respects to you and Coll. Humpherys. If my

Things are gone and connot be stopped I must pay the Impost, heavy as it is. I am sorry to give you this Trouble but I beg you to take the Wine, at any Price you please. Let your own Maitre D'Hotel judge, or accept it as a present or sell it at Vendue, i.e. let Petit dispose of it as he will, give you an Account of proceeds and give me credit, and then order me to pay the Stockdale or any Body here for you to the amount.

My esteem, & Regards as due. Yours affectionately

John Adams

TO ADAMS

Dear Sir   Paris June 2. 1785.

Your favours of May 23, and the two of May 27. came safely to hand, the first being open. That of the 22d. from Montreuil sur mer had been received and answered on the 25th.

The day before the receipt of the letter of the 27th, we had had your cases brought to the barrier of Paris in order to get the proper officer to go that far to plumb them. From there they were put on board the boat for Rouen and their portage paid. In the instant of receiving your letter I sent Petit off to try to stop them if not gone. The boat was just departing and they declared it impossible to reland them: and that could it be done, a new passport from the C. de Vergennes would be necessary for the part not landed. I now forward your letter to Mr. Garvey, countermanding your order of the wine from him, and praying him to retain all the cases of wine now sent except that which has the Madeira and Frontignac, till he shall receive your orders. These therefore you will be so good as to send him as soon as convenient. I was very sorry we could not stop the wine. It would have suited me perfectly to have taken it either at the price it cost you, if known to Petit, or if not known, then at such prices as he and Marc should have estimated it at; and this would have saved you trouble. I inclose you Petit's note of disbursements which I immediately repaid him. You will know the exchange between London and Paris, which is considerably in favour of the former. Make the allowance for that and either retain the money in your own hands or put it into Stockdale's as most convenient. Can you take the trouble of ordering me the two best of the London papers (that is to say one of each party) and by any channel which will save me postage and the search of government?

Th: Jefferson

In his Account Book for 2 June, 1785, T. J. recorded that he had "repaid Petit for portage &c. of Mr. Adam's things 173f 8."

FROM ANTHONY GARVEY
[U. S. Consul]

Sir   Rouen the 5 June 1785.

I received your Excellency's letter of the 2d. Inst. I shall take care of the Effects that you have addressed to me, and forward them agreable to orders on board the first vessel that sails for London after their reception, except the Cases of Wine, which I shall keep here for Mr. Adams' further orders; the one containing Madeira and Frontignac shall be sent. Be so good as to let me know how many Cases of Wine there are, and what particular mark or numbers the one containing Maderia and Frontignac bears, that no mistake may happen. If you cannot give me these informations I shall have them opened here, this in order to prevent mistakes.

I shall be always happy to be favored with your and Friends Commands in this City, and request you will imploy me on every occasion that I can be of use; being with the greatest respect & truth Your Excellency's most Hume. & obedient Servant,

Anthy. Garvey

(Jefferson noted in his log. of letters, Paris, 6 June 1785, "Received Mr. Garvey's June 5. and answered it same day. 8 caisses of wine.")

FROM ADAMS
(colorful background included)

Dear Sir   Bath Hotel Westminster June 7. 1785.

I have received yours of 25. May, and thank you for the News of My Son, and for the News of Paris. I wish to have seen the Queens Entrance into Paris, but I saw the Queen of England on Saturday, the Kings Birth day, in all her Glory. It is paying very dear to be King or Queen to pass One such a day in a year. To be obliged to enter into Conversation with four or five hundred, or four or five Thousand People of both Sexes, in one day and to find Small Talk enough for the Purpose, adapted to the Taste and Character of every one, is a Task which would be out of all Proportion to my Forces of Mind and Body. The K. and Q. speak to every Body. I stood next to the Spanish Minister, with whom his Majesty conversed in good French, for half or Quarter of an Hour, and I did not loose any Part of the discourse, and he said several, clever Things enough. One was *Je suis convaincu que le plus grand Ennemy du Bien, est le mieux.* [I am convinced that the greatest enemy of good is the better.] You would have applied it as I did, to the Croud of Gentlemen present who had advised his Majesty to renounce the Bien for the Mieux in America, and I believe he too had that Instance in his mind. Thursday I must be presented to the Queen, who I hope will say as many pretty Things to me, as the K. did.

You would die of ennui here, for these Ceremonies are more numerous and continue much longer here than at Versailles.

I find I shall be *accable* with Business and Ceremony together, and I miss my fine walks and pure Air at Auteuil. The Smoke and Damp of this City is ominous to me, London boasts of its Trottoir [sidewalks] but there is a space between it and the Houses through which all the Air from Kitchens, Cellars, Stables and Servants Appartements ascends into the Street and pours directly on the Passanger on Foot. Such Whiffs and puffs assault you every few Steps as are enough to breed the Plague if they do not Suffocate you on the spot.

For Mercy Sake stop all my Wine but the Bourdeaux and Madeira, and Frontenac. And stop my order to Rouen for 500 Additional Bottles. I shall be ruined, for each Minister is not permitted to import more than 5 or 600 Bottles which will not more than cover what I have at the Hague which is very rich wine and my Madeira Frontenac and Bourdeaux at Auteuil. Petit will do the Business.

Regards to Coll. Humphreys and Mr. Williamos. Adieu.

John Adams

TO ABIGAIL ADAMS

(wife of John Adams)

Dear Madam   Paris June 21, 1785

...The squibs against Mr. Adams are such as I expected from the polished, mild tempered, truth speaking people he is sent to. It would be ill policy to attempt to answer or refute them. But counter-squibs I think would be good policy. Be pleased to tell him that as I had before ordered his Madeira and Frontignac to be forwarded, and had asked his orders to Mr. Garvey as to the residue, which I doubt not he has given, I was afraid to send another order about the Bourdeaux lest it should produce confusion...

Th; Jefferson

TO MRS. ADAMS

Dear Madam   Paris July 7, 1785.

I had the honour of writing you on the 21st. of June, but the letter being full of treason has waited a private conveiance. Since that date there has been received for you at Auteuil a cask of about 60. gallons of wine. I would have examined it's quality and have ventured to decide on it's disposal, but it is a cask, and therefore cannot be got at but by operations which would muddy it and disguise its quality. As you probably know what it is, what it cost, &c. be so good as to give me your orders on the subject and they shall be complied with...

Th: Jefferson

FROM ADAMS

Grosvenor Square Westminster, the Corner of
Duke and Brook Streets July 16th. 1785

Dear Sir

I have been so perplexed with Ceremonials, Visits, Removals and eternal applications from Beggars of one Species and another, besides the real Business of my Department, that I find I have not answered your favour of the second on June, which I received in Season. I have received from Mr. Garvey [Consul at Rouen] all but my wine and have written him to day to forward that and will run the risque of it, as I believe I shall easily obtain an order to receive it without paying duties. Petits Note of Expences which you paid, you either omitted to send me or I have lost it in the Confusion of a Removal, so that I must trouble you to send it again...

[At this point in R C, T J made a note of the amount, "173f 8."]

TO ADAMS

Sir   Paris July 28. 1785

...(footnote) You say nothing in your letter (July 16 and 18) about your wine at Auteuil. I think I sent you Petit's bill for I do not find it among my papers. It's amount was 175^{tt} [sic] 8s.

Th: Jefferson

FROM ADAMS

Grosvenor Square Westminster Aug.7.1785

Dear Sir

As to the Cask of Wine at Auteuil, it is not paid for. If you will pay for it and take it, you will oblige me. By a sample of it, which I tasted it is good Wine, and very, extremely cheap...

John Adams

FROM PLOWDEN GARVEY

(Summary: from Rouen, 13 August 1785, on request of Mr. Adams, the last of his seven cases of wine have been shipped via the *Sophie*, Captain Knight...bill of lading and note of charges 96l. 16s.6d., sent to Adams and sight draft payable to John Fred: Perregaux has been drawn on Jefferson.)

TO MRS. ADAMS

Dear Madam   Paris Sep. 25. 1785

....P. S. The cask of wine at Auteuil, I take chearfully. I suppose the seller will apply to me for the price. Otherwise, I do not know who he is, I shall not be able to find him out...

Th: Jefferson

FROM GAZAIGNER DE BOYER

(Gaillac, 9 Nov. 1785. Recorded by Jefferson as received 1 Dec. 1785. Account book, for 21 Dec. 1785 contains entry,

"Paid Mr. Andrier for le sieur gazaigner 74^{tt}-8-9 for a barrique of wine de Gallac dit du Cocq which contains 215 bottles. It took [?] bottles of Bordeaux to fill it up. Note this is the wine which Mr. Adams had bought, and which he desired me to take. I am still to pay him 40f paid by Horatener & co. of Rouen for expences of transportation duties &c."

FROM MRS. ADAMS

Sir   Grosvenor Square Novr. 24th. 1785

...Inclosed is a Letter which I found a few days ago respecting the Wine which you was so kind as to take. Mr. Adams is uncertain whether he requested you to pay Mr. Bondfeild on his order 319 Livres for a Cask of Wine which he procured for him and of which he never received any account untill his arrival here. If Mr. Barclay has not done it Mr. Adams would be obliged to you to pay it for him...

A. Adams

And so this little bit of historical wine drama involving two of America's greatest patriots and future presidents came to a close over two hundred years ago. Afterwards they returned to the United States where Adams became Vice President under Washington and Jefferson Secretary of State. Except for an interlude when they became political oponents, the two were close friends over a period of 50 years. How many times over a good glass of wine they must have chuckled and recalled the episode of the unwanted wine shipment. They both died on the same day, Independence Day, July 4th 1826.

JEFFERSON'S GERMAN WINE CHOICES
His Vineyard Tour 1788

By Dr. Jurgen Kalkbrenner[1]

"...if you ever revisit Monticello, I shall be able to give you a glass of Hoch or Rudesheim of my own making." to Major von Geismer.

When on April 3, 1788, Thomas Jefferson reached Cologne, after having travelled from Paris via Holland to the Northern parts of the Rhine country, his first entry into his travel journal was not about wines. It was about Westphalian hams, of which Cologne was the principal export market at the time. He noted: "Well informed people here tell me there is no other part of the world where the bacon is smoked." And he added, "They do not know that we do it."[2]

As in this case, Jefferson's knowledge was superior to his contemporaries' in many respects. After his return from his post as American Ambassador to France, he was certainly one of the greatest experts on German wines living in the young United States. He obtained the knowledge that qualified him as such in the spring of 1788 on his tour through the Rhine valley, where he became acquainted, if not with all, with most of the German winegrowing areas.

How exact and how detailed were his observations! About the wines of Cologne he remarked, "Here the vines begin, and it is the most Northern spot on the earth on which wine is made. Their first grapes came from Orleans [France?]...It is 32. years only since the first vines were sent from Cassel, near Mayence [Mainz], to the Cape of good hope, of which the Cape wine is now made.... That I suppose is the most Southern spot on the globe where wine is made and it is singular that the same vine should have furnished two wines as much opposed to each other in quality, as in situation."

The present-day traveller would still find plenty of Westphalian ham and plenty of Rhine wine in the shops of Cologne. In vain, however, he would look for vines and vineyards, the northern border of the vine growing country of the Rhine valley having receded south to Niederdollendorf, on the slopes of the Siebengebirge near Bonn. When passing through this area and travelling further south to Coblenz on April 4, 1788, Thomas Jefferson observed that the vines "...are planted in rows 3. feet apart both ways. The vine is left about 6. or 8.f. high, and stuck with poles 10. or 12.f. high. To these poles they are tied in two places, at the height of about 2. and 4.f. ...The hills are generally excessively steep, a great proportion of them barren, the rest in vines principally ... the plains yield much wine, but bad. The good is furnished from the hills."

Tying the vines to poles is still practiced in the Middle Rhine area and in the Moselle valley, while in other parts of Germany wires are preferred as holds for the vines.

1783 WAS A GREAT YEAR

In Coblenz, where the Moselle enters the Rhine and which the Romans called Castrum ad confluentes, Jefferson discovered that in the Elector of Trier's palace "are large rooms very well warmed by warm air conveyed from an oven below through tubes which open into the rooms [the first central heating?]." He was also introduced to the wines of the Moselle valley, wines that are grown on almost vertical cliffs and are famous for their delicacy. Distinguishing various qualities he stated, "The 1st. quality (without any comparison) is that made on the mountain of Brownberg, adjoining to the village of Dusmong, and the best crop is that of the Baron Breidbach Burrhesheim grand chambellan et grand Baillif de Coblentz ... The last fine year was 1783. which sells now at 50. Louis [$1200] the foundre ... about 1100. bottles." 50 Louis was the price of a pair of good horses, as Jefferson noted later. He also learned that a day's labour of a man was paid the equivalent of 3 pounds of beef, a woman's the half of that.

The "Brownberg" wine impressed Jefferson so much, that, after his return to Paris, he mentioned it in a lengthy and detailed letter of advice written by him for two young American friends, John Rutledge, son of Governor Rutledge of South Carolina, and Lee Shippen, son of Dr. Shippen of Philadelphia. Both expected to travel the same route later in the year. Under

The Jefferson tour route of 1788

"Coblentz", he advised them, "Here call for Moselle wine, and particularly that of Brownberg and of the Grand Chambellan's crop of 1783. that you may be acquainted with the best quality of Moselle wine."

As a tavern Jefferson recommended "The Wildman ou l'Homme sauvage. A very good tavern." But Jefferson, a highly considerate man, was not thinking only of the gastronomic quality of the place. "The tavern keeper furnished me with the Carte des postes d'Allemagne. I paid his bill without examining it. When I looked into it, after my departure I found he had forgot to insert the Map. ...Pray pay him for me with this apology...He is very obliging." He was very obliging also to Rutledge and Shippen as Shippen reported in a letter of July 31, 1788. "At Coblentz we found the Wild man a very civil one to us, and having no true Brownberg in the house, he sent out and got some for us. It is the best Moselle I ever drank. He was very much pleased to hear that you remembered him and as grateful for the re-imbursement of the post map."

Three years later, at the end of 1791 or early 1792, Jefferson sent an extensive list of European wines to Henry Sheaff, a Philadelphia merchant. This list was based on Jefferson's notes taken during his trips through France and Germany. Under "Moselle" he stated, "The best of these is called Brownberg ...15 leagues from Coblentz... It is really a good wine."[3]

Is it still a good wine since Jefferson saw the predecessor of modern central heating at the Elector's palace and tasted "Brownberg" wine in the tavern "A l'Homme Sauvage"? The Brauneberger wines, with their vineyards Juffer and Falkenberg, are today listed among the first of the Moselle valley. In his book on great German wines, Stefan Andres calls them the "peaks" of the Moselle and he praises a "1953 Brauneberger Juffer, Riesling, Hochfeine Auslese, Weingut Freiherr von-Schorlemer, Lieser" as "a wine of great quality. Its bouquet is rich. ...On the palate it distributes a longlasting, full-fruity taste of berries ...altogether clear and polished ...like a sonnet."[4] The only change that has taken place is that the wine has now given its name to the village which Jefferson knew as

"Dusmond" (actually Dusemond after the Latin dolcis mons meaning "sweet or gentle hills"), some 75 kilometers southwest of Coblenz. It is now called Brauneberg.

At Coblenz, Jefferson crossed the Rhine and continued via Nassau, Schwalbach, Wiesbaden to Frankfort. He thus missed a part of the Rhine, which he advised his friends Rutledge and Shippen not to by-pass, "You will see what I am told are the most picturesque scenes in the world, and which travelers go express to see."

On his way to Frankfort and later from Mayence, where he stayed from April 10 to April 12, 1788, he explored the wines of the Rheingau. Here Germany's best and most famous wines are still grown. Of this area he noted, "Though they begin to make wine, as has been said, at Cologne, and continue it up the river indefinitely, yet it is only from Rudesheim to Hochheim, that wines of the first quality are made. The river happens there to run due East and West, so as to give to it's hills on that side a Southern aspect." Of the grapes he remarked, "...there are three kinds in use for making white wine... 1. The Klemperien, of which the inferior qualities of Rhenish wines are made, and is cultivated because of it's hardness. ... 2. The Rhysslin [Riesling ?] grape which grows only from Hochheim down to Rudesheim. This is small and delicate, and therefore succeeds only in this chosen spot. ...The mass of good wines made at Rudesheim below the village being of the 3d. kind of grape, which is called the Orleans grape."

Today most of the vineyards of the Moselle valley and of the Rheingau are planted in Riesling grapes, while the Klemperich grape is still used on lesser sites. Among the wines of the Rheingau, Jefferson gave his preference to those of Johannisberg, "Johansberg is a little mountain [berg signifies mountain] wherein is a religious house, about 15. miles below Mayence, and near the village of Vingel....This wine used to be put on a par with Hochheim and Rudesheim; but the place having come to the Bp. of Fulda, he improved it's culture so as to render it stronger, and since the year 1775, it sells at double the price of the other two. It has none of the acid of the

Hochheim and other Rhenish wines."

To Rutledge and Shippen he suggested, "Stop on the road at the village of Rudesheim, and the Abbaye of Johnsberg to examine their vineyards and wines. The latter is the best made on the Rhine without comparison, and is about double the price of the oldest Hoch. That of the year 1775 is the best."

WINE FOR BREAKFAST

Well, they stopped on the road and reported, "On our way we lodged at Reidesheim and breakfasted the next morning on samples of Johannesberg wine. What a delicious liquor Sir it is! But I found it too expensive for us to think of importing it. The price on the spot is between 5 and 6 shillings sterg. [one shilling equals 22 cents] a bottle by the Stuck which holds about 4 pipes [one pipe equals 110 gallons]."

Let us hope that later they returned to coffee and tea for their breakfast beverages.

The former abbay, now the Schloss, and its vineyards no longer belong to the Bishop of Fulda. Napoleon gave it to one of his Marshalls with the appropriate name of Kellermann. In 1816, after the Congress of Vienna, it was granted by the Austrian Emperor to Prince Clemens von Metternich. The present owner is his descendant Prince Paul-Alfons von Metternich-Winneberg.

The wines of the Rheingau have not ceased to find adoration. Hugh Johnson praises them, "superlatives become tiring in an account of the Rheingau. Yet if the qualities of great white wine mean anything to you the peculiar sort of wine these growers make offers more to taste, consider and discuss than any other in the world. ...The Rheingau's raison d'etre must be understood. It is wine for wine's sake."[5]

And of Johannisberg he writes, "Schloss Johannisberg, standing above a great apron of vines, dominates everything between Geisenheim and Winkel. The enormous prestige of its production...tends to overshadow the excellent vineyards of the rest of Johannisberg."[6]

Second best to the Johannisberger wines Jefferson listed

those of Rudesheim, "Rudesheim is a village about 18. or 20. miles below Mayence. It's fine wines are made on the hills about a mile below the village, which look to the South, and on the middle and lower parts of them. They are terrassed....These wines begin to be drinkable at about 5. years old. ...They are not at all acid, and to my taste much preferable to Hocheim, tho' but of the same price."

To the hills, "Which look to the South", the Rudesheimer Berg, a present-day expert pays tribute, "At their best (which is not always in the hottest years, since the drainage is too good at times) these are superlative wines, full of fruit and strength and yet delicate in nuance,"[7]

HOCK VINES FOR MONTICELLO

In third rank for Jefferson were the wines from Hochheim, the "Hocks". Although he alluded to them twice as being "acid", his judgement on them in the travel notes and in subsequent letters was altogether positive. In his journal he referred to Hochheim as "a village about 3. miles above Mayence, on the Maine where it empties into the Rhine. The spot whereon the good wine is made is the hill side from the church down to the plain." In his hints to Rutledge and Shippen he proposed, "stop there half an hour to see its vineyards." For their stay at Frankfort he recommended the hotel of John Adam Dick and Son, "You may taste at their tavern genuine Hoch, and of the oldest."

Jefferson even nourished the hope of transferring vines from Hochheim to Monticello, as expressed in a letter from Paris a few months later, to Major von Geismar, a Hessian officer then living in Frankfort, whom he had befriended as prisoner of war at Charlottesville, "I take the first moment to inform you that my journey was prosperous: that the vines which I took from Hochheim and Rudesheim are now growing luxuriously in my garden here [Paris], and will cross the Atlantic next winter, and that probably, if you ever revisit Monticello, I shall be able to give you there a glass of Hoch or Rudesheim of my own making." And in another letter to von Geismar he mentioned that his vines from Hochheim "succeed to admiration."

JOHN ADAM DICK & SON

Merchants, Inkeepers & Proprietors of the
Hotel , called

The Great Red Houſe

Frankfort ont the Mein.

Beg leave to acquaint the Nobility Gentry and the
Public in general; that they deal in all Sorts of
Genuine Hock or Rheniſh Wine.
Whereof the following are moſtly demanded and
to be had from them, at moſt moderate Rates.

	Places	Vintages	pr. Tun		L. Steil.
Hochheim.		1726	. . .	262 .	. 327
		1748	. . .	160 .	. 196
		1760	. . .	72 .	. 105
		1761	. . .	72 .	. 105
		1762	. . .	72 .	. 105
		1766	. . .	66 .	. 98
		1775	. . .	59 .	. 105
		1779	. . .	59 .	. 105
		1780	. . .	50 .	. 79
		1781	. . .	50 .	. 114
		1783	. . .	50 .	. 92
Rüdesheim.		1726	. . .	262 .	. 327
		1748	. . .	160 .	. 196
		1760	. . .	72 .	. 105
		1761	. . .	72 .	. 105
		1762	. . .	72 .	. 105
		1766	. . .	66 .	. 98
		1775	. . .	59 .	. 105
		1779	. . .	59 .	. 105
		1780	. . .	50 .	. 79
		1781	. . .	50 .	. 114
		1783	. . .	50 .	. 92
Johannesberg.		1775	. . .	66 .	. 262
		1779	. . .	66 .	. 262
		1780	. . .	59 .	. 104
		1781	. . .	66 .	. 230
		1783	. . .	59 .	. 104
Markebrunn.		1726	. . .	262 .	. 327
		1748	. . .	164 .	. 196
		1760	. . .	72 .	. 105
		1761	. . .	72 .	. 105
		1762	. . .	72 .	. 105
		1766	. . .	66 .	. 98
		1775	. . .	59 .	. 105
		1779	. . .	59 .	. 105
		1780	. . .	50 .	. 70
		1781	. . .	50 .	. 114
		1783	. . .	50 .	. 92
Nierſtein Laubenve Bodenheim.		1760	. . .	52 .	. 82
		1761	. . .	52 .	. 82
		1762	. . .	52 .	. 82
		1766	. . .	52 .	. 82
		1775	. . .	40 .	. 70
		1779	. . .	45 .	. 79
		1780	. . .	40 .	. 50
		1781	. . .	45 .	. 70
		1783	. . .	47 .	. 79

(Side note, vertical:) in Aums or Quarter Casks 42½ Gallons each; from the very beſt Qualities, & of the very beſt Qualities, in Aums or Quarter Casks 42½ Gallons each; from the Continuance of their Care & Attention to render themſelves worthy of the Continuance of their Prices & at proportionable Prices & of the very beſt

(Side note, bottom right, vertical:) Theſe and al other Sorts of Hock may alſo be had at proportionable Prices & of the very beſt Qualities, lovers of Hock, that they will exert every Care & Attention above J. A. Dick & Son. Aſſuring the reſpect. lovers of Hock, Orders, if once favoured with them.

A Tun contains 8. Aums . . .
An Aum contains 42½ Gallons . . .

Wine list of Frankfort hotel where Jefferson stayed in 1788

Obviously, Jefferson must have been convinced that the Hochheimers were good wines and worth planting at Monticello. However, three years later, in the list for Sheaff, he comments on "Hocks", " It is to be observed of the Hock wines that nobody can drink them but Germans or the English who have learned it from their German kings," And in contrasting the "Hocks" with wines of more southern climates he uses the comparison of an olive to a pineapple.

What had brought about this change from fair credit to utter condemnation? Was he disappointed that the vines he had brought from Hochheim did not grow in Monticello? Had the first yield been as sour as vinegar? We must leave the answer to speculation.

[His German Vinifera vines would surely have suffered the same fate from disease as did French ones. If he tried to force a premature vintage, over-acidity could have destroyed the slightly sweet taste he so admired in German wines.]

GOOD HOCH KEEPS OFF THE DOC

Before we see Jeffeson continue to Nierstein, where he studied the Rheinhesse wines only casually, and then to Mannheim, Heidelberg, Karlsruhe and finally to Strasbourg in France, we should cast a look at the present-day wines of Hochheim. They are well repected by wine connoisseurs. The wines of the vineyards Domdechaney, Hinter der Kirche (Jefferson's "the hill side from the church down to the plain"), Daubhaus are called by Stefan Andres fine, forceful and of rich bouquet. Also Hugh Johnson places good Hochheimers "on a level with the better, not the best, wines of the Rheingau."[8]

Obviously the statement made by Queen Victoria, whose name is borne by one of the best estates in Hochheim, Konigin Victoria Berg is still valid, "Good Hock keeps off the Doc."[9]

Ed. Note: On his return to France, Jefferson wrote about an unusual winemaking process,

April 16. 17. 18. Strasbourg. The Vin de paille is made in the neighborhood of Colmar in Alsace about [blank] from this place. It takes it's name from the circumstance of spreading the grapes on straw where they are preserved till spring, and then made into wine. The little juice then remaining in them makes a rich sweet wine, but the dearest in the world without being the best by any means. They charge 9[tt] the bottle for it in the taverns of Strasbourg. It is the caprice of wealth alone which continues so losing an operation. This wine is sought because dear, while the better wine of Frontignan is rarely seen at a good table because it is cheap.

References:

[1]Dr. Kalkbrenner, former Counselor of Embassy, Federal Republic of Germany, Washington, D. C., is a connoisseur of his country's wines and has a firsthand knowledge of the vineyards that Jefferson visited.

[2]*The Papers of Thomas Jefferson*, Boyd, Princeton, N. J., 1956, Vols. 13 and 14.

[3]Chicago 1965, privately printed, with an introduction by Lawrence W. Towner "Thomas Jefferson on Wines".

[4]Translated from: Stefan Andres, *Die grossen Weine Deutschlands*, Berlin, Frankfurt-Main, 1960, p.56.

[5]Hugh Johnson, *The World Atlas of Wine*, New York, 1971, p.141.

[6]Ibid., p.40.

[7]Ibid., p.138.

[8]Ibid., p.141.

[9]Hans Ambrosi, *Wo grosse Weine wachsen*, Munich.

CHAMPAGNE: A CHOSEN SPECIALTY
But Non-sparkling Was Preferred!

Long before his tour of vineyards in northern France in April 1788, Jefferson expressed his special fondness for wines of the Champagne region. The records he kept of his cellar in Paris, April 7, 1787, showed that he had on hand 29 bottles of "champagne. Chevr. Luaerne." By the next month, however, they had all been consumed, none being listed the next May, indicating his preference.

Strangely, he stated in his many future orders, that the Champagne be "non-mousseux" or non-sparkling. The "brisk" wines as he referred to them sometimes, were drunk only in countries outside France. The demand was high which increased the price by ⅛th, and this added to loss of bottles by breakage, made the true Champagne more expensive. Expense did not trouble Jefferson in those times of affluence. He truly preferred the still Champagnes and influenced the desires of President Washington who also ordered them non-sparkling.

The sparkling process in Champagne-making produces great internal pressure on the bottles, thus the thicker glass that makes the heavier bottle now. Two centuries ago, the art of glass-making was far inferior to the methods used today, consequently there was a much higher incidence of breakage. Jefferson, in his precise way of record keeping, noted when any wine bottles were broken which was not often. However, in his Memorandun Book, December 1, 1803, when he was President, he noted, "...champagne d'Aij. (153. broke)..." This was an extremely high percentage out of a total of 400 bottles. In July of 1804, he recorded a breakage of 23 bottles out of 400. If his Champagne was non-sparkling, exerting little pressure, why such a high breakage?

May 1, 1787, in his notes of his southern tour into Italy, he recorded from the region south of Monaco a mention of sparkling wine made in Italy, "A superb road might be made along the margin of the sea from Laspeze where the champagne country of Italy opens..." An excellent sparkling wine is made in Italy today, but called "spumante", not Champagne.

HOW TO GROW AND MAKE CHAMPAGNE

The conciseness of Jefferson's journals is remarkable. For an example of his style consider his comments on Champagne, which then, as now, was marketed chiefly around the area of Epernay. On his visit there in 1788 he wrote,

Apr. 22. Epernay. The hills abound with chalk. Of this they make lime, not so strong as stone lime, and therefore to be used in greater proportions. They cut the blocks into regular forms also like stone and build houses of it. The common earth too, well impregnated with this, is made into mortar, moulded in the form of brick, dried in the sun, and houses built of them which last 100 or 300 years. The plains here are a mile wide, red, good, in corn, clover, Luzerne, St. foin. The hills are in vines, and this being precisely the canton where the most celebrated wines of Champagne are made details must be entered into. Remember however that they will relate always to the white wines unless where the red are expressly mentioned. The reason is that their red wines, tho much esteemed on the spot, are by no means esteemed elsewhere equally with their white, nor do they merit it.

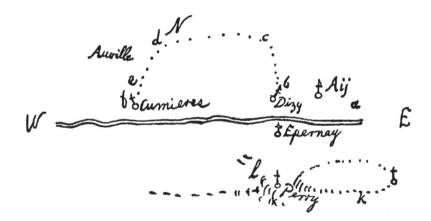

A topographical sketch of the positions of the wine villages, the course of the hills, and consequently the aspect of the vineyards.

Soil. Meagre mulatto clay mixt with small broken stones, and a little hue of chalk. Very dry.

Aspect. May be better seen by the annexed diagram, observing that the wine of Aij is made from a. to b. Dizy b. to c. Auvillij d. to e. Cumieres e. to f. Epernay g. to h. Perry l. to k. The hills from Aij to Cumieres are generally about 250f. high. The good wine is made only in the middle region. The lower region however is better than the upper because this last is exposed to cold winds and colder atmosphere.

Culture. The vines are planted 2f. apart. Afterwards they are multiplied (*provignés*) when a stock puts out two shoots they lay them down, spread them open and cover them over with earth so as to have in the end about a plant for every square foot. This operation is preformed with the aid of a hook formed thus Υ and 9.I. long which being stuck in the ground holds down the main stock while the laborer separates and covers the new shoots. They leave two buds above the ground. When the vine has shot up high enough, they stick it with oak sticks of the size and length of our tabacco sticks and tie the vine to them with straw. These sticks cost 2^{tt} [^{tt} livre. One ^{tt} equals 20 cents] the hundred and will last 40 years. An arpent, one year with another in the fine vineyards gives 12. peices and in the inferior vineyards 25. pieces. Each piece is of 200. bottles. An arpent of the first quality sells for 3000^{tt} and there have been instances of 7200^{tt} (the arpent contains 100 verges of 22 pieds square). The arpent of inferior quality sells at 1000.^{tt} They plant the vines in a hole about a foot deep, and fill that hole with good mould to make the plant take. Otherwise it would perish. Afterwards if ever they put dung it is very little. During wheat harvest there is a month or 6. weeks that nothing is done in the vineyards. That is to say that from the 1st. Aug. to the beginning of vintage. The vintage commences early in Sep. and lasts a month. A days work for a labourer in the busiest season is 20s. and he feeds himself. In the least busy season it is 15s. Cornlands are rented from 4^{tt} to 24,^{tt} but vinelands never rented. The three *façons* of an arpent of vines cost 15.^{tt} The whole years expence of an arpent is worth 100.^{tt}

Grapes. The bulk of their grapes are purple, which they prefer for making even white wine. They press them very lightly (without treading them or permitting them to ferment at all) for about an hour, so that it is the beginning of the running only which makes the bright wine. What follows the beginning is of a straw colour and therefore not placed on a level with the first: the last part of the juice produced by strong pressure is red and ordinary. They chuse the bunches with as much care to make wine of the very 1st. quality as if to eat. Not above one eighth of the whole grapes will do for this purpose. The white grape, tho not so fine for wine as the red, when the red can be produced, and more liable to rot in a moist season, yet grows better if the soil be excessively poor, and therefore in such a soil it is preferred: because there indeed the red would not grow at all.

WINEMAKING

Wines. The white wines are either 1. mousseux (sparkling) or 2. non mousseux (still). The sparkling are little drank in France but are alone known and drank in foreign countries. This makes so great a demand and so certain a one that it is the dearest by about an eigth and therefore they endeavour to make all sparkling if they can. This is done by bottling in the spring from the beginning of March to June. If it succeeds they lose abundance of bottles from $^1/_{10}$ to $^1/_3$. This is another cause encreasing the price. To make the still wine they bottle in September. This is only done when they know from some circumstances that the wine will not be brisk. So if the spring bottling fails to make a brisk wine, they decant it into other bottles in the fall and it then makes the very best still wine. In this operation it loses from $^1/_{10}$ to $^1/_{20}$ by sediment. They let it stand in the bottles in this case 48. hours with only a napkin spread over their mouths, but no cork. The best sparkling wine decanted in this manner makes the best still wine and which will keep much longer than that originally made still being bottled in September. The brisk wines lose their briskness the older they are, but they gain in quality with age to a certain length. These wines are in perfection from 2. to 10. years old, and will be very good to 15. 1766 was the best year ever known, 1775. and 1776 next to that. 1783 is the last good year, and that not to be compared with those. These wines stand icing very well.

Aij. M. Dorsay makes 1100 peices which sell as soon as made at 300.^{tt} and in good years 400 in the cask. I paid in his cellar to M. Louis his homme d'affaires for the remains of the year 1783. 3^{tt}-10 the bottle. Brisk champaigne of the same merit would have cost 4.^{tt} (The piece and demiqueue are the same. The feuillette is 100. bouteilles.) Mr. le Duc 400 to 500 pieces. M. de Villermont 300. pieces. Mr. Janson 250. pieces. All of the 1st quality, red and white in equal quantities.

Auvillij. Les moines Benedictins, 1000 peices red and white but three fourths red. Both of the first quality. The king's table is supplied by them. This enablels them to sell at 550^{tt} the piece tho' their white is hardly as good as Dorsay's, and their red is the best. L'Abbatiale belonging to the bishop of the place 1000 to 1200 pieces red and white, three fourths red at 400^{tt} to 500.^{tt}because neighbors to the monks.

Cumieres is all of a 2d quality. Both red and white 150^{tt} to 200^{tt} the piece.

Epernay. Mde Jermont 200 pieces @ 300.^{tt} —M. Patelaine 150 pieces. M. Marc 200 peices. M. Chertems 60 pieces. M. Lauchay 50 peices. M. Cousin 100 pieces (Aubergiste de l'hotel de Rohan á Epernay.) M. Pierrot 100 pieces. Les Chanoines regulieres d'Epernay 200. pieces. Mesdames les Urselines religieuses 100, pieces. M. Gilette 200. p. All of the 1st. quality red and white in equal quantities.

Pierrij. M. Casotte 500 pieces. M. de la Motte 300 pieces. M. de Failli 300 pieces. I tasted his wine of 1779 which was really very good tho not equal to that of M. Dorsay of 1783. He sells it at 2—10 to merchants and 3.^{tt} to individuals. Les Semnaristes 150.p. M. Hoquart 200.p. all of 1st. quality, white and red in equal quantities. At Cramont also there are some wines of 1st. quality made. At Avize also, and Aucy, Le Meni, Mareuil, Verzy-Verzenni. This last place (Verzy Verzenni) belongs to the M. de Sillery, the wines are carried to Sillery and there stored, whence they are called Vins de Sillery, tho not made there.

All these wines of Epernay and Pierrij sell almost as dear as M. Dorsay's, their quality being nearly the same. There are many small proprietors who might make all wines of the 1st. quality if they would cull their grapes: but they are too poor for this. Therefore the proprietors beforenamed, whose names are established buy of the poorer ones the right to cull their vineyards, by which means they increase their quantity, as they find about ⅓ of the grapes fit to make wine of the 1st. quality.

The lowest priced wines of all are 30^{tt} the peice, red or white. They make brandy of the pumice. In very bad years when their wines become vinegar they are sold for 6^{tt} the peice and made into brandy. They yield $^1/_{10}$ brandy.

White Champaigne is good in proportion as it is silky and still. Many circumstances derange the scale of wines. The proprietor of the best vineyard, in the best year, having bad weather come upon while he is gathering his grapes, makes a bad wine, while his neighbor holding a more indifferent vineyard, which happens to be ingathering while the weather is food, makes a better. The M. de Casotte at Pierrij formerly was the first house. His successors by some inperceptible change of culture have degraded the quality of their wines. Their cellars are admirably made, being about 6. 8. or 10f. wide vaulted and extending into the ground in a kind of labyrinth to prodigious distance, with an air hole of 2.f. diameter every 50. feet. From the top of the vault to the surface of the earth is from 15. to 30f. I have no where seen cellars comparable to these, In packing their bottles they lay a row on their sided, then across them at each end they lay laths, and on these another row of bottles, heads and points on the others. By this means they can take out a bottle from the bottom or where they will.[1]

CHAMPAGNE FOR WASHINGTON

In 1789 Jefferson, then age 46, returned to Washington to

assume the position of Secretary of State under President Washington. After spending four years in the premier wine nation of the world, he was respected for his knowledge of fine wines and was entrusted to order for the Chief Executive. He thought highly of Champagne, but non-sparkling, and devoted this entire letter to that subject which he wrote to William Short, Chargé des Affaires, Paris,

New York Aug. 12, 1790

Dear Sir

Being just now informed that a vefsal sails this afternoon for a port of Normandy, and knowing that the President wishes to have some Champagne, & that this is the season to write for it, I have been to him, and he desires 40. dozen bottles. The execution of this commifsion I must put upon you, begging the favor of you to procure it of the growth of M. Dorsey's vineyard at Aij opposite to Epernay in Champagne, and of the best year he has, for present drinking. his homme d'Affaires when I was there was a M. Louis, and if the same be in place it will perhaps be best to write to him, and it may give him the idea of a more standing customer if he knows that the application comes through the person who bought the remains of his wine of 1783 in April 1788. being in company with a M. Cousin. it is to be *Non-Moussuex*. M. Dorsay himself lives in Paris. We have not time to procure a bill to inclose you herein, but I will take care to forward one immediately by some other convayance. I am anxious this wine should not move from Champagne till the heats are over, and that is should arrive at Philadelphia before the spring comes on. it will of course be in bottles. Adieu Dear Sir

P.S. call for the best possible, and they   Yours affectionately

may be sure of a continuance of such an

annual demand as long as it comes

of the best.

Th: Jefferson

Jefferson was apparently concerned about moving Champagne from his cellar on a hot June day, when he wrote to Tobias Lear regarding President Washington's wines,

June 24, 1791

"Thomas Jefferson presents his compliments to Mr. Lear. He has been endeavouring this morning, while the thing is in his mind to make a statement of the cost and expences of the President's wines, but not having a full account of the whole from Fenwick he is unable to do it but on sight of the account rendered by him to the President. If Mr. Lear, the first time any circumstances shall give him occasion of doing Th: J. the honour of calling on him, will put that account in his pocket, the matter can be completed in two or three minutes.—The cloudiness of the present day renders it favourable to remove the 4. hampers of Champagne from Th: J's cellar, if Mr. Lear thinks proper to send for them. It wouls be well to open a case of every kind and place the bottles on their shelves that they may be settled before the President's return."

By now the seat of government had moved from New York to Philadelphia, and Jefferson writes William Short again about Champagne for the President,

Philadelphia July 28, 1791

"Young Osmont arrived here safely, and is living with Colo. Biddle in a merchantile line. He appears to me a young man of extraordinary prudence, I am endeavouring to help him in the case of his purchase of le Tonnelier, if the latter had any right to the lands he pretended to sell.–Mazzei's debt may rest between him and me, and I shall endeavour to arrange it here. He was certainly a good hand to employ with the abbé Morellet, from whom I understand there is no hope, and but little from Barrois who is the real debtor. Perhaps Barrois would pay me in books. If he has a complete set of the Greek Byzantine historians this would balance the account.–The wines from Champagne and Bordeaux, dress from Houdon, press from Charpentier, reveille and carriages are arrived. So is Petit. You have not informed me of the cost of the Champagne, and of it's transportation to Paris, so that my account with the President remains still open. I inclose you a bill of exchange for £131-5 sterl. drawn by John Warder of this place on John Warder & co. merchants..."

Twelve years later when Jefferson himself was President, his preference for Champagne was further stated in a letter to Mr. Fulmar Shipworth in France. He gave exact directions where the best might be found, the route it should travel, and the best time of the year when it should leave the wineries and embark on the long voyage to America,

Washington May 4, 1803

Dear Sir,

"I am about to ask from you the execution of a troublesome comifsion, without being able to encourage it's undertaking by an assurance that it may not be repeated hereafter. The meannefs of quality, as well as extravagence of price of the

French wines which can be purchased in this country have determined me to seek them in the spot where they grow. When in France, I visited all the remarkable wine cantons, went into the vineyards, & cellars of these, whose crops were of the first variety noted their names, qualities & prices, & after my return to Paris took my supplies regularly from the owners of the best vineyards whose interest for the character of his wine ensured his fidelity to quality and price, The wines of Champagne can be best got by the way of Paris, where the agency of a friend becomes necefsary. This agency I take the liberty of solliciting from you. The following were the places, persons & quantities for Champagne of the 1st quality, when I was there in 1788. at Sig Mons'r Dorsay made 1100. pieces. M. le Duc 400. M. de Villermont 300. M. [?] 250 at Auevillaj The Benedictines made 1000. pieces, & L'Abbatiale 1100. at Pierrij M. Casotte made 500. pieces, de la Motte 300. de Failli 300. Voguant 200. les Samineni 150. at Verzy Verzenni, the property of the Marquis de Sillery, were made the wines called de Sillery. of all these the wines of Aij. made in M. Dorsay's vineyards were the best, & from him I always afterwards took my supplies. his homme d'affaires was then a M. Louis, & I paid always from 3^{tt}. to

3^{tt}-10s. the bottle for the best, & of the best years. I am told wines have considerably rison since that. M. Dorsay lived in Paris during winter I believe on the Quai Dorsay. I think there is little reason to doubt that the culture of so great a property, & of such established reputation has been kept in perfection, but this presumption is submitted to the control of your information & enquiry: my object being to get the best, & only from an old customer of preference, if his wines maintain their relative excellence. I would wish 400 bottles of the white Champagne non-moufseux of the best year now on hand, for which purpose I shall inclose herein a bill of exchange for 400 Dollars, which, not being yet received shall be explained in a postscript. The package of the wine on the spot should be recommended to be made with great care, & some attention is required on their passage from Aij to Havre, that they may not be exposed to a hot sun at Havre be so good as to addrefs them to mr Barrett our Consul, if there, & if not, then to M. de la Motte, either of whom will take the charge off your hands at that place. it is efsential that they should leave Havre by the middle of July, or they will not be here in time to save me from the necefsity of buying here bad & dear. consequently there will be no time to lose after you recieve this letter. The wines of Burgundy would be very desirable, & there are three kinds of their red wines. Chambertin, Voujeau, & Veaune, [sic] & one of their whites, Monrachet, which, under favorable circumstances will bear transportation, but always with risk of being spoiled of exposed, on the way, to either great heat or cold, as I have known by experience since I returned to America. unlefs the Champagnes have rison in price more than I am informed, there may be something left of my bill, which I should like to recieve in Chambertin & Monrachet in equal, & ever so small quantities, if you can take the trouble of getting it for me merely as an experiment. If it succeeds I may ask a quantity the next year. It should leave it's cellars in Chambertin & Monrachet about the beginning of October, & come through without delay at either Paris or Havre. There was living at Beaune, near Chambertin & Monrachet, a tonnelier named Parent, who being a taster & bottler of wines by trade, was my conductor through the vineyards & cellars of the Cote, & ever after my wine broker & correspondent. if living, he will execute for me faithfully any order you may be so good as to send him. The only wines of first quality made at Monrachet were in the vineyards of M. de Clermont, & of the Marquis de Sarsnet of Dijon. I shall be happy to recieve a line of information as soon as the Champagne is underway. Epernay the center of the wine villages is but a day's journey from Paris. We are just now learning from a mefsage of the British king to parliament that war with France is probable...

Th: Jefferson

Champagne was the *creme de la creme* of wines in his time, but in his later years Jefferson turned to other wines that were his regular stand-bys. These required less cellar and transportation care, fewer bottles broken, and were lower in price. Furthermore, if he didn't care for the bubbles—always ordering non-sparkling—was the taste all that superior to the still wines of Bordeaux and Burgundy?

Or, was Jefferson's taste behind the wine times? In 1819 the English ambassador to the United States reported that in Washington society, "You will be judged of by your Champagne of which the Americans prefer the sweet and sparkling."

---

[1]Boyd, "Tour Through Holland 1788."

FRONTIGNAN: A JEFFERSON FAVORITE
A Challenge To Grow In The U.S?

Even before his lengthy tour–largely a wine and vineyard tour–of Burgundy, Southern France, Italy and the Bordeaux region, Thomas Jefferson had expressed his fondness for Frontignan wine. His tour was from March 3, 1787 to June of that year.

On May 12th he arrived in the town of Frontignan, the next one he visited after Montpelier in Southern France where the famous college of viticulture is located today. "The territory in which the vin [wine] muscat de Frontignan is made," he wrote, "is about a league of three toises long, and one fourth of a league broad."

He described the best grade and how it was made and sold, "The first quality is sold, *brut*, for one hundred and twenty livres the piece [cask, equal to 200 bottles]; but it is then thick, and must have a winter and the *fouet*, to render it potable and brilliant. The *fouet* is like a chocolate mill, the handle of iron, the brush of stiff hair. In bottles, this wine costs twenty-four sous, the bottle, &c. included. It is potable the April after it is made, is best that year, and after ten years, begins to have a pitchy [resininous?] taste, resembling it to Malaga. It is not permitted to ferment more than half a day [at least ten days is required for wine to ferment completely, so he may have been referring to the practice of fermenting on the grape skins and pulp for a half day, then completing the fermentation on the juice only], because it would not be so liquorish. The best color, and its natural one is the amber. By force of whipping, it is made white, but loses flavor..."

The wine is well known in Europe today and is described by Hugh Johnson,[1] "The most famous of France's many muscats is that of Frontignan, from the Mediterranean coast not far north of the Pyrenees. It is usually sold under the name of Frontignac.

"There is a special variety of the muscat grown at Frontignan, which gives the wine more delicacy than most, but it is intensely sweet; one glass is about as much as most people can drink. It is slightly fortified [added alcohol], enough to bring it up to 15 per cent alcohol, which puts it into the official category of *vin de liqueur*—the same as port. In fact, it is considerably less strong than port."

Jefferson does not indicate whether the wine was sweet in his time, nor if it was always fortified. It may be that his reference to it not being permitted to ferment more than half a day refers to a special winemaking process that included fortification.

The grape Frontignan is not listed by Winkler (Univ. of California, Davis), nor described in detail by P. Wagner. However it has been propagated successfully by the late Dr. Konstantin D. Frank, Vinifera Wine Cellars, Hammondsport, New York. He distributed Frontignan plants from his nursery to several locations in the eastern United States, as a table (eating) as well as a winemaking variety. It has done well experimentally at Highbury Vineyard, The Plains, Virginia.

Jefferson recommended Frontignan along with a few other wines to his friends in Europe and America, some of whom were in high offices and even to become presidents.

In a shipping inventory, amounting to scores of boxes and items, he notes a range from macaroni to a chariot, and from a guitar to cork oaks. He listed 12 bottles of Frontignan to Monticello, 12 to Richmond, 10 to "Seastores" [enjoy on the voyage?], and 15 to Philadelphia.

George Washington relied on his advice for what wines to purchase for the President's table and for official functions. Jefferson wrote from Philadelphia (the seat of government) to his former secretary William Short in Paris, September 6, 1790 saying that the President had left for Mount Vernon that morning and had requested him to order a selection of French wines which included 10 dozen bottles of Frontignan.

The following extracts relating to Frontignan are from "The

Papers of Thomas Jefferson", Julian P. Boyd, Editor, Princeton University Press, Princeton, New Jersey, 1950:

From Jefferson, Paris, Aug. 8, 1786, to Stephen Cathalan, Jr., U. S. Consul, Marseilles,

"Sir,

I have been duly honoured with your favor of July 28...I shall readily lend my aid to promote the mercantile intercourse between your port and the United States whenever I can aid it. For the present it is much restrained by the danger of capture by the pyratical states [in North Africa]...P. S. If very good Frontignac wine can be procured at Marseilles I would be obliged to you for six dozen bottles, the price of which I will pay on your bill."

From John Bondfield, Consul, Bordeaux, Nov. 30, 1787,

"Sir,

I received in due course your favor of the 13 Instant, the Vin de Frontignan for Monsr. le Comte de Moustier shall be carefully forwarded to New York by the first vessel after its arrival here...

"The Exports from this Port to the United States have been confined to two or three small Cargoes of Wines and Brandys objects of small value..."

From Bondfield,

"Bordeaux, 19 Apr. 1788 [summarized by Boyd]. Acknowledges TJ's letters of 22 Feb. and 3 Mch.; forwarded TJ's letter to Pichard; hearing nothing from Pichard, wrote him and received the enclosed reply. The 'Vins d'hautbrion belonging to Monsr. Le Cte. De fumel' are esteemed as next in quality and a few hogsheads of this of the 1784 vintage are available. Has received 'two Cases vin de frontignac from Mons. Lambert' which he will forward to Moustier in New York. The 'check occationed by the overstock of Tobacco' at Bordeaux the previous fall having given 'another channel to the American Navigation, it may be twelve months before any imports of consiquence come this way'; nevertheless, the 'market at present presents the most favorable sales.'"

"...Pichard to Bonfield, Libourne, 13 Apr. 1788, asking him to inform TJ that he has no *'vin de la fitte de l'annee 1784';* that he is sorry and hopes to serve him in the future; that he would have written TJ immediately if 'Mr. Jefferson *avoit datte sa lettre et meut envoye son adressé'* [had dated his letter and sent his address]; and that, though he had some *'vin de la fitte de l'annee 1786,'* it was not yet potable."

From Jefferson in Paris, April 28, 1788, in French, to M. Cabanis, Banker, Frontignan,

"Monsieur,

"Monsieur Lambert de Frontignan, by a letter dated 22 February has asked me to pay the sum of 129 livres for 100 bottles of wine which he has sent to Monsieur le Comte de Moustier in America by my order. Unfortunately, his letter did not arrive until March 3rd when I was leaving Paris for the Low Countries and Germany. I find it here on my return after only four or five days. I am sending you this sum Sir, and I ask you to be assured that it would not have been delayed one moment if it had not been for my absence..." Boyd states in a footnote, "Dr. Lambert's letter of 22 Feb. 1788 has not been found. Tj made the following entry in his Account Book under 28 Apr. 1788; 'pd Cabanis banker fro Lambert of Frontignan 100 bottles of wine sent to the Count de Moustier 129 livers,' A draft for the sum was evidently enclosed in the present letter."

From William Short, on tour at Toulouse, April 20 1789,

" Dear Sir,

" I had the pleasure of writing to you from Marseilles...

"I forgot to mention to you, that not being able to see the home d'affaires [manager] of M. Rochegude at Avignon [near Frontignan], I was obliged to execute your commission by chusing at his hotel the wine you desired, and leaving a memorandum for it to be sent to you to Paris. The wine is kept in the country where it is made. That which I tasted of which kind you are to have is six years old. It costs 21s [sous] instead of 24s as you imagined the bottle included. It is to be paid when received at Paris together with the price of carriage and duty. It should arrive in a short time from this and will be sent to your address. They told me that they often sent it to Paris and that you might be sure of being well served. You may be the more sure still as it is considered only as a trial and they have hopes of continuing to supply you..."

Boyd in a footnote states, "...Recorded in SJL as received 27 Apr. 1789. Short was obliged to write Daqueria Rochegude again about the 6 dozen bottles of white wine ordered for TJ, and on 26 May 1789 Rochegude replied that they had been sent in two baskets by a carter with a way-bill..."

Jefferson made a note of the receipt of Frontignan wine August 12, 1790 (Library of Congress, 57-9707) which indicated the price that year:

Sauterne 30 doz. 432 [dollars?]

Segur 20 doz. 3 bl. 720

Frontignan 10 doz. 1 144

Champagne 40 doz. 3.10 1680

Mem'm wine Aug. 12, 1790

Jefferson noted in his Garden Book March 25, 1807, that he planted "10. white Frontignac." grape vines in the South West vineyard at the North East end, third terrace.

Two hundred years after Jefferson's visit to Frontignan, the fine wines are still being grown and made there. He left such detailed records that a visitor today could well retrace his steps and perhaps visit some of the same vineyards and wineries. This could offer another dimension to a tour of southern France by the American visitor who admires an old and noble wine name. For the wine farmer in eastern United States, now that fungal and other diseases are controllable, it can be a challenge to grow and make the Frontignan wine that Jefferson tried so hard to do.

Blanquette De Limoux Today

In May 1787, when Jefferson was making his tour of south-

Jefferson and Wine

ern France and had admired the wines of Frontignan in the Carcassonne region, he was also attracted to the good wines at good prices nearby of Bergasse, Ledanon, Rivesalt, and Blanquette de Limoux. His final inventory a few months before he died almost 40 years later, listed a supply of wines from all four of those areas.

The Blanquette de Limoux has an especially ancient and fascinating history, and is a popular wine made today. The Mauzac grape variety formed the basis of this sparkling white wine made in the Champagne method. Blanquette is one of the few *Appelation d'Origine Controllé* wines produced in the Midi, and indeed, the oldest "brut" in the world.[2]

Blanquette de Limoux was first produced by the Benedictine monks at the Monestery of Saint Hilaire, some five miles from Limoux, itself nearly twenty miles south of Carcassonne. The famous French chronicler, Froissart, in an account of a journey in the Languedoc in 1388 spoke of "delightful drinking sessions where we sampled the white wine of Limoux." The name "Blanquette' derives from a slightly white underside of the Mauzac vine leaves. The oldest known document referring to this wine by name is dated 1544. In it the administrators of the town of Limoux dispatched to the Sieur d'Argues (who today gives his name to the highest quality bottles of the wine and whose ruined chateau can still be seen a few miles from the town). Thirty-four years later another document refers to a gift of Blanquette to the King's Provost-General, and in 1584 the Duc de Joyeuse and his troops celebrated the capture of Brugairolles, a village nearby Limoux, with "a few loads of Blanquette". A load was equivalent to about 31 imperial gallons! By the late 18th century Blanquette was being drunk extensively beyond the borders of the Languedoc. There exists a document dated 1774 which states that Blanquette was consumed in "all the good towns of the kingdom". It had already been established in the 16th century as a grand cru of the Languedoc. Today it is a grand cru of France.

MAUZAC GRAPE

On the eve of the second world war Blanquette became

established as an A. O. C. wine. The area in which it may be grown is confined to 42 communes around Limoux in the upper valley of the Aude; and only those holdings within this area which are formally approved as suitable may be planted with Mauzac vines. A 1955 law, indeed, prohibits the growing in the area of any other type of the vine which produces a sparkling wine. The Mauzac vines are normally grown on slopes facing south and sheltered from the wind. The soil in the area is largely chalk and clay. The whole area, which is actually more southerly than the French Riviera, enjoys a mild winter climate with hot sunny summers. The only other type of vine now used for Blanquette is Chardonnay. You are allowed to devote 10% of the area you have under Mauzac to Chardonnay, which ripens somewhat earlier than Mauzac and therefore stretches the time available for harvesting. Only 6,000 kilos of the Mauzac grapes may be harvested for Blanquette per hectare, and their average alcoholic content must be at least 10 degrees. They may only be transported to the Blanquette de Lemoux Co-operative in special wooden or plastic boxes containing some 35 kilos each to prevent the grapes from getting crushed, which might cause premature fermentation. Harvesting normally takes place in late September and early October.

The ripe grapes are subject to light pressure so that 150 kilos give 100 litres of juice. All juice remaining in the marc is sold for *vin ordinaire*. The must is decanted into vats where it is left for several hours before being drawn off into barrels. Here is is allowed to ferment for several weeks at a low and constant temperature. Later it is decanted several times until the wine is perfectly clear. Qualified wine tasters then blend together wines of different ages and origins. The cuvee, or blended wine, is then bottled and the bottles are stacked in galleries where the temperature is maintained at between 9 and 13 centigrade. It remains in these bottles for at least nine months during which its second fermentation takes place. The sediment from this fermentation settles on the lower side of the bottles, which are then inverted at an angle on racks and turned every day by hand so that the sediment collects against the cork. This is eventually "disgorged" when the cork is sharply expelled. About a quarter of a glassful is then extracted from each bottle and replaced by wine from the same cuvee plus a few grammes of the *liquer d'expedition*, a mixture of the finest quality of old wines from the best years. The bottles, which are of the traditional Champagne type, are finally corked with Champagne corks held down with a wire frame.

Blanquette de Limoux is an attractive sparkling wine with a distinctive flavour of its own. It is described in the admirable "Guide du Vin" by Raymond Dumay as "*mousseux, spiritueux, agreable, de saveur douce et assez caracterisse.*" The Co-operative de la Blanquette produces sweet, semi-sweet and dry varieties. The amount of "*liquer d'expedition*" which is introduced into the wine in its final stage of development determines the category. They are all of course blanc de blancs since both Mauzac and Chardonnay produce white grapes.

The Co-operative produces about three quarters of the total output of Blanquette and has a membership of some 650 producers. A handful of them have very large properties but the majority have only a few acres and many less than an acre. Although few bottles of Blanquette are currently sold in the United States a more serious attempt to interest the American market is being made.

Curiously, although Blanquette was a favorite of his, Jefferson did not like the sparkle in his Champagne, and always ordered it "*non-mousseaux*". However, no record has been found where he specified that his Blanquette must be a "still" wine.

References:

[1]**Hugh Johnson, "Modern Encylopedia of Wine", N. Y.: Simon and Schuster, 1987, p.212.**

[2]**Richard Scott, "Blanquette De Limoux, Making A Jefferson Favorite Today", *VWGA, Journal*, Fall 1977, pp.380-383. Mr. Scott is retired correspondent, *Manchester Guardian*, has planted a Mauzac vineyard, Domaine de Carliqui, 11300 Limoux, France.**

L'AFFAIRE COUNT MOUSTIER
"A Painful Embarrassment"

When Thomas Jefferson was serving as Ambassador to France, he became a close friend to a member of the Royal Court who served him as a trusted advisor on good buys in wines, the Count de Moustier.

Over a period of several years, both when they were on the European continent and when one or the other was in the young United States, they corresponded and helped each other in obtaining wines. It may have been Moustier who introduced Jefferson to the wines of Frontignan which became a longtime favorite of his. The taste was pleasant and the price was one of the lowest.

At one point he gave glowing recommendations of Moustier to his friends in America, however his close attachment turned into painful embarrassment with international implications. And all this happened around the time of the worsing political situation in France, ending in the beheading of the King (Louis XVI) and leading to the Revolution.

Jefferson and Moustier had been friends for some time, when in early 1787 he reported the public disturbances in his usual vivid way to his chief in New York (then the seat of the U. S. Government) John Jay, Secretary of State:

"THE QUEEN SINS ON..."

"...the Queen, going to the theatre at Versailles with Madame de Polignac, was received with a general hiss. The King, long in the habit of drowing his cares in wine, plunges deeper and deeper. The Queen cries, but sins on...The Marechal de Segur retired at the same time (yesterday), prompted to it by the court. Their successors are not yet known. Monsieur de St. Priest goes ambassador to Holland, in the room of Verac, transferred to Switzerland, and the Count de Moustier goes to America, in the room of the Chevalier de la Luzerne, who has a promise of the first vacancy...the parties are ordered to prepare for thier destination..."

In a later letter to Jay, Jefferson praises Moustier who was single, and also his traveling companion, Madame la Marquise de Brehan.

"...but I beg leave to present him to you, on account of his personal as well as his public character. You will find him open, communicative, candid, simple in his manners, and a declared enemy to ostentation and luxury. He goes with a resolution to add no aliment to it by his example, unless he finds that the dispositions of our countrymen require it indispensably. Permit me, at the same time, to solicit your friendly notice, and through you, that also of Mrs. Jay, to Madame la Marquise de Brehan, sister in law to Monsieur de Moustier. She accompanies him, in hopes that a change of climate may assist her feeble health, and also, that she may procure a more valuable education for her son, and safer from seduction, in America than in France. I think it impossible to find a better woman, more amiable, more modest more simple in her manners, dress, and way of thinking. She will deserve the friendship of Mrs. Jay, and the way to obtain hers, is to receive her and treat her without the shadow of etiquette."

Jefferson continued his report taking one of his usual swipes at royalty and offering to purchase wines for Jay,

"...There has long been a division in the Council here, on the question of war and peace. Monsieur de Montmorin and Monsieur de Breteuil have been constantly for war. They are supported in this by the Queen. The King goes for nothing. He hunts one half the day, is drunk the other, and signs whatever he is bid. The Archbishop of Thoulouse desires peace. Though brought in by the Queen, he is opposed to her in this capital object, which would produce an alliance with her brother. Whether the Archbishop will yield or not, I know not. But an intrigue is already begun for ousting him from his place, and it is rather probable it will succeed. He is a good and patriotic minister for peace, and very capable in the department of finance, At least, he is so in theory. I have heard his talents for execution censured. Can I be useful here to Mrs. Jay or yourself, in executing any commissions, great or small? I offer you my services with great cordiality. You know whether any of the wines of this country may attract your wishes. In my tour, last spring, I visited the best vineyards of Burgundy, Cote-rotie, Hermitage, Lunelle, Fontignan, and white and red Bourdeaux [sic], got acquainted with the proprietors, and can procure for you the best crops from the vigneron himself..."

Jefferson received a friendly letter from Moustier just before sailing for America, September 3, 1787 (in French),

"At the moment of departure, Sir, nearly everything is ready for sailing tomorrow morning. I have just realized my negligence in not obtaining the Frontignan wine for you. I am getting it especially for American ladies as well as the gentlemen to whom I wish to be accepted in every respect and I would not want to be without it. I have the honor therefore of asking you, Sir, if you have not already ordered it, to procure for me 100 bottles of the good Frontignan wine and you will know the best way of obtaining it as you have already had the kindness to indicate. I will make payment in the most convenient way for you. The bad weather seems not to be presenting a problem towards my trip to America as a true minister of peace....

Le Cte. de Moustier"

Although no enclosure is mentioned, Moustier must have sent with this letter the following unsigned note, addressed to Madame la Presidente de Pichard at her hotel in Bordeaux, dated at Brest September 3, 1787, (in French) "Mr. Jefferson, Minister of the United States of America, desires, dear cousin, to have your best wine, and I would like to ask that you treat him as you would ourselves. It is the Sauterne that he wishes especially to have. I do not know when he needs this, but as we are about to sail, tomorrow, I wanted to send you a note about this,and take advantage of this opportunity to renew the assurances of my tenderest and most enduring friendship."

We next read about Moustier in a letter to Jefferson from his Bordeaux agent Bondfield, November 30, 1787, acknowledging Jefferson's letter of November 13th and stating that the Frontignan wine for Monsr. le Counte de Moustier shall be forwarded to New York by the first vessel.."

The next communication which mentions the Count, comes, oddly enough from Germany. Jefferson during the tour through the Rhineland vineyards, noted at Coblentz, April 5, 1788, "The Moselle is here from 100. to 200. yds. wide, the Rhine 300. to 400. A jessamine in the Ct. de Moustier's garden in leaf." Perhaps Moustier owned a residence there, and Jefferson stayed overnight in his house.

In a letter dated April 19, 1788, to Jefferson from Bondfield, he notes that two cases of Frontignan were received from M. Lambert in Marseilles and will be forwarded to Moustier in New York. April 28, 1788 Jefferson wrote to Mr. Cabinis at Marseilles he would pay for the 100 bottles of Frontignan wine at 129 livres for the Count Moustier.

Meanwhile, in America, the Count and Madame Brehan were settling down, he in his new appointment as French Ambassador. As might be expected of a new chief of mission, he also was traveling to acquaint himself with the people and countryside, and apparently taking Madame Brehan with him.

A DEVELOPING SCANDAL

In a letter headed "Private" from New York, November 25, 1788, John Jay informs Jefferson about the attitude of Congress on several matters, then politely declines his offer to buy French wines, and finally discusses a scandal that is developing around the French couple,

"...I should have availed myself my Dear Sir, of your friendly offer to supply me with french winnes, if I could have been certain of remaining some Time where I am. But the unceasing Efforts made to remove Congress from hence, have from Time to Time rendered my Residence here so uncertain, that I thought it better to postpone increasing my Stores of any kind, than be at the Trouble of removing them. I sincerely wish that this Question of Removal was finally determined, for besides other Inconveniences resulting from its frequent agitation, the Injury it does to the Dignity of Government is not inconsiderable.

The Count de Moustier found in this Country the best

Dispositions to make it agreable to him, but it seems he expected more particular and flattering Marks of minute Respect than our People in general entertain Ideas of, or are either accustomed or inclined to pay to anybody. This added as I suspect and believe to Insinuations from persons who have no Desire that he should be very agreable to us, or we to him, have led him to Errors relative to men and things which naturally dispose him to give and receive Disgust. Appearances (whether well or ill founded is not important) have created and diffused an opinion that an improper Connection subsists between him and the Marchioness. You can easily concieve the Influence of such an opinion on the Minds and Feelings of such a People as ours. For my part I regret it; she seems to be an amiable woman; and I think if left to the Operation of his own Judgement and Disposition his Conduct relative to this Country would be friendly and useful. These are things that I have not said or written to any other Person. Nor is it pleasant to say or write them, but in the situation you are in, Information of this Kind may have its uses. With great Esteem and Regard I am Dear Sir Your most Obt . & hbl. Servt.,

John Jay

This criticism by the urbane, sophisticated head of American foreign affairs must have caused Jefferson considerable discomfort. But, strong as it was, it was rather mildly stated compared to the following letter from James Madison, writing from Philadelphia, December 8, 1788, which, after reporting that George Washington would be the first President and John Adams his probable Vice President, launched into the Moustier affair with vigor and in cypher,

...Moutier [sic] proves a most unlucky appointment. He is unsocial, proud and niggardly and betrays a sort of fastidiousness toward this country. He suffers also from illicit connection with the Madame de Brehan which is universally known and offensive to American manners. She is perfectly soured toward this country. The ladies of New York (a few within the official circle excepted) have for some time withdrawn their attentions from her. She knows the cause, is deeply stung by it, views every thing thro the medium of rancor and conveys her impressions to her paramour over whom she exercises despotic sway. Latterly their time has [been] chiefly spent in [travelling]. The first vis[it] was to an Indian treaty at Fort Schuyler and thence to the Oneida town. The next to Boston and thence to N. Hampshire. The last to Mount Vernon from which they but lately returned. On their journeys it is said they often neglected the most obvious precautions for veiling their intimacy. At Boston he imprudently suffered etiquette to prevent even an interview with governor Hancock. The inhabitants taking part with the governor neither visited nor invited the count. They were the less apprenhensive of a misinterpretation of the neglect as the most cordial intercourse had just preceded between the town and the French squadron. Both the count and the marchioness are particularly unpopular among their countrymen here. Such of them as are not under restraint make very free remarks and are anxious for a new diplomatic arrangement.—It is but right to add to these particulars that there is reason to believe that unlucky impressions were made on the count at his first probably by de la Forest, the Consul, a cunning disciple I take it of Marbois' politics and by something in his communications with Jay which he considered as the effect of coldness and sourness toward France..."

After having recommended the couple so highly to his best friends and high political figures in the United States, Jefferson must have been distressed indeed to receive this second and stronger criticism.

What the immediate and final results of all this were will have to wait until further research reveals more about L'Affaire Moustier. His *liaison dangereuse* in the U. S. may have been responsible for his transfer to a European post. His name was mentioned when M. Lambert, Jefferson's agent in Frontignan, wrote to him February 10, 1791, saying he had recently communicated with Moustier who was ambassador in Prussia. Perhaps this correspondence, and many to follow, were about good wine. *(Boyd and T. J. Randolph, "Memoirs and Papers...")*

WINE ADVISOR TO FIVE PRESIDENTS
Jefferson The Premier Connoisseur

The position of advisor to the President of the United States on wine quality and purchases today would be quite an honor in the trade. What a distinguished tribute it is then to our third President, Thomas Jefferson, who, if we include his own eight years in office, was the respected wine expert to the first *five* American heads of state.

This important social role which he both cultivated and enjoyed, meant that Jefferson's choices would not only have to satisfy the President himself, but be also of such quality as to please official guests at formal executive banquets and ceremonies. Many of the guests and members of the diplomatic corps were from European countries and had enjoyed the finest wines in royal courts. They had to be pleased.

At this point in our early history too, the young nation was striving for respectability and a high cultural image that would match its recent military and political achievements. No chance could be taken that important guests would be served poor wine. Excellent wine at social events, especially on the Presidential level, was necessary.

This educated, handsome, distinguished patriot possessed a palate that was as sensitive to good taste as his violin and harpsichord were attuned to the minuets of the period.

Jefferson had the unique experience of having tasted, tested and recorded some 200 wines of all types from many countries, white and red, sweet and dry, fortified and natural, cheap and expensive. Additionally, and most important in those nearly primitive days, he by virtue of having lived in Europe for several years knew the vineyard owners and wine merchants. He was well aware from experience of the vast problem of shipping fragile bottles and delicate wines over thousands of miles of storm-threatened waters—and often pirate infested—in tedious sailing vessels. He knew the time of year to transport wines this way and the seasons when adverse winds could send ships and their precious wine cargos off course "to fret" (as he said) in hot, tropical ports where they might remain for months until the winds were favorable.

In his meticulous and exacting way, Jefferson had computed all the data on the cost of bottles (expensive), corks, packing, wagon transport, and whether a certain wine from a particular vineyard should be shipped in bottle or cask.

It is little wonder then, that Jefferson was considered the premier wine connoisseur extraordinaire and his advice sought and followed by the country's leaders. It can be safely surmised that for about 35 years the Presidential cellars contained the wines he had recommended, approved their quality, and probably also arranged the ordering and transport details.

The passage of about two centuries of time means that the data now is often fragmented, but until continuing research reveals more explicit information the meaning is clear from what we have about the important part that Jefferson played.[1]

PRESIDENT GEORGE WASHINGTON

George Washington assumed the office of President of the United States April 30, 1789 and served to March 3, 1797.

Jefferson and Washington, both Virginia Tidewater planters, became associated in mutual wine interests as early as April 1774, when they engaged in forming "The Wine Company". Washington, together with Jefferson, Peyton Randolph, George Mason, Benjamin Harrison, John Curtis and others bought one share each at fifty pounds sterling to finance a business for raising wine vines, making wine, and for other agricultural pursuits.

During the Revolutionary War, Washington carried with him silver camp cups from which to enjoy occasional wine, and once prescribed it to the Marquis de Chastellux in the amount of three or four cups of Madeira as a prescription for ague.

A few days before leaving Paris, September 17,1789, to return to the United States, Jefferson wrote John Jay, Secretary for Foreign Affairs, in New York (then the capital) about wine that he was sending to President Washington:

TI. No. 30. These are hampers containing samples of the best

TI. No. 31. wines of this country, which I beg leave to present to the President and yourself, in order that you may decide whether you would wish to have any, and which of them for your table hereafter, and offer my service in procuring them for you. The kinds are 1. Monrache (the best kind of White Burgundy) 2. Champagne non mousseux (i.e. still) much preferred here to the sparkling, which goes all to foreign countries. 3. Sauterne (a white Bordeaux) 4. Rochegude from the neighborhood of Avignon, somewhat of a Madeira quality 5. Frontignan. I have brought all these from the Vignerons who made them, the 1st, 2d. and 5th. when on the spots myself, the 3d. and 4th. by writing to them. The Vigneron never adulterates his wine, but on the contrary gives it the most perfect and pure possible. But when once a wine has been into a merchant's hands, it never comes out unmixed. This being the basis of their trade, no degree of honesty, of personal friendship or of kindred prevents it. I must beg the favor to you to deliver one hamper to the President with my offers of service, and the preceding explanation...

I send the present letter to the person at Havre to whom I have consigned the packages, desiring him to forward it with them and to inclose to you the bill of lading. Hoping they may come safely to hand, I beg leave to assure you of the sentiments of sincere esteem and respect with which I am Dear Sir Your most obedt. & most humble servt,

Th: Jefferson

P.S. Every bottle is marked (with a diamond) with the initial letter of the wine it contains. [There were no stick-on labels, therefore this may request etching by wheel engraving.]

TO WILLIAM SHORT

Dear Sir   New York Aug. 12.1790.

Being just now informed that a vessel sails this afternoon for a port of Normandy, and knowing that the President wished to have some Champagne, and that this is the season to write for it, I have been to him, and he desires 40. dozen bottles. The execution of this commission I must put upon you, begging the favor of you to procure it of the growth of M. Dorsay's vineyard at Ay opposite to Epernay in Champagne, and of the best year he has, for present drinking. His homme d'Affaires when I was there was a M. Louis, and if the same be in place it will perhaps be best to write him, and it may give him the idea of a more standing customer if he knows that the application comes through the person who bought the remains of his wine of 1783. in April 1788. being in company with a M. Cousin. It is to be *Non-mousseux* [not sparkling] M. Dorsay himself lives in Paris. We have not time to procure a bill to inclose you herein, but I will take care to forward one immediately by some other conveyance. I am anxious this wine should not move from Champagne till the heats are over, and that it should arrive in Philadelphia before spring comes on. It will of course be in bottles. Adieu Dear Sir Your's affectionaley,

Th: Jefferson

P.S. call the best possible, and they may be sure of the continuance of such an annual demand as long as it comes of the best.

There is a memorandum in T J's hand, endorsed "Washington Presidt," reading: Sauterne, 30. doz. 1, 432; Segur, 20. dox. 3, 720; Frontignan, 10. doz.,1, 144; Champagne 40. doz.,3. 10s 1680. "At the bottom of this memorandum are TJ's calculations of costs of the wines named, with shillings, transposed into livres, so that all of the totals are in the latter currency.

TO WILLIAM SHORT IN PARIS

Dear Sir,   New York, August 25, 1790

The President will leave this[city?] on the 30th for Mount Vernon... I probably shall not write to you till my return to Philadelphia, unless it be merely to cover a bill of exchange for the President's wine as soon as I recieve it from him...

Th; Jefferson

TO JOSEPH FENWICK

Dear Sir   Philadelphia Sep. 6, 1790

According to your permission I trouble you with a commission to recieve and forward to me some wines for the President and myself. They are written for in the inclosed letters to the respective owners of the vineyards, and are as follows.

M. la comte de Lur- Saluce	30. doz. Sauterne for the President 10. doz. do. for myself 20. doz.. vin de Segur for the President
M. de Mirosmenil Madame de Rozan	10. doz. vin de Rozan for myself.
Monsieur Lambert at Frontignan	10. doz. Frontignan for the President 5. doz. do. for myself

To these I must beg you to add 10. dozen for me of a good white vin ordinaire, or indeed something better, that is to say of such quality as will do to mix with water, and also be drinkable alone. Such I suppose may be obtained at Bordeaux for ten sous the bottle. I would wish you to buy it of the person who makes it, and give me his name and address, that, if it suits me, I may always be sure of the same quality. This letter will go under cover to Mr. Short, who will furnish you with the means of paiment. Be so good as to have the wines delivered immediately and forward them by the first safe vessel bound from Bordeaux to Philadelphia. I have directed those for the President to be packed separately and marked G. W. and mine T. I. You will recieve them ready packed. Those from Fontignan cannot probably be forwarded so soon as the others. You need only send the letter to Dr. Lambert at Frontignan, with a note of your address, and he will forward them to Bordeaux and draw on you for the amount of the wine and expences. I am with great esteem Dear Sir your most obedt. humble servt.

Th; Jefferson

TO MADAME DE RAUSAN

(in French)

6 Sep, 1790

Since I did not have the honor, Madame, of knowing you personally, I have had the opportunity in a tour I made during my stay in Paris of visiting the canton of best Bordeaux wines, among which was de Rozan, your cru, of excellent quality. Would you please send me ten dozenbottles of the best for drinking now, bottled and packed at the vineyard. I would also like to ask, Madame, How I might describe my orders in the future so that I might buy the same wines from time to time.

Th: Jefferson

TO COUNT MIROMENIL
(in French)

6 Sep. 1790

Although I have not had the honor of meeting you personally, I have had the opportunity of visiting the canton of the best wines of Bordeaux and of having seen your vineyard which produces the wines known as Segur and know that it is one of the best cru of this canton. I am writing for our President General Washington, and he has asked me to see if you would be so good as to send him twenty dozen bottles of your best wine for drinking now, to be bottled, packed, and marked "G.W." at the vineyard; he said it was more than probable that he would renew the order each year and he wants to be assured that future orders may be so identified as being truly from your own cellars.

Th; Jefferson

TO MONSIEUR DR. LAMBERT, FRONTIGNAN
(in French)

6 Sept. 1790

Although now being a long way from you, Sir, I still remember your excellent wines. Could you kindly send me as soon as possible ten dozen bottles for our President General Washington, and five dozen for me, of white and red, but the last in proportion. The packing of the ten dozen must be separate, and labelled [etiquette's] G. W. and the five dozen T.I. Decide the best way for a rough voyage. (for me, the five dozen should be put in half bottles if you have them, which would make them ten dozen of half bottles). Mr Fenwick, American Consul at

Bordeaux, will receive them and pay all costs.

Th: Jefferson

Excerpt of original letter showing how the packages should be labelled.

dernier en bonne proportion. les emballages des dix dou-
-zaines doivent etre separemment faites, et etiquetées
G.W. et des cinque douzaines TI. pour decider la parte
que doit supporter les malheurs de voiage. (j'aimais
meme que les cinque douzaines pour moi sient mises

TO COUNT DE LUR-SALUCES OF CH. D'YQUEM
(in French, in part)

6 Sep. 1790

The white wine of Sauterne, of your cru, that you have been kind enough to send me in Paris early in 1788 has been so well accepted by Americans [in France] who know good wines that I am sure that now I am back in the United States my country-men here will admire them. Our President, General Washington would like to try a sample. He would like for you to send him thirty dozen, Sir, and for myself, I would like to have ten dozen, to be bottled, packed separately, and marked as indicated above, shipping in a way that will insure their protection against breakage. Please send then to Mr. Fenwick who will pay all costs and inform him when sent.

Th; Jefferson

TO WILLIAM SHORT

Dear Sir   Philadelphia 6 Sep. 1790

I am here on my way to Virginia, to which place I set out tomorrow. The President left this morning on his way to Mount Vernon. He engaged me some time ago to get some wines from France, to wit 40. dozen of Champagne, 30 doz. of Sauterne, 20. dozen of Bordeaux de Segur, and 10. doz. of Frontignan, and he took a note of their prices in order to furnish me with a bill of exchange sufficient to cover the cost and charges. In the multiplicity of his business before his departure he has forgot to do this: and it remains that we do not permit him to be disappointed of his wine by the omission. But how to do it? For the amount of the whole I suppose will be 3000. and the being obliged to set up a house in New York, then to abandon it and remove here, has put me out of condition to advance such a sum here. I think however it can be done, without incommoding you, by drawing on the bankers in Amsterdam. On the President's return here (about the 1st. of December) bills shall be remitted you, and by using these for your own purpose instead of making new draughts for your salary on the bankers, all will stand right without any special mention in the public accounts. I will make any necessary explanations at the Treasury, should any be necessary.

I write for wines for my own at the same time. These will amount to about 550. livres. I have sent out to seek for a bill of exchange to that amount. If it arrives today I will inclose it herein. If not, I will charge the person with whom I leave the present letter, not to send it off till he has got such a bill and to inclose one herewith, and forward a duplicate by some other opportunity. I leave the letter to Fenwick open, to the end that you may see the arrangements I take to leave you no other trouble than to forward it to him and let him know how he shall be furnished with money to pay for the wines. The bill for my part shall be made paiable to you.

The new constitution of this state has passed. The chair of the government was to have been disputed between Morris and Mifflin. But the former has declined, and his friends set up Sinclair in opposition to Mifflin. I am, my dear Sir Your's affectionately,

Th; Jefferson

FROM WILLIAM SHORT

Dear Sir   Amsterdam Dec. 23, 1790

This letter accompanying my No. 50. will be sent by the English packet. By your desire I make use of this conveyance, although from hence it is a very uncertain one as the weather at this season of the year frequently keeps the mail several days at Helvoetsluys and thus prevents letters arriving in time for the Packet. I fear this was the fate of mine of Nov. 26.

I have lately recieved from Paris your letter of Sep. 6. from Philadelphia inclosing a bill of exchange for 589.6s. and a letter for Mr. Fenwick. I read it agreeably to your desire and forwarded it to him with advice that I would accept and pay at sight his bill for the disbursements and charges respecting the wine. No delay can therefore arise on that score. I have already advice of the Champaign you had ordered being already recieved at Havre, and I hope it is now on the sea. I have advice also that the Mis. de la fayette's picture is finished and I have directed it to be sent also to Havre. The price is 16. guineas for the painting, 3½ for the gilt frame; and 12. for box and packing. The painter is Boze, who I think has taken by far the best likenesses of the Marquis...

W: Short

FROM WILLIAM SHORT

Sir,   December 29, 1790

...The bill which I received from you, and the price of the Mis. de la fayette's picture are not contained in it as the former is for your wine and the latter will be joined to some trifles that I shall have to pay for you for the dress from Houdon, *echelle de bibliotheque* &c. This account is dated Dec. 30. because that will be the date of my order on the bankers here for the balance which I shall give them to-morrow...

... I mentioned to you in my last that the Champagne was recieved at Havre. I have since heard nothing of it, but hope it has been long sent off from thence. M. Fenwick I hope will soon dispatch the Bordeaux. I have written to him that I would pay immediately his disbursements on that account. M. Vernon was with him when he last wrote me on the 18th. He was then to embark in a fortnight for Norfolk, Virga...

W: Short

TO SHARP DELANY
(Customs Agent)

Sir,   Philadelphia Jan. 15, 1791

...[Delany had written Jefferson Jan. 12, 1791 to furnish the value of wall paper and wine imported from France which arrived from Havre on the Henrietta, Benjamin Wickes, master] If you will be so good as to let me know the amount of the duty on the wine and paper, I will call with it or send it to you...

Th: Jefferson

The cutoms declaration dated Oct. 22, 1790 signed by Jefferson stated in part:

"Twelve Cases Containing Fifty six dozen & Eight Bottles Wine	Galls. 145 - 10 - Bottles 18.00 - 5pCt. -	14.50 0.90
61. One Case Containing 145 Rolls Paper Hangings	Livres 300 adv. 30 ———— 330 Doll. 61.05 - 7½ -	 4.58
		19.98
	disct. 10pct.	1.99
	dollrs.	17.99"

(Jefferson noted in his Account Book Feb. 4, 1791 that he paid Delany an order on the bank for 28.39 duty and portage of wines and papers.)

FROM COUNT MIROMENIL
(in French)

Paris 18 January 1791

I received, Sir, the letter that you did me the honor of

writing the 6th of September last on the part of your President General Washington, who desired 20 dozen bottles of the Grand Wines Named Segur du Medoc. The reputation of this General is well known in France and it is the desire of all good Frenchmen to take this oppertunity to show their respect and especially to carry out his orders. I pary you, Sir, to give him our respects, and for me personally express my gratitude for the opportunity to be of help to the most respected General. I was indeed the owner since 1765 of part of these vineyards through my first wife whose name was Segur who I lost in 1774. She left me with two daughters I married off in 1786 and to whom I returned their mother's property. Thus the land of La Tour in Medoc they enjoy in common today, belongs to their husbands. However, I maintain a friendly correspondence with Le Seigneur Domenger who is the manager, to whom I am going to send your letter and ask him to fill this order which to me is important because I wish to please General Washington. I will also make sure to inform Count de la Pallu and the Marquis de Beaumont, my sons-in-law who will be just as anxious as I am to give orders accordingly and I can assure you every effort will be made as regards the quality of the wines to make sure your wishes are fully implemented.

I shall also request Messrs. Fenwick, Masson & Co of Bordeaux who wrote to me and sent me your letter of the 7th of this month to forward my reply to you and to inform them that M. Domenger would have the honor to see them and make arrangements with them. Be assured Sir, of the very sincere feeling with which I have the honor to be your very humble and very obedient servant,

Le Count de Miromenil, Marshall de Camp

(received by Jefferson 21 June, 1791)

FROM LAMBERT

(in French)

Monsieur   Frontignan 10e. *fevrier* 1791

...I hope that your friend The Honorable General Washington finds the wine I sent you as good as he desired. Following the taste of your country as described by Mr. De Moustier, I have chosen a wine less "Liquoreux" that that previously sent to you...

The case of 60 bottles for you is marked ["marquée", refers to almost any type of labelling or even engraving on metal or glass, but for a shipping package it probably refers to a cloth or paper label. T.J.N.I. and the two sent for your respected General are under the mark of G.W.N.2. and 3...

Lambêrt D.m.–maire

FROM FENWICK MASON & CO.

Sir   Bordeaux 10 feby. 1791.

We have the honor of your favor of the 6th. Sepr. addressed to our J. F. containing letters to several proprietors with a request to pay for and expedite the several parcels of wine you ordered, which shall be complyed with by the first vessel in Philadela. Tho' as oppertunities direct from here are very rare, we shall venture to expedite your Wines when received by the first good vessel to Boston N. York or Charleston with directions to our correspondent to send them immediately on to Philadelphia. This mode of conveyance we shall adopt as the most probable to insure their arrival this Summer.

We have received Madam de Rausan parcel and advice from the Countess de lus Salucethat she shoud immediately prepare and forward us the parcel ordered from her. M. de Miromenel has also wrote us that his Son in Law the Count de la Pallu, at present the proprietor of the Estate of Segur wou'd comply with your order but we have since seen his homme d'affair who says he has no wine on hand proper to ship as a sample that will do justice to his estate, therefore cannot execute your order. Shoud this prove to be the case we shall venture to send for the president some of our own chusing. We fear we shall be in the same situation respecting the frontignac as we have heard nothing of Mr. Lambert. We have wrote him twice to frontignac. Shoud we not hear from him before an oppertunity offers, we shall send you the frontignac from among the best to be produced in Bordeaux.

Monsieur de Pechard is the proprietor of the Estate of *La fite* (formerly Segur) and onsieur de fumel of *Obrion and Chateau-margeaux*. These are three of the first four growths of wine in this provence, the owners of which are residents here and generally provided to supply their friends. The Miromenel estate *La Tour* (formerly Segur also) is the fourth, of which there are three proprietors Count de la Pallu, Marquis de Beaumont and the Count de Segur. Their homme d'affaire here is M. Domenger who has the management of the Estate...

We have the honor to be Sir Your most obd & Hble Servants,

Fenwick Mason & Co.

P. S. Since writing the above we have received the frontignac Wine from Mr. Lambert. There is now a vessel here for Chas. Town. If none offers for Philadela. before this is ready, we think to ship your wines by her. We are   F. M. & Co.
18 feby. 1791

Note by Boyd, addressed: "the Honourable Thomas Jefferson Esquire Secretary of State Philadelphia Minerva [Capt.] Cooper via London", endorsed by TJ as received 6 July 1701. This was the duplicate: its original [not found] is recorded in as received 21 June 1791.

FROM COUNTESS DE LUR-SALUCES

(in French)

Bordeaux 25 February 1791

Having had the misfortune of losing M. le Comte de Lur Saluces, and therefore being in charge of Chateau d'Yquem and its white Sauternes, Mr. Fenwick has sent me the letter you addressed to the Count. I hope you will be satisfied with the shipment I am sending which consists of 10 cases of 50 bottles each, 150 bottles for you, and 350 bottles for General Washington...

FROM FENWICK MASON & COMPANY

Bordeaux March 29, 1791

(Summary by Boyd)

Enclose duplicate of theirs of 10 Feb. and invoice for 14

cases of wine for TJ and 14 for the President as ordered by TJ 6 Sept 1790, shipped on *Eliza,* Capt. Tilden, via Charleston, to Robert Hazelhurst & Co. with request to forward by first packet. "The proprietors of the Mirosmenil Estate...declined shipping the wine of Segur order for the President. We therefore have replaced it out of the wines of Lafite, the Estate of Mr. Pichard (formerly Segur) the growth of 1786. which we hope will prove perfect and giive intire satisfaction. The white graves wine we have shipped you generally costs 500 or 600 per Ton at an age proper to bottle, is made on the Estate of Mr. Dulamont to whom you may in future apply for the same quality if it pleases. He may perhaps give it something lower.— We think the Comsse. de Lur Saluce has charged a very extraordinary price for the parcel shiped you. The same quality here never costs more than 600 at 800 per Ton of 4 hogsheads and she we observe has charged you 30 Sols per bottle, glass included.—The carriage of the frontignac wine from Mr. Lambert also is at least equal to one third the first price of the wine." They have asked him for better terms in future. They enclose account which will enable TJ to settle with the President. Hazelhurst & Co. have been asked to pay freight there and draw on TJ for that and duties, if any.

(Received by Jefferson June 21, 1791)

FROM SHORT

Paris May 2, 1791

The wines &c. have been paid for by M. Grand on my order. These sums will be deducted from the 9405.^{tt} and the bill of exchange of 500 and odd livres you sent me last winter. The rest will be remitted to V. Staphorst & Hubbard to be kept for you. You may therefore settle this matter with the P[resident] as to the wines: when his bills of exchange shall arrive they shall be deposited also with Staphorst & Hubbard, at your disposition or that of the P—according as you may direct...

TO MR. [?] IN THE U.S.

May 15,1791

I expect some parcels of wine from Bordeaux for the President and myself. Mr. Lear will recieve the President's as also a parcel for him from Havre. I do not know the quantity of mine, which with the incertainty of it's coming at all prevents my leaving the duties. If it should arive as there would be danger of it's spoiling in a warehouse, perhaps Mr. Delany will let it come to my own cellars, on assurance that I will settle the duties on my return.

I expect 3 doz. of wine (as a sample) from Baltimore. Perhaps part of it may come by the stage. Also some cyder from Norfolk. The freight will be to be paid.

FROM HENRY REMSEN, JR.

Philadelphia June 16 1791

...Four baskets and four boxes covered in oil cloth have come from France for TJ. He presumes they are wine and has placed in cellar. Also the Chariot and sulky came by same vessel, the carriage of the first damaged by sea water. Carr, the coach-maker who was employed by Francis to unpack and house them, says this was due to improper packing and should be attended to at once. If TJ stays a day or so in New York and thinks it necessary for him to do what is proper, he asks for directions. The duty on these items has not been paid, but he has given bond to the collecter for the amount and oath that a due entry will be made. Lear took charge of the President's wine. Also, 14 cases of wine for TJ have come via Charleston and placed in cellar, with freight paid. He has inquired at Baltimore stage office about wine from there, but has not heard of it...

TO DELMOTTE

(in Paris)

Philadelphia Aug. 30. 1791

I am now to acknolege the reciept of your favors of Feb.9. Mar.25. and Apr.24. as also of the several packages of wine, carriages, &c. which came safe to hand, and for your care of which be pleased to accept my thanks.

Th; Jefferson

TO MADAM DE RAUSAN

(in French)

Philadelphia 1 Sept. 1791

I have received, Madam, the wines of Rauzan that you have been kind enough to send, in good condition, without any being broken; and I am very pleased. I have the honor of asking you now to send 500 bottles of the year 1785. *in bottles*, and two barrels of 250 bottles each, of the harvest of 1790, *in casks*, and I ask that you kindly send it all to Mr. Fenwick, who will make payment to you.

[TJ was apparently ordering for his own cellar and not Washington's because he did not ask that the shipment be "etiquette']

Prc (MHi); at foot of text: *Madame Briet de Rauzan, locataire au conenet de Notre dame, rue Dutra, à Bordeaux.*

TO WILLIAM SHORT

(in Paris)

Philadelphia Sep.1. 1791

Finding it necessary to send to Bordeaux for my year's stock of wine, I inclose herein a bill of exchange of Mr. John Vaughan of this place on Messieurs Le Coulteux & co. for a thousand livres Tournois. Besides this, being in the moment of my departure for Virginia, I leave my letter open with a friend to put into it another bill of £40. sterling on London, which a broker is now in quest of for me. I make them payable to you, because if you will be so good as to negociate them, it will save a good deal of time, which would be lost by their going to Bordeaux and back again, and I have therefore, in the inclosed, mentioned it to Mr. Fenwick, to whom I must ask you to write a line...

Th: Jefferson

PrC (MHi): at head of text: "Private." TJ's letter of this date to Fenwick, recorded in SJL, has not been found, but TJ's accounts for 1 Sep. 1791 indicate he was asking Fenwick to use the £40 bill of exchange to pay for wine he had purchased.

According to another entry under the same date, the bill on John Vaughan was to buy for Henry Knox 250 bottles of 1785 wine and a "cask of equal quality of 1790, from Mde. de Rauzan."

Towards the last of the eight years that he had served as Secretary of State under President Washington, Jefferson began making plans for his return to Monticello and his family. Shipments of wine were being directed there instead of his place in Philadelphia,

TO COL. ROBERT GAMBLE

Philadelphia Aug. 8, 1793

Having just received information from Archibald Campbell Mercht. of Baltimore of the arrival there of 14. cases of claret for me, I have taken the liberty of desiring him to forward it to Richmond to your addrefs, he drawing on me here for the freight to Richmond. I take this liberty because you will best know of the conveyances up to Monticello, to which place I would pray you to send it by the first *safe* conveyance...speedily as can be done *safely* as I know it is not every waggoner who merits to be trusted...

Th; Jefferson

TO JOSEPH FENWICK

Philadelphia Aug. 22, 1793

I have just received your favor of May 16 [!] and at the same time learnt the arrival of my wine at Batimore [sic], from which place I have ordered it to Virginia, whether I shall follow it at the close of the year...

Th: Jefferson

TO COL. ROBERT GAMBLE

Monticello Sep.26. 1793

In pafsing through Baltimore I received the Skippers' receipt for the 14. cases of wine, which have been shipped from thence on board the sloop Polly, James Fibbitt master, on the 7th inst. is I hope arrived at Richmond by this time, in which case I shall be happy to receive them, or part of them by the first waggon...the receipt for the wine is inclosed.

Th: Jefferson

TO JOSEPH YZARDI

Philadelphia Dec. 3, 1793

I have just received your favors of the 29th inst public and private & being in the moment of giving in my resignation I shall only answer the last by thanking you for the order for the wine, and informing you that Richmond is my nearest port & that to which both letters & things had best be addrefsed for me in future.

Th: Jefferson

PRESIDENT JOHN ADAMS

John Adams, elected in 1796, held office from March 4, 1797 to March 3, 1801.

Adams, from Boston, was about eight years older than Jefferson. The two became good friends in early 1776 when both spoke out strongly for independence in Congress, and Adams advocated Jefferson's ideas of a formal declaration. He was the likely one to write it, but he deferred to Jefferson whose literary talents were well respected and support from the southern state of Virginia was important.

Taverns in those days were like clubs where those who could afford it could gather for religious and political discussions, enjoy the wine, and they also served as the forerunners of modern hotels by offering a few rooms for traveling guests. In Philadelphia, Jefferson proceeded to the Indian Queen Tavern where he composed much of the draft of the Declaration of Independence. Shortly befor this, his Journal notes in his careful hand, "Broached a pipe (about 125 gallons) of Madeira, 1770 vintage." Contemporary pictures of the historical event with Declaration committee members Franklin, Livingston, Adams, and Jefferson, June 28, 1776, when he presents his draft, show in the background on the mantelpiece a wine pitcher and wine glass.[2]

In 1784, Jefferson was appointed Ambassador to France to work with Franklin and Adams in Europe on trade and other matters. He served as the chief advisor to Adams on the purchase and transportation of fine wines, which has been covered in detail in the chapter of Adams and the large quantity of "unwanted wines" following him to London. The two families spent a holiday in England together, Mrs. Adams at one time taking care of one of Jefferson's daughters.

The question of a treaty of commerce with Portugal was of considerable importance at this time when neither the United States nor the Portugese nation were very happy with their relations with Great Britain. Adams wrote from London to Jefferson November 5, 1785, discussing the needs of both countries listing first of all for America, "...Considerable Quantities of Maderia, Lisbon and Port Wines..." These "Island Wines" were much desired for the better tables in the United States because, being sweet and fortified, they endured the long sea voyages better then the dry table wines.

Jefferson replied in detail from Paris November 27, 1785,

"...Wines. The strength of the wines of Portugal will give them always an almost exclusive possession of a country where the summers are so hot as in America. The present demand will be very great if they will enable us to pay for them; but if they consider the extent and rapid population of the United States they must see that the time is not distant when they will not be able to make enough for us, and that it is of great importance to avail themselves of the prejudices already established in favor of their wines and to continue them by faciliitating the purchase. Do this and they need not care for the decline of their use in England. They will be independent of that country..."

Three years later Adams returned to the United States. Jefferson wrote him August 2, 1788, from Paris, "I have received with a great deal of pleasure the account of your safe arrival and joyful reception in Boston..." Adams became Vice President under George Washington and Jefferson Secretary of State, marking a period when political differences cooled their friendship. In the next election they ran against each other for the Presidency, Adams won, and by the rules his opponent Jefferson became Vice President. Jefferson won in the next election. In later years they renewed their friendship through their mutual friend Dr. Benjamin Rush.

Adams also advised Jefferson on wines, introducing him to Cahusac, a popular white. Cahusac today is a dry white which may be obtained under the regional name Gaillac. "Occasionally, bottles listing Cahusac as their home reach Washington (D.C.) usually labelled legally as "Vin d'appelation d'origine simple,' which might be translated as "Anonymous," according to John R. Hailman, "A Toast to Mr. Jefferson," *Washington Post*, July 1, 1976.

Both men died on the same day, July 4, 1826. From his deathbed at Monticello, Jefferson could see the marble bust of his old friend, Adams. At Braintree, Mass., Adams' last words were, "Jefferson still lives," not knowing he had died a few hours earlier.

PRESIDENT THOMAS JEFFERSON

Jefferson was President of the United States for two terms, from March 4, 1801 to March 3, 1809.

There was no question about Jefferson being the most influential wine connoisseur of his time. Not only did he advise people from many states, governors, military leaders, cabinet members, planters, and laymen, but it was only natural that he should help four of his best friends too, who should just happen to be Presidents!

This book is the testimony to the good advice he gave also to himself.

PRESIDENT JAMES MADISON

Madison served as the fourth President of the new nation from March 4, 1809 to March 3, 1817.

Jefferson corresponded more probably with his "devoted friend" Madison on agricultural and horticultural matters than with any of the other four Presidents as indicated in the "Garden Book". However, references to wine have undoubtedly been edited out in many of these letters by Jefferson biographers. Unfortunately, too, Boyd's monumental work of 19 volumes carry only to about the year 1791 and most of the Jefferson-Madison correspondence came after that which means that a great deal of wine-related data is not presently easily available.

One letter he wrote to Madison from Frontainebleau, October 28, 1785, stands out as one of the most poignant and revealing of Jefferson's character and sensitivity to the sufferings of his fellow man. His colorful, "She burst into tears...", descriptions of the peasants as well as the royal Court in this beautiful French city, give an insight into his impressions better than any other letter of this type. Although it contains only a short item about wine vines at the last, it is quoted here in full:

"Dear Sir

Seven o'clock, and retired to my fireside, I have determined to enter into conversation with you; this is a village of about 5,000 inhabitants when the court is not here and 20,000 when they are, occupying a valley thro' which runs a brook, and on each side of it a ridge of small mountains most of which are naked rock. The king comes here in the fall always, to hunt. His court attend him, as do also the foreign diplomatic corps. But as this is not indispensably required, and my finances do not admit the expence of a continued residence here, I propose to come occasionally to attend the king's levees, returning again to Paris, distant 40 miles. This being the first trip, I set out yesterday morning to take a view of the place. For the purpose I shaped my course towards the highest of the mountains in sight, to the top of which was about a league. As soon as I had got clear of the town I fell in with a poor woman walking at the same rate with myself and going the same course. Wishing to know the condition of the labouring poor I entered into conversation with her, which I began by enquiries for the path which would lead me into the mountain: and thence proceeded to enquires into her vocation, condition and circumstance. She told me she was a day labourer, at 8. sous or 4d. sterling the day; that she had two children to maintain, and to pay rent of 30 livres for house (which would consume the hire of 75 days), that often she could get no emploiment, and of course was without bread. As we had walked together near a mile and she had so far served me as a guide, I gave her, on parting 24 sous. She burst into tears of gratitude which I could preceive was unfeigned, because she was unable to utter a word. She probably never before received so great an aid. This little *attendrissement*, with the solitude of my walk led me into a train of reflections on that unequal division of property which occasions the numberless instances of wretchedness which I had observed in this country and is to be observed all over Europe. The property of this country is absolutely con-centered in a very few hands, having revenues of from half a million guineas a year downwards. These employ the flower of the country as servants, some of them having as many as 200 domestics, not labouring. They employ also a great number of manufacturers, and tradesmen, and lastly the class of labouring husbandmen. But after all these comes the most numerous of all the classes, that is, the poor who cannot find work. I asked myself what could be the reason that so many should be per-mitted to beg who are willing to work, in a country where there is a very considerable proportion of uncultivated lands? These lands are kept idle mostly for the sake of game. It should seem then that it must be because of the enormous wealth of the proprietors which places them above attention to the increase of their revenues by permitting these lands to be laboured. I am conscious that an equal division of property is impracticable. But the consequences of this enormous inequality producing so much misery to the bulk of mankind, legislators cannot invent too many devices for subdividing porperty, only taking care to let their subdivisions go hand in hand with the natural affections of the human mind. The descent of property of every kind therefore to all children, or to all the brothers and sisters, or other relations in equal degree is a politic measure, and a practicable one. Another means of silently lessening the ine-quality of property is to exempt all from taxation below a certain point, and to tax the higher portions of property in geometrical progression as they rise. Whenever there is in any country, uncultivated lands and unemployed poor, it is clear that the laws of property have been so far extended as to violate natural right. The earth is given as a common stock for man to labour and live on. If, for the encouragement of industry we allow it to be appropriated, we must take care that other employment be furnished to those excluded from the appropriation. If we do not the fundamental right to labour the earth returns to the unemployed. It is too soon yet in our country to say that every man who cannot find employment but can find uncultivated land, shall be at liberty to cultivate it, paying a moderate rent. But it is not too soon to provide by every possible means that as few as possible shall be without a little portion of land. The small landholders are the most precious part of a state.—The next object which struck my attention in my walk was the deer with which the wood abounded. They were of the kind called 'Cerfs' and are certainly of the same species with ours. They are blackish indeed under the belly, and not white as ours, and they are more of the chestnut red: but these are such small differences as would be sure to happen in two races from the same stock, beeding separately a number of ages.— Their hares are totally different from the animal we call by that name: but their rabbet is almost exactly like him. The only difference is in their manners; the land on which I walked for some time being absolutely reduced to a honeycomb by their burrowing. I think there is no instance of ours burrowing.— After descending the hill again I saw a man cutting fern. I went to him under the pretence of asking the shortest road to the town, and afterwards asked for what use he was cutting fern. He told me that this part of the country furnished a great deal of fruit to Paris. That when packed in straw it acquired an ill taste, but that dry fern preserved it perfectly without communicating any taste at all. I treasured this observation for the preservation of my apples on my return to my country. They have no apple here to compare with our Newtown pipping. They have nothing which deserves the name of a peach; there being not sun enough to ripen the plumbpeach and the best of their soft peaches being like our autumn peaches. Their cherries and strawberries are fair, but I think less flavoured. Their plumbs I think are better; so also the gooseberries, and the pears infinitely beyond any thing we possess. They have no grape better than our sweet-water. But they have a succession of as good from very early in the summer till frost. I am tomorrow to go to Mr. Malsherbes (an uncle of the Chevalr. Luzerne's) about 7. leagues from hence, who is the most curious man in France as to his trees. He is making for me a collection of the vines which the Burgundy, Champagne, Bourdeaux, Frontignac, and other the most valuable wines of this counrty are made. Another gentleman is collecting for me the best eating grapes, including what we call the raisin. I propose also to endeavor to colonize their hare, rabbet, red and grey partridge, pheasants of different kinds, and some other birds. But I find that I am wandering beyond the limits of my walk and will therefore bid you Adieu. Yours affectionately,

Th: Jefferson

In another letter to Madison (Monticello, June 18, 1813) many years after his diplomantic tour in France, Jefferson was less the radical and more philosophical when he stated,"...in the lotteries of human life you see that even farming is but gambling." This proved especially true in his "gamble" with the European wine vines he imported and planted, a venture in which he lost.

PRESIDENT JAMES MONROE

Jefferson was overjoyed when his dear friend and neighbor James Monroe assumed the office of the Presidency March 4, 1817, to serve two terms until March 3, 1825.

President Monroe's home was "Ash Lawn" next door to Monticello, and these two notable patriots were not only acutely attuned to political events but their interests were also both rooted deeply in the soil. They exchanged correspondence on farming as early as March 11, 1794, and Monroe planted a vineyard at his home.

Monroe was charged with a special mission to the government of France and Italy and, Jefferson gave him a letter to Madame Noailles de Tesse January 30, 1803, with whom he corresponded on numerous horticultural matters. It may be that Monroe brought back wine vines on that trip.

Jefferson wrote John David from Monticello, January 13, 1816, "... Colo.Monroe, our Secretary of State, whose seat is within 2 or 3 miles of me, has a fine collection of vines which he selected & brought with him from France with a view to making wine. perhaps that might furnish something for you..." It is improbable that Vinifera vines brought from Europe in 1803 could have survived fungi and phylloxera for 13 years, but Monroe may have had successive shipments during that period. Jefferson also noted in a letter to Monroe, January 16, 1816, "...I have an opportunity of getting some vines planted next month...will you permit me to take the trimmings of your vines, it shall be done by him so as to insure no injury to them...?" Records show they were received and planted. The most detailed notes on wine choices given to any President by Jefferson existing today were contained in the following letter to Monroe from Monticello, April 8, 1817:

"Dear Sir,—I shall not waste your time in idle congratulations. You know my joy on the commitment of the helm of Government to your hands.

I promised you when I should have received and tried the wines I had ordered from France and Italy to give you a note of the kinds which I should think worthy of your procurement; and this being the season for ordering them, so that they may come in the mild temperature of autumn, I now fulfil my promise.

They are the following: *Vin blanc limuoureux d'Hermitage de M. Jourdan a Tanis.* This costs about eighty-two and a half cents a bottle put on shipboard.

Vin de Ledarion (in Languedoc) something of the port character but higher flavored, more delicate, less rough. I do not know the price, but probably about twenty-five cents a bottle.

Vin de Rousillon. The best is that of Perpignan or Rives alte of the crop of M. Durand. It costs seventy-two cents a gallon, bears bringing in a cask. If put into bottles there it costs eleven cents a bottle more than if bottled here by an inexplicable and pernicious arrangement of our tariff.

Vin de Nice. The crop called Bellet, of Mr. Sasterno, is the best. This is the most elegant every-day wine in the world and costs thirty-one cents the bottle. Not much being made it is little known at the general markets.

Mr. Cathalan of Marseilles is the best channel for getting the first three of these wines and a good one for the *Nice*, being in their neighborhood and knowing well who makes the crops of the best quality. The *Nice* being a wine foreign to France occasions some troublesome forms. If you could get that direct from Sasterno himself at Nice, it would be better. And, by the bye, he is very anxious for the appointment of consul for the United States at that place. I knew his father well, one of the most respectable merchants and men of the place. I hear a good character of the son, who has succeeded to his business. He understands English well, having passed some time in a counting house in London for improvement. I believe we have not many vessels going to that port annually and yet as the appointment brings no expense to the United States, and is sometimes salutary to our merchants and seamen, I see no objection to naming one there.

There is still another wine to be named to you, which is the wine of Florence called *Montepulciano*, with which Mr. Appleton can best furnish you. There is a particular very best crop of it known to him and which he has usually sent to me. This costs twenty-five cents per bottle. He knows, too, from experience how to have it bottled and packed as to ensure its bearing the passage which in the ordinary way it does not. I have imported it through him annually ten or twelve years and do not think I have lost one bottle in one hundred.

I salute you with all my wishes for a prosperous and splendid voyage over the ocean on which you are embarked, and with sincere prayers for the continuance of your life and health."[3]

THE MODERATE PRESIDENTS

Washington, Adams, Madison, Monroe, and Jefferson were all good friends of many years standing. No other five American leaders did more for the successful birth of our nation. They enjoyed countless glasses of wine together. It was Jefferson who guided their tastes to the best quality. What part the mild beverage played in motivating their dreams into action programs for a free and prosperous United States of America will never be known. We do know that they were moderate consumers of man's oldest medicine. They were never known to be "disguised in drink". All being scholars of the ancient classics they probably knew the early Greek admonition, "Methan Argan", meaning *nothing too much.*

References:

[1]"The Papers of Thomas Jefferson", Julian Boyd, et al, 1950, Princeton University, unless otherwise indicated.

[2]The Christian Brothers Collection, San Francisco, California.

[3]"Writings of Thomas Jefferson," A. E. Berg, Wash., D. C., 1903, Vol. 19, p. 243.

WINE AND FOOD AT THE WHITE HOUSE
The Presidential Table

By Lucia C. Stanton[1]

*"Never before had such dinners been given in the President's
House, nor such a variety of the finest and most costly wines."*

On March 4, 1801, after walking to the Capitol to take the
oath of office, the new President returned to his New Jersey
Avenue lodging for dinner. Thomas Jefferson took his usual
place, "the lowest and coldest seat," at the bottom of a long
table where he and thirty others dined on boarding-house fare.
Later that spring, after he set up his own household on Pennsylvania Avenue, he began to offer meals of a very different
sort to Washington residents. As one observer wrote,"Never
before had such dinners been given in the President's House,
nor such a variety of the finest and most costly wines." President Jefferson's entertainments—for legislators, administrators, and diplomats, citizens of Georgetown, European
philosophers, and Cherokee chiefs—were unprecedented in
their frequency and bountiful elegance.

Before he took up residence in the unfinished stone palace
lately vacated by John and Abigail Adams, Jefferson began to
assemble the largest domestic staff he had employed since his
years as minister to France. Two Frenchmen as butler and
cook and three Irish servants as coachman, valet–porter, and
housekeeper formed the skeleton crew for his first months at
the President's House. Later he added footmen, apprentice
cooks, a scullion, a stable boy, and a washerwoman, bringing
what he called his Washington "family" to a fluctuating total
often to twelve servants.

He turned to Philipe Létombe, French envoy at Philadelphia, for assistance in filling the two most critical staff positions. Acknowledging that a suitable *maître d'hôtel* did not
exist "among natives of our country," he said he found "as great
difficulty in composing my household as I shall probably find
in composing an administration," adding that "honesty and
skill in making the dessert are indispensible qualifications."

Létombe found the perfect household administrator in Etienne Lemaire, a "portly well mannered" Frenchman who had served both European aristocrats and wealthy Americans. Létombe's second discovery, forty-two-year-old *chef de cuisine* Honore Julien, brought experience from his years in the presidential kitchens of George Washington .

CHIEF CHEF JULIEN

Writing from Monticello in April 1801, Jefferson hoped that Julien had arrived and that everything at the President's House was ready "for the entertainment of company." He returned to Washington at the end of the month to inaugurate the new regime of hospitality, and, in December, members of the Seventh Congress arrived in the capital for the first session. Among the many innovations they found at the Republican court were the informal dinners that had replaced the weekly levees of Washington and Adams. Since each legislator was invited at least once, and many more often, the bulky Congress of almost 150 men dictated a crowded social calendar at the President's House—three dinners a week during the session.

Three times a week, therefore, Jefferson sent up to Capitol Hill a dozen printed invitations, which specified a dinner hour of "half after three, or at whatever hour the house may rise." Most of the congressional diners gathered in what is now the Green Room. This small dining room, with its chintz curtains and green floorcloth, was also used for intimate dinners with cabinet members and close friends and family. Margaret Bayard Smith applauded the use here of a round or oval table, "a great influence on the conversational powers of Mr. Jefferson's guests." The room was equipped with a number of tiered dumbwaiters, from which food was taken without the need of servants. Many witnesses reported that Jefferson himself did the serving. "He performed the honors of the table with great facility," observed one guest, while another noted that "Mr. Jefferson said little at dinner besides attending to the filling of plates, which he did with great ease and grace for a philosopher."

Now came the moment to display the art of Julien, who

labored invisibly in Jefferson's basement at a large coal-burning
range. Mrs. Smith stated that "the excellence and superior
skill of his French cook was acknowleged by all who frequented
his table." Between 1802 and 1809, some of Jefferson's dinner
guests left accounts of what they found at the President's
House.

Excerpt from Jefferson's records in his own hand, "Analysis of expenditures from Mar. 4, 1801 to Mar 4, 1802." He paid $2,797.38 for wines
and $2,003.71 for "Groceries" (not wines). "Provisions totalled $4,504.84
and probably included food supplies also. (Library of Congress)

1802 Feb. 6. Federalist congressman, Mannaseh Cutler:
"Rice soup, round of beef, turkey, mutton, ham, loin of veal,
cutlets of mutton or veal, fried eggs, fried beef, a pie called
macaroni which appeared to be a rich crust filled with the

strillions of onions, or shallots, which I took it to be, tasted very strong, and not agreeable. Mr. [Meriwether] Lewis told me there were none in it; it was an Italian dish, and what appeared like onions was made of flour and butter, with a particularly strong liquor mixed with them. Ice cream very good, crust wholly dried, crumbled into thin flakes: a dish somewhat like a pudding–inside white as milk or curd, very porous and light, covered with cream sauce–very fine. Many other jimcracks, a great variety of fruit, plenty of wines, and good." Every day, in order to provide the ingredients for Julien's creations. Lemaire took a horse and cart to the Washington and Georgetown markets. A list of all his market purchases from January 1806 has survived, itemizing payments for seafood (shad, sturgeon, rockfish, oysters); immense quantities of meat and poultry; wild game (venison, duck, pigeons, squirrels, vegetables according to the season (lettuce, asparagus, and peas in spring, and tomatoes, squash, and eggplants in the fall); fruits ranging from local currants, strawberries, and watermelons to exotic oranges and pineapples; and chestnuts, black walnuts, hickory nuts.

"WINE IN GREAT VARIETY"

1802 Nov. 24. Architect and engineer Benjamin H. Latrobe: "The dinner was excellent, cooked rather in the Franch style (larded venison), the dessert was profuse and extremely elegant, and the knicknacs, after withdrawing the cloths, profuse and numberless. Wine in great variety, from sherry to champagne, and a few decanters of rare Spanish wine, presents from (Spanish envoy) Chevalier D'Yrujo." These "knicknacs," consisting mainly of nuts, dried fruits, and confections, were standard accompaniment to the decanters of wine that followed the meal. Many of these items had to be imported from Europe. In 1806 Jefferson received a large shipment of French delicacies to stock the pantry, including three kinds of almonds, seedless raisins, figs and pruned, olives and olive oil, artichoke hearts, tarragon vinegar, Maille mustard, anchovies, Bologna sausage, and Parmesan cheese.

1802 December 24. Federalist senator, William Plumer of

New Hampshire: "We had a very good dinner, with a profusion of fruits and sweetmeats. The wine was truly the best I ever drank, particularly the champagne—it is delicious indeed." The popularity of champagne with his guests caused Jefferson to monitor its consumption. He recorded that, between 1 Dec. 1803 and 20 Mar. 1804, 207 bottles served 651 guests, which was "a bottle to 3 1/7 persons. Hence the annual stock necessary may be calculated at 415. bottles a year or say 500." This scale of hospitality was a considerable expense. In his first year in office Jefferson spent more than a third of his presidential salary of $25,000 on food and wine. In 1807 he calculated that Lemaire's daily trips to market cost him an average of $526 a month during the Congressional sessions.

1803 January. Republican congressman and botanist, Dr. Samuel L Mitchill: "The dinners are neat and plentiful...Among other things ice-creams were produced in the form of balls of the *frozen* material inclosed in covers of *warm pastry*, exhibiting a curious contrast, as if the ice had just been taken from the *oven*."

1804 Feb. 23. Manasseh Cutler again: "dined with his Democratic Majesty. Dinner handsome, not elegant. Good soup and *Boulli*; Ice cream." Ice cream seems to have been always present, even—thanks to an ice house—in the summer. Lemaire once had to hire an extra servant to turn the crank of the ice cream maker on the Fourth of July. A recipe for vanilla ice cream, in Jefferson's own hand, is in the Library of Congress.

1804 Dec. 3. William Plumer again: "The dinner was elegant and rich—his wine very good—there were eight different kinnds of which there were Hungary, and still richer *Tokay*—for this he in formed me that he gave a *guinea a bottle*(little more than a quart).— There was also exposed on the table two bottles of water brought from the river Mississippi, and a quantity of the Mammoth cheese. This cheese, was one made by some Democrats in Massachusetts two three years since, and presented to Mr. Jefferson. It weighed 1200 lb. and is very far from being good. His table furnished a great variety of pies, fruit and nuts." At this dinner Plumer was benefiting from

Jefferson's decision to turn from American merchants to European producers for his wine purchases. "The meanness of quality, as well as extravagance of price of the French wines which can be purchased in this country have determined me to seek them in the spot were they grow," he had written in May 1803 to his Paris agent. By 1804 the presidential wine cellar had received additions of still Champagne, Chambertin burgundy, Chateau Filhot sauternes, and Chateau Rausan Margaux.

GOBLETS WELL FILLED

1806 Jan. 13. Thomas Jefferson Randolph, the President's thirteen year-old-grandson was present at this meal with the French and Tunisian ambassadors. The latter, a flamboyant Turk named Mellimelli, brought his two attaches, between whom young "Jeff" was placed at the foot of the table, "with a large silver goblet on each side me, and a bottle of wine to be replenished when exhausted. I had orders to keep the goblets well filled. Altho' Mohametans, watching their master at the other end of the long table, they emptied them repeatedly and seemed to enjoy and feel their wine.," This ceremonial dinner no doubt took place in the large "public" dining room in the northwest corner of the President's House. It had a rectangular table and a second kind of dumbwaiter—a revolving serving door similar to one Jefferson installed at Monticello. Hetty Ann Barton in 1803 found it second only in interest to the "mammoth cheese," still on display in the East Room. The dumbwaiter was "so contrived that but a few minutes and all appeared or disappeared at once. This machine, fixed in the wall, held all *one course*, and was turned into the room in a minute."

For this meal Lemaire had spent $68.63 that morning at the market, for 120 pounds of beef, 90 pounds of mutton, 35 pounds of veal, 27 pounds of pork, a pig's head, 3 turkeys, 18 quail, 30 "small brids," a fish, 17 dozen eggs, 25 pounds of butter, 30 pounds of rice, 2 gallons of chestnuts, 2 dozen oranges, unspecified amounts of celery, spinach, cabbage, hominy, and lemon essence. Nothing is known of the dishes Julien concocted from these ingredients, but it is probable that macaroni in some form was served, as Jefferson and Mellimelli, long a resident of Naples, shared a love of pasta.

1809 Feb. 5. Margaret Bayard Smith reported a dinner which certainly took place in the small dining room. The only guests, just arrived from Philadelphia, were geologist William Maclure and Quaker philanthropist Caleb Lownes. Maclure, fresh from residence in Paris where espionage among servants was a fact of life, spoke in an undertone inaudible to Jefferson, who chided him; "You need not speak so low. You see we are alone, and *our walls have no ears*." Ingredients for this muted meal, revealed in Lemaire's shopping list, included ham, suckling pig, mutton, beef, veal, venison, rabbit, wild and domestic ducks, turkey, partridges, pheasants, dried peas, and "different vegetables."

Whatever the menu, it was at the end of the last course, when the tablecloth was removed and the "jimcracks" and nuts brought in, that the social harmony Jefferson sought to promote through his entertaining began to be most felt. Decanters of French wine followed the French cuisine, and, as his grandson related, "The fashion was to sit long at table after the cloth was removed, sip their wine and converse. Mr J, oft remarked that the easy flow of after dinner conversation around the table was the most agreable amusing and instructive and he was very fond of it."

TEMPERATE PRESIDENT

William Plumer noted the effect of the wine course on the dinner table conversation with the President: "My usual course, when invited to dine with him, is to converse very little with him, except on the weather and such common topics, until I come to the dining table, nor even then untill after the more substantial dishes are disposed off—and we have drank a glass to two. I do *not* mean, that the President is under the influence of wine for he is very *temperate*. But as I am generally placed next to him—and at that time the company is generally engaged in little parties eagerly talking—and thereby gives him and me More freedom in conversation—and even two glasses of wine oftimes renders a temperate man communicate."

The wonderful influence of wine and conversation is also illustrated in one of Manasseh Cutler's accounts. In 1803 two Federalist congressmen, Roger Griswold and John Rutledge, whose virulent attacks on Jefferson had evidently convinced him they were unfit for the circle of social harmony in his dining room, had not received a dinner invitation from the President in the session. when four Federalists, making commoncause with their neglected colleagues, refused a dinner invitation, it was necessary at the last moment to draft some gentlemen from Georgetown to fill the empty chairs, The atmosphere at the table was strained. Cutler related that "to get rid of the awkwardness we all seemed to feel, a subject occurred to me which I well knew the President always delighted to talk about. I began inquiries about his travels in France, the quality of different kinds of fruit, what their usual desserts were at table, their great varieties of dishes, etc. We went on with the conversation very pleasantly, with scarcely a word from any other person, till we had finished our ice cream. When the wine began to pass round the table a little more freely, all their tongues began to be in motion. We spent the evening tolerably agreeably."

For eight years French food, French wine, and his French servants lightened Jefferson's political labors. After he returned to Monticello in 1809 he wanted to continue the European style of entertainment established in the President's House. He sent off annual orders for French wine and foodstuffs to his agent at Marseilles, but he had more difficulty maintaining the culinary standards set by Julien at the President's House. Two of Jefferson's slaves, Edy and Fanny, had been trained under Julien in the Washington kitchens, and in 1809 the Frenchman travelled to Monticello to give them additional instruction and to help set up the kitchen. But dinners were evidently never quite the same. In 1821 Jefferson wrote: " I envy M. Chaumont nothing but his French cook and cuisine. These are luxuries which can neither be forgotten not possessed in our country."

Honoré Julien, who remained in Washington and established a successful catering dynasty, kept in touch with the President he had served so well. In 1812 he mailed Jefferson his recipe for cream cheese, and in later years he accompanied his New Year's wishes with delicacies unavailable in the Virginia Piedmont —a Swiss cheese and garden seeds in 1818 and wild ducks in 1825. Jefferson responded to the gift of canvasbacks: "They came sound and in good order, and enabled me to regale my friends here with what they had never tasted before. Their delicious flavor was new to them, but what heightened it with me was the proof they brought of your kind recollection of me...I hope you will continue to be prosperous, and I pray you, with my thanks to accept the assurance of my just rememberance of your faithful service to me and my constant and affectionate attachment to you."

Among the handful of surviving recipes in Jefferson's hand (in the Library of Congress) are those for making noodles, vanilla ice cream, brandied peaches, and Madeira jellies. Several of Etienne Lemaire's and Honoré Julien's recipes also survive. Lemaire's notes on the use of wine in French dishes from boeuf à la mode to fricasse de lapin are in the Library of Congress (undated, #42200). His method of economizing in the use of vanilla beans and his recipe for syrup of vinegar as a substitute for Jefferson's favorite syrup of punch are in letters to Jefferson, 6 and 25 May 1806, Massachusetts Historical Society and Library of Congress. At Jefferson's request Julien provided a recipe for cream chese in a letter dated 2 July 1812, Library of Congress. Lemaire's recipes for boeuf à la mode, bouili, breast of mutton, and pancakes, and Julien's recipe for burnt cream are in Marie Kimball, "Thomas Jefferson's Cook Book (Charlottesville, 1987), pp. 61-2, 64, 104-5.

(Ed. Note)

All through the years, and especially when ordering for the White House encumbent, Jefferson would take time and great pains to instruct the American Embassy in Paris what the best wines were and their prices, as in this letter to Alexander Donald, from Philadelphia May 13, 1791,

Bordeaux wines,

1. Red. There are 4. crops which are best and dearest, to wit Chateau-Margaux, all engaged to Jernon a merchant. Tour de Segur belonging to Monsieur Miromenil, 125. tons. Hautbrion, two thirds of which are engaged; the other third belongs to the Count de Toulouse, and De La Fite belonging to the President Pichard at Bordeaux. The last are in perfection at 3. years old, the three first not till 4. years. The cost about 1500.^{tt} the tun when new, and from 2000.^{tt} *to* 2400.^{tt} when ready for drinking.—The best red wines after the 4. crops are Rozan belonging to Madame de Rozan (who supplies me), Dabbadie ou Lionville, la Rose, Quirouen, Durfort. These cost 1000.^{tt} new, and I believe 1500.^{tt} to 1750.^{tt} fit for use. These wines are so nearly equal to the 4. crops that I do not believe any man can distinguish them when drank separately.

2. White wines, The wines made in the Canton of Grave are most esteemed at Bordeaux. The best crops are 1. Pontac belonging to M. de Lamont, 400.^{tt} the ton, new. 2. St. Brise belonging to M. de Pontac, 350.^{tt} the ton new. 3. de Carbonius belonging to the Benedictine monks. They never sell new, and when old they get 800.^{tt} the ton.—But the white wines in the three parishes above Grave are more esteemed at Paris than the vins de Grave. These are 1. Sauterne, the best of all, belonging to M. de Luz-Saluce (who supplies me) 300.^{tt} the ton new and 600.^{tt} old. 2. Prignac. The best is the President du Roy['s]. Same price. 3. Barsac. Best is the President Pichard's. same price.

Add to all prices 5. sous for bottles and bottling. You have no occasion for a letter. The only introduction and the sufficient one is the cash. If you should apply to Madame de Rosan or Monsieur de Luz-Saluce, if their stock of good wine should be low, it may add an inducement to them to name me. In all cases the owner is the person to apply to. He will either send you none, or good. He never adulterates, because he would be a felo de se to do it. All the persons live in Bordeaux where not otherwise mentioned.

Lemaire's wine types for different meats.[2]

```
          facon Demployer different sorte de vin -
          A Lusage de la Cuisinne francaise -
```

Boeuf a la mode	1/2 pinte de vin bla[nc]
Veau a lestoufade	1/2 idem de <rouge> blanc
Dindon ala daube	1/2 idem idem
Matelote de poicon	1/2 idem de rouge
Salmi de Gibie	un Goblet idem
Un poicon de 9 a 10# au four	une bouteille de blanc
une fricasse de lapin	1/2 idem de rouge
un Gasteau au ri	une peinte de Sherry pr. la sauce
les Begn'ais de pomme	1/2 Goblet dau vie pr. les marine
les begn'ais de pain	1/2 peinte de madeira
poutain al'angloise	1 peinte pr. la sauce

Reference:

[1]*Director of Research, Thomas Jefferson Memorial Foundation, Monticello, P. O. Box 316, Charlottesville, Virginia 22902.*

[2]*Annotated by TJ, "Le maire, wine in cookery," Library of Congress #42200, undated.*

ORDERS SHIFT TO SOUTHERN FRANCE
The Ageing Jefferson 1815-1819

In his later years, Jefferson made a dramatic change in his orders for wines from Europe. He had developed a taste and respect for the civilized beverage in his late teens, which carried on to a very sophisticated degree as he came into regular contact with the Nation's leaders—both social and governmental—as he progressed as proprietor of the Monticello mansion, Member of the Virginia House of Burgesses, attended the Continental Congress, became Governor of Virginia, and then U. S. Minister and Commercial Representative in France, Secretary of State under Washington, and President . During this period, roughly 1770-1810, he sought and discovered the finest table wines. For about four decades he desired and was able to pay for the finest vintages of Bordeaux, Burgundy, Champagne, and Germany.

His admitted professional love in life was farming, but his loyalty to public service over such a very long period had understandably caused him to place the management of his plantation in the hands of others. He found on his return to the family fireside at Monticello for permanent residence, that without his previous regular salaries and now with a struggling farm operation, he was forced to watch his finances much more closely. As the highly efficient manager of the many aspects of his wide range of interests, he had also to see how he could economize on that other devotion of his, wine. Knowing the excellence and reasonable prices of wines in Southern France and Northern Italy after his 1787 tour there, he turned to those old favorites which he could order through his trusted friends in the Marseilles Consulate, Stephen Cathalan; Victor Sasserno, in Nice, and Thomas Appleton, Florence.

TO STEPHEN CATHALAN

July 3, 1815[1]

It is so long that I have heard from you that this letter seems almost as if written to the dead, and you have the like grounds for recieving it as from the same region. Wars &c &c.

I resume our old correspondence with a declaration of wants. The fine wines of your region of the country are not forgotten, nor the friend thro' whom I used to obtain them. and first the white Hermitage of M. Jourdan of Tains, of the quality having 'un peu de la liqueur' as he expressed, which we call silky, soft, smooth, in contradiction to the dry, hard or rough. What I had from M. Jourdan of this quality was barely a little sweetish, so as to be sensible and no more, and this is exactly the quality I esteem. Next comes the red wine of Nice, such as my friend Mr. Sasserno sent me, which was indeed very fine. That country being now united with France, will render it easier for you I hope to order it to Marseilles. There is a 3d kind of wine which I am less able to specify to you with certainty by it's particular name. I used to meet with it at Paris under the general term of Vin rouge de Roussillon; and it was usually drunk after the repast as a vin liqueur, as were Pacharetti sec, & Madeira sec: and it was in truth as *dry* as they were, but a little higher colored. I remember I then thought it would please the American taste, as being dry and tolerably strong. I suppose there may be many kinds of wine of Roussillon; but I never saw any but that particular quality used at Paris. I am certain it will be greatly esteemed here, being of high flavor, not quite so strong as Pacharetti or Madeire or Xxeres, but yet of very good body, sufficient to bear well our climate. There is a name of Rivesalte which runs in my head, and almost identifies itself with the red wine of Rousillon, but without sufficient distinctness or certainty of recollection that it is the same: and should the wine of Rivesalte, from what you know of it, answer the description here given, you may conclude it is that I mean. All this I leave to you. To these I add 50. lb. of Maccaroni, an article not to be bought in the United states.... Have placed $200 at Paris for you to draw on. Taking from it first the cost of the 50. lb. of Maccaroni, and reserving enough for all charges till shipped, I would wish about a fifth of the residue to be laid out in Hermitage, and the remaining $^4/_5$ equally divided between the wines of Nice and Roussillon. Reshipment.(According to his tabulations at the base of the letter he expects about 42. b. hermitage, 217 do. Nice and 284 do. Roussillon)

It is interesting to note in the next letter that Jefferson timed his orders for European wines with the arrival of the swallows (birds!) in the spring at Monticello.

It is also obvious that he was missing his old red Bordeaux favorites, but was finding satisfaction in a replacement grown by Mr. Bergasse in Southern France whose "imitations were perfect". He enjoyed wine "daily"...as the Europeans do.

TO CATHALAN

June 6, 1817

My last to you was of Feb.1.16. since which I have recieved your several favors of Feb. 15. Mar. 19. June 1. 4. 19. & July 12. & the several parcels of wine and Maccaroni, came safe to hand. All of them were good; but those particularly esteemed for daily use are the Nice, Ledanon & Roussillon. The Nice de Bellet is superlatively fine, for which I am particularly obliged to M. Spreafico. The vin de Ledanon too is excellent, and the Roussillon of M. Durand very good. This last will be most sought for from this quarter, as being lower priced, & more adapted to the taste of this country, artificially created by our long restraint under English government to the strong wines of Portugal and Spain. The Ledanon recalled to my memory what I had drunk at your table 30. years ago, and I am as partial to it now as then. The return of the first swallow, just now seen, reminds me that the season is now arrived when the provision of another year should be attended to. I therefore am now directing a remittance to Mr. Vaughan, my friend and correspondent at Philadelphia, requesting him to transmit 200. Dollars of it for myself and 65. Dollars for my grandson Thomas Jefferson Randplph, either to yourself directly, or to place at Paris at your command. When you shall have recieved it, I will pray you to procure for me the wines and other articles stated in the invoice inclosed, and to extend your kindness to my grandson also, who is this day leaving us with his wife and child to commence separate housekeeping, and prays me to present him to your good offices. I do it with greater satisfaction, because I can conscientiously assure you of his most solid integrity honor and diligence. When I shall be no more, all my affairs will be left in his hands. I state his invoice separately, and will pray you to have his parcels separately packed, that we may each know our own. In your letter of June 19. you remind me of Mr. Bergasse's former establishment at Marseilles, and that his son continues the business of compounding the wines of the country in imitation of others, and particularly that he can furnish the quality of Bordeaux claret at a franc per bottle, box included, and 3. years old. It is this which my grandson asks for, on my assurance to him that Mr. Bergasse's imitations were perfect, of which I had tasted several, and that they contained not a drop of any thing but the pure juice of the grape. If you will have the goodness to have my parcels marked T.I. [he continues to use this style to mark his wines] & his T.$^{R.}$I. they will be taken care of by the way as if they were all mine, and still be easily separated when they come to our hands...

There is a number of my friends who have tasted these wines at my table, and are so much pleased with their qualities and prices that they are about forming a company, and engaging an agent in Richmond, to import for them once a year what each shall direct. I have promised, when their association is made up, to recommend their agent to you, & to warrant them faithful supplies. Our new President, Col. Monroe, has asked from me some information as to the wines I would recommend for his table and how to get them. I recommended to him the vin blanc liqoureux d'Hermitage de M. Jourdans, the Ledanon, the Roussillon de M. Durand; and the Nice de Bellet of M. Sasserno, and that he should get them thro' you, as best knowing the particular qualities to which I refer. I am anxious to introduce here these fine wines in place of the Alcoholic wines of Spain and Portugal; and the universal approbation of all who taste them at my table will, I am persuaded, turn by degrees the current of demand from this part of our country, and that it will continue to spread *de proche en proche*. The delicacy and innocence of these wines will change the habit from the coarse & inebriating kinds hitherto only known here. My own annual demand will generally be about what it is this year; the President's probably the double or treble. The wine of M. Jourdan being chiefly for a *bonne bouche*, I shall still ask for it occasionally...

Vin de Perpignan de M. Durand. 100. gallons, en double futaille.

Vin de Ledanon. 100. bottles. say, one hundred

Vin de Nice de Bellet. 200. bottles. say, two hundred.

best Olive oil. 5. gallons in bottles.

Maccaroni. 100. lb.

Raisins. 50. lb. those of Smyrna, sans pepins, would be preferred.

Anchovies. 1.doz. bottles.

The above are for Th: Jefferson

The following articles are for Thomas J. Randolph.

60. gallons of Vin de Perpignan of M. Durand, in double casks.

100. bottles vin de M. Bergasse of the quality of Bordeaux claret. 50.lb. Maccaroni.

Jefferson was beginning to feel the effects of financial pressures as returns from his plantation were in decline,

TO CATHALAN

Jan.18, 1818

...The maccaroni, anchovies, oil, and Vins rouges et blancs de M. Bergasse, announced in your letter of Aug. 27. are all recieved and approved; and I am in the daily expectation of hearing further from you and of recieving the wines of Rivesalte, Ledanon & Nice. I find from the consumption of the stock sent in 1816. that that asked in 1817. will not carry me thro' the present year. I must therefore request you to send me without delay, say by the 1st. vessel bound to the Chesapeake, or any port North of that, 200. bottles of the Vin rouge de M. Bergasse of the Bordeaux quality, such as you sent to my grandson. Within three months from this time I shall make you a remittance for the supply of another year, in which shall be included the 200.f cost of what I now ask. I say *three months* hence, because my property consisting in farms, my rents and profits come in in the month of April only; which is the reason of your recieving my invoices so late generally as to make it difficult for the wines to get here before the winter sets in; and that the last written for are not even yet arrived...

TO CATHALAN

April 5, 1818

The Rivesalte & Nice wines arrived at New York about the beginning of January: but so dangerous is our coast in winter that they could not be brought round to Richmond till lately and arrived here two days ago. The Rivesalte will require time to settle before it can be fairly tested. The Nice is good, but is not exactly that of the preceding year, which was a little silky, just enough to be sensible, & to please the palate of our friends beyond any wine I have ever see. That now recieved is dry, but well flavored. The Ledanon is arrived at Alexandria, but not yet got to Richmond. I find you have been in advance for my grandson as well as myself. This proceeds chiefly from the advance in the price of the Rousillon beyond that of the preceding year. I now make thro' Mr. Vaughan a remittance of 420.D. to cover the previous advances for my grandson & myself, the 200. bottles of M. Bergasse's claret I wrote for in mine of Jan 18. and to furnish the new supplies requested on the back hereof, and shall certainly never fail to cover any deficit in our remittances occasioned by unexpected rise of prices in our first subsequent call. The packages for myself are to be marked T.I. and those for my grandson T^{R}I as on the former occasion. I write for my supplies earlier this year than usual, in the hope they may arrive in autumn, or certainly before the winter sets in.

Verso: 64. gallons of Rivesalte

300. bottles of Nice wine

5. gallons of the best olive oil of Aix

12. bottles of Anchovies

50. lb. raisins of Smyrna, sans pepins

100. lb. Maccaroni

The above are for myself to be marked T.I.

The following are for Thomas Jefferson Randolph to be marked T.^{R}I.

30. gallons of Rivesalte

50. bottles of M. Bergasse's claret

[The major part of this letter is in "Reforming His Nation's Taste" chapter],

In a P. S. he ordered:

60. gallons Rivesalte

150. bottles vin de Bellet de Nice

150. bottles of Ledanon

150. bottles vin rouge de Bergasse, qualité de Bordeaux

50 bottles vin muscat blanc de Lunel

5. gallons Oil of Aix

100. lb. Maccaroni

12. bottles of Anchovies

50. lb. raisins de Smyrne sans pepin, if to be had; if not then of others

---

Reference:

[1]**Library of Congress.**

SEARCHING FOR THE BEST VINES
The Adlum Correspondence
By Mary M. Bowes[1]

"...I have little doubt but that grapes of a good quality for making wine may be found in every state in the Union." John Adlum

What prompted Thomas Jefferson, the statesman, educator, inventor, democrat and philosopher, to get involved in experimenting with and promoting American wines? It was his love of the soil and his scientific curiosity that prompted it; Jefferson was also a farmer.

He was born in a farmhouse in Shadwell, Virginia, and all his early influences were of the farm. He carried these influences with him throughout his life; agrarianism was the most significant aspect of his entire philosophy. He loved farming more than anything else, and once wrote, "I have often thought that if heaven had given me choice of my position and calling, it should have been on a rich spot of earth, well watered, and near a good market for the production of the garden. No occupation is so delightful to me as the cultivation of the earth."[2]

Jefferson's concern for American agriculture led him to experiment with fertilizers, crop rotation, animal husbandry, and farm tools. He introduced the threshing machine to America from Scotland, and encouraged his son-in-law to introduce terraced and horizontal plowing in the United States. He once said that the greatest service that could be rendered any country was the addition of a useful plant to its culture.[3] He preformed this great service, then, many times over, by promoting the culture of the fig, mulberry, and olive trees in America. He once had sacks of a high-quality species of rice smuggled out of Italy and sent to South Carolina and Georgia to improve the crops there. At Monticello one year he cultivated 32 vegetables, 22 crops and 13 grasses, and at times Monticello was the only place in America where some of these plants were growing.

From 1766 to 1824 Jefferson kept a Garden Book which is

a highly detailed memorandum showing Jefferson's great concern for agriculture and the process of nature. Listings in it include times of planting, sprouting, and ripening; diagrams and drawings of plots and beds; accounts of weather. It is no wonder that his curiosity and enthusiasm for agriculture led him to also investigate American wine. Jefferson's experiments with wine were some of his earliest ones at Monticello, and his interest continued with these for about sixty years. At the same time, he strongly supported the experimental efforts of his contemporaries, and vigorously promoted U.S. wine growing.

Jefferson is recognized by many as the father of American wines, for he not only cultivated his own vineyard for many years, but he also did much to promote the winemaking efforts of other early American winegrowers.

One of his first experiments at Monticello was in 1773, when Dr. Filippo Mazzei of Tuscany brought some Italian winegrowers and ten thousand European vine cuttings in a chartered ship in order to establish wine growing in Virginia. The experiment, however, was not too successful. After only a few years, many of Mazzei's laborers either died or left him, and the interruption of commerce during the Revolutionary War prevented Mazzei from obtaining others from Italy. Mazzei was then sent on a special assignment for the government, and while he was away his vines were ruined.[4]

Jefferson, however, was not always so highly approving of producing wines in America. In 1787, after a tour of the South of France, he wrote that he had paid particular attention to the crops growing there. He spoke of adopting the cultures of many of them in the Southern United States, as the two climates were similar. But of wines he said:

"We should not wish for their wines, though they are good and abundant. The culture of the vine is not desired in lands capable of producing anything else. It is a species of gambling, and of desperate gambling, too, wherein, whether you make much or nothing, you are equally ruined. The middling crop alone is the saving point, and that the seasons seldom hit. Accordingly, we see much wretchness among this class of cultivators.[5]

Jefferson went on to say that the vine was a resource for land with barren spots and a surplus of people. He continued saying that, perhaps, when America's population increased productions beyond demand, "Instead of going on to make an useless surplus of them, we may employ our supernumary hands on the vine. But that period," he wrote, "is not yet arrived."[67]

Again in the same year he wrote his former law instructor at William & Mary College, George Wythe, from Paris, September 16, 1787, with a tinge of doubt about growing wine vines in America, "...I do not speak of the vine, because it is the parent of misery. Those who cultivate it are always poor, and he who would employ himself with us in the culture of corn, cotton &c. can procure in exchange for that much more wine, and better than he could raise by it's direct culture..."

Even though that period had not yet arrived, Jefferson continued his winemaking and wine growing experiments at Monticello, and must have been somewhat encouraged by them in 1808 when he wrote in a letter, "We could in the United States, make as great a variety of wines as are made in Europe, not exactly the same kinds, but doubtless as good.[7]

Actually, Jefferson had little success in winegrowing. Plant diseases and insects, a result of the humid weather, were the primary causes of crop failure. Jefferson used imported [Vinifera] vines for the most part, and they were not resistant to these in America.

"For thirty years Jefferson continued trying to grow Vinifera (European varieties), importing some of his vines from Chateau d'Yquem, and he is said once to have even imported some French soil...." He finally admitted failure with Vinifera when he recommended in a letter in 1809 that native vines be planted instead.

PARISES ADLUM'S WINE

The letter was written to John Adlum, who owned an estate he named "The Vineyard" which is now part of Rock Creek

Park in Washington, D. C. The wine that Jefferson writes of was made with a grape called Alexander, or Taskin.[8] The letter reads in part:

"I think it would be well to push the culture of that grape, without losing our time and efforts in search of foreign vines, which it will take centuries to adapt to our soil and climate."

Jefferson's enthusiasm in promoting American wines greatly increased after this success with a native grape, so much so that in describing the Charlottesville area in a letter he wrote:

"It's soil is equal in natural fertility to any highlands I have ever seen..., excellently adapted to wheat , maize and clover...I will add that both soil and climate are admirably adapted to the vine, which is the abundant natural production of our forests, and that you cannot bring a more valuable laborer than one aquainted with both its culture and manipulation into wine."[9]

The year 1819 found Jefferson still testing wines for John Adlum. By then a 74-year old man, Jefferson continued as the leading American authority on wines. It must have been a joyous day for Jefferson when, in 1819, he sipped a cup of American wine made from a native grape by John Adlum and thought, "This is it." In a letter to John Adlum describing that wine, Jefferson wrote: "The quality of the bottle you sent me before satisfies me that we have at length found one native grape innured to all the accidents of our climate, which will give us a wine worthy the best vineyards of France."

Jefferson's greatest contribution to the American wine industry was probably his encouragement and promotion of the American wines. Formal history may not remember him for this contribution, and instead remember him as a politician, scientist and educator, but American winegrowers will always recall him first as a vinyardist and promoter of American wines. While others may quote the Declaration of Independence, winegrowers will remember the spirit of Thomas Jefferson that never failed in trying to grow the vine.

The correspondence between Jefferson and Adlum ranged over approximately 15 years until the Monticello viticulture scientist was in his 80's. The letters so vividly reveal the hopes and heart aches as the two men struggled to find the best vines that would make the finest wines, that they are all printed here for the first time.

We know that these two dedicated horticulturists were fighting an enemy impossible to conquer, fungi. Even if they had employed root grafts on the Vinifera vines, various forms of fungi like Black Rot and Powdery mildew would have killed the vines. Modern sprays and grafts now protect the European wine vines and vineyards, home and commercial. They have sprung up in Virginia as Jefferson had dreamed they might. But there is still much more experimentation to be carried on and the spirit of Thomas Jefferson can be a decisive motivation to the scientists of the present time.

The Jefferson and Adlum correspondence follows:

TO MAJOR JOHN ADLUM

Monticello Oct. 7,09

Sir:

While I lived in Washington, a member of Congress from your state (I do not recollect which) presented me two bottles of wine made by you, one of which,of Madeira colour he said was entirely factious [?], the other, a dark red wine was made from a wild or native grape, called in Maryland the Fox grape, but was very different from what is called by that name in Virginia. This was a very fine vine, & so exactly resembling the red Burgundy of Chambertin (one of the best crops) that on fair comparison with that, of which I had very good on the same table imported by myself from the place where made, the company could not distinguish the one from the other. I think it would be well to push the culture of that grape without losing our time & efforts in search of foreign vines, which it will take centuries to adapt to our soil & climate. The object of the present letter is so far to trespass on your kindness, & your disposition to promote a culture so useful, as to request you, at the proper season to send me some cuttings of that vine. They should be taken off in February with 5 buds to each cutting, and if done up first in strong linen & then covered with paper & addressed to me at Monticello near Milton, after committed to the post, they will come safely & so speedily as to render their success probable. Praying your pardon to a brother-amateur in these things, I beg leave to tender you my salutations & assurances of respect.

Th; Jefferson

FROM ADLUM

Wilton Farm near Have De Grace, Feb. 15, 1810

Sir,

Your favour of the 7th of October came duly to hand, and I would have answered it sooner to let you know that I would send you the cuttings desired, but I wished, with the answer to send you a bottle of wine made a few days before the reciept of your letter. After it was done fermenting I racked it off and I thought it rather tart, and having read in the memoirs of the Philada. Agriculture Society, an account of wine made by Mr. Joseph Cooper. wherein he mentions, that having racked off some of his wine which he found too tart he added some sugar to it and it became the best wine he had made, I did the same, and put three pounds of loaf sugar to nine gallons, (which was all the wine I made this year) which caused another fermentation to take place. I then racked it off again, and put about one twelfth part of good French brandy to it, and when it became fine, I found it (to my great dissapointment) much too rich & sweet, and different from what I made before, wanting it neat-nefs.

The colour I think rather paler than heretofore which I think is owing to the grapes not being so ripe as they ought to be. There are some peculiarities, different in the cultivation of this grape necessary, with which I will acquaint you, when I send you the cuttings.

You mentioned that the grape is different from what is commonly called the fox grape in Virginia., It is a black or deep purple grape, with the pulp of the Fox grape grape with some of that smell peculiar to such grapes, and the History Mr. Bartram gave me of it is this: a person of the name of Alexander, gardener to the late John Penn, formerly governor of Pennsylvania, discovered the vine growing somewhere near the Schuylkil river, from whence he planted it into Mr. Penns garden from which some of them are yet cultivated in & about the neighborhood of Philada. The berry of the grape is not quite so large as Fox grapes generally are.

One bottle of the wine I sent you to Washington by Mr. Christie was made from this grape, the other bottle was made from currants. I made three kegs of currant wine two of the red and one of the white currant. After I had the wine fined, two gentlemen called on me one day, and I asked them to stay to dinner with me as it was near the time I usually dine. One of them was bred in a wine store the other in the habit of drinking good wines, and when I was getting wine for dinner, I drew off a tumbler of the red currant wine and brought it to them, and asked them what kind of wine that was. After they had tasted it, they both pronounced it to be a new madeira, I made some objections, which they endeavoured to argue me out of, and insisted that all new madeira wine had that high colour and flavor. I took the hint as to the colour, and next morning I put the contents of the three kegs into a madeira quarter cask recently emptied, and the white currant wine corrected to colour of the red, and the quarter casks communicated in a small degree the smell of the madeira, which afterward puzzled some good judges, and I believe some that I carried to Phila. out of curiosity would have passed for madeira if Mr. Therf had not detected it, but though he could say it was not madeira, ha could not say what it was, but said it was worth two dollars pr. gallon. None of the gentlemen who tasted the wine at that time had the least knowledge of its being a home made wine, and the Fox grape wine I had with me at that time they said was worth one dollar pr. bottle, When I mentioned I made the wine, I had a great many applications from different quarters, for a little of the wine to taste, and I generally sent the currant wine, but evaded telling what it was made of by saying it was a mixture the produce of my farm, but a gentleman from the Island of Jamaica an acquaintance, wished a few bottles to carry home with him as a curiosity, and in American Wine, When I gave it to him he put such pointed questions to me as to how it was made the kind of grape, etc. that I was obliged to tell him it was made of currants . (or be guilty of ill manners.) And after I told him I generally told every person who asked me. And from that time. I never was asked for another bottle. I mentioned this circumstance to shew you the force of prejudice for before it was known to be made of currants every one who tasted it said it was very good wine for this Country and nearer madeira, than any wine they had tasted. It was made from a receipt taken from the first volume of the American Philosophical transactions, with the addition; one sixteenth of very good French brandy added to it. The Fox grape wine had also one sixteenth of brandy in it.

I intend agreeable to your advice to plant out a number of cuttings this spring. I have only about 50 vines of the kind growing. I had upwards of 1200 foreign vines, but scarcely ever got a good bunch of grape from them, owing in the first instance in the Spring to the rose [?] bugs, who eat the blossoms, and afterwards other bugs eat and otherwise injure the grapes, some became mildewed and would not ripen and were subject to such a variety of injuries that I had them grubbed up.

This native grapes are not subject to any of these accidents or diseases—except when they do not hang in the shade of their own leaves. They are apt to be scorched by the sun, and then will never ripen well.

I intend sending you the cuttings the first week in March and will send some wine with them. I would have sent you the wine sooner, but as I mentioned above I was disappointed in it.

It will give me great pleasure at anytime to furnish you or any of your friends with cuttings that I have to spare for I think with you it is best to propogate the culture of our native grape in preference to foreign. They are already adapted to our culture, and I have little doubt but that grapes of a good quality for making wine may be found in every State in the Union; I have eat an excellent grape growing in an Island of Tobys creek a branch of the Allegany river, and have I eat very good white grapes growing along the said river. And in the neighborhood of Presque Ile, there is a very good black grape of a good size and very juicy. And a person of the name of Hick's who was a prisoner of the Indians when the French has Presque Ile informed me he afsisted in gathering considerable quantities for the French officers, and that they made considerable quantities of wine of them—I have seen grapes there about the size of the Miller Burgundy grapes and grew much like them— Along the North East branch of Susquehanna I have eat of a very good and juicy black grape called the beach grape, as the grow along the beach of the river between Wyoming & Tyaga. Some of them have a peculiarity different from any grape that have come under my observation, the branches of the vines are almost every year cut close off by the ice leaving only an old stump, which puts out shots and bears grapes the same season. There is also good grapes on the Island in the Susquehanna between the head of the Tide & Bald Fryar ferry—And if persons living in the neighborhood of the different kinds of grapes would try experiments in making wine, I have no doubt, but excellent wines may be made in a great many parts of our Country. When the grapes are juicy and not rich, add some brandy. When they ripen late and the juice is thick add water and sugar, and if the vines of the best kinds of native grapes were cultivated in different parts of the Country with care I have little doubt that in a few years, wine of a good quality, might be plenty and cheap (nearly) as cider is.

I have drunk a very decent wine at Mr. Thomas Gauls, who lived at Spring Hill and at Isaac Pott's at the Valley Forge made out of what they call the fall grape and they both told me that they made about a hogshead every year; from the grapes that grew in their fields and along their fences. By the time you read this far I expect you must be tired! I shall therefore conclude.

John Adlum

FROM ADLUM

Wilton Farm March 13th, 1810

Sir:

With this days mail I send you a number of cuttings of the vine from which I made the wine I had the honor of sending you by Mr. Christie.

I also enclose a bottle of the wine made last season.

There is one peculiarity in those vines different from any I am acquainted with. They will not bear pruning in the same manner that foreign vines do. When I had them first cultivated, my gardener (when the grapes were set about the size of a swan shot) cut the vine at the joint or bud beyond the last bunch of grapes, which he informed me was the manner of trimming the fruit bearing vines in Europe, that the nourishment might go into the grapes. But the last bud immediately put out a new shot, blofsomed and bore grapes, these he cut in the same manner as the first, and the cut again put out a new shoot, blofsomed and the fruit set. So that there was at the same time, ripe grapes, full green grapes, and the last about the size of swan shot. The ground they were planted in was well manured, and frequently watered while the grapes were growing. But since that discovery I do not suffer the vines to be trimed in the manner mentioned. These grapes grow much larger and ripen much better when they are suffered to hang in the shade of their own leaves, than when tied to strait sticks, they then are frequently scorched by the sun, and then they never ripen well afterwards.

Mr. Gale who lives a few miles from me got a number of cuttings from me, and trains them in the manner mentioned by Forsyth in his book on fruit trees, and it is astonishing to see with what strength the shoots grow but he has not yet made any wine from them. It is his opinion that they ought to be planted a rod apart (that is) 16½ feet.

I shall be glad to hear of your receiving the cuttings safe. Also your opinion of the wine.

I have been some days later forwarding you the cuttings

than I intended, owing to the indisposition of my family. But if no accident happens them by the way and you have them well watered I have no doubt of them succeeding.

John Adlum

FROM ADLUM

Wilton Farm near Havre de Grace April 10th, 1810

Sir:

About the middle of last month I sent you a number of cuttings of the grape vines you requested. As I have not heard, that you have received them, I am fearful they may have been lost on the way. If so! and you will send me word: I will forward on to you a smaller number of cuttings, and see that they are put in the mail. So that there can be no question of their getting safe to you.

John Adlum

P. S. There was a bottle of wine with the cuttings, made of grapes, but made too rich by adding sugar.

TO ADLUM

Monticello Apr. 20, 1810

Sir

Your favors fo Feb. 15 & March 13 were recieved in due time, but were not acknoleged because I was daily in expectation of the cuttings which should have accompanied the latter on the 15th inst. I recieved yours of the 10th & concluding the bundle of cuttings had been rejected at some post office as too large to pass thro that line, I had yesterday, in despair, written my acknolegements to you for the kind service you had endeavored to render me but before I had sent off the letter, I received from the State office of Milton the bundle of cuttings & bottle of wine safe. Yesterday was employed in preparing ground for the cuttings, 165 in number & this morninig they will be planted their long passage gives them a dry appearance, tho I hope that out of so many some will live and enable me to fill my ground. Their chance will be lefsened because living on the top of a mountain I have not yet the command of the water, which I hope to obtain this year by cisterns already prepared for saving the rain water. Supposing the wine may acquired some time to settle, it has not been opened, but I have invited some friends to come & try it with me tomorrow, however the putting sugar into it may change the character of this batch. The quality of the bottle you sent before satisfies me that we have at length found one native grape, in ured to all accidents of our climate, which will give us a wine worthy of the best vineyards of France. When you did me the favor of sending me the former bottle I placed it on the table with some of the best Burgundy of Chambertin which I had imported myself from the maker of it, and desiring the company to point out which was the American bottle, it was acknoleged they could discover no sensible difference. I noted Cooper's recipe for making wine which you mention in your letter, and regretted it because it will have a tendency to continue the general error in this country that brandy always, & sugar some times, are necefsary for wine. This idea will retard & discourage our progress in making good wine, be afsured that there is never one atom of anything whatever put into any of the good vines made in France. I name that country because I can vouch the fact from the assurance to myself of the vignerous of all the best wine cantons of that country which I visited myself. It is never done but by the exporting merchants & then only for the English & American markets where by a inhaled taste the intoxicating quality of wine, more that it's flavor, is required by the palate.

I pray you to accept my thanks for your kind attention to my request, it was made with a view to encourage the example you have set, of trying our native grapes already acclimated, rather than those which will require an age to habituate them to our climate, & will disappoint & discourage those who try them, and with many thanks I render the assurances of my great esteem & respect.

Th: Jefferson

Grafting was being considered by Jefferson at this time, Jan.1,1816. The confident French viticulturist Jean David wrote, "What you say of the wild vines that grow in your woods

confirms me in my opinion [i. e. that viticulture in the US would succeed], because if those vines themselves produce a grape proper for making good wine, what might one expect from those which would be cultivated. This same vine being grafted [*etant greffé*] would perhaps be the best plant to use."
[13]

TO ADLUM

Monticello Jan. 13.16

Dear Sir.

While I lived in Washington you were so kind as to send me 2 bottles of wine made by yourself, the one from currants, the other from a native grape, called with you a fox grape, discovered by Mr. Penn's gardener. The wine of this was as good as the best Burgundy and resembling it. in 1810. you added the great favor of sending me many cuttings. These were committed to the stage Mar. 13. on the 27th of that month I set out on a journey the cuttings arrived at our post office a day or two after & were detained there till my return. They were recieved Apr. 19. and immediately planted, but having been 6 weeks in a dry situation not a single one lived. disheartened by this failure and not having any person skilled in the culture, I never troubled you again on the subject. but I have now an opportunity of renewing the trial under a person brought up to the culture of the vine & making wine from his nativity. am I too unreasonable in asking once more a few cuttings of the same vine? I am so convinced that our first success will be from a native grape, that I would try no other. a few cuttings, as short as you think will do, put into a light box, & mixed well with wet moss, if addressed to me by the stage to the care of Mr. William F. Gray in Fredericksberg, will be forwarded by him to Milton without delay, where I shall be on the watch for them. I must find my apology in this repeated trouble in your own patriotic disposition to promote an useful culture and I pray you to accept the assurance of my great esteem & respect.

Th: Jefferson

FROM ADLUM

George Town District of Columbia

Feby. 27th, 1816

Dear Sir

I did not receive your favour of the 16th inst. until yesterday. I now reside in the neighborhood of this Town, and have lived here near two years. I heard by accident of your letter being in the Post Office of Havre de grace, and wrote to the Post master fot it, it was very neglectful of him not to forward it to me, as he knew. I resided in this vicinity.

As I suspose the person to whom I sold my farm at Havre de grace had grubbed up all the grapevines I left there, I have written to Livin Gale Esquire son to my late friend Mr. George Gale who got the grape from me to forward you a number of the cuttings of the grape you want, which I am very sure he will do with a great deal of pleasure, and I have requested him that when he forward them to you to write that no time may be lost, in planting them & I have also written him something since to save a number of cuttings for me, and expect to be at his house some time next month. and if it is not too late. I will send you an additional number of cuttings. I hope you will believe that I do not think it any trouble, where I can be in any manner useful in promoting the culture of any thing useful in my country.

John Adlum

FROM LEVIN GALE

Levin Gale to Jefferson, Chesapeake Md. March 30, 1816

I received sometime ago a letter from Major John Adlum near George Town D. C. requesting me to forward you some cuttings of a particular grape which was orginally got from him. The same day this goes by the mail there will be put in the stage a box containing 150 cuttings of the kind mentioned Directed to you to the Care of Mr. Wm. F. Gray Fredericksburgh Virginia. I have to apologize for not complying sooner with his request but being from home at the time his letter reached this together with other circumstances prevented attending to his request with alacrity I could have wished. Should you wish more cuttings next year shall be happy to forward them and regret that our vines from neglect furnished so few...

                                          Levin Gale

FROM ADLUM

                                    Near George Town D. C.
                                    June 5, 1822

Dear Sir.

I went last week to see the Baltimore cattle show, with a view to get the members of the Agricultural Society of Maryland to recommend the cultivation of the vine, and the making of wine.

I had previously sent four kinds of wine to the President of the society, and which was drank at the Societies dinner, and generally spoke favourably of—Particularly the kind made from a grape called the Bland, to which I have added Madeira, and is said to have been originally found in Virginia.

The enclosed letters were shown to the President of the Society Mr. Skinner and others, Mr. Skinner has a desire to publish them in his American Farmer, Which I could not consent to without your leave. I have therefore taken the liberty of sending them to you, (that if you should consent to their publication) you may strike out such parts as you may think proper—Or if your inclination and leisure permit to write one with the substance more condensed.

I have now about four acres of vines now planted—about two of which are in bearing, and the other two acres I expect will bear fruit next year—And I planted out about 14000 cuttings this season, and to my great mortification. I observed to day hundreds of the buds that were just putting out schorched by the heat of the Sun which must have happened on Friday, Saturday and Sunday last. Where the leaf was fairly formed they resisted the heat of the sun and are growing, And I hope the number will be sufficient to plant out ten acres, with what I have growing.

From present prospects, I hope to make six or seven hundred gallons of wine this year, last year while I was on a trip to the West Indies upwards of three hundred gallons of my wine turned to vinegar, for want of proper attention to racking.

My desire to promote a new article of culture in our Country, and which I think of great importance, will I hope plead my excuse for troubling you—

I am Dear Sir, With great respect, Your most Obedt. Serv.

John Adlum

TO ADLUM

Monticello June 13, 1822

Sir,

Favor of the 5th has been duly recieved, covering my two letters to you of Oct. 7. 1809, and Apr. 10. 1820 which I now return of these be pleased to make whatever use you think proper. but I should think the first half of the last letter had better be omitted, as it would encumber Mr. Skinner's column, with matter entirely uselefs & uninteresting to his readers. I am very glad to learn that you are pushing that culture, and I hope you will particularly that of what I would call the Caumartin grape, as it's wine resembles so exactly that of the Caumartin Burgundy. I presume you know that a wine of remarkable merit is made in considerable quantities in a district of N. Carolina on Scuppernon Creek. This wine, when it can be obtained unbrandied would be drank at the first tables of Europe in competition with their best wines. What of it however is sent to the general market at Norfolk is so brandied as to be unworthy of being called wine. to get it with out brandy requires a troublesome correspondence & special agent. until this fatal error is corrected, the character of our wines will stand low. Accept the assurance of my great esteem and respect.

Th: Jefferson

FROM ADLUM

Vineyard near George Town, D. C.

March 14th, 1823

Dear Sir.

I send for your acceptance through the Post Office a bottle of wine made last September, from a grape I call Tokay. A German Priest who saw the grape ripe said they were the true Tokay, such as he had been growing in Hungury, I have no doubt but that these grapes are like them, but I have a strong suspicion that they are native—I found them at Clarksberg in Montgomery County at a Mrs. Scholls, and she does not know where they came from—Mr. Scholl in his life time—called them the Catawba grape—This wine is made without brandy but there was twenty five lbs. of sugar to the barrel—This was the first year of the vines bearing, but I have no doubt that in two years more no sugar will be required—In a few days I will send you a bottle of my Burgundy also made last September—And I send a small book on the cultivation of the vine and making wine—After you have received both bottles of wine, I will thank you for your opinion of them—These wines are rather green yet. they would be much dryer two years hence—

John Adlum

P. S. If you wish to have any grape cuttings I will send you some of the Tokay and others—The Tokay is the most abundant bearer of any grape I am acquainted with.

John Adlum

FROM ADLUM

Vineyard near George Town, D. C.
March 24, 1823

Dear Sir

I sent you some days since a bottle of domestic wine that I call Tokay—I now send you a bottle of what I call Burgundy, neither of these wines have had any brandy in them—I will after I have bottled it send you a bottle of my Champaign, made of the miller [?] Burgundy grape, which will have to be kept perhaps two months before you drink it, when I expect it will be brisk and sparkle—I have but about five gallons of this quarter cask of my Burgundy wine left—but I have a barrel & quarter cask more but not so good as this—I will be glad to

TO ADLUM

Dear Sir   Monticello Apr. 11. 1823

    I received successively the two bottles of wine you were so kind as to send me. the first called Tokay, is truly a fine wine, of high flavor. and, as you assure me there was not a drop of brandy or other spirit in it, I may say it is a wine of a good body of it's own. the 2d. bottle, a red wine, I tried when I had good judges at the table. we agreed it was a wine one might always drink with satisfaction, but of no peculiar excellence. of your book on the culture of the vine it would be presumption in me to give any opinion, because it is a culture of which I have no knolege either from practice or reading. wishing you very sincerely compleat success in this your laudable undertaking, I assure you of my great esteem and respect.

                                     Th. Jefferson

Maj.r John Adlum

Example of a Jefferson letter.

have your opinion of the wines and also of the book I sent you—I called last spring upon Mr. Robert Smith, President of the Agricultural Society of Maryland to endeavour to get a premium offered for the cultivation of the grape and making wine; but I believe it is not yet acted on, and I presume will not until some persons above the common prejudices take it up.—If a premium was offered, I could not look upon myself a candidate as I have three years advantage of any person now beginning— But I have the pleasure of seeing a considerable interest taking place in Virginia, this spring, on the cultivation of the Vine etc and have sold at least ten times the number of cuttings to Virginians, that I have to other persons—If you think it would be of any advantage to this Country to recommend to Mr. Madison to patronize this object. I would thank you to recommend it to him, not as an individual, but as President of an Agricultural Society—And as I said above I will not consider myself a candidate for the premium if one is offered—I intend in a few days to send Mr. Madison, the same wine, I have the pleasure of sending you—I am sorry, to take up so much of your time; but, I hope my anxiety to promote an object which I hope will produce a new era in this Country for the better, will plead my excuse—

                                        John Adlum

References:

[1]Former Editor, *The Bulletin*, Virginia Department of Agriculture and Commerce, Richmond, Va.

[2]*The Writings of Thomas Jefferson*, letter to Mr. Peale, Aug. 20, 1811 (Taylor and Maury, Washington, D. C., 1853), VI.

[3]A. C. Miller, Jr., "Jefferson as an Agriculturist", *Agricultural History*, XVI, (April, 1942), 65.

[4]Chapter 3, Mazzei.

[5]Taylor, op cit.

[6]Ibid.

[7]Ibid., V, pp. 314-315.

[8]John Adlum, *A Memoir on the Cultivation of the Vine in America*, (Washington, D. C., 1828, p.151.

[9]Taylor, op cit.

NORTH CAROLINA SCUPPERNONG
Jefferson's "Exquisite Wine"

By Annette A. Penney[1]

North Carolina has the distinction of being the home of the grape that to Jefferson was a superb specimen from which was produced a fine wine and declared one of his favorites. Also, with his taste in wines being a well educated one, he felt that this wine from North Carolina would surely be at home on the finest tables of Europe. He commented in this manner in a letter to his good friend William Johnson,[2]

Monticello May 10, 1817

Sir,

"...the pamphlet you were so kind as to send me manifests a zeal, which cannot be too much praised, for the interests of agriculture, the employment of our first parents in Eden, the happiest we can follow, and the most important to our country. while it displays the happy capabilities of that portion of it which you inhabit. it shews how much is yet to be done to develop them fully. I am not without hope that thro' your efforts and example, we shall yet see it a country abounding in wine and oil. North Carolina has the merit of taking the lead in the former culture, of giving the first specimen of an exquisite wine, produced in quantity, and established in it's culture beyond the danger of being discontinued. her Scuppernon wine, made on the Southside of the Sound, would be distinguished on the best tables of Europe, for it's fine aroma, and chrystalline transparence. unhappily that aroma, in most of the samples I have seen, has been entirely submerged in brandy ...we, of this state, must make bread, and be contented with so much of that as a miserable insect will leave us. this remnant will scarcely feed us the present year, for such swarms of the Wheat-fly were never before seen in this country..."

General Cocke, Bremo, Fluvanna County, Virginia, noted March 27, 1817, "...sent to Monticello for some Marseilles figs and Paper Mulberry, and at the same time sent Mr. Jefferson some wine made from the Scuppernong grape of North Carolina, a fruit which must be well worthy to be cultivated. The wine is of delicious flavour, resembling Frontinac..."

Jefferson points out in a note to General John H. Cocke about his pleasure in the Scuppernong wine,

Monticello, March 27, 1817

Thomas Jefferson is very thankful to Genl. Cocke for the sample of Scuppernong wine which he has been so kind as to send him, and which he considers as being as fine, as it is a singular wine. He sends him plants of the Marseilles fig & of this [?] Paper [?] or Olaheite mulberry, & cuttings of the Lombardy poplar which he brought from France, very different from the common one. being a tree of some shade. he adds a couple of plants of the prickly locust [*Robinia hispride*] a rich blooming shrub, rarely to be met with;...he will expect the pleasure of seeing Genl. Cocke on the court day, & salutes him with friendship & respect.

An amusing sidelight to the Carolina wine trade is succinctly expressed by Francis Eppes, son of Jefferson's daughter Maria who died April 17, 1804. He was left to care for the family estate and his father. From his letter to his grandfather Jefferson, October 31, 1822, it is apparent that the whole Jefferson family was intimately interested in the progress of the wine industry in the Carolinas.

"...I obtained from Col. Burton the address of several gentlemen who make the Carolina wine. he was much opposed to giving the information being willing & indeed anxious to procure it for you, but upon my insisting told me that Thomas Cox & Co. commission Merchants Plymouth, would be more likely to please than any others. The makers of the wine are persons in easy circumstances, who do not care to oblige, generally keeping the best for themselves. It was from Cox that your last & (I believe) my Fathers which you admired, were obtained. In case however, that you might still prefer the wine makers themselves, he informed me that Ebinezer Pettigrew P. O. Edenton, & George E. Spruce P. O. Plymouth make the best. The former will not always sell being very wealthy. The latter is not in as good circumstances, and owns the famous vine covering an acre of ground.[3] Col. B. informed us that the vine does not grow from the slip, which accounts for the failure of yours.

"If you can conveniently, I wish you would answer this as soon as it comes to hand. I am compelled to go down to Richmond on the 17th of Nov. at fartherest, which will leave me two mails, the 14th & 16th..."

It is believed that the grape so enjoyed by Jefferson was discovered on the Roanoke island, N. C., by Sir Walter Raleigh's colony and that the original vine is still in existence, Jefferson described the scuppernong grape. It was said to be a direct offspring of the muscadine grape (*Vitis Rotundifolia*). Jefferson also comments about this wine in his letter to Samuel Maverick of South Carolina, May 12 1822. Much later, the origin of this grape caused an extensive search by horticulturist F. C. Reimer, early in the 1900's. He made special trips to all of the old vineyards in North Carolina and investigated the records of early grape growers. He could find no authentic records on the Scuppernong's origin, but he believed that the original vine was found in northeastern North Carolina, probably in Tyrrell County. The earliest record reveals the grape came from Tyrrell County about 1760, and was planted near New Bern, being given the name of the man who brought the grape vine there, Mr. Hickman.

The most reliable information regarding the finding of the original plant came from generations of lore in the family of Isaac Alexander who in the middle of the 18th century went from Mecklenburg to Tyrrell County to take possession of a tract of land granted to him by the English King. He found, near Albermarle Sound, the wild grapevine bearing luscious white grapes. Thus, it is believed, this was the original vine which later was named Scuppernong. As early as 1809, there were extensive plantings of this vine reported near Lake Scuppernong, (Indian name) and the grape that was commonly known as the White Grape assumed the name of its surroundings, thus, Scuppernong was born.

MAKING SCUPPERNONG WINE

How to make the Scuppernong wine and the origin of the name back in Indian times is discussed in the N. C. Agriculture Experiment Station, West Raleigh Bulletin 201, April 1909 by F. C. Reimer,

"...The grape is large and sweet, of the species of the Fox grape, but white; has been cultivated a number of years in the neighborhood of Lake Phelps, but it is not clearly understood whence it originated. It is supposed to be a Nateri. There are few settlers about the lake but what have a grapevine, which is generally planted at the root of some large mulberry, beech or oak tree, or trained along an arbor of poles lying on forks high enough for a person to walk under and gather conveniently. The vines are never pruned, but suffered to run in a rude state, and many people have vines that will make them a barrel of wine.

"The wine is made by gathering the ripe grapes, picking out all those which are green or bruised, and squeezing the juice from a cider press as soon as they are gathered (for if they lie from one day to another the juice will sour and the wine will always have that taste). Then it is put in a clean barrel. In every three quarts of grape juice one quart of brandy is added. After three or four days the wine is raked off till it is clear, and when it gets age is much approved of.

"The process above mentioned is that now followed, but as there are several gentlemen of information sending to the people in that neighborhood to make wine for them, a better process my be discovered. Some have tried fermentation but it did not answer."

NAMING THE SCUPPERNONG

On January 31, 1811, *The Raleigh Star* published under the heading, "North Carolina Wine from Native Grapes," part of a report made by James Blount, of Scuppernong, North Carolina, who had been appointed to take a census of Washington County. In this report he states that Washington County produced thirteen hundred and sixty-eight gallons of wine from native grapes during 1810. Mr Blount in his report further says:

"Having taken an account of the wine in my division, I think it my duty to relate the results of my inquiries on this small but very interesting branch of our infant manufacturers.

"The large white grape from which most of this wine is made is said to be a native of America, and probably of North Carolina, as no person can tell its origin; and I feel inclined to join in this opinion, having about three years ago found a vine with ripe fruit on it of this kind in the woods, where it is very improbable it could have been planted. I am told the grape from the seed will be purple and larger than from the cuttings of the vine, though not as sweet. These vines thrive well on various kinds of soil, but delight most in that which is loose and sandy, and if care is taken to manure them for two or three years it will afterwards only be necessary to keep the weeds clear, prune and scaffold them; and one vine is worth more than fifty apple trees."

The editors of *The Star* add the following comments to Mr. Blount's report:

"Our readers will recollect a communication on this singular and excellent species of grape (which for the sake of distinction, until we are better instructed, we shall denominate the Scuppernong Grape). In the 239th page of our first volume. That communication excited considerable interest and procured for us another favour of the same kind from Mr. Cooper, which will be seen on page 38 of our second volume."

"The grape was named 'Scuppernong' because of the numerous plantings of this variety along the Scuppernong River at the time. The name was also given as a compliment to James Blount, who lived near that river and whose excellent articles on this grape attracted much attention...

"At that time, Dr. Calvin Jones and Thomas Henderson were editors of *The Star*. The honor, then, of naming this grape belongs to the editors of the Raleigh (North Carolina) newspaper. It is very probable that it should properly be given to Dr.

Calvin Jones, who was a noted naturalist, and edited the agricultural part of *The Star*.

"The writer feels certain that this is the first time that this grape was designated as *Scuppernong*. He has not been able to find this name used in any of the earlier writings; and Blount, in his report two years previous to that date, speaks of it as 'the large White Grape.' The following extracts from a letter written by James Saunders of Chowan County, North Carolina, to the editors of *The Star* and published in that paper April 17, 1812, under the title "Scuppernong Grapes and Wines," also lead to the same conclusion,

"Your publishing with such lively interest the properties of that excellent fruit you have named the 'Scuppernong Grape,' while it appeard you were yourselves quite a stranger to it, has induced me to endeavor to prepare and convey to you, this fall, a few slips of that valuable and most luxurious article.

"The usual or common name given those grapes here is the 'White Fox.' So far as my information goes, I think it is most probably a native of Roanoke Island, near Roanoke Inlet, where some have conjectured Sir Walter Raleigh either found or left them. However, I have heard no person object to the name you have given, nor do I expect that any will, for the neighborhood about Scuppernong for several years has abounded with them, and for some time past the inhabitants have been turning them to good account, and, with the help of the encouraging *Star*, this branch of economy and industry may be brought to high perfection."

AN INDIAN NAME

The word Scuppernong is a corruption of the Indian word *ascuponung*, meaning place of the ascupo, ascopo, or askopo. The word *ascopo* was the Algonquin Indian name for the Sweet Bay (*Magnolia glauca*). This tree is very abundant along the Scuppernong River.

On the old maps of the State we find that the word *ascuponung* was gradually changed until it has become badly corrupted. Eman Bowen gives it as *cuscoponung* in 1752. On a map by Joshua Fry, published a little later, it is given as *cusponung*. In 1770 John Collet changes it to *Scuponung*. In 1771 James Cook again changes it to *Scuponing*. Some time between 1775 and 1800 it was finally changed to *Scuppernong*...

The largest (trunk circumference 7 feet 6 inches) vines were reported in the mid 1800's to have produced from 50 to 100 bushels of fruit, which sold to the wine makers and other consumers at an average of one dollar per bushel and were considered the main crop by the bankers and islanders. They grow in clusters of six or eight berries generally about the size of a common marble, and are pale yellow when ripe. The Scuppernong became very popular and many people had at least one in their yard during the 1800's. But, interest fell off until the early 1960's when reports about Muscadine grapes were stimulated by the formation of the New River Grape Growers Association in Raleigh. A breeding program to develop higher yielding varieties of excellent quality was undertaken headed by Dr. Carlos Williams of N. C. State University in cooperation with the U. S. Department of Agriculture.

By 1961 five, new perfect flowered varieties were released with Magnolia now being the leading commercial variety. Today this North Carolina industry has grown from almost nothing to a half-million-dollar agricultural enterprise with expansion still possible. The Carlos variety developed at N. C. State has a high yield potential and is adaptable to mechanical harvesting which will benefit growers. The newer Noble variety is expected to show promise for making wine. Experts emphasize that the natural sweet wine should be marketed as an aperitif or dessert wine, and not as a dry table wine.

Muscadine grapes have several desirable features to offer North Carolina farmers. Prices are good and if a reasonable management program is carried out, cash returns per acre can be high. Some growers, after the initial establishment period of 3 to 4 years, are realizing yields of 5 to 10 tons and acre. At over $300 per ton, many are netting more money per acre with grapes than with tobacco. Numerous vineyards in the hills are now growing Vinifera, and they can bring as high as $1,000 per ton! The largest by far is Biltmore Estates, Ashville. A promising wine growing co-op has been established bear Greensboro headed by Dr. Scott Lawrence.

Grape growing can also be almost completely mechanized. Except for the first year they do not compete for summer labor. Weeds can be controlled chemically and harvesting and pruning are done after the tobacco season is over. Many farmers are looking to grapes to gainfully employ their seasonal help throughout the fall and winter, and in this way prevent their dependable farm labor from seeking employment elsewhere. Grapes are very well suited to a farm diversification program, and the climate, soil, and terrain are good.

There are no acreage controls, no price supports—consequently, the farmer should become informed of the latest cultural practices and markets and try to coordinate efforts in developing this industry. Of course, this is the purpose of the North Carolina Grape Growers Association and anyone interested in growing grapes should join and actively support and participate in this organization, % Guildford County Extension Service, 3309 Burlington Rd. Greensboro, N. C. 27400, tel. 919/375-5876. Producers and marketing firms must work together. There is no reason that can be imagined that would prevent the grape industry in North Carolina from doubling or tripling, with Scuppernong for sweet wine and Vinifera for dry wine. Mr. Jefferson might say, "I told you so."

References:

[1] A resident of Upperville, Virginia, Mrs. Penny has for many years been associate Editor of the *Journal*, Vinifera Wine Growere Association. She manages her own public relations firm in Washington, D. C.

[2] Jefferson's Garden Book, p.572.

[3] Ibid., p.22.

MUSCAT VINES TO SOUTH CAROLINA
Searching For Good Varieties
By Annette C. Penney

The Carolinas were especially focused upon by Jefferson in his constant search for different types of plants for the new States, food varieties being the most important. Both North and South Carolina's soil conditions were quite familiar to Jefferson, more so than the other states, thus he recognized the potential of developing several kinds of commercial crops. In his travels through Europe, he observed everything in the plant life and selected what he felt could enhance the crops of America.

To South Carolina he sent rice, olive trees of Aix and to William Drayton, Chairman of the Agriculture Society of S. C., he sent 43 pieces of muscat vines (Vinifera grapes used in making wine and raisins). Both the rice and the grapes were compatible with the southern soil and climate of South Carolina, but to his dismay the olive trees failed to enjoy the soil as it was too rich. Jefferson considered the olive plant the "...worthiest plant to be introduced into America." In fact, he stated, "Of all the gifts of heaven to man, it [olive] is next to the most precious, if it be not the most precious. Perhaps it may claim a preference even to bread, because there is such an infinitude of vegetables, which it renders a proper and comfortable nourishment." He sent about 500 plants of the olive trees to South Carolina in 1791, but 25 years later he bemoaned the fact that: "...If any of them exist, it is merely as a curiosity in their gardens, not a single orchard of them has been planted."[1]

It was in 1788 that Jefferson wrote from Paris to his friend John Rutledge, Jr., about the possibility of the grape being grown in South Carolina. Then a year later a good size shipment arrived and the grape industry potential was launched. Shipping plants from Europe proved a tremendously difficult job in that too many would die along the way, probably standing on wharves, unwartered and awaiting shipment. But, typical of Jefferson, he took elaborate precautions in packing his precious wine vines—as he did all other plants, of course. This was learned from a letter he wrote Richard Cary, "Take the plants up by the roots, leaving good roots. Trim off all the boughs and cut the stems to the length of our box. Near the tip end of every plant cut a number of notches which will serve as labels, giving the same number to all plants of the same species. Where the plant is too small to be notched, notch a separated stick and tye it to the plant. Make a list on paper of the plants by their names and number of notches. Layer the plants in thick banks of moss, wrapping large roots separately."[2]

In his meticulous way, Jefferson never left anything to chance, but carefully explained any project or idea he was involved in and this applied to his great love, horticulture. The same is true of many of his correspondents in those days, particularly when it came to conveying exactly how someone should plant something, thus causing a grape vine to be either healthy or modestly so. The following letter will give some idea about the correspondence between gentlemen farmers during the early 1800's,

FROM SAMUEL MAVERICK

Montpelier, Pendleton Dist: S.C.

Aug.11,1821

For many years past I have been in the habit of Cultivating the Grape Vine and with various Success, owing to some cause or other they very generally Rotted, and which has allmost allways happened Just at he moment as it were when they attained their full size, they then take a drab Coloured spot on one side which spreads in a few days over the Grape and has the appearance of being scalded and in that state they readily part fom the Vine, that is they are easily shook off, this phenominon is most comon to the large Dark purple or Black Grape, the white Chasilas and several other Kinds of Grape are infested with the same Brown spot, drys a way flatning on one side, and the Branches fall off. I have a Valuable Grape now in Bearing, which is said to have been procured from you some years past. it has made its appearance in this part of the

Country or Rather I have procured it in two ways. One from Col. Hawkins from the Creek Nation, and in another from a Mr. Booth from Virginia. this has ripened well and is a good Bearer, I now have Inclosed two Leaves from that Vine in order that you may be better inabled to give me Information what grape it is, and where Imported from, for several reasons, One of which is to compair the similarity of Effect in perhaps different Latitudes, and for a further Importation of Vines, the Bunches on this vine contain generally from 20 to 40 Grapes, and after attaining ½ to ¾ Inch in Diameter, they turn light Coloured, then gradually assume the Colour of Madarah wine or light brick Colour, the Grape is nearly round, flattened a little at the ends, and rather most at the stem, the fruit is verry Excelent, but leaves a verry slight astringent tast in the skin.

I am in Latitude 34.20 the Land lays pleasantly Rolling, perhaps one of the Best watered Countrys in America, about 30 miles below the Table Mountain which forms part of the Great Chain running threw this Continant our soil is various, and in my particular neighbourhood and farm we have a mixture of sand and Blck Loom from 4 to 12 Inches on a Greasy Red Retentive Clay, on which I have tryed various Methods to Cultivate the Vine, on Arbours, Aspilliers and frames 2½ foot high training them Horisontally, but I find to train them on Poles about 10 foot high, running them up in single stems and Exposing them to the sun and air, answers best with me and occasionally pulling off the Leaves, on a Gradual South Exposiour, I have Laid of Horisontal Beds 5 foot wide, with 10 foot space Between from which I have taken off all the Soil, I carted on Top soil, Cow manure and sand on the Beds and Incorporated them with a Portion of the Clay and soil from 2½ to 3 foot deep, and planted one Row of Vines about 6 to 8 foot apart on Each Bed, in this way alone I have been inabled to rase the Large Black Grape, which has allmost invariably rotted in every other way, the only appology I have to offer for this paper to you is the Emence Importance to this Country in the Introduction of a New and Valuable Article of Commerce, as well as a most delicious and agreeable fruit, the Introduction of which may perhaps ameliorate the awful effects of spiritual

Liquor. I have in my Colection a Small Grape in Tolerable size Bunches say ¼ to ½ lb in weight which Ripens well, very sweet and delicious flavour, wild grapes are plenty and Consist of the Large Black Muscadine small thin Leaf groes on Rich Bottom Lands—Fox Grape Black Red and White—the summer Grape on high land the small winter Grape on water Coarses and a new kind I have just discovered, but some what similar to the summer Grape and I supose of that kind the Bunches and Berrys Larger ripens well, if there is any thing in this way, which strikes your fancy, you will please to order me to whom and where I shall send them by way of Charleston to you, to which place I will forward them by a waggon.

I shall consider it a great favour for any information Relitive to the Grape Vine as to Soil, Manure, Climate, Exposier, prooning, Kinds, or any thing else, I once had the pleasure of speaking to you on the Road, my Uncle Wm. Turpin and myself met you in passing through Virginia on our way to Carolina about 13 years ago, since when he has settled himself at New Rotchell New York.

are thay not Various other plants that might be Introduced for the great Convenience and Cumfort of the Inhabitance of this wide Extended Country, even Tea and other Luxerys to sasiate the avorice of Comerce, or at least to spair the Ne[ce]essity of the Millions yearly Expended in Protecting the Introduction of scarce articles which we might have in great profusion at home, it appears to me that there is no Excuse Except to keep up a nursery of seamen and follow the old plan of those Nations of Europe differently situated from us, they from Ne[ce]ssity have become Amphibious, but we are Land Animals, and will perhaps indanger our political Existence by following them too far into the water...[3]

DRUNKENESS A MORTAL VICE

Jefferson, still very busy with the University of Virginia, wrote to Maverick on May 12, 1822, "...the grape you inquire after as having gone from this place is not now recollected by me. as some in my vineyard have died, others have been substitud without noting which, so that at present all are unknown.

that as good wines will be made in America as in Europe the Scuppernon of North Carolina furnishes sufficient proof. the vine is congenial to every climate in Europe from Hungary to the Mediterranean, and will be bound to succeed in the same temperatures here wherever tried by intelligent vignerons. the culture however is more desirable for domestic use than profitable as an occupation for market. in countries which use ardent spirits drunkeness is a mortal vice; but in those which make wine for common use you never see a drunkard.

On March 4, [1823?] Samuel Maverick wrote to Jefferson, "...the Cultivation of the Vine has commenced on the Black warrior River by the Settlement of Frenchman, but with what success I am unable to say, as I did not go so low by 70 miles, I saw several of the frenchmen. they appear confident of success of the Vine...any Ideas respecting or on the Culture of the Vine, will thankfully recd..."

Jefferson took notes on almost every phase of agriculture ad he passed through the rural sections of France and Italy...Grape vines, rice and olives received his closest attention. He was interested first of all in finding a dry rice to supplement or supplant the wet rice of the Carolinas and Georgia, because he thought wet rice "a plant the sows life and death with almost equal hand." Secondly, he considered the olive the worthiest plant to be introduced to America. But, his love of fine wines and his preoccupation with obtaining the best grape vines for America were the basis for the great strides made in developing vineyards in the eastern U. S. over the centuries.

LETTERS TO SOUTH CAROLINIANS

Following are excerpts from some of Jefferson's letters to or about friends of South Carolina in which he tells about his constant attention to the wine aspects of those countries he visited during his stay in Europe.

Traveling notes for Mr. Rutledge and Mr. Shippen June 3, 1788,

...When one calls in the taverns for the *vin du pays,* they give what is natural and unadulterated and cheap; when *vin etrangere* is called for, it only gives a pretext for charging an extravagant price for an unwholesome stuff, very often of their own brewery. The people you will naturally see the most of will be tavern keepers, valets de place, and postilions. These are the hackneyed rascals of every country. Of course they must never be considered when we calculate the national character.

To William Drayton of Charleston, July 30, 1787,

"...I was induced, in the course of my journey thro' the South of France, to pay very particular attention to the objects of their culture, because the resemblance of their climate to that of the Southern part of the United States, authorizes us to presume we may adopt any of their articles of culture which we would wish for. We should not wish for their wines, tho they are good and abundant. The culture of the vine is not desirable in lands capable of producing anything else. it is a species of gambling, and of desperate gambling too, wherein, whether you make much or nothing, you are equally ruined. The middling crop alone is the saving point, and that the seasons seldom hit. Accordingly we see much wretchness amidst this class of cultivators. Wine too is so cheap in these countries that a labourer with us, employed in the culture of any other article, may exchange it for wine, more and better then he could raise himself. It is a resource for a country, the whole of whose good soil is otherwise employed, and which still has some barren spots and a surplus of population to employ on them. There the vine is good, because it is something in the place of nothing. It may become a resource to us at a still earlier period: when the increase of population shall increase our production beyond the demand for them both at home and abroad. Instead of going on to make a useless surplus of them, we may employ our supernumerary hands on the vine. But that period is not yet arrived..."

To Major Geismar in Frankfort, Germany [old friend from the Revolutionary War days],

My dear Sir   Paris July 13, 1788

On my return to this place I found such a mass of business

awaiting me that I have never been able to write a letter of which friendship was the only motive. I take the first moment to inform you that my journey was prosperous: that the vines which I took from Hocheim and Rudesheim are now growing luxuriously in my garden here, and will cross the Atlantic next winter, and that probably, if you ever revisit Monticello, I shall be able to give you there a glass of Hock or Rudesheim of my own making. My last news from America is very encouraging. Eight states have adopted the new constitution and we are pretty sure of three more. New York is a little doubtful, and Rhode island against it. But this will not prevent it's establishment, and they will come into it after a while.—Mr. Rutledge, son of Governor Rutledge of S. Carolina, and Mr. Shippen, son of Dr, Shippen of Philadelphia and nephew of the late President of Congress, being to pass thro' Frankfort, I have desired them to wait on you, in confidence that you will advise them what there is to be seen in that neighborhood and procure them the facilities of doing it, as well as shew them any other civilities their situation may need. This I pray you do for those very worthy and sensible young men for the love of him who is with sincere esteem & attachment My dear Sir your affectionate friend & servt., Th; Jefferson.

To John Rutledge, Jr.   24 September 1788

I learned with pleasure from Parent [see Burgundy Chapter] that this year would be still better for wine than 84. He begged me to assure you of his zeal for your service and the fidelity with which he would continue to furnish you. I ate of the grape of which the Volnais is made. I was struck with its resemblance to some of our wild grapes in Virginia and particularly some that grow in Surry [County} on my fathers estate. The shape of the bunch, the size and color, and still more the taste of the grape, so absolutely the same, that I think it would be impossible to distinguish one from the other. The vine at my fathers grew on an oak tree which stood in an old field quite separate from any other, so that the sun acted on it with its full force. I could wish much to see a fair experiment made on the grapes of that tree. I recollect my father made one year by way of experiment some wine, of what grapes however I know not. The wine was very sweet and very agreeable to my taste, but not at all resembling Volnais...

FROM JOHN RUTLEDGE, JR

Note by Boyd:

Strasbourg, 1 Aug. 1788. Arrived yesterday after pleasant journey along route TJ had proposed, which he found even more delightful than he expected. At Coblence I paid the Landlord for your Map. He had entirely forgot it, and says you are the best Man in the world for remembering it. As you recommended, I embarked at Coblence to avoid the mountainous Road; I found it slow ascending the Rhine, but was compensated by the romantic and picturesque Scenes. On my passage I visited the Vineyards at [Johanne]sberg. The wines were the most [delicious] I ever tasted: but I fear we can never [import] them in America: the keeper of the Cave, if I recollect well, told me the wine would cost four shillings on the Spot. Although much pressed in time Major Geismer prevailed on me to stay three days at Frankfort. He presented me at Court at Philipsbourg, overwhelmed me with Civilities and by his attentions, rendered Frankfort so dear to me that I left with much regret...He said much of the friendship which you shewed him while he was a Prisoner in Virginia and seemed happy in having an Opportunity of being kind to one of your friends.

1820, Jefferson wrote on September 30th to Charles Pickney, Charleston, about his poor health, "...To threescore and seventeen add two years of prostrate health, and you have the old, infirm, and nerveless body I now am, unable to write but with pain, and unwilling to think without necessity."[4]

References:

[1]*The Garden Book*, p. 121.

[2]op cit.

[3]Op cit., p.597.

[4]"Papers of Thomas Jefferson", Boyd, Princeton University Press.

THE FARM BOOK [1]
Manufactures 2500 Barrels

Jefferson's Farm Book" is a collection of memorandums he began in January 1774 at the age of thirty and continued until May 1826 the year of his death. Like his "Garden Book", it was never published by him, but in 1953 the American Philosophical Society assembled it (and some missing pages from various libraries) and with extensive commentary by its editor Edwin M. Betts, produced the well documented "Thomas Jefferson's Farm Book" which provides the data for this article. [2]

THE LETTERS

Jefferson left all his personal papers to his grandson, Thomas Jefferson Randolph, and after the latter's death they passed on through purchase to his great-grandson Thomas Jefferson Coolidge who gave them in June 9, 1898 to the Massachusetts Historical Society where the original Farm Book now resides.

Logically, the records deal with crops, plantation management, land, etc., whereas the "Garden Book" is more about horticulture, vines and wines. However, although there are only a few references to the latter, his writings about such wine related items as cellars, barrel-making, and corks that are of interest and must have occupied much of Jefferson's thoughts as they were so important for his dream of home wine growing.

Mr. Betts describes the master of Monticello, "He must have felt wonderfully in harmony with his world...when he walked and rode through his farms, vineyards, gardens, and orchards, laying ambitious plans...and habitually singing as he went, not the melodies chanted by his servants at work, but the more sophisticated music of Italy and France, which he and his daughters would play together during the lengthening evenings in the beautiful house he was remodeling at Monticello...If ostentation was foreign to him, so was familiarity. No one ventured to take liberties with the tall, spare, erect gentlemen, who reminded his overseer of a race horse in training..."

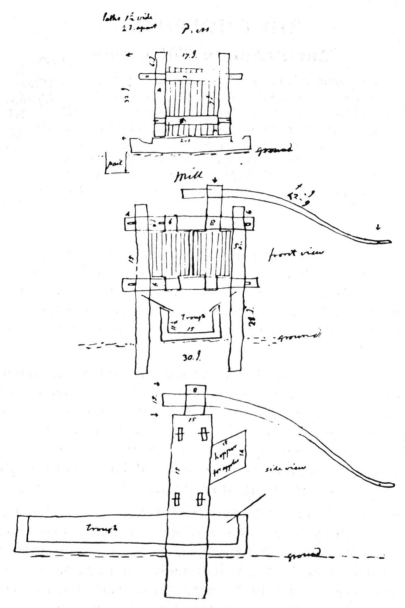

A Jefferson Press

Diagram of a press designed by Jefferson shown in the Farm Book. Basically designed for apples, it was probably used for grapes as well. The mill has two corrugated iron rollers between which the fruit is crushed when the long handle is revolved, similar to sorghum cane presses of today. After crushing, the pomace would be placed in the round basket where the "laths" are measured at 1½ inches wide and placed ¼ inches apart.

Alderman Library, University of Virginia

DEMOCRACY FOR FARMERS

Jefferson held that farmers were the chosen people of God and it has been said that he loved democracy because it gave free expression to farmers. For many years he believed that the states should remain argricultural, arguing that the manufacturers and the corrupt cities which they bred should remain in Europe. However, he changed his opinion in the later years of the 18th century after French and British blockades, trying to make his farms as selfsufficient as possible and to import nothing but books. This reflected in his increased interest in wines made from native American varieties of vines.

His knowledge of wine-making sometimes colored his language as shown in a letter to the Englishman Rev. Richard Price, Aug. 7, 1785, "...and could you still trouble yourself with our welfare, no man is more able to give aid to the labouring side...our country is getting in a *ferment* against yours..."

The editor of the Farm Book has included brief references to wine, corks, cooperage, cider, beer, spirits, and overindulgence. They will be taken up in this order.

Jefferson wrote George Jefferson in Richmond, Feb. 8, 1803, "...be pleased also to send these by the first *safe boatman* because nothing is so liable to adulteration by them as molasses. the wine should also be confided to trustworthy hands..." His manager Joel Yancey, wrote him Dec. 31, 1819, "Your waggon arrived here on the 24th. by it I received a cask of cyder and wine which I stored away in the deep cellar..." No mention was made of what kinds of wines they were or where they originally came from.

Good corks were an expensive rarity in those days, and Jefferson knew their value for preserving sound wines of good taste and bouquet, They all came from Europe as they all do today, and during the blockade years of the War of 1812 there must have been a severe shortage at Monticello.

TO THOMAS NEWTON

Nov. 20, 1802

...your kind offer respecting the procuring cyder for me is

accepted with thankfulness. if there were people at Norfolk who follow the business of bottling as in most of the large cities, I am persuaded it would be better done there than here. my people (who are foreigners) know nothing of it, nor is there any body in this place who does. hence a great inequality in the bottles, from some being better or worse corked, and an inequality in the casks from their not understanding the true state of the liquor for bottling. if there be persons in Norfolk who follow this & are skilful, I should prefer it's being done there, & forwarded after it is done. if not, I shall still be glad to recieve it in cask and do it ourselves, 6. casks sent on to this place, and three to Gibson & Jefferson in Richmond to be forwarded to Monticello will be sufficient. the main article is to have it of superior quality. but for this I rely with satisfaction on your friendship...

TO BERNARD PEYTON

Richmond March 11, 1817

"I must ask the favor of you to purchase for me 6 gross of the best corks to be had in Richmond, and to send them by the stage to Milton to the address of Mr Vest postmaster, the season for using them being now actually upon us..."

FROM PEYTON

March 17, 1817

"...I have searched the City for the best Velvet Corks, & have succeeded in procuring the six Gross wished of excellent quality, which shall be forwarded by tomorrow's stage, to the address of Mr. Vest, Milton..."

It is interesting to note that Mr. Betts has included a footnote, "There are several other letters pertaining to corks. They are omitted here , but copies of them are in the Library of the American Philosophical Society, Philadelphia, Pa."

LARGE COOPERAGE PRODUCTION

In keeping with his policies of self sufficiency on the farm, Jefferson maintained a large cooperage operation. This was mainly for flour and tobacco, amounting to thousands of barrels, and it is assumed that he made his own casks for wine. His forests provided the finest oak staves and Barnaby and Nace were his chief coopers.

He expressed his concern for good cooperage in a letter from Washington, D.C., to George Jefferson, Feb. 11, 1805, "...will you be so good as to send to Monticello a hogshead of best molasses but in a double case in sound & good condition or it will be no better than a hogshead of water when it arrives there..."

He noted in his Account Book, Dec. 21, 1806, "gave Barnaby ord. on T. E. Randolph for the price of 18. Barrels to wit 1. in every 31. see ante Mar. 17. 1813 (in which he promised Barnaby one out of every 31 barrels he made) note he has delivered (with 72. to be delivd. this day) 563 barrels from Oct. 9 to yesterday inclusive."

Cooperage became a big business with Jefferson as noted in his letter to Mr. Colclaser August 8, 1817,

You enquired the other day what number of barrels I should be able to furnish. we have barrel stuff enough in the woods ready cut off to serve two seasons. I have now set mr. Goodman's force to riving and dressing ready to put up, and mean that they shall always get and dress the timber, so that Barnaby & the other two with him shall do nothing but set up. I count on their setting up ready for delivery from 90. to 100. a week, & that they will do this at least 40. weeks in the year, as nothing but harvest or sickness will ever take them a day out of their shop. I therefore count on delivering you 4000. barrels a year. they have 50. in the barn ready for delivery and will begin on Monday to prepare their 90. or 100. a week. I have instructed mr Bacon to give the hauling necessary in this business a preference over every other call....

On June 26, 1821 in the Account Book he noted. "Barnaby has delivd. 1203 barrels this year. I gave him an order for 26. some time ago, & now for 13 (equals) 39 his allowance. Nace has delivered 1380. bar., and I now give him an order for 45. of them. his part. "The cooper's house was near the mills, and he may have done his work in the joiner's (carpenter) shop.

Dimensions of the tobacco hogsheads were, "4 f. 6. I. long. the head 34. I. in the clear with an allowance of 2. I. more for the prizing head." For the flour barrels Jefferson used staves, "28 I. long and dress to 27 I. it takes 16. or 17. staves to a barrel & 6. heading pieces. 22. or 23. in all. a cut of a middle sized tree yields 16. or 17. bolts, which give 4. staves each. such a tree, midling good will yield 18. or 20 cuts. a cut will make 3. barrels, staves & heading. one tree with another will make 50. barrels."

CIDER AND BEER

Of all the beverages, Jefferson preferred wine. He probably rarely ever took other alcoholic drinks. He had a highly developed taste for good wines especially after his years in Europe, but his difficulties in planting the European vines in America perhaps turned some of his interests to wine's first cousin, cider. April 22, 1810 he wrote in his Memorandum Book, "Statement of cyder made in November last. 1. cask of Taliaberro (apple variety) cyder was bottled & served thro' the winter to this day. in March we bottled 460. bottles of Taliaberro 72. of red Hughes (total) 532. making in the whole 175. gallons."

Jefferson wrote Fanny Brand Dec. 16, 1815,

"I was unfortunately from home when you were so kind as to send information of your having cyder to spare. I returned yesterday only, and now send the bearer to ask the favor of some samples of your best casks of cyder. he carried 6. phials with numbers on their corks, and if you will be so good as to give a sample from each good cask, and number the cask correspondingly with the number on the vial into which it's sample is put, I can chuse with certainty what I prefer. if your cyder is as good as what I had before I shall willingly take two or three hundred gallons. the quantity will depend on the quality..."

The serious shortages of imports caused by the War of 1812 which made it difficult, tho not impossible, for Jefferson to obtain foreign wines, had a side effect by giving him an opportunity to make beer. An English captain, Joseph Miller, who had been a brewer in London, was confined to Albemarle County in that year for political reasons. He was invited by Jefferson to live at Monticello and while there he taught his servant the processes of malting and brewing.

Jefferson wrote William D. Meriwether, Sept. 17, 1813, "I lent you some time ago the London & Country brewer and Combrun's book on the same subject. we are this day beginning, under the directions of Capt. Miller, the business of brewing malt liquors, and if these books are no longer useful to you I will thank you for them, as we may perhaps be able to derive some information from them..."

Then to Nicholas Gouin Dufief, Sept. 18, 1813, "...in the Aurora of Sep. 7. I see a book advertised as under publication at N. York under the title of "the American brewer & Malster which, as teaching the method of malting Indian corn I should be very glad to get. could you procure it for me if published or when published..."

TO RICHARD RANDOLPH

Jan. 25, 1814

"Will you be so good as to send me two gross of your beer jugs; the one gross to be quart jugs, and the other pottle do. they are to be delivered to a mr. William Johnson a waterman of Milton, who will apply for them about a week..."

TO JOSEPH COPPINGER

April 25, 1815

...I am lately become a brewer for family use, having had the benefit of instruction to one of my people by an English brewer of the first order. I had noted the advertisement of your book in which the process of malting corn was promised & had engaged a bookseller to send it to me as soon as it should come out. we tried it here the last fall with perfect success, and I shall use it principally hereafter. during the revolutionary war, the brewers on James river used Indian corn almost exclusively of all other. in my family brewing I have used wheat also as we do not raise barley. I shall still desire my bookseller to send me on your book when printed...

TO CAPTAIN JOSEPH MILLER

June 26, 1815

...our brewing of the last autumn is generally good, altho' not as rich as that of the preceding year, the batch we are now using is excellent. that which Peter Hemings did for mr Bankhead was good, and the brewing of corn which he did here after your departure would have been good, but that he spoiled it by over-hopping. a little more experience however will make him a good brewer. my absence in Bedford in the spring prevented our preparing some malt then, which I now regret...

Correspondence continued with Miller two years later, when Jefferson wrote March 11, 1817, "...Peter's brewing of the last season I am in hopes will prove excellent. at least the only cask of it we have tried proves so. altho' our hopes of your settling among us are damped by your long absence, yet we do not despair altogether...." Jefferson obviously wanted to hold on to the brewing expert.

On April 11, 1820, he wrote his devoted friend James Madison who had succeeded him as President in 1809,

"Our brewing for the use of the present year has been some time over. about the last of Oct. or beginning of Nov. we began for the ensuing year, and malt and brew 3. 60 galln casks *successively* which will give so many successive lessons to the person you send. on his return he can try his hand with you in order to discover what parts of the processes he will have learnt imperfectly, and come again to our spring brewing of a single cask in order to perfect himself, and go back to you and try his hand again on as much as you will want. you will want a house for malting, which is quickest made by digging into the steep side of a hill, so as to need a roof only, and you will want a haircloth also of the size of your loft to lay the grain in. this can only be had from Phila or N.Y. I will give you notice in the fall when we are to commence malting and our malter and brewer is uncommonly intelligent and capable of giving instruction ..."

Another fellow Virginian and friend from the Piedmont

region, Governor James Barbour of Barboursville, wrote Jefferson April 30, 1821 inquiring about the brewing of ale.

"Some years past I recollect to have drunk some ale at Monticello which I understood was of your own brewing. The manner of doing which you had obtained by a recipe from some intelligent Briton. Being desirous to introduce that kind of drink and having a facility in preparing the materials of which it is made, you will oblige me much by furnishing me with a copy of the recipe as soon as your convenience will permit."

TO GOVERNOR BARBOUR

May 11, 1821

...I have no reciept for brewing, & I much doubt if the operations of malting & brewing could be successfully performed from a reciept. if it could Combrune's book on the subject would teach the best processes: and perhaps might quide to ultimate success with the sacrifice of 2. or 3. trials. a Capt Miller now in Norfolk, but who passes much of his time with Charles Bankhead in Spotsylva, was during the late war, confined by the executive to our neighborhood, perhaps indeed by yourself. I took him to my house. he had been a brewer in London, and undertook to teach both processes to a servt. of mine, which during his stay here & on one or two visits afterwards in the brewing season, he did with entire success. I happened to have a servant of great intelligence and diligence both of which are necessary. we brew 100. gallss. of ale in the fall & 100. galls. in the spring, taking 8. galls. only from the bushel of wheat. the public breweries take 15. which makes their liquor meagre and often vapid. we are now finishing our spring brewing, if you have a capable servt. and he were to attend our fall brewing, so as to get an idea of the manual operation, Combrune's book with a little of your own attention in the beginning might qualify him...

Little did either one of them have any idea to predict, but 155 years later in the Bicentennial year of the United States, Barbour's 800-acre farm was to become the start of the largest

Vinifera (European) vineyard and commercial winery in Virginia. Jefferson is said to have designed the stately mansion with large columns, the ruins of which are preserved.

HOME MADE SPIRITS

It was a custom during the colonial days for farmers to give their workers spirits during the heavy work of harvest time and for some special festive occasions. Jefferson was opposed to giving whiskey to slaves and workmen, excepting under rare conditions and only when they were doing in cold weather certain kinds of labor, because it greatly reduced their efficiency.

TO J. HOLMES FREEMAN

Dec. 21, 1805

...as to whiskey to be given to the labouring hands, it is right when they work in the water in cool weather. on other occasions in general it is an injurious & demoralizing practice. they do more for a day or two but less afterwards as we see where a harvest is lengthy. confine therefore if you please, the giving them whiskey to those occasions which might otherwise produce colds & sickness...

As early as March 14, 1774 he noted in his Account Book, "recd from the Forest 4 Doz. 10. bott. of Jamaica rum (note I shall keep a tally of these as we use them by making a mark in the margin in order to try the fidelity of Martin."

TO GEORGE DIVERS

Philadelphia, Nov. 26 1792

As I propose to purchase a still here for the use of my plantations, & understand there is good deal in the size, proportion & number of the vessels, I take the liberty of requesting you to inform me what particulars I had better provide. I make this appeal to you the rather, as you can judge of the extent & manner in which I am to carry on the business, proposing nothing more than the distillation my own grain & fruit..

FROM DIVERS

Albemarle County, Va., Jan. 1, 1793

...I would advise you to purchase One Still that will work 85 one of 45 and a Copper Kettle of Sixty Gallons with these Stills and Boiler you may make from 70 to 80 Gallons of whiskey p Week & feed 60 or 70 Hogs, [corn mash left over from distilling] the feeding that number of Hogs will be an object to you as it will save a considerable quantity of Indian Corn, from which consideration I have been induced to recommend it to you to purchase Stills of the above size, that you may be able to keep them at work for 7 months in the year in which time they will Distill about 900 Bushels of grain. If you wish to carry on the business to a greater extent you can add 10 or 15 Galls. to each Lott but I would not exceed 100 Galls. for the large or 70 Galls. for the Small one. a pewter worm [tubing] is better than Copper...

It is not known if Jefferson made any purchase as the result of this exchange.

Some years later, he wrote Michael Krafft, Dec. 21 1804, "Th: Jefferson presents his compliments to mr Krafft and his thanks for the volume on distilling which he has been so kind as to send him. he owes him particular acknowlegements for the obliging terms in his dedication; but is sensible that the book possesses, it it's own merits, the best of all titles to the public esteem."

In instructions he gave to farm manager Edmund Bacon in 1805-06, Jefferson noted, "Whiskey is wanted for the house, some for Mr. Dinsmore, and some sometimes for the people. About 30 gallons will last a year. Mr. Merriwether or Mr. Rogers may perhaps each let us have some for nails, (made at Monticello) or will distil it out of our worst toll wheat."

Captain Miller started Jefferson's distillery, apparently for the first time in the fall of 1813. Corn, rye, wheat and barley were used at various times. On occasions when grains could not be sold for food, it was converted into alcohol.

TO JAMES MADISON

March 10, 1814

...Our agriculture presents little interesting. wheat looks

badly, much having been killed by the late severe weather. corn is scarce, but it's price kept down to 3. D. by the substitute of wheat as food for both laborers and horses, costing on 3/6 to 4/. they begin to distill the old flour, getting 10. galls. of whiskey from the barrel & consequently more than we can get at Richmond for the new..."

Jefferson's notes covered a wide range of subjects in the Farm Book, and he was an eager follower of John A. Binns who in 1803 published his "Treatise on practical farming" which recommended "deep plowing". Jefferson thought of it in relation to his regualr crops, but he was probably aware of the value of this method in European vineyards because of the deep growing nature of wine vines. Newly established vineyards must be deep plowed first.

ABHORRED DRUNKENNESS

Jefferson abhorred drunkenness and at times over-indulgence by his workers gave him problems. Writing to Edmund Bacon, Dec. 28, 1806 about personnel problems at the "toll-mill", he commented, "...in the mean time I should think Davy the best for the purpose. I believe he is honest: but he is addicted to drink at times. you can try him however..." Bacon wrote in later years about the Monticello blacksmith ship, "...A man named Stewart was at the head of that. He was a fine workman, but he would have his sprees——would get drunk. Mr. Jefferson kept him a good many years longer than he would have done, because he wanted him to teach some of his own hands."

Whether it be for wine, cider, beer or spirits, Jefferson had to guard his supplies at all times even as modern man does now. He made this clear in a letter from Philadelphia, Feb. 4, 1800 to his son-in-law Thomas Mann Rnadolph, "...I must get Martha or yourself to give orders for bottling the cyder in the proper season in March. there is nobody there but Ursula who unites trust & skill to do it. she may take anybody she pleases to aid her. I am in hopes if any keys had been delivered to Jupiter that they have been taken care of. mr. Richardson may perhaps be useful in seeing to the cyder. when I say that Ursula may have anybody she pleases to help her, I mean to except John, who must have nothing to do with drink..."

Although the following letter from his daughter Martha was not included in the Farm Book, it significantly relates to home winemaking which she knew he was deeply interested in having done properly. As it refers to bottling only, this could have been done from a cask or wine made at Monticello or one he had purchased. It was common practice to order wine in casks from Europe and bottle it in America. The letter, written to Jefferson in the last year of his Presidency, also shows the warm affection she held for her father,

FROM MARTHA RANDOLPH

My Dear Father   Edge Hill Oct. 27, 1808

...it was cork, & not bottles that were wanting to bottle the rest of the wine. my orders were that they should continue untill their corks gave out. which they did not do for Ellen told me there were still some corks left but as these were not enough for the whole cask they would not make a begginning but prefered using a water cask, that may or may not answer I shall send often to inspect them. having been greatly decieved in 2 of the same description once before. I am truly concerned to hear that your rheumatism has fixed in so dreadful a part of the back. you will be obliged to try flannel next the skin in which I have very good confidence particularly as you have never abused the use of it. adieu My Dear Father I am with tenderest affection, your

M. Randolph

References:

[1]Massachusetts Historical Society, Boston.

[2]*Thomas Jefferson's Farm Book*, edited by Edwin M. Betts, Princeton University Press, 1953, p.552.

[3]University of Virginia Library, Charlottesville, Virginai.

MONTICELLO WINE CELLAR & REMINDERS
The "Mystery" Vessel

Was the cellar the first work in the construction of the main house?

Jefferson's discriminating tastes for fine art, music, architecture, food, literature, and gentlemanly manners also extended to his fondness for wine and all the related aspects to its fullest enjoyment.

At the age of 17, he entered William and Mary College, Williamsburg, capital of the colony. His principal teacher was a Scot, William Small, who introduced him to Francis Fauquier who was the acting Governor, and to George Wythe, a prominent local lawyer. Later on these four dined at the Governor's Palace where they enjoyed good food, wine, musicales and discussed the classics, theories of the ancients and politics.

Jefferson lived with the Wythe family from 1762 to 1767 while studing law and here made his first written comments on wine quality. Dr. Dumas Malone, a Jeffersonian historian,

has described him as tall, sandy-haired, not prepossessing in appearance, a skilled horseman, played the violin, and seems to have been a popular companion. "The strain of seriousness in his nature, however, was soon apparent; it may have been accentuated by the unhappy outcome of his love affair with Rebecca Burwell."

His father Peter Jefferson had died in 1757, leaving Thomas, age 14, the elder of two sons, about 5,000 acres of land. At age 21 he came into his inheritance, and in 1769 he began to work on his own home which he called "Monticello" (Italian for Little Mountain), Albermarle County, in the Peidmont region near the Blue Ridge Mountains.

Architectual historians say that the wine cellar was the first stage of Monticello construction. This is not to say that Jefferson placed wine related matters in the "first things first" category in regard to his cellar, but merely a building fact that foundations for a house must go in before the upper construction begins. Historians arrive at this conclusion because the

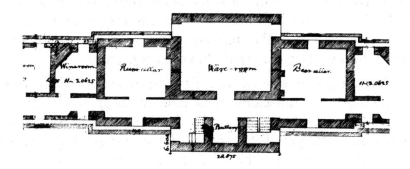

Jefferson's drawing of the floor plan for the ground level elevation. The corridor runs north (right) and south, placing the cellars on the west side.

Passageway on which the cellars opened, running south to the vineyards nearby. Jefferson planted his vines on the south side of the hill as was the custom in Europe, in order to obtain maximum sunlight and warmth for full ripening and best vintages. In the U. S.—on a much more southernly latitude—vineyards are usually placed on the east side of hills.

wine cellar is built of brick, and according to records left by Jefferson, he started with brick but finding that this was more expensive than common field stone he thereafter made the rest of the foundation in stone. He had the opportunity to study the Palace cellars in Williamsburg and must have gained much useful data to help construct his own cellars.

Originally, in one of the first architectual drawings by Jefferson, the wine cellar was labeled "beer room" and was situated on a long corridor that ran under the top of the hill connecting two pavillions (outer house wings) with the main house in the center. The wine cellar was located under the dining room, a fact that made it convenient for him to have wine come promptly by a pulley arrangement that will be described later. He gave the width of the "Wine room' as 11 feet 3.0625 inches, carrying the latter measurement to four decimal points, a good example of his careful attention to details and accuracy. Next to the wine cellar was a "ware room" located about under the parlor and next to that the "wine room" which was approximately under his bedroom. This room was later used for other purposes than storing wine and is not the wine cellar that Jefferson used and the one we know today.

The door (next page) to the cellar is large, double thickness, banded and studded with steel, swinging on long strap hinges of the period. The treasured contents of the room were protected by a strong lock, the keys to which were entrusted to one or two people in whom Jefferson had full confidence.

The original wine racks and bins have deteriorated, however new ones have been built on the north wall of the cellar. No original wines of Jefferson's day have been preserved, but the bins have been filled with similar bottles which are supposed to be of Jefferson's day: a neck from a wine bottle, the bottom and side of a wine bottle, and the neck from a demi-jon jug. Along the west wall opposite the entrance are placed various tools and objects of the type used at Monticello and associated with wine making there. The floor is of the original plantation-made brick, like the walls. A small window on the top of the west wall indicates the ground level which places the cellar

Probably the original wine cellar door. The opening made wide which allow large casks to be brought into the cool enviornment.

about three-fourths underground. This insures an average temperature of about 55 degrees F., dropping perhaps to about 40 degrees in the winter and no more than approximately 65 degrees in summer. The hill on which Monticello is located is about 500 feet above sea level.

Floors and walls being made of brick indicate that the wine cellar was part of the first work on foundations of his mansion. There was only one opening to the outside, facing west, and protected by an iron door. No original bottles have been found on French vintages, but replicas of the period have been placed on restored shelves.

Down the corridor south is another cellar on which there is a plaque placed by the Thomas Jefferson Memorial Foundation which reads, "Rum Cellar 1772, Rum...was used mainly...by Jefferson slaves, Jefferson prefered wine and cyder for his own use."

Another room on the wine cellar level is the old kitchen, restored and furnished in the original style. There are a few wine bottles and a small screw down press that could be used for grapes or fruits. There have been reports of the existance of the original Jefferson wine press, but these have not been substantiated. Research has not revealed any detailed records of his home wine making procedures, however hundreds of his documents in various repositories in several states may one day bring this to light, a challange for the wine historian.

On the main floor of the house, as the visitor enters the door in the East Front, there is a large reception hall. On the left is Jefferson's bedroom and next to that his study where on the floor rests his wooden traveling wine chest. (above) Five or six of the decanter type bottles are said to be originals The chest is on loan from the Honorable Prentis Cooper, Nashville, Tennessee.

Monticello was sold when Jefferson died, and his household effects and furnishings were all dispersed. The Thomas Jefferson Memorial Foundation has restored the mansion and has performed a notable task of bringing back as many of the original artifacts and furnishings as possible.

The dining room is located on the opposite side of the reception hall from the bedroom and at a point over the wine cellar. At both ends of the graceful period mantel, Jefferson concealed small dumbwaiters behind paneled doors, just wide enough to bring single bottles of wine up from the cellar. This may have been the reason he shifted his wine cellar from the original plan to the area just below the dining room—in order to serve the dumb waiter.(below)

The famous Jefferson wine cups may be seen in a mahogany china cabinet in the dining room. In 1806 Jefferson was willed by his friend and teacher, George Wythe, two large silver beakers of about 20 ounces weight and of an undetermined design. After using them for several years, Jefferson sent them to John Letelier, a Richmond silversmith, with directions to make eight smaller cups of about 5 ounces weight and 2⅝ inches high with rounded bottoms. He further stipulated that they be gilded inside and four be marked "G.W. to T.J." and four "T.J." These were received at Monticello in October, 1810, and used there until his death.

His daughter Martha Randolph in later years distributed seven of the cups to seven of her children. The eighth cup is believed to have been given to Dr. Robley Dunglison, Jefferson's physician. Of the original eight cups seven have been located and two of them may be seen at Monticello. The Stieff Company, Baltimore, Maryland, has exclusive rights to reproduce the cups both in regular and miniature sizes and in silver and pewter. (below)

Charles Matheson

The only silver cup believed to be designed by Jefferson may be purchased in replica.

Another wine related object in the dining room is a porcelein monteith. A 17th century type of large punch bowl, often of silver, with a scalloped rim, was named after its inventor. The vessel was used for holding, rinsing and cooling of wine glasses. The open work rim keeps the fragile glasses apart. (below)

Monteiths, invented by a Scot of that name, are known to have been used 300 years ago. There is a significant collection of fine very old silver ones at Colonial Williamsburg.

"MYSTERY" WINE VESSEL

Like any other wine interested traveler to the vineyard regions of France, Jefferson while stopping at Nimes near the southern town of Frontignan—home of a favored wine of his— was fascinated by a curiously shaped bronze vessel excavated from the ruins of the Maison Carree (square house), a Roman Temple. A wooden model was made for him and in later years he ordered a silver replica from the Philadelphia firm of Anthony Simmons and Samuel Alexander, adding a hinge cover. Somewhat resembling a shoe with a delicate curved handle over the lace part, the vessel was called an "Askos" and now resides in the dining room, being handed down by the family. "Askos" is a Greek word meaning "a wine skin", a small vase or jug shaped like "a wine skin or leather bottle." The word also means in Greek the second day of the "Rural Dionysia" [god of wine] festival, held in the autumn when the wine is first tasted, when they danced upon the wine skins, hence to dance as at the "Ascolia". Because of its Greek name the object probably predates the later Roman period. Exactly how it was used sometimes, and how Jefferson employed it, has been a subject of considerable speculation and cause for it to be regarded as a mystery wine vessel.

"This graceful model," wrote Julian P. Boyd in *Antiques Magazine*, July, 1973, "...possibly the earliest copy of a classical artifact to be brought to the United States—has acquired both symbolic meaning and a rich cluster of associations..." Jefferson called it at various times, an "antique vase," "charming vase" and referred to it as a "Roman Ewer" (wide mouth vase, sometimes with a handle attached) when he directed the makers of his silver model to inscribe the top of the lid, "Copied from a model taken in 1787 by Th. Jefferson from a Roman Ewer in the Cabinet of Antiquities at Nimes." The Monticello Foundation has surmised that it was used as a chocolate pot.

The *Antiques* article continues, "The object was indeed one of compelling beauty and interest, obviously not created for any ordinary Roman citizen but for somon proconsul or person of similar powers and diginity. Its flowing lines, its handsomely cast handle terminating in an animal's head, its antiquity, and its provenance associating it with the vicinity of the Maison Carree caused Jefferson, as he later declared, to decide at once to have it copied...George Dennis, in his "Cities and Cemeteries of Etruria", was unquestionably correct in concluding that such vessels 'seem to have been employed for the toilet alone.'" Boyd also concluded that "perhaps he used it at the table for cream or syrup or honey," and refers to the old folk saying, "the ingnorant would not have noticed and the knowing would not have commented."

Considering that Jefferson for his well known enjoyment of wine, probably ordered the lid top added to keep the wine gnats from his Madeira, and because of the fact that the Greeks not only had a word for it, "wine container", and used it for that, visitors might agree that it is one of the most unusual wine associated artifacts in the world.

ITALIAN FAVORITES AND ORDERS
"Light And High Flavored"

Jefferson first began to note his interest in Italian wines, when, on his tour of France in 1787, he headed east from Toulon on the coast towards Nice which was then not part of France. April 10th he found in the Antibes and Nice region that, "The wine made in this neighborhood is good, tho' not of the first quality." Later he was to find Italian wines of very high quality that he admired. (see pp. 123-124). Moving north towards Turin, he noted vines together with other crops. When he arrived there he saw, "somewhat more of vines". At Racconigi he recorded the way they planted and staked the vines, and eastward in the Milan area he began to see more vineyards and commented on a surprise freeze that put a half inch of ice on the rice fields. April 28th he was ready to travel south to Genoa on the Mediterranean coast and a milder climate, "Wherever there is soil on the lower parts it is principally in olives and figs, in vines also..." The wine he found at Noli to be white and "indifferent". At Albenga "The earth furnishes wine..." but he did not describe the quality. Here was planted a great deal of cane and reed which were used to espalier the vines.

"A superb road might be made along the margin of the sea from Laspaze where the champaign (sic) country of Italy opens..." A quarter of a century later found Jefferson making regular orders every year, well versed in their vintages, qualities and prices. He was well organized with Thomas Appleton at Genoa and Victor Sasserno in Nice, who could handle his purchases and shipments efficiently. He could recall the "Arna, Artiminiano, Barbaresco, Barolo, Carmigniano, Chianti, Gatina, Montepulciano, Montferrat, "Nebiule" (Nebbiolo), Salusola, and Tuscan wines.

TO THOMAS APPLETON[1]

Jan. 14, 1816

...For the present I confine myself to the physical want of some good Montepulciano; and your friendship has heretofore supplied me with that which was so good that I naturally address my want to you. In your letter of May 1. 05. you mention that what you then sent me was produced on grounds formerly belonging to the order of Jesuits and sold for the benefit of the government in 1773. at the time that that institution was abolished. I hope it has preserved it's reputation, & the quality of it's wines. I send this letter to my friend John Vaughan of Philadelphia and inclose with it to him 50.D. to be remitted to you and I pray you to send me it's amount in Montepulciano, in black bottles, well corked & cemented, and in strong boxes, addressed to the Collector of any port from Boston to the Chesapeak, to which the first opportunity occurs: Norfolk & Richmond being always to be preferred, if a conveyance equally early offers. But the warm season will be so fast advancing, when you receive this, that no time will be to be lost. Perhaps I may trouble you annually to about the same amount, this being a very favorite wine, and habit having rendered the light and high flavored wines a necessary of life with me. I salute you with assurances of my constant esteem & respect.

TO APPLETON

Jan. 31, 1816

(Repeats request for wine of preceding letter; This letter being carried by gentleman setting out directly for Paris, TJ worried about approach of warm season)

FROM APPLETON

Apr. 15, 1816

...Previous to recieving your letter, I had written to Montepulciano, for samples of the last growth of wine; but generally the vintage of the last year, has been greatly inferior to preceeding ones and in a particular manner, I found it so with that of Montepulciano which induced me entirely to relinquish the intention I had, to purchase of that kind for my own use.— We have, however, many other wines equally light, and very nearly as well flavour'd at about one half the price, for the former is transported in flasks, nearly 150 miles over land, before it arrives at Florence.—Not willing, therefore, to send you a quality, inferior to that formerly sent, I shall defer complying with your order; until the next vintage, which however, is not drawn from the lees, until January ; but should you prefer some of the other qualities, I shall be able to send it much earlier...

FROM APPLETON

May 30, 1816

...I then likewise [i.e. in letter of 10 May] mention'd that owing to the failure in quality, of the wine of Montepulciano of the last vintage, I should defer sending of the growth of that place, until the next season.—In the mean time I have procur'd from a friend, a barrel of Carmigniano wine, which though not equal to that of Montepulciano, is nevertheless one of the best flavour'd of Tuscany. I have had it carefuly bottled and sealed with pitch, so that I have good reason to believe it will arive to you, free from injury.—Our barrel contains fifty-seven bottles, which are pack'd in one case, and shipp'd on board the Schooner Fanny, Capt: Selby for New York, and address'd to the care of the Collector. I cannot precisely say the price, as my friend is in the country, and the vessel will sail in the course of this day; but it will be at a very moderate expence.—Towards the latter part of the next month, I have the promise of a barrel of Arna wine, to which none is superior, except Montepulciano; and it the estimation of many, they are on a lever.—By the first vessel which will sail afterwards, I shall forward it to you.—These wines can always be procur'd, at a much less price than that of Montepulciano, as they are convey'd by the Arno, while the letter is transported 150 miles over land.

(TJ notes; N. York. 57 bottles Carmigniano recd. Aug. 14.)

TO APPLETON

July 18, 1816

...If a sober goodhumored man understanding the vineyard & kitchen garden would come to me on those terms, [i.e. $100 a year and board and lodging] bound to serve 4. years, I would advance his passage on his arrival, setting it off against his subsequent wages. But he must come to the port of Norfolk or Richmond, & no where else. If such a one should occur to you, you would oblige me by sending him.

I remark the temporary difficulty you mention of obtaining good Montepulciano, and prefer waiting for that, when to be had, to a quicker supply of any other kind which might not so certainly suit our taste. It might not be amiss perhaps to substitute a bottle or two as samples of any other wines which would bear the voyage, and be of quality and price to recommend them. You know we like dry wines, or at any rate not more than silky...

FROM APPLETON

July 30, 1816

My last respects, Sir, were in date of the 30th. of May, and which went by the Schooner Fanny, Capt: Selby for New York; at the same time I shipp'd to the care of the collector for that port, in order to be forwarded to you, a case containing 57 bottles of Carmigniano wine.—I have now shipp'd on board the ship Von-Hollen Capt: Ralph Porter, bound to Baltimore, two cases of Tuscan wine—No. 1. contains 57 bottles of Artiminiano—No. 2. contains an equal number of bottles of Chianti wine, this latter is of a very high flavor: and both are directed to the care of the Collector for that port. By the next vessel, I am in hopes, to be able to forward the Arna: a wine of a very superior quality, indeed.—The vessel unexpectedly departing in the course of the day, allows me only the time, to renew the expressions of my very sincere respect & esteem.

TJ notes on verso: Baltimore. No.1.57. bottles Artimignian
No.2 57. do Chianti

FROM APPLETON

Sept. 27, 1816

...I have now shipp'd on board the Brig Saucy Jack, Richard Humfries, Master and to the care of the collector of Charleston, So. Carolina two cases of Arna wine No. 1 containing 57 bottles & no. 2. 30.—inclos'd is your little account which you will percieve precisely balanc'd for the fifty dollars you remitted me for this purpose.—The last mention'd wine, is esteem'd the first quality of all I have sent and the next after Montepulciano. ...(continues re unusual weather and expected poor vintage).

FROM APPLETON

Oct. 20, 1816

I have shipp'd on board the Brig Saucy Jack, Capt: Humphreys for Charleston. S. Carolina two Cases containing together 87. bottles of Arna wine which I hope you will find greatly to your satisfaction. By the brig Othello Capt: Gladding, & who sail'd 10 days since, I wrote you... [and] inclos'd your little account for the wines sent, which you will percieve exactly balanc'd by the two cases now sent...

FROM APPLETON

March 5, 1817

. . . . (shipped Lupinella grass, via Boston; hasn't heard from TJ Since Mch. 1816; repeats news of shipment of Arna wine).

TO APPLETON

Aug. 1. 1817

(long letter on various matters)....The wines you were so good as to send me were all recieved exactly as you described them.   The Arna was the best, but still not equal to the Montepulciano, and as I learn from your letter of Sep. 27. that the crop of wines for that year was desperate I have not applied to you for any this year. If however it has proved that any good Montepulciano (of the growth formerly sent me) has been produced, contrary to your expectation, the of balance of the 400.D remaining after payment of the interest, might be invested in that. It will give us a taste...

Th: Jefferson

Reference
[1]**Library of Congress, Appleton Letters.**

Historic Meeting At Monticello Cellar

Filippo Mazzei, Robert Coles, and Dr. Lapo Mazzei (left to right), descendants of Thomas Jefferson and his Patriot vigneron Philip Mazzei, rekindle their ancestors' friendship in the wine cellar at Monticello, during a 1981 visit. Dr. Mazzei is Chairman, The Chianti Classico Consortium, Italy, with offices in Florence. (see Mazzei chapter)

Philip Mazzei was born near Florence in 1730 into a family of merchants, and in 1767 met Benjamin Franklin in London. This led to a project with Thomas Jefferson to bring 1000 vines and 10 vignerons to Virginia and plant at Colle near Monticello, in 1773. Jefferson reportedly gave him the original draft of the Declaration of Independence. President John F. Kennedy once wrote that Jefferson paraphrased some of Mazzei's writings in the Declaration.

JEFFERSON'S CHOICE MEDICINE, WINE
Last Words Recorded by Doctor

By Bernard E. Nunez, M.D.,F.A.C.P.,D.T.M.&H.[London]

Medicine during the years of the American Revolution was clearly overmatched by disease. With no antiseptics, antibiotics or anesthesia, medicine was only edging away from the dark ages. Wine was used in all these modalities.

Disease was decisive in many of the battles of the Revolution. John Adams blamed smallpox rather than the British Fleet for the general retreat from Quebec to Montreal. Dr. James Thatcher who served as a regimental surgeon from Boston to Yorktown, wrote that 70,000 died, 10,000 a year. Most physicians at the time thought that for every death in battle there were ten from disease. Typhoid fever, dysentery, malaria, the "bloody flux" and typhus were the real killers.

Wine was deemed a capital remedy in every stage of typhus according to Dr. James Tilton of Delaware, who aquired the disease himself. "In my own case," he wrote, "besides an obstinate delirium, I had a crust on my tongue as thick as a blade of a knife, and black as soot. The skin was worn off my hips and dorsal vertebrae as to make it necessary to patch those parts with a common plaster. My friend, Dr. Rush [by then the leading military surgeon] paid kind attention to me, and a benevolent lady of the neighborhood sent me several gallons of excellent wine. My tongue soon began to moisten on the edges, and in the course of some days the whole crust fell off and left it so raw and irritable that I was obliged to hold skinned almonds in my mouth to abate the irritation." Dr. Tilton was also responsible for the "Indian Hut" hospital for continental troops, replacing large open wards with small isolation units. The "Tilton huts" reduced the appalling rate of dysentery and typhus in the unhygienic army hospitals.

On the day of surrender, the Americans and French had a combined sick list of more than 1,400, the British more than 1,200. In contrast, the American loss in battle was 26 killed and 56 wounded; the British 146 killed, and 326 wounded; the

French 52 killed and 134 wounded.

JEFFERSON AND DR. RUSH

The health of the troops was a primary concern of General Washington and his staff. He understood that his own reputation, the protection of the country and the success of the campaign were dependent upon the health of the army. Dr. Benjamin Rush became Surgeon General to the Continental Army during the first two years of the Revolutionary War. He was a great organizer and became a dear friend and advisor to Thomas Jefferson. Dr. Rush was never able to grasp, however, Hippocrates' ideas of the healing power of nature. He had extreme faith in the curing power of blood letting. He also believed in giving huge doses of calomel-and-jalat, known as "Rush's Thunderbolts." He was devoted to wine for Thomas Jefferson mentions his name in this connection in a letter to President James Monroe, January 11, 1819, when he writes of his daily routine at the age of 76,

"Like my friend Dr. Benjamin Rush I have lived temperately, eating little animal food. I double, however, the doctor's glass and a half of wine, and even treble it with a friend, but halve its effect by drinking the weak wines only, the ardent wines I cannot drink nor do I use ardent spirits in any form."

After Jefferson's years in France as Minister, his feelings about wine were heightened because of its salutary effect and his aristocratic associations. Wine was not only a medicine it was an aristocratic vehicle to the good life. Rather oddly, for one of his great strength and stature, he was always painfully sensitive to cold. He wrote to William Dumbar in 1801, no doubt with vivid memories of the climate of Paris, specially in the notable winter of 1788 which nearly finished him, that "when I recollect on the one hand all the suffering I have had from cold, and on the other, all my pains, the former predominates greatly," and it was often a matter of wonderment to him, "that any human being should remain in a cold country who could find room in a warm one." It must have been the beneficial effect that wine had on his general health that caused him to later encourage the planting of the vine in America. "Good wine is a necessity of life for me," he once wrote.

As a strong indication of his faith in wine as a medicine, Jefferson while President in Washington, D. C. wrote to his son-in-law John W. Eppes, (who married Maria) at Monticello, March 15, 1804, upon hearing that she was critically ill:

"The debility of Maria will need attention, lest a recurrence of fever should degenerate into typhus...The sherry at Monticello is old and genuine, and the Pedro Ximenes much older still and stomachic...The house, its contents, and appendages and servants are as freely subjected to you as to myself...My tenderest love to Maria and Patsy [older daughter, Martha] and all the young ones."

He was grief-stricken when Maria died April 17, 1804, "My loss is great indeed," he wrote, "Others may lose of their abundance, but I, of my want, have lost even the half of all I had."

Jefferson likened friendship to old wine. In a letter to his enduring friend Dr. Rush, August 17, 1811, from Poplar Forest, another home near Monticello, he commented:

"My journey to (Poplar Forest) in a hard-going gig gave me great suffering...The loss of the power of taking exercise would be a sore affliction to me...The sedentary character of my public occupations sapped a constitution naturally sound and vigorous, and draws it to an earlier close. But it will still last as long as I wish it. There is a fullness of time when men should go, and not occupy too long the ground to which others have the right to advance. We must continue while here to exchange occasionally our mutual good wishes. I find friendship to be like wine, raw when new, ripened with age, the true old man's milk and restorative cordial."

WINE FOR WELL BEING

Jefferson's reputation as a wine believer was, of course, generally known throughout the country, so it was not surprising for him to receive letters such as the one written by Peter Carr (married Jefferson's sister) on Feb. 2, 1815,

"My inexorable rheumatism still confines me, and has for the last three weeks bound me hand and foot. A violent ague and fever super added, has reduced me to a state of disability never before experienced. I am beginning today to take the warm bath from which I hope for beneficial effects. If I weather the storm, I must endeavor to spend the winter in some milder climate. My physician recommends some tonic remedies— sound port or claret or wine of that character. I have sent to Richmond for some which has not yet arrived. If you have any such, I should in the mean time be much obliged by the favor of a couple of bottles."

Jefferson was convinced that wine, like food, was necessary for man's general well being. He enjoyed a moderate amount almost every day, not just as a mild pick-me-up, but as a necessary ingredient for sound fitness. In this vein he wrote Monsieur de Neuville, December 13, 1818,

"...we can drink wine here as cheap as we do grog, and who will not prefer it? It's extended use will carry health and comfort to a much enlarged circle..."

A flaw in Jefferson's health appeared at the time he became President; a persistant diarrhea, occasionally violent. He mentioned the complaint to Benjamin Rush who prescribed the usual regimen of diet, wine, exercise, bathing and medication, together with cessation of Jefferson's practice: his prescript against colds, of bathing his feet every morning during the winter. Said Rush, "The bowels sympathize with the feet above any other external part of the body, and suffer a peculiar manner from the effects of cold water upon them." With little trust in physic and less in physicians, "three of them together were enough to bring buzzards to the neighborhood," he jested, and continued the practice of bathing his feet in cold water and was remarkably free of colds. For his diarrhea he preferred the "trotting cure," as perscribed by Dr. William Eustis of Boston, who obviously believed that the bowels sympathized with that part of the body exercised by the horse. Jefferson kept the practice of horse back riding the rest of his life.

In his last years, the Sage of Monticello appeared twenty years younger than his age. The ravages of age appeared more evident to him than to his visitors, but his mind remained lively, his senses sharp, his countenance warm, his manners as bright and urbane as ever. He attributed his good health, generally to temperate habits of living, eating, and drinking. He ate moderately, an essentially vegetable diet, and drank light wines only. In his last years, when he had recruited Dr. Robley Dunglison, a London physician, for the chair of anatomy and medicine at the University of Virginia, he began to suffer from a urinary illness; the prostatic hypertrophy of old age. For long intervals he lay on a couch in pain. The urinary problem combined with his recurrent diarrhea drained the life from his body. It is most probable that this two edged sword, the urinary retention and the diarrhea brought on a state of uremia from which he lapsed into a coma and died.

Feb. 1. 26	old stock on hand	now rec'd.	total
vin rouge de Bergasse	142.	. . . .	142
Red Ledanon	37	180	
blanquette de Limoux	49	. . .	49
muscat de Rivesalte	36	150	
Scuppernon quant. suff			
Claret from Richmᵈ.	22	. . .	22
Virgin oil of Aix.	2	36	
Anchovies	*	12	
Maccaroni.	*	113	
	286		

Jefferson's last known "purchasing list" for wines which indicates what he possessed in his cellar at Monticello a few months before he died. This refutes published claims that he had only Scuppernong wine at that time.

Courtesy James Monroe Memorial Library, Fredericksburg, Va.

Dr. Dunglison who was at his bedside, remarked on the clarity and vigor of his mind to the end. Jefferson made all the arrangements with his grandson Mr. Randolph and spoke freely of his approaching death. Dr. Dunglison writes: "In the course of the day and night of the 2nd of July, he was affected with stupor, with intervals of wakefulness and consciousness; but on the 3rd, the stupor became permanent. About seven o'clock of the evening of that day, he awoke, and seeing my staying at his bedside exclaimed, `Oh, Doctor, are you still there?' in a voice, however, that was husky and indistinct. He then asked, `Is it the fourth?' to which I replied, `It soon will be.' Those were the last words I heard him utter."

References:

Betts, Edwin Morris, *Thomas Jefferson's Garden Book*, Philadelphia, The American Philosophical Society, 1944.

Peterson, Merrill D., *Thomas Jefferson and the New Nation,* New York, Oxford University Press, 1970.

Boyd, *Papers of Thomas Jefferson*, Princeton University Press, Vol. 1-6.

Battlefield Medicine in the American Revolution, *Medical World News*, 1976, June 28.

Mayo, "Jefferson Himself, " University of Virginia.

The Wine Museum, "Thomas Jefferson and Wine in Early America," San Francisco.

WILLIAMSBURG'S PALACE CELLARS
Jefferson Enjoyed Their Wines

By Brock W. Jobe[1]

The present restoration of the Palace cellars means that they resemble what they were when Thomas Jefferson lived there as Governor. He had the opportunity to see them, and the records show that he enjoyed the wine that was stored there. Jefferson was in Williamsburg as a student at William & Mary College, 1760-1762; studied law under George Wythe, 1762-1767; member of the Virginia House of Burgesses, 1769-1776; and Governor of Virginia, 1779-1781. The last Royal Governor John Murry [Earl of Dunmore] fled the Palace in June, 1775.

When the new Commonwealth came into existance, the Palace served for five years as the executive mansion for Governor Patrick Henry, then Jefferson. In 1780, the capital of the state moved to Richmond. It was then used as a military headquarters and during the Yorktown campaign, as a hospital. The Palace burned in 1781. Jefferson, when Governor, made detailed drawings of the floor plans which were invaluable to the restoration of the main structure in the 1930's. The cellars were restored in 1981.

The Governor's Palace in Williamsburg is one of Virginia's best known colonial structures. Begun in 1705, completed about 1720, and destroyed by fire in 1781, the building enjoyed a brief lifespan of only seventy-six years. Yet it housed seven royal and two state governors and throughout its history served as a symbol of elegance and wealth. Today a careful reconstruction of the Palace as it appeared during the second half of the 18th century stands on its original foundations at the head of Palace Green. Inside the building, fourteen furnished rooms, ranging from parlor to pantry, are open to view, and beneath the main floor ten surviving cellar rooms can be visited.

A thorough furnishings plan for the area was prepared by the Curatorial Staff of Colonial Williamsburg.[2] Fortunately, a record of the contents of these rooms survives. In October, 1770, shortly after the death of Lord Botetourt, the Royal Governor of Virginia since 1768, a detailed room-by-room inventory of the Palace was taken. Using this document as well as contemporary information pertaining to cellars and their uses, the Palace cellars were restored to their appearance of 1770.

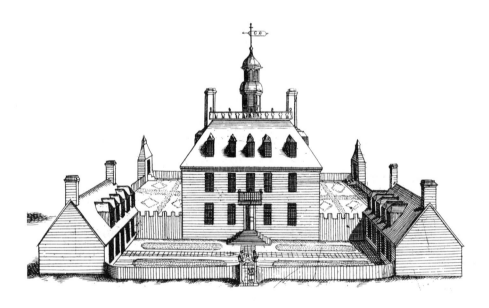

THE GOVERNOR'S PALACE. From a restrike of the "Bodleian Plate", copper plate engraving, c. 1740.

COLONIAL CELLARS

Cellar plans in colonial Virginia included both simple and complex designs. In Williamsburg, small houses such as the George Reid House, erected between 1789 to 1792, contained a single basement room which ran under the entire dwelling. Larger, two-room deep houses had between two and five rooms. The George Wythe House, a handsome Georgian structure built about 1750, has a cellar plan which duplicates the symmetrical arrangement of the first floor—two flanking each side of a central passage. Large country seats were sometimes outfitted with even more subterranean rooms. At Mansfield, the Spotsylvania County home of Mann Page, six cellar rooms were constructed. In a plan of Mount Vernon drawn in 1773, George Washington sketched ten cellar rooms divided by a passage spanning the length of the building. Though the design was not totally implemented, six rooms and the passage were completed.

After the Revolution complex cellar plans became more common. Benjamin Henry Latrobe produced sophisticated designs for several Virginia clients during the 1790's. Colonel Harvie's House, for example, included a "Basement Story" composed of a school room, housekeeper's room, wine cellar, store cellar, common passage, pantry, and larder. Latrobe's 1818 plan of the Stephen Decatur House in Washington, D.C. listed seven rooms, a passage, and a stair hall.

The Construction of cellar rooms varied considerably. Packed earth, brick, stone, and sometimes wood were used for cellar flooring. Of the four, earthen floors were the least expensive and most common; yet they rarely survive in extant cellars. Stenton, built by James Logan in Germantown, Pennsylvania, between 1728 and 1730, is one of the oldest houses to retain its original dirt floors.

Cellar ceilings were usually formed by joists and floorboards of the floor above. However, rooms for the storage of wines were often built with vaulted ceilings of brick. In Virginia, vaulted cellars were in use by the last quarter of the 17th century. During excavations at Jamestown, a narrow building

was discovered dating from about 1675 to 1700 which contained
a vaulted cellar room. This structure is thought to have been a
tavern, possibly that of Thomas Woodhouse, a late 17th century
Jamestown innkeeper. At least one 18th century Williamsburg
inn also contained a vault. Beneath the oldest section of the
King's Arms Tavern was a large vaulted area with brick flooring. In multi-room cellars, a single vaulted wine cellar was
often erected beneath the entrance hall of the main floor. Such,
for example, was the case at Mansfield, Stenton, and Rosewell,
the Page family mansion in Glouster County. Cellars were
sometimes built with several vaulted rooms. At Mount Vernon,
Washington ordered the construction of three vaulted rooms
in 1774.

In colonial Virginia, cellars served many purposes. Kitchens
were sometimes located there. The *Virginia Gazette* of April
29, 1737, for example, carried the following advertisement:

*To be Lett or Sold, at the Capitol Landing (near Wil-
liamsburg) a House, 40 Feet Long, and 20 feet wide, having a
porch, and Brick Chimneys with Fireplaces above and below a
Brick Cellar from End to End, Part whereof is a Kitchen..*

In most dwellings cellars provided storage space for non-
perishable foodstuffs, wines, paints, liquors, and empty bottles
and casks. Colonel Edwin Conway of Lancaster County owned
"in the Seller" in 1763:

> Bottle (,) 1 Jar with Hogs Lard
>
> Bottles (,) 1 Jar with Hogs Lard,
>
> 8 Small Casks with about 150
>
> Gallons of Brandy (,) 1 New Rundles
>
> 14 Gamons of Bacon and 2 Middlens.

In Williamsburg in 1754 the shoemaker George Wells stored
only a gross of bottles, a cask of cider, a jar of soap, a cask of
soap, and a parcel of empty casks in his cellar. The inventory
of Doctor Nicholas Flood listed in the "large Cellar" an
enormous array of wines and spirits including maderia, white
wine, "Frontiniac," malmsy, sherry, "old Mount(ai)in" wine, red

port, Barnados rum, Antiqua rum, gin, cherry bounce, orange peal cordial and peach brandy.

These three inventories of men of different economic levels reveal the varied assortment of goods found in Virginia cellars.

In addition to functioning as a kitchen and storage facility, cellars provided an area for bottling of wines and liquors. Often imported wines and beer were shipped to Virginia in casks and then drawn off into bottles, sealed with corks, packthread, and wax, stored in binns, and, as Ephraim Chambers stated in his 1753 supplement to the *Cyclopaedia*, allowed to "ripen and improve." Evidence the Virginians followed such a procedure appears in the diary of Landon Carter (1710-1778), the affluent owner of Sabine Hall in Richmond County. On June 15, 1764, he "Bottled off Mr. I[saac] W[illiam] G[iberne]'s cask of red Wine. 14 dozen [bottles]." In 1773 he commoented that "Beale bottling of the pipe of wine this day, quantity 43 dozen," and again, two years later, rendered "My own pipe of wine bottled off last week 42 dozen." On the average Carter drew off one pipe per year. Unfortunately he does not state what tools or supplies were required for the operation. Eighteenth-century treatises on wine making reveal that funnels, drip pans or tubs, wooden buckets, brass cocks, corks, packthread or wire, sealing wax, a mallet, and empty bottles were needed for the operation.

THE GOVERNOR'S INVENTORY

The cellar plan at the Governor's Palace represents the most elaborate one known from colonial Virginia. Archaeologists discovered the remains of ten cellar rooms during excavation between 1930 and 1932. Every room was paved with stone or brick. Three rooms were found to have had vaulted ceilings and a fourth room, based on circumstantial evidence, is thought to have had one.

During Lord Botetourt's administration, and probably throughout the colonial period, the cellars contained one of the largest supplies of wines and spirits in Virginai. In 1770 eight of the ten rooms were reserved for wine, beer, and spirits, The wealthy Dr. Nicholas Flood left at his death 609 bottles of wine and 261 empty bottles in addition to a small number of filled hogsheads, casks, and jugs. Yet Botetourt possessed in one room alone (the Binn Cellar") a total of 2369 bottles of wine and beer. The Curatorial Staff has refurbished the Palace cellars according to the Botetourt inventory in which each of the ten cellar rooms and their furnishings is described .

Nearest the staircase leading into the cellars are a narrow passage and two small rooms paved with stone. The room to the left was probably that named the "Cooks Cellar" in the Botetourt inventory while that to the right was the "Stone Cellar."

Both rooms served as storerooms for foodstuffs, candles, and medicines. The stone cellar contained" abt 11 doz[en] [bottles] of Hatwell water. 4 doz gallipots english moist sweet Meats—2 potts Virg^{a}sweet meats.— box & paper of twisted glass & frost—3 entire & 5 broken Potts of sweet meats—part of a pot of pickled mangoes, 1 whole & 1 broken pot of Tamarin, 4 entire pots of Walnuts. 2 full Jars of Currants—3 full Boxes of Sperma Caeti Candles—11 Bottles of Capers—3 d[itt]° Olives; 2 d° anniseed Water 1 d° english Ginn; Whole Box mould tallow Candles 1 p^r of d°, 1 p^r dipt d° a Parcel of old Boxes.

The Hatwell an anniseed waters were non-alcoholic potions distilled from seeds of aromatic plants and were primarily used as remedies or cordials. The foods included a host of eighteenth century delicacieis preserved in sugar or vinegar. Sweet meats was a general term applied to foods rich in sugar. Twisted glass and frost referred to sugar candy. In addition to pickled mangoes, a popular West Indian fruit, it is likely that the walnuts, olives, and capers were pickled. Temarind, a common import from the Carribean, and currants, an English import, could have been preserved in sugar or vinegar. Spermacaeti candles were expensive but long lasting and brilliantly white in color. Tallow, extracted from the fat of animals, produced a slightly darker and faster burning candle.

The substantial number of bottles, pots, and jars in the room suggests that shelves lined the walls. A row of holes in the surviving portions of the south wall confirm this and today three shelves supported on brick piers have been reconstructed. The cooks cellar, by comparison, contained far fewer objects. The Botetourt inventory listed the following:

> Bottles gooseberries; 3 Bottles d[ou]ble distill
>
> Vinegar—⅓ of a Cask Currents—⅔ of
>
> Cask brown Sugar—half cask Rice—
>
> 3 parts of three Pots Lard—

With three casks and only a small number of bottles in the room, it is likely that few shelves were installed, perhaps only a pair in the relieving arch at the base of the west chimney stack.

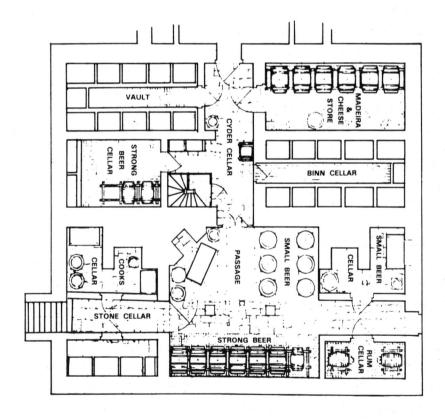

PLAN OF THE CELLARS. The room designations appearing on the plan were chosen by Earnest M. Frank, formerly of the Architect's Office, Colonial Williamsburg, after careful study of the inventory of Lord Botetourt.

JEFFERSON'S PALACE DINNERS

Botetourt reserved the remaining eight cellar rooms for the storage of liquors and wines. Thatea so many rooms should be designated for this use is not surprising when considering the amount of entertaining at the Governor's Palace. Botetourt, like all governors, regularly celebrated events such as the birthday of the reigning monarch by inviting numerous towns-people to the Palace for supper. An account of 1727 listed a pipe of wine, "Cold Treats", and a "Ball...for ye [La]dys" as *The Necessarys Requisite for ye birth night*" celebration.

Dinners, both formal and informal, required substantial amounts of wines. One can visualize the many bottles uncorked by household servants at a series of dinners given by Botetourt in 1769 at the conclusion of the April session of the General Court. "Fifty two dined with me Yesterday," he commented, "and I expect at least that number today." Likewise at a small meal for close associates one can imagine the Governor sharing a bottle of madeira or a bowl of rum punch. Such must have been the case when Governor Francis Fauquier invited George Wythe, Dr. William Small, and the student Thomas Jefferson, to the Palace for dinner and conversation during 1760 and 1761. At these meals, Jefferson [age 17] later recalled, "I have heard more good sense, more rational and philosophical conversation, than in all my life besides."

Many guests were impressed by the quality of the wine served at the Palace. In 1733, John and Charles Carter wrote to merchants in Madeira requesting two pipes of "Mountain Wine" of the type that "We formerly drank...at Governor Drysdale's an[d] colonel Spotswood's Tables."

Governors occasionally presented wines to friends. William Nelson, the influential merchant of Yorktown, received a gift of wine from Governor Fauquier in November 1767, considering it "a Mark of the Gentleman's Politness & Civility."

To satisfy the needs of entertaining, dining, and gift-giving, governors of the colony maintained well-stocked cellars. In Botetourt's case, the largest of the wine cellars, the "Passage", located east of the entrance hall, contained the following:

> 6 Casks strong & 6 d° small Beers
>
> unopen'd
>
> 1 Barrel of Cranberries
>
> 1 Hogshead Molasses Beer
>
> 2 empty Hhds—2 powdering Tubbs

Strong and small beer were similar beverages of different strengths. The former often contained more malt and was brewed for a longer period of time than the latter. The origin of the beer, and the size of the casks, and their placemnt in the room are difficult to determine. Beer was occasionally brewed in Virginia. The Reverend Hugh Jones reported in 1724 that "Some raise barley and make malt there, amd others have malt from England, with which those that understand it, brew as good beer as in England," He added, however, that most of the beer drunk in the colony was imported "Bristol beer" and it is likely that Botetourt's casks contained beer from England. The term cask is a general one which gives no indication of size. Quarter casks, thirty-gallon containers, may well have been used for the beer. These vessels were probably stored in an upright position rather than on their sides on racks. This method is recommended when the casks are unopened for it allows, according to one popular mid-18th century treatise, "a large Cover of Yeast [to form], that greatly contributes to the keeping in the Spirit of the Beer...and, by its broad level Bottom, gives a better Lodgment to the fining and preserving Ingredients, than any other Cask whatsoever that lies in the long Cross-form."

Molasses beer was brewed with molasses instead of malt. The unopened barrel in the passage probably stood upright like the strong and small beer casks. The barrel of cranberries and empty hogsheads were no doubt also set on their ends. The powdering tubs, a common item in many Virginia cellars, were used for the salting and pickling of meats and vegetables.

Beyond the passage in the south-east portion of the basement story were small rooms of about the size of the cooks cellar and stone cellar. They probably corresponded to the "Rum Cellar" and "small beer Cellar" of the Botetourt inventory. The latter, which is thought to refer to the north room, contained in 1770:

> 1 empty Carboy; 7 Iron Hoops—
>
> 1 empty cask—2 Bushel
>
> Cask of Split Pease

The Rum cellar was filled with: 1 Hhd Rum & ab^t ⅓ [Hhd Rum]. 2 brass Cocks. 2 earthen pans—1 stooper—

Funnel, shallow earthen pan, brass cock, corks, and bottles in the restored cellar at Colonial Williamsburg, Governor's Palace.

The contents of these rooms offer an interesting comparison. At the time the inventory was taken, the smaller beer cellar contained no beer and served instead as a storeroom for miscellaneous materials, some of which may have been placed on shelves. Both bottles and casks of small beer were stored elsewhere in the cellars. The rum cellar, however, functioned as the main repository for rum. Both hogsheads and been tapped, brass cocks inserted, and shallow earthenware pans placed on the floor to catch any drips. The inventory gives no clue as to where the hogsheads stood. They probably lay horizontally along the south wall on a pair of wooden beams on the floor or on a more elaborate frame. A related 18th century rack has survived in the cellars of Stenton.

2369 BOTTLES IN BINN CELLAR

To the north of the central passage was a narrow passage flanked by a pair of rooms on either side. The Botetourt inventory listed five rooms in this area; The "Binn Cellar," the "Vault," the "Cyder Cellar," the "Strong beer Cellar" and the "Madeira & Cheese Store." Of these, we can only be certain of the location of one—the binn cellar. located in the southeast corner of the rear cellar area, the room today contains eleven brick receptables which correspond to the number of binns listed in tthe room in the inventory. A total of 2369 bottles filled these binns. They were divided as follows:

N° 1. contains

17 doz & 4 bottles old Hock—Ben Hinton

8½ doz d° M^r. Fauquier

2. 7½ doz:—Madeira—

3. 37 doz & 7 Madeira—

4. 9 doz & 3 Bottles English small Beer

5. 37½ doz. strong beer very fine

6. 14 Bottles old Madeira

7. 9 doz & 4 Bottles of Porter

8. 27 doz & 5 Bottles Claret—

9. 11 doz & 2 Bottles Burgundy

10. 18½ doz red Port—

11. 12 doz & 2 Bottles Madeira

The bottles were stored on their sides with a cushion of sawdust, sand, or straw between each layer. A similalr network of binns survives in two cellar rooms dating from the 1740's, at Rousham, an English country house in Oxfordshire.

Another part of the restored Williamsburg Governor's Palace cellar.

Most of the wines listed in the binn cellar were popular throughout Virginia during the third quarter of the 18th century. Madeira, here listed in greater quantities than any other wine, was a favorite of the colonists. William Byrd praised it as a "splendid wine from Madeira (a Canary Island), which is very delicious, and strong, and [which is] far better and more healthful than all other European wines, not only because of its agreeable sweetness but because of its soothing quality." Claret from France and port from Portugal were also common beverages as were small beer, strong beer, and porter, a strong dark beer introduced from England by mid century. French Burgundy and old hock, a white wine from the Rhineland of Germany, however, were rarely found in local homes, probably because they did not preserve as well as the fortified wines. Botetourt purchased a portion of his hock in 1768 from the estate of Francis Fauquier, the preceding governor. The remainder came from unidentified "Ben Hinton."

The vault, like the binn cellar, housed only bottled wines and liquors, probably laid on their sides on shelves or in binns. Unfortunately, no trace of either form of receptical has survived in any room except the binn cellar. For exhibition purposes, the northwest room has been designated as the vault.

The total number of bottles in the vault amounted to only 384, a figure far below that for the binn cellar. They were divided into the following categories:

> 6 doz & 8 Bottles of Claret—
>
> 2 doz 1 Bottle white Wine
>
> 16 Bottles Arrack—
>
> 4 doz malmsay Madeira—M^r. Fauquier
>
> 11 doz peach Brandy—2 Bottles Honey
>
> 6 Bottles old Claret—3 Bottles Champaine
>
> 14 Bottles old Spirits—6 Bottles fine Arrack
>
> 11 Bottles french Brandy—3 doz & 4
>
> Bottles old Spirits

Here again, except for champagne, all of the wines and liquors in the inventory were popular Virginia beverages. Peach brandy was a perennial favorite, second only to cider as a household drink. No doubt the peach brandy listed here was made locally. Peach orchards dotted the Virginia landscape and brandy production was extensive. Josiah Quincy, Jr., a visitor from New England, wrote in the spring of 1774 of seeing throughout Virginia "large fields (from ten to thirty acres extent)...planted with peachtrees, which being all in bloom made my journey vastly agreeable. The purpose of raising these trees is the making of brandy, a very favorite liquor."

French brandy, arrack, and malmsey were also favored by Virginians, Even cognac, the finest of French brandies, was sold in the colonies. William Avlett, for example, advertised in Williamsburg in 1777 that he "hath on hand...best *coniack* BRANDY, in baskets of two bottles each." After the Revolution, the importation of brandy, like other French liquors, increased significantly. According to George Washington, at least 24,000 gallons were shipped to Virginia in the year 1788 alone. Arrack, an expensive East indian import, was used primarily in punch. Malmsey, a sweet dessert wine, was made in Spain and the Canary Islands.

CHAMPAGNE, "SWEET AND SPARKLING"

The reference to champagne in the inventory is one of the few from the colonial period. Like burgundy, it was considered a special treat which few could afford. During the early 19th century, however, its popularity grew and by 1819 the English ambassador to the United States could report that in Washington society "You will be judged of by your Champagne of which the Americans prefer the sweet & sparkling."

The remaining two rooms and passages housed barreled and bottled beverages, cheese, and hops. Listed in the "Madeira & Cheese Store" were:

> 6 Pipes of Madeira Wine—
>
> small part of a Hogshead of Molasses
>
> a Case wth about forty Pound of Hops
>
> 2 dbl Golster Cheeses—37 single d°
>
> a small Box of Corks & Bottle
>
> Stopper
>
> 1 Step Ladder & old Chair
>
> 3 Horses—2 large Shelves

Surely madeira must have been Lord Botetourt's favorite wine with six pipes here, measuring over 750 gallons, in addition to hundreds of bottles in the binn cellar. The presence of a box of corks suggests that madeira was transferred from pipes to bottles in the room. Additional items needed for bottling, such as packthread and funnels, were located in other areas of the Palace and could easily have been brought down when needed. Molasses and hops may have been used for brewing molasses beer somewhere on the Palace grounds.

Single and double Gloucester cheese were often imported from England. Usually they arrived in twelve to sixteen pound units. Of the two varieties, the latter was generally preferred. An American encyclopaedia of 1798 describes the double Gloucester as "a cheese that pleases almost every palate." The large shelves which no doubt rested on the three wooded horses, provided storage space for the cheese. Fixed shelves may also have been installed over the doorway. The old chair in the room is the only piece of furniture listed in the entire cellars.

The final two rooms noted in the cellar inventory were the "Strong beer Cellar" and the "Cyder Cellar." The first contained in 1770:

> 3 doz 9 Bottles damaged Ale—
>
> 1 Hh^d of Rum; ab^t half of Hhd of Spirits
>
> 24 doz & 8 Bottles of strong Beer.

No doubt the bottles of beer and ale were stored on shelves or in binns. The Hogsheads probably rested on a wooden rack or a pair of parallel beams. The cider cellar held:

> 1 Barrel peach Brandy—
>
> 1 Brass Cock in an old Cask—
>
> 3 doz & 5 Bottles english Cyder—
> 2 gr [Oss], & half Virg^a Cyder.

Here the barrels and bottles were probably stored in a similar fashion to those in the strong beer cellar.

Of all the beverages consumed in Virginia, none was more popular than cider. While it was occasionally imported from England, enormous quantities were also produced locally. Indeed, visitors often commented on the delightful taste of Virginia cider "Hewes's crab-apple is much cultivated in Virginia," wrote Josiah Quincy, Jr. in 1773. "I have tasted better cyder made of it than any I ever drank made from Northern fruit. The Cyder is quite pale and clear, but of most exquisite flavor."

In historic house museums today little attention is devoted to cellars. Rarely are they shown to the public and only occasionally are they mentioned by interpreters. Usually they serve as offices for curators or the interpretative staff or simply as an area to hide such modern conveniences as hot water heaters or air conditioning units. Yet their historic importance should not be overlooked. They provided necessary storage space for non-perishable foodstuffs, offered an exellent climate for the aging of wines and liquors, and sometimes functioned as kitchens as in the long cellar complex under Jefferson's Monticello.

A view of the restored vaulted ceiling in the cellars of the Governor's Palace, Williamsburg, Virginia.

Using the Botetourt inventory as a principal guide, the

Curatorial Staff of Colonial Williamsburg has furnished it as authentically as possible so that the general public will be able to appreciate the major role of the cellars in eighteenth century America.

References;

Illustrations courtesy of the Colonial Williamsburg Foundation, P. O. Box C, Williamsburg, Virginia 23187, tel. 804/229-1000.

[1]Mr. Jobe was Associate Curator, Exibition Buildings, The Colonial Williamsburg Foundation, whose motto is "That The Future May Learn From The Past."

WINE: ORIGIN OF FREE TRADE POLICY

High Taxes Encourage Strong Drink

*"I think it is a great error to consider a heavy tax on wines
as a tax on luxury. On the contrary, it is a tax on the health
of our citizens." —Th: Jefferson*

A "trivial shipment" of wine for Thomas Jefferson probably altered his views on interstate commerce and resulted in the establishment of a policy which has been essential to the prosperity of the United States.

Jefferson during the course of his wine orders in France was obviously appalled at the high taxation levied on all goods going from one princely state or country to another. These duties were often as much as the transportation of the wine.

Julian Boyd[1] draws attention to this historical fact in an extensive footnote to a letter written to Jefferson (in Paris) from John Bondfield, Bordeaux, April 19, 1785 concerning the shipment of four cases of wine to Mr. Eppes in Virginia. (see also pp.62-63.)

Footnote by Boyd:

Recorded in Jefferson's log as received 24 Apr. 1785. Enclosure missing, but in the Massachusetts Historical Society there is a printed form from Bondfield & Gireaudeau to R. Durand & Cie., directing them to receive, "A la garde de Dieu et conduite de Revore de Blois", each of the four cases containing 36 bottles of wine, to be delivered to TJ within 24 days. This form contains on its face the marks given on the cases, the rate of transportation (to be paid by TJ to the carrier), and TJ's former address as "Hotel d'Orlean, rue des Augustins." On its verso is recorded the total of costs involved in the shipment, which tallies with TJ's statement in Account Book under 13 May 1785: portage and duties on wine Bourdeaux 90-1-3. Documents supporting these charges are also in MHi; (1) Receipt for payment of customs at Monleu, 22 Apr. (2) Same for Ruffec, 26 Apr., endorsed by TJ on verso: Bonfeild. 12 doz. bott. wine recd. May 8. 1785: (3) A receipt for charges paid a "Notaire Royal" at Angersville-la-Gaste, covering the entire shipment in the conveyance, including quatre caisses pour Mr. Javerson, 7 May. (4) Receipt to TJ for duties paid, 10 May.

This sheaf of documents, representing as it did something unknown in the American colonial experience under the mercantile system and only lately cropping up in the form of retaliatory imposts among some of the states, must have impressed TJ at this particular moment when he was engaged in promoting the idea that nations were "wealthy and populous nearly in proportion to the freedom of their commerce; and... were it perfectly free, they would probably attain the highest points of wealth and population of which their circumstances would admit" (Commissioners to De Thulemeier, 14 Mch. 1785). An otherwise trivial shipment of wine became a matter of significance in the larger diplomatic task and in a comparative view of the French and American states when it was observed that internal duties accounted for almost as much of the total as actual transportation expenses did (the costs for the "voiture" and "Commission" amounted to only 481.12s. of the total of 901.2s.3d.) This was an experience new to an American but long suffered by the French, and represented, as TJ must have later observed, one of the striking differences between the roots of revolution in the two nations. It is in light of such a personal experience as this mere shipment of wine, too, that one must view TJ's reply to James Monroe's letter of 12 Apr. 1785 in which he was aspleased as Monroe was fearful of the proposal to vest in Congress control over trade between the states—an opinion quite different from that he had expressed several years earlier (TJ to Monroe, 17 June 1785; TJ to John Adams, 17 Dec. 1777).

The Bill of Loading (sic) that Bonfield promised to send to Eppes also came to rest in TJ's papers (MHi) and is dated 25 Apr. 1785. (Boyd)

EQUATING WINE WITH SPIRITS

Jefferson in his lifelong drive to bring the beverage of culture to young America, constantly encountered the persistance of lawmakers to lump wine in the same high alcohol package as hard spirits. Now, in the late 20th century, legislators are advocating higher taxes on wines, wineries, and related aspects.

Jefferson proclaimed, "It is an error to view a tax on wine as merely a tax on the rich. It is a prohibition of its use to the middling class of our citizens, and a condemnation of them to the poison of whiskey...Fix but the duty at the rate of other merchandise...Its extended use will carry health and confort to a much enlarged circle."

In modern times, Peter J. Morrell has written The New York Times in the same vein, addressing everyone who favors a new tax on wine, "I propose it is better to let our citizens pay what they must through income and corporate taxes, so they know when, how much and how long to scream at their elected reprsentatives, than to place hidden burdens on one of life's sublime everyday pleasures." He continued with the proposal, "A 50 cents per gallon tax on imported gasoline and oil would probably raise more money and better serve the interests of the American people than all excise tax proposals combined..." Mr. Jefferson possessed innate and timeless good sense.

The question of the relationship of wine in trade, taxes, duties, etc. was noted in Jefferson's correspondence as early as April 11, 1787 when he was making his tour of France. He wrote his good friend the Marquis de la Fayette from Nice,

Your head, my dear friend, is full of Notable things; and being better employed, therefore, I do not expect letters from you. I am constantly roving about, to see what I have never seen before, and shall never see again. In the great cities, I go to see what travellers think alone worthy of being seen; but I make a job of it, and generally gulp it all down in a day. On the other hand, I am never satiated with rambling through the fields and farms, examining the culture and cultivators, with a degree of curiosity which makes some take me to be a fool, and others to be much wiser than I am...The articles of your produce wanted with us, are brandies, wines, oil, fruits, and manufac-tured silks; those with which we can furnish you, are indigo, potash, tobacco, flour, salt fish, furs and peltries, ships and materials for building them...[2]

FROM FENWICK

Bordeaux, March 29, 1791

The carriage of the frontignac wine from Mr. Lambert also is at least equal to one third the first price of the wine (provincial princes often charged duties on goods shipped through their provinces, adding much to transportation costs).

FROM PIERRE GUIDE

Baltimore, May 5, 1791

Grateful for TJ's wishes for the success of his venture in extending trade with Sardinia...high duties fall heavily on some articles...appreciates order for wine, figs and raisins...sending a dozen bottles of the Vin Vieux Rouge de Nice...by the first occasion he will send the other two dozen bottles of wine, which he sells at four gourdes per dozen...

TO MADISON

Bennington, Vt. June 21, 1791

While at Hudson, Jefferson sought to persuade Captain Seth Jenkins, principal founder of the port, that better spirits could be made from wine than from molasses. This would have had the double advantage for the U.S. of increasing trade with France and of lessening dependence upon the British West Indies for sugar. Jenkins remained unconvinced because of the higher cost of imported wines...the very fact that Jefferson advanced the suggestion shows that he was thinking of trade as an instrument of politics.

FROM C. W. F. DUMAS

The Hague, 1 Oct. 1791

News from the Netherlands...Thirty million florins have been used to assist "la Compagnie des Indes orientales." As the result, taxes on wine, coffee, tea, tobacco, servants, horses, crossing gates will be raised in the province of Holland.

FROM CATHALAN

Marseilles, 4 Sep. 1791

The price of brandy has risen throughout France because

of the poor prospect of the crop of wine; it cost (£) 45^{tt} p. ql. Brut at Cette and might rise to (£) 60^{tt}, and only costs (£) 42^{tt} here because of imports from Naples and Trieste.

Washington, 1791[3]

Jefferson left an accounting of the cost of wine, freight, and other charges on a large shipment of wine for President Washington. He had ordered Frontignan, Sauterns, La Fite, and Champagne. The charges were about one third the cost of the wines themselves.

FROM DAVID GELSTON

New York, Oct. 22, 1803

Itemizes the costs of 13 cases of wine coming from Bordeaux: Duties, $27.55; Freight, $25.55; Permits, carting, and storing, $2.52, for a total of $55.62. The cost of the wine was not given.

TO SAMUEL SMITH, BALTIMORE

Monticello, May 3, 1823

At the very old age of 80, Jefferson was still trying to obtain better tax and other breaks for wine, fully convinced that it was not only the health reasons to be considered, but practical for the U.S. Treasury. In his letter he recommends tax on whiskey to discourage consumption, but not on imported wines. He stated his belief in support of infant industries only when they can in the future become strong.

Jefferson was then fighting the same battle for lower wine costs, just as wine devotees are trying to hold back the neo-prohibitionist pressures today. The great leader who did so much in charting the direction of his new Nation, felt that an inexpensive wine could be a "...gain for the treasury, and to the sobriety of our country."

There were many other perils besides high taxation to be encountered in shipping wines. Some of these were pilferage, storms at sea in small sailing vessels, severe cold, as these letters indicate:

FROM JOHN STEELE

Custom House, Philadelphia

Feby, 22, 1820

The wine mentioned in yours of the 17th instant was yesterday laden on board the Schr. Industry, Carson Master, and accepted to the care of Mr. Gibson at Richmond

Soon after the arrival of the Emma Matilda in our waters I received Mr. Dodge's letter on the subject and would have forwarded the wine to Mr. Gibson, as formerly, at an earlier day; but the vefsel, being detained by ice for some weeks, did not reach our port until the 18th.

Supposing the Boxes not sufficiently secure to sustain the land carriage from Richmond I directed them to be strapped— Enclosed you will receive a memorandum of the Duty & charges

FROM FRAN. O. MEARS

Norfolk Feby 21, 1803

It was customary to brand casks of wine to identify them for shipment, as noted in this bill of lading sending two pipes (1 pipe=110 gallons) to Alexandria. In this case Jefferson was identified by the initials TN,

Wine was probably enjoyed by the watermen (longshore men today) when the opportunity permitted as they loaded and unloaded ships at the harbors, resulting in such losses that casks had to be enclosed in an outer cask to protect the liquid assets,

FROM PATRICK GIBSON

Richmond Feby 22, 1816

I sent you by Gibsons boat a Cask Teneriffe Wine rcd. of Dr. Fermanoes throuogh Fox & Richardson. I have by your directions inclosed it in a rough cask to secure it from the watermen.

The [?] mark (as you will observe at the head of the sack) is twenty-nine Gallons, one Gal. Majr. Gibbons has just judged of the wine & Mr. Richardson informs me that the Majr. says it is the best Teneriffe he has ever tasted. P. S. Enclosed is Majr. Gibsons certificate.

Lost wine: Jefferson writes his agent in Richmond,

TO JAMES BROWN[4]

Monticello Jan. 3, 1790

I received duly your favor of Dec. 21 and with it the several articles noted to be sent therewith , except No. 1 a box of wine. I had observed in my mem'm [memorandum] that there were two No. 1s. and had desired both to be sent; and both are so marked in your letter; but the waggoners concurring in their declarations that only one was delivered. I am in hopes it was omitted by error, & that it may now come by my waggon unless it is on the way in the canoes...

...Articles to be sent by my waggons...

6. gallons good French brandy. If none, send good rum...

6. half pint tumblers. 12 wine glasses...

Th. Jefferson

Dealing in international trade and without established banks to handle the currency transactions were a very difficult and worrysome process as this letter indicates,

TO VICTOR DUPONT

Washington May 4, 1803

Mr. Dupont your father informed me he should have occasion to remit considerable sums of money from France to the U. S. The small matter for which I have occasion cannot be proposed as a convenience to him, but to myself alone. I wish to place 400. Dollars in Paris for the purchase of some wine, and know not how to remit it there. if it be convenient for you to give me your draught on your father for the equivalent of that sum in money of France, I shall be obliged to you for it; and for that purpose now enclose you four bills of the U. S. bank of this place of one hundred dollars each. To wit n°s 4000. 4045. 5818, 5864. Should you know of any vefsel bound to any port of France direct, I would thank you for the information for the conveyance of my letters. Accept my friendly salutations & respect.[5]

Th: Jefferson

References:

[1]Boyd, Princeton University Press.

[2]Thomas Jefferson Randolph, *Memoir, Correspondence of Thomas Jefferson,* Vol.II, Charlottesville, 1829, pp.104, 114.

[3]Probably Massachusetts Historical Society, Boston. (not Library of Congress, nor U. of Va.).

[4]Beinecke Rare Book Library, Yale University, New Haven, Conn.

[5]University of Virginia Library, Charlottesville, Virginia.

JEFFERSON'S ACCOUNT BOOK
A Fascinating List Of Purchases

Comparing the brands that he bought with their contemporaries on the market today, provides a clue to his tastes, except some wines may have changed greatly, for better or worse. And the "coolers" were surely not the type we know today.

A typed copy of the "Acount Book" has been prepared and indexed, and a copy may be seen at the Alderman Library, University of Virginia, Charlottesville. Drawing his information largely from this data, John R. Hailman[1] wrote in the Washington Post, about these wines and how some of them are on the market today,[2]

"...In his everyday table wine selections, Jefferson was very much a precursor of 1980's Americans. When his favorite Bordeaux, Burgundies and Champagnes became too expensive, he turned to the thriftier wines of Italy and Provence and Languedoc in Southern France. A particular favorite among these was a light, dry, claret-like red made in Marseille by Henri Bergasse, a wine grower and personal friend of Jefferson. This forthright imitation of Bordeaux was accepted by Jefferson as such. While no wine of that name is made now, the Bergasse family still thrives in Marseille, a direct descendant recently having been mayor. There also exists a wine made near Marseille which fits excellently the character of Bergasse claret described by Jefferson. It is called *Palette,* and now has its own controlled placename under French law. It was once generally available at Calvert Wine & Cheese Shop on Wisconsin Avenue, Washington, D. C., which sold an excellent *Palette* from the Chateau Simone for a very reasonable price. It should still appear in Washington from time to time and is worth watching for.

"Jefferson's acknowledged favorite red table wine was that of *Bellet,* a small region north of Nice, which he called "the best everyday wine in the world." Today *Bellet* is little exported, but may be drunk with dinner at La Niçoise restaurant in Washington. It is hardly as good as Jefferson proclaimed it, but is still a very pleasant wine.

"John Adams introduced Jefferson to *Cahusac*, a favorite everyday white, by selling him a cask he did not want. Today *Chausac* is a dry white of no distinction which generally sells under the broader, regional name of Gaillac. Occasionally, bottles listing *Cahusac* as their home, reach Washington usually labelled legally as "Vin d'appellation d'origine simple," which might be translated as "Anonymous." One such which I bought from a barrel display in a liquor store on M Street was barely worth the $2 I paid for it.

"Even more evil days have fallen upon *Ledanon* (also *Ledenon*), a full-bodied red from Languedoc which Jefferson drank in great quantities at Monticello after his retirement, and even recommended to his neighbors. Today it is unflatteringly known as "tank" wine, and used mainly for blending.

"Of Italian wines Jefferson drank a variety, Including: Chianti, Orvieto, Lacryma Cristi, Gattinara, Marsala, and Est-Est-Est, as well as the ancestor of Soave. His favorite of all was Montepulciano, a wine now much in decline and seldom seen in America, whose closest relations here would be the Chiantis, of which Jefferson like Carmignano. It is sometimes available at Woodley Liquors.

"Among Spanish wines Jefferson mentioned Sherry and "St. Lucar." the wine then named (as were many) after the port from which it was shipped, but which today is called *Manzanilla,* and which is available in most American wine shops. Jefferson also served to American guests great quantities of "*Mountain,*" a heavy, sweet dessert wine obtainable today at the Wine & Cheese Shop in Georgetown as *Malaga*. He once served Monticello visitor Daniel Webster a "Grecian Islands" wine which Webster called "*Samian,*" undoubtedly the once-famous Muscat of Samos, recently available at Central Liquors.

"One of Jefferson's favorite Portuguese wines which does still exist, the golden *Setubal,* was noted on his 1787 Paris cellar list. Made now in the dramatically beautiful area between beach and mountain across the bay from Lisbon, *Setubal* is one of the oldest and finest dessert wines in the world.

"Indeed, if Thomas Jefferson returned to Washington today, he would recognize most wines in local shops by name and taste. And while he would find neither white Chateau Lafite nor the half pint Lafite tasting-bottles he ordered in the 1780's, most of his favorite wines would still be around. In fact, of all the many objects of his insatiable curiosity, he would probably find that wines have changed least of all in the century and a half since his death."

Partial Index To Typescript of Account Book

white ordinaire, 418

Wine cellar, Monticello, addition to, '94, 590

   bottles in '94, 589

   contents, 51, 52, 79, 96

Wine company, 161, 163, 260

Wine coolers, purchased, 388

   glasses, purchased, 378, 758

Wine room, not at Monticello, 286

References:

[1]Mr. Hailman lives at 810 Lincoln Ave., Oxford, Miss. 38655.

[2]*The Washington Post*, July 1, 1976, Washington, D. C.

JEFFERSON'S ONLY BOOK
Saved By Some Strong Madeira?

To Alexander Donald, Sep. 17, 1787, "Sending Mr. Madison in N.Y. 57 copies of a bad book called Notes on Virginia, the author of which has no other merit than that of thinking as little of it as any man in the world can." Th. Jefferson.

Although Thomas Jefferson's literary documents numbered in the thousands, he wrote only one book for publication, *Notes on the State of Virginia*. By a very wide stretch of the wine devotee's imagination, it could be conjectured that he might not have authored that had it not been for the timely administering of some strong Monticello Madeira to one of our least known Revolutionary heroes, and thereby hangs a tale.

But first, more about his other writings which have indicated inaccurately that he had published more than one book. "The Garden Book" and "The Farm Book" cited in previous chapters were longhand, detailed records and notes compiled by Jefferson over many years for his own reference in informal notebook fashion. In recent decades, these were compiled, edited and annotated and published by the American Philosophical Society in book form. His "Account Book" and other so-called "books" were not published in book form.

Jefferson was far too modest about his writing ability, as noted by Lance Morrow, *Time Magazine*, 1978 (?), "The men who invented the country 200 years ago have long since been enshrouded by the myths of textbooks and the mists of hagiology. The most elusive figure in that gentlemen's club of revolutionaries was Thomas Jefferson. Henry Adams wrote that every other American statesman could be portrayed with a `few broad strokes of the brush,' but Jefferson `only touch by touch with a fine pencil, and the perfection of the likeness depended upon shifting and uncertain flickers of semitransparent shadow...'..He possessed a resplendently Baconian intellect, a mind with all its windows open..."

Notes on the State of Virginia covers almost every subject that he could probably think of: geography, shipping, population data, number of inhabitants, Indians, education, politics, argriculture, and of course grape vines, although very brief, about the last;:

"Grapes, Vitis. Various kinds; though only three described by Clayton".

Jefferson noted there were 191 taverns in the state, a pretty high number if we consider there were only about 25 towns, the largest of which was Norfolk with a population of 6000. Taverns were friendly places where wine could be enjoyed while politics, religion, business and everyday affairs were discussed. For enough wine to supply the tavern and home usage too, it is little wonder there were laws on the state books to encourage wine growing. After all, taverns were the clubs, pubs and debating halls of the times.

Back to our hero and the strong wine, at the end of 1780 the Revolution was going badly against the Americans. The secretary of the French legation, Francois Barbe-Marbois, became anxious and requested information on the states. It befell to Jefferson to compile the data on Virginia. In October a British fleet invaded Hampton Roads but withdrew the next month. Governor Jefferson wrote he was compiling the information for Marbois. In January another invasion took place when the British reached Richmond under the traitor Benedict Arnold. The General Marquis de Lafayette arrived and met Jefferson for the first time and soon the British were retreating down the James River. The Governor wrote Marbois he was continuing work on the *Notes*.

The Commonwealth government removed to Charlottesville, Jefferson at their head (his term soon to expire), but General Cornwallis reversed and sent a detachment of mounted British regulars to ride to Charlottesville to take them by surprise. "...they covered seventy miles in twenty-four hours, but at "Cuckoo Tavern," some forty miles from Charlottesville, their movements were observed and their objective surmised by a daring young Virginian, known to history as Captain John "Jack" Jouett.

John Jouett, the "Paul Revere of the South," raced through 40 miles of thickets and swamps, and arrived in Monticello in the nick of time to warn Jefferson of the oncoming British attack.   Loudoun County News Photo

British General Cornwallis had selected the infamous Colonel "Bloody" Banastre Tarleton to head the small swift unit of dragoons to capture Governor Jefferson and the Virginia Legislature. Tarleton was known for his slaughter of American Colonial Abraham Buford's men in 1780 *after* they had surrendered their swords. Tarleton was still smarting from his defeat by General Daniel Morgan at the Battle of Cowpens and was looking for revenge. He commandeered the finest thoroughbred horses from Virginia's Tidewater plantations, to "literally mount his men on race horses." Jefferson could have suffered Colonel Buford's fate.

"Riding desperately through the night, along trails that no stranger could have found in this rugged country, Jouett reached Monticello before sunrise on Monday, June 4. Jefferson had been unable to assemble a meeting of the Council, but the Assembly had finally achieved a quorum for a fruitless meeting on May 28. The speakers of the two houses and a few other guests were at Monticello when Jouett arrived. According to tradition, the exhausted horseman was revived with old Madeira and rode on to arouse the sleeping legislators in Charlottesville. Cornwallis's trick had failed.

His term as Governor had now expired and Jefferson and his family moved to his rural retreat "Poplar Forest" about ninety miles southwest. He took his voluminous data with which to prepare answers to Marbois' questions, and in early August the manuscript was virtually completed and in December he wrote Marbois the task was finished.

Perhaps the old Madeira helped play a part in saving the records and making all that possible!

Alas, although Jefferson hid Virginia state papers, and escaped, the frustrated dragoons further delayed their failed pursuit when they broke into the Monticello wine cellar.

WINE STOCKS AT THE WHITE HOUSE
Presidential Mansion Burned in 1812

When Jefferson was President, he listed his expenditures during these years. On March 4th of each year he summarized his expenses for wines as well as other items. In those days wine was regarded as a food, and he points up this fact in one instance by noting in parentheses after "groceries" that this did not include wines.

We will probably never know much about the cellars under the White House during his term of office because the Presidential residence was destroyed during the War of 1812. Reports have appeared in recent times indicating special attention to the construction of the cellars by Jefferson, however, the basic sources of this claim has not been verified. Another news article has stated that when Jefferson died under severe financial stress there was only scuppernong wine in his Monticello cellars. On the contrary, his "Stock of Wine" record shows that a few months before he died there was only a small amount of Scuppernong, about which he wrote that the quantity was sufficient, while his stock of red and white French wines numbered over 500 bottles.

There is much to learn from these rather routine figures if time is taken to analyze them, especially if they are considered in relation to data in other chapters, We not only learn the names of the wines he preferred, but their costs, and even down to the taxes, transportation charges, commissions, etc. He obviously kept these highly detailed records in order to form the basis of his theories for establishing commercial tax policies for the young Nation during its early formative years. His recommendations to the Secretary of the Treasurer Gallatin on import duties must have been based on some of this data.

We might also learn from these figures just how much the average White House guest consumed of wines. Jefferson noted how many bottles of Champagne were enjoyed by a certain number of people.

He very nearly expressed a little humor – a quality not often found in his writings – when he noted the date a cask of Madeira was opened, how many months it lasted, and exactly how many weeks and days he was away from the White House during the overall period in which it was consumed!

THE ACCOUNT BOOK

Wine related entries are excerpted as follows from the "Account Book":

Analysis of Expenditures from Mar. 4, 1801 to Mar. 4, 1802, Groceries, 2003.71; Wines, 2797.38; Charities, 978.20; Servants, 2675.84

Mar. 10, (1802) – inclosed the check of 590.72 to Yznardi to pay his bill of wines.

June 6, My second pipe of Maderia is out this day, broached Nov. 3, has lasted 6. months

July 23, (trip to Monticello from D. C.) Barnet's breakfast & wine 2.67

Dec. 20, Note a hamper of Champagne of 50. bottles opened Dec. 7. is finished

Dec. 19th in which time 125, gentlemen have dined, which is 2. bottles to 5. persons.

Jan. 11, (1803) paid Monsr. de Casa – Yrujo 150.d. for 200. bottles Champagne

Apr. 10, the 3d. pipe of Madeira broached June 6, 1802, is out. it has lasted 10. months of which I was absent 3.

Apr. 14 inclosed the said note for 42.42 to messrs. Smith & Buchanan of Baltimore for duties. freight from Lisbon & porterage of two hhds of wine d'Oeyras sent me by mr. Jarvis.

Expenses from Mar. 4, 1802 to Mar. 4, 1803, Wines – 1296.63; Groceries – 1624.76

Oct. 27, desired mr. Barnes to pay David Gelston of N. York 55.62 for freight & duty of 300. bottles of wine from Bordeaux.

Nov. 17, desired mr. Barnes to remit to Genl. Muhlenberg for 400. bottles champagne duties 29.66 which is 7½ cents per bottle freight 40.26 which is 10 cents per bottle – 69.92 – 17½ cents a bottle

Mar. 20, (1804), there remains on hand 40. bottles of the 247 of champagne recd from Fulwer Skipwith Decl. the consumption then has been 207. bottles, which on 651. persons dined is a bottle to 3 1/7 persons. hence the annual stock necessary may be calculated at 415. bottles a year or say 500. to wit con re 65.272. vacation(?) 143.

May 28 the pipe of Madeira broached Apr. 10.03 is out. it has lasted 13M - 18D of which I have been absent 3M-2D.

July 19 inclosed to Joseph Yznardi the 2d bill for 200.D for a pipe of dry sherry recd. last Dec.

Inclosed to Wm. Jarvis at Lisbon the 2d bill of 300.D. for 2 pipes of Termo, & a half pipe of Oeysas recd heretofore, inclosed to Thomas Appleton of Leghorn the 3d bill of 250D. for 138 bottles of Florence wines recd. last month and for a supply of Montipulciano now ordered.

Sept. 15 pd. for 1 doz wine glasses 1.40 for butter 1.66.

Dec. 6 recd from do. a draught on bk US. at Phila. for 132.25 inclosed the same to Henry Sheaff for wines furnished 4. months ago.

Feb. 11, (1805) drew on bk U.S. in favor of Thos. W. Pairo 24.D for wine

Mar. 2 received of J. Barnes 200.D. – pd Genl. Jackson Yznardi's bill 195.D. for wine

May 15 drew off the remains of the 5th pipe of Madeira 76 bottles & sent them to Monticello, and broached the 6th pipe. the 5th broached 1804. May 28.

Dec. 5 J. Barnes has remitted 212.D. to Nicklin & Griffith of Philadelphia in discharge of my acceptance of William Higgins bill on Rob. Smith for 2. pipes Marseille wine.

Dec. 25 pd. Isaac Norris, casing 2 pipes Marsalla 16.D.

Feb. 5 (1806) drew ord. on bk U.S. in favr. J. Oakley 69.60 duty 2 pipes Marsalla recd from bk U.S. 50.D.

May 5 recd from do. (Jones & Howell) an ord. on bk at

N.York in favr David Gelston for 22.22 to repay frt. & duties of wine. which I indorsed to him.

red from do an ord. on bk N.Y. in favr. of Ebenezer Stevens 94.13 for 2. casks wine for myself & Natl. Gordon which I inclosed to Stevens.

July 12 recd from bk U.S. 11.68 by order on bk at Philalda, & inclosed it to P. Mulenberg Phila for duties on wines & books

Mar. 7 (1808) drew on bk U.S. in favr. of Gabriel Christie for 60.94 to wit for duties & charges on wines & c from Marseilles 46.94.

May 21 gave James Davidson ord. on bk U.S. for 421.21. to discharge Cathalan's excha. on me for wines & fruits.

Nov. 25 the last pipe of Madeira is broached this day, & is to be bottled. the preceding one was broached July 06.

Jan 5 (1808) drew on bank in favr Isaac A. Coles 219.73 to wit 150 for a quarter's salary + 69.73 to pay Philetus Havens for 3. cases St George wine

Mar. 24 drew ord. on U.S. in favr J. Davidson for Cathalan for 87.10 for wines & groceries.

June 25 pd mr. Coles 25.d for a box (60 bottles) of St. George wine.

June 27 inclosed to John Hollins of Baltimore 35.D.40 to wit wines 7.50

Jan. 9, (1809) inclosed to Genl Sam. Smith ord. on the bk. US for 200.68 to pay a draught of Peter Kuhn in favor. of mr. Patterson of Baltimore for Mabiouli wine heretofore furnished.

[Jefferson made notes on these wines for 1805 through 1808 in a separate summary]:

Apr. 17 (1805) 38. bottles Aleatico, 3. &. Santo. 3 &. Artemino. 19 &, Chianti. 10 &. Montepulciano. from Joseph Barnes = 73 &.

May 30 100 bott. vins del Carmine. Appleton

1 hhd (i.e. half pipe) Marsalla. Preble.

Oct. 19. 1.2r. cask old Termo from Jarvis 26.20, 1. do cask

old Bucello. from.do 28.60 + fr. duties of 73.83

Nov. 9 473 – bottles Montepulciano cost Leghorn .25 = 118.50 = .25 bottle, duties 35.60 freight 46.38 port charges 6.08 = 88.06 = .18 ½ pr bottle

Jan. (1806) 2. pipes Marsella wine. Higgins 212. cost + 69.60 duty

Apr. 22. 100. bottles White Hermitage cost at Marseilles 76.62 + duty fr. 21.6. do vin de paille – do – 7.82 + 1.22

June 7. 100 do white Hermitage cost at Marseilles 76.62 c + fr. 8.91 + dut. 12 B 35 + 98 (?)barrique 45 gall. Cahusac. cost (at) Bordeaux 22.89 + 14.725 + dut 22.275 = 60 (?)

July. 50. bottles Nebioule shipped by Thos. Strom for Kuhn cost 200. bottles Nebioule from Kuhn. cost delivered at Genoa. 54 cents pr. bottle.

Feb. (1807) 200 bottles Hermitage from Marseilles.

June 4, 350 bottles (80 gall.) Montepulciano from Leghorn 91.55 D + fr. 40.42 + duties 29.85 + port charges 2.25 = 164.07 or .47 pr bottle

June 13 A cask Cathusac (23. gall.) cost at Bordeaux 29.51 +fr. 4.88 + duties 7.36 + port charges 4.83 = 46.58 or 2 D. .02 c pr gallon. 120. bottles St. George sent to Monto. cost at Cette (?) at .24 pr bottle 42.875

Oct. 8 do from Mr. Barnes. 60. bottles charges .15 equals 26.847 (total) 69.722

Dec. 2 3 kegs Nebioule yielding 134. bottles.

Apr. 4 (1808) 100. bottles wine of Nice cost there 30.D.84, 1.96 freight to Marseilles, 24.42 to Phila., 17.69 duty & permit, .67 portage = 75.58

MEMORANDUM BOOK

The "Account Book" was primarily a financial record. The "Memorandum Book" while including some costs, was mainly a description of varieties and quantities. Note the mention of insurance, and in another entry the breakage of 153 bottles [1].

1801 Wine provided at Washington

May 3. a pipe of Brazil Madeira from Colo. Newton	350.
20. a pipe of Pedro Ximenes Mountain from Yznardi. 126. galls. at 2.	252.
424 bottles of it sent to Monticello. Feb. 1803	
a Quart. r. cask of Tent? from do. 30. galls. at 1.50	45.
a keg of Pacharetti doux. from do.	
doz. of claret from do.	
15. doz Sauterne from H. Sheaff. at 8.D.	120.
[two lines crossed out]	
(148. bottles claret at 10.D. pr doz.)	
(6. doz. do. at 12.D.)	
June. 12.2. pipes of Brazil Maderia. from Taylor & Newton	700.
148. bott. claret at 10.D. pr doz. 123.33	
72. do. at 12.D. - 72.	195.33
Sep. 28. 2. pipes of Brazil Madeira from Taylor & Newton	700.
Nov. 28. 30. doz - 360. bottles of Sauterne from Sheaff	240.

1802

Jan. 7. Atierce (60. galls.) Malaga from mr. Yznardi. Lacryma Christi	106.
the above is 45. years old viz. vintage of 1755	
2. doz. bottles of claret from mr. Barnes. at 8.D.	16.
Feb. 24. 1. pipe dry Bacharetti. from mr Yznardi	202.
1. pipe sherry of London quality 10.y.old	188.
½ pipe of sherry of a different quality	94.
278 bottles of it sent to Monticello. Feb. 1, 1803	
½ pipe of white sherry	d 84.
insurance on the wines of Feb. 24. 22.72	
May. 6 duties pd Yznardi on do. 156.	178.72
claret from J. Barnes.	
Nov. a half barrel of Syracuse from Capt. Mc. Neil	
Dec. 1. 100. bottles Champagne from the Chevalr. Yrujo	172.50

1803

Jan. 10. 100 do. at .86¼ viz. .75 pint cost + 11¼ duty

    2. half pipes of wine of Oeyras? from mr. Jarvis at Lisbon   98.17

    sent to Monticello

Mar. 3. 2 pipes of Brazil Madeira from

        James Taylor at Norfolk   700.

        21. 12. doz. Sauterne. from Sheaff. at 8⅔D.   104.33

Oct. 21. 50. bottles white Hermitage at 73⅓ cents

    + 8¾ duty – 82. + 9½ freight   45.80

    23. 150. bottles Rozan Margau at 82½ cents

    + 8¾ duty – 91¼ 8¾   150.00

    150. do. Sauterne at 64 1/6 + 8¾ duty – 8¾ –

81¾ cents   122.57

Dec. 1. 400. do. Champagne d'Aij. (153. broke) 63¾ cents   07½ cents duty

    .19 cents fr. – 84½.95

    100. do. Burgundy of Chambertin .59½ cents –

07½ cents duty — .19 fr. – 77.86   484.

    10. a quarter cask Mountain of crop of 1747.

    from Kirkpatrick of Malaga ft. 10

Monticello do. 30. 2. pipes Fermo one of the crops of Carrasqira,

    the other of Arruda.

    Jarvis. 170 –   196.35

    1. butt of Pale sherry 6 from Yzardi   194.85

1804

Mar. 19. a pipe of Brazil Madeira from Taylor   354.07

    a box Champagne from do. 5. doz. at .62½ cents   37.50

June 20. 138. bottles of wines from Florence (123 Montepulciano) frt. duty. 25 1/2 cents – cost .26   33.17

July. 400. bottles Champagne from N.Y. same as Mar. 19 at 1.D. (23 broke) 400.

   July 20. 98. bottles claret from Sheaff 82.

   Nov. 28 240. bottles of Hungary wine at 1.70

     36. do. of Tokay – 3.31

     12. do. other wines – 4.36 from Bollman 546.23

   Monticello – Dec. 1. pipe dry Pacharetti prime cost 194.85

     1. sherry 15. y. old

   Monto. 147. bottles Port from Fernandez 152.25

     53. Bucellas. 10. y. old

     1. pipe Arrudae wine from Jarvis. Lisbon.

     36. bottles Chateau Margaux of 98. at 7^{tt}

     72. Rozan Margaux of 98 at 4^{tt} 10s   778 f – 50(leo)

     72. do. Salus Sauterne at 2^{tt} – 5s

1805

Apr. 17. 38. bottles Aleatico. 3.do. Santo. 3.do. Artemino. 19. do Chianti. 10.d0. Montepulciano from Joseph Barnes – 73.D.

May 30. 100. bott. vins del Carmine. Appleton, 1. hhd (i.e. half pipe) Marsalla. Preble.

Oct. 19. 1.2r. cask old Fermo from Jarvis 26.20 — fr. duties &c. 73.83; 1.do – Bucellas from do. 28.60

Nov. 9. 473 – bottles Montepulciano: cost Leghorn .25 – 118.50 – .25 pr bottle, duties 35.60, freight 46.38, port charges 6.08 – 88.06 – .18½ bottle

100 bottles hermitage

1806

Jan. 2. pipes Marsalla wine. Higgins 212. cost – 69.60 duty ? fr. Apr. 22. 100. bottles white Hermitage cost at Marseilles 76.62 21.6.do vin de paille – do. – 7.82 – 1.22

June 7. 100.do. white Hermitage cost at Marseilles 76.62 – fr. 8.91 – du. 12.835 – 98.865, barrique 45. galls. Cahusace. cost at Bordeaux 22.89 – fr. 14.725 – dut. 22.275 – 60.D.

July. 50. bottles Nebioule shipped by Thos. Storm for Kuhn cost 200. bottles Nebioule from Kuhn. cost delivered at Genoa .54 cents pr. bottle.

1807

Feb. 200 bottles Hermitage from Marseilles. June 4. 350. bottles 180. galls. Montepulciano from Leghorn 96.55D. - fr. 40.42 - duties 29.85 - port charges 2.25 – 164.07 or .47 pr. bottle; 13. a cask Cahusac (23. galls.) cost at Bordeaux 29.51 – frt. 4.88 – duties 7.36 – port charges 4.83 – 46.58 or 2.D.02c pr. gallon; 120 bottles St. George sent to Monto. cost at Cette at .24 pr. bottle. Oct. 8. do. from mr Barnes. 60. bottles – 42.875 charges .15–26.847 – 69.722

Dec. 2. e kegs Nebioule yielding 134. bottles. D

1808

Apr. 4. 100. bottles wine of Nice cost there 30.84, .196 freight to Marseilles, 24.22 to Phila, 17.69 duty & freight, .67 portage – 75.58

A SUMMARY OF HOW LONG MADEIRA LASTED AT THE WHITE HOUSE

Madeira			lasted exclus.
No. rec.	broached	finished	absence
1. 1801. May 3.	01. May 15.	01. Nov. 3.	3½ months
2. 1801. June 12.	Nov. 3	02. June 6.	6. months
3. do.	02. June 6.	03. Apr. 10.	7. months.
4. – Sep. 28	03. Apr. 10.	04. May 28.	10. months
5. do. –	04. May 28.	05. May 15.	
		sent remains 76.b. Montico.	
6. 1803. Mar. 3.	05. May. 15.	06. July	10 – 17
7. – do. –	06. July	07. Nov. 25.	10 – 19
8. 1804. Mar. 19	07. Nov. 25.		

ACCOUNT BOOK EXCERPTS 1817-1826

For the year [fiscal?] 1817-1818 Jefferson noted in his "Account Book" "wines $442.00, books 433.75 Taxes 294.87".

For the year 1818-1819, he listed, "(?)320.00 for wines, 481.62 for books, and 255.91 for taxes."

Jan. 3 (1822) desired Bernard Peyton to remit for me to Gervey A. S. Dearborne Collector of Boston 18.23 duties, freight, etc. of 25. boxes of wines, oil, maccaroni, & anchovies from Joshua Dodge of Marseilles.

Jan. 7. (1822)

Gave Edm. Meeks ord. on James Leitch for 20.D.

Stock of wines on hand	bottles
Roussillon of Rivesalte, dry. a cask of 62 gall.	25
Muscat de Rivesalte	6
Ledanon	145
Claret of Bergasse	55
Limoux	25
Old Muscat 18.vin cuit 3.vin cuit de Provence 17.	38
Barsac	20
Scuppernon 45 + 26. + 1	72
	386

received this day from Marseilles as follows

Muscat de Riversalte	150
Ledanon	150
Claret of Bergasse	144
Vin blanc de Limoux	150
	594

Whole stock on hand 62. gall. +   980

Statement of wines on hand Nov. 26. (1822)

	Jan. 7	Nov. 25	rcv'd Nov. 25	Total on hand
Ledanon	295	216	100	316
Claret	199	none	144	144
Limoux	175	114	75	189
Mouscat-				

Rivesalte 156	66	100	166
Scuppernon 72	31	–	31
Barsac 10	20	–	20

955	447	419	866

[1823 missing]

(Jan.) 9. (1824) Recd. of Raphael 85.D.

Rec. wines from Dodge & Oxnam

	old stock on hand	now rec'd	total
Ledanon	83	100	183
Claret	0	100	100
Limoux	4	25	29
Muscat	53	50	103
Suppernon	11	--	11
Barsac	20	--	20

	171	275	446

_Feb. 8. I desired Bernard Peyton to remit 62.85 to John Steele Collectr. Phila. duty & on wines.

Feb. 25, (1824) desired B. Payton to remit 146.D. to E. Copeland of Boston for Dodge and Oxnard for wines, etc. Note, Th. J. Randolph, part of this is 74.61

Dec. 9. (1824) desired B. Payton to remit to E. Copeland for Dodge and Oxnard 123..70-659-30 for wines & other articles just arrived from them, also 37.72 to Jonathan Thompson Collector of N.Y. for freight duties etc.

Dec. 18, (1824) – desired B. Peyton to remit 52.10 to E. Copeland for 5. cases of 50. bottles each of the wine of Bergasse and a cask of 30. galls. of table wine, or win. ordinaire from Dodge & Oxnard, and to Henry A. S. Dearborne 31.30 freight duties, etc.

Jan. 4, (1825) The wines, rec'd from Dodge & Oxnard Dec. 14 & this day

	for myself	for T.I.R.	Total
vin rouge de Bergasse	150	100	250
red wine of Ledanon	100	--	100
blanquette de Limoux	75	25	100
Muscat de Rivesalte	50	25	75
	375	150	525

My preceeding stock was all but out.

Jan. 21 (1826) desired Bernard Peyton to remit 39.37 to Jonathan Thompson N.Y. freight duties and charges on 300 bot. wine and 5. cases oil, anchovies, maccaronie, from Dodge & Oxnard Marseilles.

Feb. 1 – Stock of wine

	old stock on hand	now received	total
vin rouge			
de Bergassee	142	--	142
red Ladanon	37	150	187
blanquette de			
Limoux	49	--	49
Muscat			
de rivesalte	36	150	186
Claret from Richmond	22	--	22
	286		586

Scuppernon quant. suf.

References:
[1]Thomas Jefferson Memorial Foundation, Monticello.

MONTICELLO WINE GLASS ARCHAEOLOGY
Excavations Reveal Jefferson's Taste
By Anna Gruber & Hal Sharp[1]

Deposits deep underground and undisturbed since the time of the third President, have revealed an amazing number of wine glass and bottle artifacts...in 1794 he recorded having 1,600 bottles on hand.—Ed.

Since 1979, The Thomas Jefferson Memorial Foundation, Inc. has sponsored archaeology at Monticello as part of a continuing program of research and restoration. Excavations have revealed many thousands of artifacts relating to everyday life at Jefferson's home, and of these many involve the storage and serving of wine. Among the most common is the dark green glass of wine bottles, abundant on almost every site. In view of a typical entry from Jefferson's account books, this abundance is not surprising:

[July 24, 1794] Stacked the following empty bottles. English 261 long do. 160. French 670=1091...there are besides about 500 full bottles in the house...call the whole stock 1600.

These English and French bottles can be identified by form (Fig.1, a-d). Generally, English wine bottles during the early to mid-eighteenth century have wide stout bodies with short thick necks, while those of the late eighteenth to early nineteenth century are taller, with thinner bodies and long necks. The lips and the string rims (a band of glass just beneath the lip) are carefully worked. Eighteenth century French bottles, as Jefferson might note, are more graceful, usually broader at the shoulder than at the base and have tall thin necks, oftenwithout a lip at all. The string rims on French bottles, though, are not so carefully applied. A third variety, not positively identified because the differences are subtle, may be Dutch (Fig. 1, e); its most distinguishing features are rather crudely formed bodies and string rims.[2]

DUTCH STYLES

Six of these possibly Dutch bottles comprised perhaps the most remarkable find on the mountain. Discovered at the

Figure 1. Wine Bottles

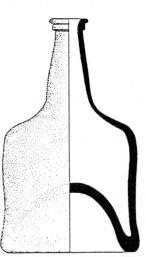 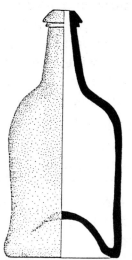 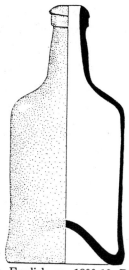

a. English, ca. 1750-70. Recovered from the dry well. Ht. 8 1/32".

b. English, ca. 1800-10. Recovered from a servant's house site. Ht. 8 1/2".

c. English, ca. 1800-10. Recovered from a servant's house site. Ht. 8 7/8".

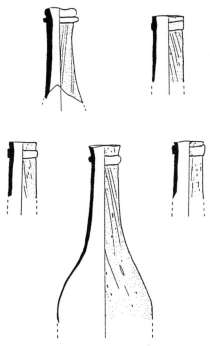 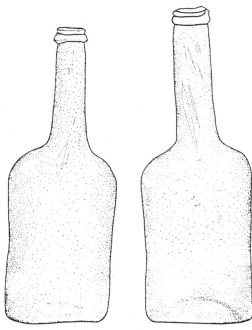

d. French wine bottle neck fragments recovered from the yard area north of the house.

e. Two of the six possibly Dutch bottles found with their contents of preserved fruit on the floor of the dry well. Ht. left 10 5/16", right 11".

bottom of a nineteen foot dry well, a storage cellar apparently constructed and abandoned in 1770-1771, five were intact and contained a quantity of preserved fruit.[3] That cherries and another fruit filled wine bottles indicates that although orginally manufactured for wine, these bottles possessed enough value to be used for other purposes as well; some wine bottles recovered from colonial sites have contained milk and paint.

While wine bottle glass is a frequent find on the mountain, wine bottle seals are quite rare. Excavators have only four of these glass insignia which possibly date to the Jefferson period (Fig. 2). Two seals are oval, marked "ST. JULIEN L. LAGUER-ENNE MÉDOC." The third is a fragment of an oval seal marked "ST. ESTE[PHE]," and the fourth is a complete round seal with a cluster of grapes on a vine and the embossed letters"CHATEAU LAFITE" beneath. All four are of green glass, and would have been pressed into the shoulder of wine bottles. We have no evidence that Jefferson ordered any St. Estephe wines, though "he did...receive in 1793, 504 bottles of a vin ordinaire called by his bordeaux agent" a Medoc of 1788."[4] Since both the St. Estephe and St. Julien communes produced Medoc wines near Bordeaux, perhaps these seals may be from the 1793 order. The source of the Chateau LaFite seal, however, is more ellusive. In 1788, Jefferson ordered 250 bottles of 1784 LaFite, but none were available. He did receive, as a substitute for an order he made in 1790 from George Washington, some 1786 LaFite, but this time, ordered none of that variety for himself.[5] If the LaFite seal is Jeffersonian, perhaps it is part of a gift.

DECANTERS

Excavations in deposits undisturbed since Jefferson's time have produced two wine decanters. Recovered from behind a section of the garden terrace retaining wall built in the spring of 1808, one survives only as a base. It is clear blown glass $4\frac{1}{16}$ inches in diameter and is rimmed with tapered ovoid facets cut into the edge. The other is an almost complete vessel from the dry well fill. This decanter is also of clear blown glass, and is in the 1760-1775 style with a wide sloping shoulder and a

Figure 3. Glass label decanter wheel-engraved "**MADEIRA**" ca. 1760-1775. Recovered from the dry well.

Figure 2. Wine Bottle Seals

    "CHATEAU LAFITE' Recovered from the kitchen yard.
Diam. 1¼".

    "St. JULIEN LAGUERENNE MEDOC" recovered from the yard
area of a servant's house

    "St. ESTE[PHE]" Recovered from the north yard area of
the North Pavilion.

slightly narrower base (Fig. 3). Its most interesting feature is the wheel-engraved design of a label, inscribed "MADEIRA," suspended from a chain around the neck and surrounded by a grape and vine motif. Unfortunately, its stopper finial still waits to be found.

Jefferson's Account Book shows that he ordered several sets of wine glasses throughout his life. Like the wine bottle glass, fragments of these goblets and glasses meet the eye on almost every site. Although only the heaviest parts usually survive intact — stems and the bottom of the bowls — archaeological work has produced a great variety of forms (Fig. 4). The bowls on this clear blown glass stemware vary from plain and undecorated styles to those which are cut and etched. The stems themselves range as well from plain forms to the more elaborate, including facets or knobs and air or enamalled twists. These stem and bowl designs provide the most important datable feature of wine glasses. Two bowl fragments, rimmed with a banded floral pattern above cut facets, appeared in excavations along Mulberry Row, and matched exactly two complete glasses said by family history to have been Jefferson's (Fig. 5). These artifacts provided conclusive evidence for the Foundation's decision to purchase the wine glasses, now on display.

VINEYARD DIGS

In addition to producing these tangible artifacts, archaeological fieldwork has examined important landscape features such as the south orchard and vineyard. excavations of these sites, located just below the terraced vegetable garden, revealed a regular pattern of dark soil stains against the surrounding red clay subsoil which in the orchard corresponded to Jefferson's plans for the distribution of fruit trees. Similarly, trenches in the vineyard area revealed "on the same axis as the orchard tree stains"[6] a less regular pattern of small post hole stains, probably made as laborers drove vine support posts into the ground. Further work uncovered more of these post holes; and based on both this archaeological evidence and the documentary sources, Jefferson's dream of a thriving vineyard on

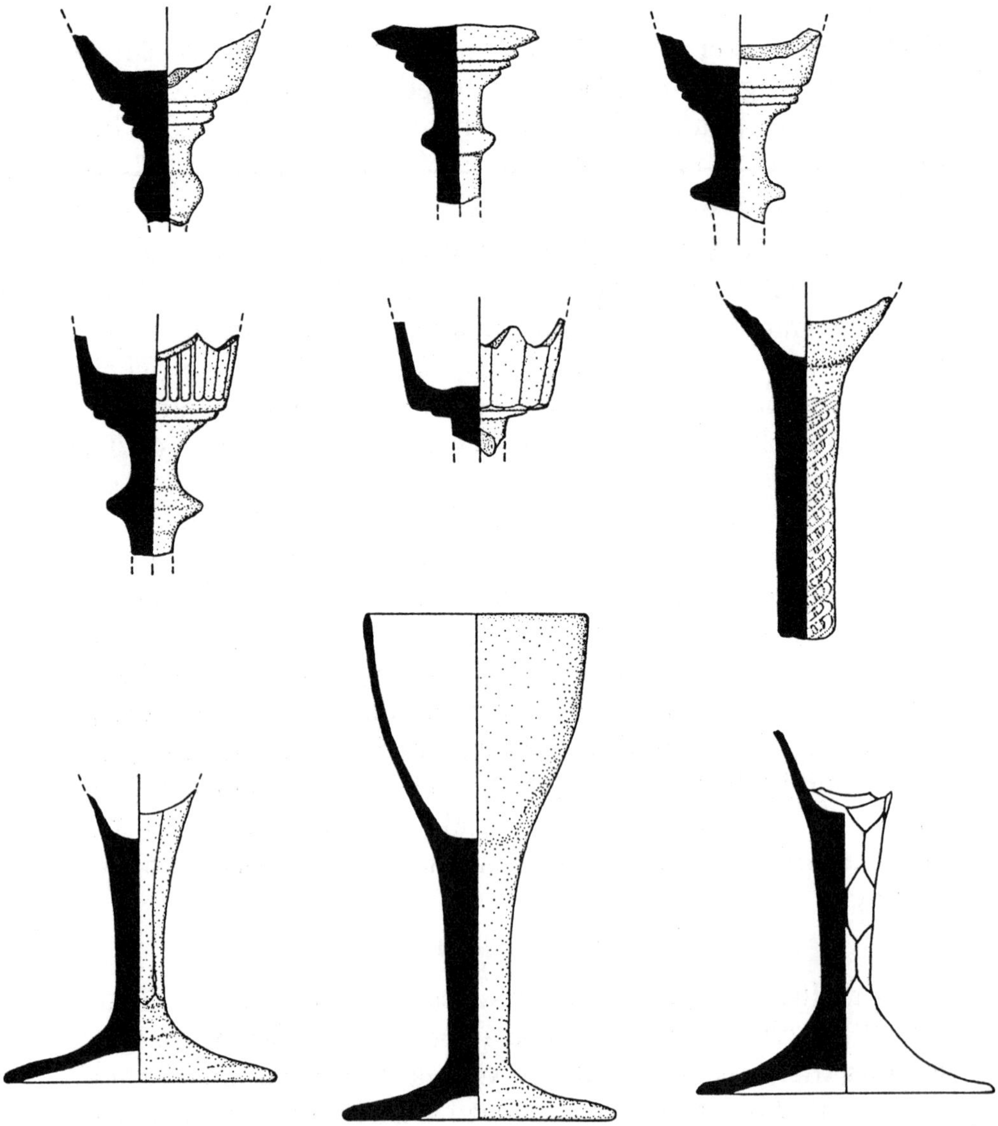

Figure 4. Wine Glasses

(top row) Knop and angular knob stems having stepped junctions with plain bowls. Early nineteenth century.

(middle row, left and center) Angular knop stem with facetted bowl and a facetted bowl fragment. Early nineteenth century.

(middle row, right) A straight stem with air twist decoration. Ca. 1735-1760.

(bottom row, left to right) A facetted stem fragment with a plain foot. A nearly complete wine glass with a plain foot and an undecorated stem and bowl. (last quarter of the eighteenth century). A stem fragment with cut hexagonal facets and a plain foot (ca. 1760-1770).

the mountain has been realized. While archaeological work at Monticello is far from complete, this method of research has been an important contribution not only to the rediscovery of Jefferson's wine related artifacts, but also to an increased understanding of plantation life in the early years of the Republic.

FIGURE 5. Two excavated wine glass bowl fragments with wheel-engraved floral rim pattern and two complete wine glasses with the identical engraved rim pattern (Possibly Irish, ca. 1780, height: 3 ⅝"). The complete wine glasses were an inheritance from Thomas Jefferson to Fanny Burke, Jefferson's great-great-granddaughter. She gave the glasses to members of the Hoes family, who are descendants of James Monroe, from whom the Foundation acquired them in 1984.

References:

[1]Archaeology Laboratory Supervisor and staff member respectively, Monticello, Dr. William M. Kelso, Director, P. O. Box 316, Charlottesville, Va. 22902, tel. 804/296-5245.

[2]Ivor Noel Hume, *A Guide to Artifacts of Colonial America*, Alfred A. Knopf: New York, 1974, pp.69-71.

[3]William M. Kelso, "A Report on the Archaeological Excavations at Monticello, Charlottesville, Virginia, 19716-1981," Manuscript: Thomas Jefferson Memorial Foundation, 1983, p.73.

[4]Lucia Stanton, "Saint-Estephe," Memorandum: Thomas Jefferson Memorial Foundation, 19. XI. 86.

[5]Lucia Stanton, "Research report: Chateau LaFite 1787, with initials 'Th. J.'," Manuscript: Thomas Jefferson Memorial Foundation, 12. XII. 85, p.2.

[6]William M. Kelso, "Archaeological Excavations, 1979-1981," p.48.

JEFFERSON'S PARIS WINES FOUND IN 1985
1787 Lafite Brings $157,500 At Auction[1]

No written evidence has been found that these particular bottles were in Jefferson's possession, however, scientific analysis says they are genuine. Monticello continues to look for evidence proving their authenticity,

Napoleon was a teenager when the 1787 vintage of Chateau Lafitte—as it was spelled then—was made in Bordeaux. Thomas Jefferson was American Ambassador to France that year, and he had for some years admired the quality of the table wines from that region. He regularly ordered wines of specific vintages he preferred.

In the spring of 1985, Mr. Hardy Rodenstock, a highly respected connoisseur and collector of fine old wine from Bad Marienburg, West Germany, was consigned about a dozen bottles of 18th century Bordeaux wines bearing Jefferson's initials etched on the bottles. He wrote the Association that the bottles were found in Paris behind a wall in a cellar. "We assume that the owner of this house at the time — Jefferson was at that time again in the U.S.A. — wanted to save the bottles from the French Revolution. The foundation walls of these houses came from around the time of 1750.

"The following wines were found: Chateau d'Yquem, Ch, Margau (Margaux,) Lafitte (today Chateau Lafite Rothschild), Brane Mouton (now Mouton Rothschild) and from the years 1784 and 1787. These vintages, as you would assume from the correspondence of Jefferson and the contemporary Chateau owners, were the best years, of that period.

"I drank with my wine loving friends one bottle each of the vintages of 1784 and 1787 of Chateau d'Yquem. Both were excellent, very dark in color, very sweet and not dry as we would have expected. I have had the corks and the wine tested in a laboratory. The cork originates from the time period of 1780 to 1800, and the wine also."

J. Michael Broadbent[2], Master of Wine and Director of the Wine Department, Christie's, was one of the distinguished few who took part in that tasting, by mainly German connoisseurs. He described the d'Yquem "...its colour as perfect pale for its age, old amber, bright and lively; bouquet perfect! Unbelievable. Scented vanilla and blancmange. On the palate, still sweet, with perfect weight, balance and acidity. Dry finish. Flavour of peaches and cream."

"LaFitte" 1787 With Jefferson"s Initials
Courtesy, Christie's London

He brought back to London with him the bottle of Lafite, having experienced difficulty in getting Mr. Rodenstock to part with it for auction. He showed it to Mr. Hugo Morley-Fletcher, director in charge of Christie's porcelain and glass department who verified the date of the bottle. More importantly, he said that the figures and letters on the side of the bottle are original and of contemporary wheel-engraving; that later engraving looks different.

Mr. Broadbent expressed the belief that Jefferson purchased the bottles in France and had them engraved for him–possibly in Paris, possibly through Mr. Bondfield (American Consul) in Bordeaux–when he placed the orders; that the engraved bottles were delivered to each respective chateau and when filled and sealed were returned to or via Bonfield who consigned them to Paris. "It would be typical," he wrote VWGA, "of Jefferson's logic: How better to identify what he bought, by vintage and chateau, and to differentiate his own stock from George Washington's." On the question of initials, Jefferson was known to have used several different abbreviations.

Mr. Broadbent added, "Incidentally–coincidentally–it was on December, 1766, that James Christie held his first ever auction. It included "Fine Claret." Lafite, spelled "Lafete" was first sold by Christie"s in 1788. The first *vintage* of claret was the 1771, at a Christie auction in 1776 and the first named *vintage* of Lafite was the 1802, sold by us in 1830."

Jefferson's bottle of 1787 Lafite is to the wine world what the Rembrandts and Renoirs are to the art world, even more so, being described by CBS television as "the most famous bottle of wine in the world." Christie's estimated the bottle might fetch $15,000. The VWGA said that it would bring more than $50,000. The highest price paid for a bottle of wine before was $38,000. This figure was smashed within a few seconds of the bidding. Marvin Shanken, New York collector of fine wines, pushed the bidding upward, but Christopher Forbes of the publishing family won the bottle at $157,500. That would come to about $1,890,000 per case!

Mr. Forbes complained of the price, Jefferson did too! Tasting of the wine would be "magical." The new owner has a collection in New York of Presidential memorabilia and placed the bottle on a table once owned by America's first viticulture scientist and premier wine connoisseur of his period.

VERY EARLY "CLARET"

Claret was the first wine to appear in a Christie Catalogue (5 December 1766) and the wines of Bordeaux have dominated the salesroom, virtually without a break, since that date. It was described simply as *Fine Claret "property of a Nobleman desceas'd"* and offered in 3-dozen lots (average lot size today), it sold for around 24 shillings per dozen.

The first Bordeaux vineyard to appear by name was *Lafete,* it was in a catalogue of 8 February 1788. Four dozen sold @66 shillings per dozen—a high price in those days.

The first *vintage* of Lafite to be catalogued was the 1802, in a sale on 30 June 1830. It was clearly English bottled for it was catalogued as *Sutton & Palmer's Lafitte* (sic) *of 1802*—and written in the auctioneer's hand *"two old on the report of Mr. Wheeler."*

Lafite tended to be spelled in various ways: *Lafete* (as in 1788), mainly *Lafitte* around the turn of the century, *La Fite* (in 1806) and even as *Ch. La Fille* (in 1802). *Chateau Margaux* also appeared variously as *Margous claret wine* (in Lord Hervey's wine accounts of 1706), *Chateau Margou* (1716), *Margon clarett* (1718), *Chatteau Margon claret* (1723), *Chateau Margoux* (1724) and in Christie's catalogues for the first time as *Ch. Margeau* (1788), *Ch. Margau* (1794), *Ch. Margot* (1802), *Ch. Margeaux,* (1822) and as now, *Ch. Margaux,* for the first time in 1833.

A Christie's Catalog reports, "Mr. Hardy Rodenstock, a collector well known to Christie's and undoubtedly the most respected connoisseur of old wines in Germany, purchased this bottle, together with other wines (mentioned in the catalogue), in Paris. They had been found in a very old bricked-up cellar.

"The precise whereabouts of the cellar is not known to us, nor is the history of the wine: whether it was from one of

Jefferson's residences; if not, how it had got there, or when.

"All we can say with certainty is that the bottle is of the correct date, the lettering and the wheel engraving are absolutely right for the period. The cork appears to be original and the cork of the 1787 Yquem from the same cellar has been checked in a German laboratory and their report is that it is original.

"There is an immense amount of circumstantial evidence supporting the ordering of this wine and its identification, but, of course, no proof.

"Jefferson's visit to Bordeaux in May 1787, though brief, was typically thorough. He quickly ascertained the finest vineyards, listing them in order of rank. He also found out the names of the leading merchants whom, incidentally, he invariably by-passed: it was his practice to order direct. Indeed, later that year, in December 1787, he wrote (for the first time) directly, to '*Monsieur Diquem*'...*for some small provision of white Sauterne wine for my own use during my residence in France, and the same after my return to America, whenever this will take place. I know yours is one of the best crus of Sauterne, and I would prefer to receive it directly from your hand,*(i.e. bottled at the chateau) *because I would be sure that it is genuine, good and sound. Permit me then Sir, to ask if you still have some of the Sauterne, finest quality, of the year 1784?...*' The bottles to be '*supplied*' and '*packaged*' '*under the inspection of your manager.*' The following month (7 January 1788) the Count of Lur-Saluces, ('*Mr. d'Yquem's son-in-law...and owner of all his assets*') replied that, having '*drawn*' from cask '*and bottled with the greatest care, the wine you ordered,*' he will be happy to handle his orders directly '*at any time you need.*'

"Jefferson, in a letter from Paris dated February 1788 referred to '*Chateau Margau, of the year 1784, bought by myself on the spot and therefore genuine.*' Around the same time he ordered direct from the proprietor '*the excellent wines called La Fite produced by your people*': 250 bottles of the 1784 if available and '*bottled at your place.*' Unfortunately, a consignment of the 1784 Haut-Brion was inadvertently shipped *'thro inattention'* with a considerable number of other wines to the *'Isl of France'* (sic). Whether a later consignment 1787 Lafitte, Ch. Margau etc. met the same fate it is hard to say, but that would not be impossible.

"When he returned to the United States, having established direct contact with all the major vineyard proprietors, he continued to order direct.

"In July 1790 he posted off a whole batch addressed in French to various chateau owners. They were sent via his former secretary in Paris and, typically methodically, he summarized his orders in a letter to his Bordeaux agents, Fenwick Mason & Co. (Joseph Fenwick was U.S. consul).

"For example, to the Count Miromenil [sic] of 'Segur' (La Tour de Segur, now Chateau Latour), requesting *'20 dozen bottles of your best wine of drinking now, to be bottled, packed and marked "G.W." at the vineyard.'* assuring the Count that if the wine was subsequently found to the President's and his (Th.J.'s) satisfaction there would be a regular annual order.

"Similarly worded letters were sent to a M. Lambert, to the Count of Lur Saluces and to other leading chateau proprietors.

"He was not always successful, for although Miromenil replied that his agent would contact Messrs. Fenwick, Mason & Co. *'to see them and make arrangements with them'* (repacking, shipping, etc.), Joseph Fenwick shortly after, in February 1791, wrote to Jefferson to say that Madame de Rausan's 'parcel' of wine had been received, and the Countess de Lus (sic) Saluces had said that hers (Yquem) was ready. However, he, Fenwick, had seen the *'homme d'affair'* at Segur who said he had *'no wine on hand to ship as a sample that will do justice to his estate,'* despite Miromenil's note to the effect that the order would be complied with.

"Fenwick added, helpfully, that *'we shall venture to send some wine of our own chusing'* (sic).

"The fact, therefore, that a wine such as Brane-Mouton (the Brane or Branne Family were then the owners of the vineyard now known as Chateau Mouton-Rothchild) was not specifically ordered by name, yet appears in bottles with his initials on, can be accounted for by Fenwick's letter. Indeed on 29 March 1791, Fenwick enclosed *an invoice for 14 cases for TJ and 14 for the President as ordered by TJ 6 Sep. 1790* noting that the wines of Lafite had replaced the Segur (Latour) which was unavailable.

PACKING AND DELIVERY

"The previous paragraphs refer to Jefferson's practice of ordering direct which, through the contacts made when he was ambassador in Paris, he continued on his return to the United States as Minister of State to George Washington and throughout his own two terms as President, from 1801 to 1809.

"In 1790 he wrote from Philadelphia to his former secretary in Paris that the President (George Washington) had requested him (Th.J.) to order a selection of French wines.

"This and subsequent letters emphasized how particular he was first to ensure that the wine was bottled at the chateau to guarantee its genuineness and condition, secondly to pack it carefully, third to identify the wine, fourthly to ship it at an appropriate time of the year when *'the heats are over, and that it should arrive at Philadelphia before the spring comes on. It will of course be in bottles'* (Th.J. to William Short, 12 August 1790).

"On 6 September 1790 he wrote from Philadelphia to his agent in Bordeaux, Joseph Fenwick: *'receive and forward some wines for the President and myself'* as per the *'inclosed letters to the respective owners of the vineyards '* and went on to summarize the quantities of each wine. Later in the letter he informed Fenwick that he had *'directed that those* (wines) *for the President to be packed separately and marked G.W. and mine T.I. (sic) You will receive them ready packed.'*

"From the owner of Segur (Latour) he ordered direct *'20 dozen bottles of your best wine for drinking now and marked* 'G.W.' *at the vineyard,'* to M. Lambert *'shipments to be marked as indicated above,'* To Count de Lur Saluces *'to be bottled, packed separately and marked as indicated above'*...all written in 1790.

IDENTIFICATION AND INITIALS Th.J.

"First of all, though it is abundantly clear from all the correspondence that Jefferson required the wines to be chateau-bottled and identified, the method of identification does not seem to be categorically specified. The word he used, in French, was 'etiquettes' (labelled).

"One can only assume that, knowing of Jefferson's meticulous attention to detail, indeed, fussiness, and that in Bordeaux they were dealing with a great connoisseur, supplying both him and the highest in the land, the President of the United States, the chateau proprietors and the Bordeaux agents, Fenwick Mason & Co. took the greatest pains to get everything right.

"Putting ourselves in Fenwick's place, we imagine that, to be on the safe side (bearing in mind that 'bottle tickets' or paper labels were not in use at that time, also that the wines were packed in large chests or hampers, not in conveniently identified 12-bottle boxes), they arranged that the bottles delivered to their cellars by the proprietors were immediately identified by getting a local artisan to engrave on the bottles themselves the name of the chateau, the vintage and whose stock it was, i.e. G.W. or T.J.

"Jefferson invariably signed letters to his former secretary, to his agents in Bordeaux and to the chateau proprietors *Th:Jefferson* (note the colon). Occasionally the initials T.I. are used, but the capital letter 'I' is really just a calligraphic version of a J with a straightened tail. This can frequently be seen in books on the subject, the tail usually being extended.

"It appears that he never wrote his initials without a colon after 'Th,' so it has been suggested that the initials 'Th.J' engraved on the bottle itself are incorrect...The initials were applied by a French engraver presumably on the instructions of either William Short or more likely, Jefferson's agent, Joseph Fenwick, and it seems logical that an artisan brought in to engrave the initials would have been used to a point or full stop after the 'Th.' rather than a colon which was, a strange affectation peculiar to Jefferson himself: it was in fact two dots either side of the upward stroke of the letter 'h.'

"It is significant that when ordering from the United States he did not specify any vintage, leaving it up to the proprietor to supply the best wine available—more than hinting that *only* the very best was good enough for himself and the President. For example, to Madame de Rausan, in 1790 *'Would you please send me ten dozen bottles of the best for drinking now.'* No mention of vintage. But the best would have been that of the 1787 vintage, still in cask but already to be bottled."

OPINIONS FROM GERMANY AND FRANCE

Opinions about the authenticity of the Jefferson wines were divided in two of the largest wine-producing nations in the world — Germany and France.

The English press had been seen to be generally favorable about the Paris cache, *The Times* of London and *Decanter* magazine reporting in detail about the tastings.[3] Noted British wine authority and author, Jancis Robinson, wrote in the former ("Sweet Taste of Legend at £5,000 a Sip"),

" ...The recent history of the wine remains a mystery, Rodenstock will not reveal how much he paid for it, or where it came from...Until now, nobody in the world had ever tasted a 199-year-old claret...far from being faded, this relic of pre-revolutionary days was richly juicy and fighting fit...It actually developed more flavour in the glass [1787 Brane Mouton] and after 20 minutes was the most exciting liquid I ever expect to drink. It was a deep blackish crimson, looking and tasting like a rather drier and lighter version of vintage port..."

Her article in *Decanter* referred to letters to the editor that questioned the circumstances of the discovery. Arthur Woods, Proprietor of Copper Beech Vineyards, Lindfield, West Sussex, expressed the opinion[4],

"...Nobody will be more pleased than I should real evidence surface that the Lafite 1787 in question was once the property of Thomas Jefferson. Until then I remain an admirer of the apostle Thomas, despite Jesus' mild rebuke, 'Blessed are they that have not seen and yet have believed.'   ...What is clear above everything is that the owner of the wines (for there are a number of bottles) Mr. Hardy Rodenstock, told nobody, least of all Christie's, where, when and by whom they were found."

Ch. D'Yquem "of The First Quality"
Vintage of 1784
Courtesy, Christie's London

The German media, being the homeland of the cache owner, published a great deal about the finding of the bottles, the tastings, and auctions of two bottles. Led by the prestigious, *Alles Ober Wein*[5], the most detailed reporting of the subject was covered, including the scientific aspects of examination by top experts of the wine, bottles, corks, and engraving,

"...The most expensive bottle in the world; 29 cm high, 9 cm wide, bright, hand made of blown, ambergreen brilliant glass, that on one side is coated with a thick dusty layer because of the long storage; on the other side clear and clean...the bottle is closed with the original seal and with a newer layer of wax seal over the original cork..." German opinion was essentially that the Paris wines were possessed by Jefferson.

French media, interestingly, while reporting the event with less coverage, have in general been more skeptical. An example being an account prepared by one of its leading experts, M. Jean-François Bazin of the *La Revue du Vin de France*[6]. Some of the questions he posed were related also to the tasting of a bottle of Chateau d'Yquem at Wiesbaden, Oct. 1985, a bottle of Brane Mouton 1787 at Mouton, June 1986 and a bottle of Yquem 1787 at Yquem,

"...When a bottle attributed to a famous person is sold for more than a million francs, it is normal to want to know the origin...Why should he [Rodenstock] protect so jealously this secret. The knowledge of the building, of its past, of the history of its occupants could easily explain the existence of these bottles...Why did this collection contain only the great growths of Bordeaux, perfectly identified and identifiable, even though the process of engraving bottles was rare? ...The engraving evidently took place at the same time for all these bottles. No doubt in Paris. But why? The possibility of the confusion with another collector with the same initials? Impossible, since the 'Th.J' engraved on the bottles was a perfect reproduction of the writing of the great man. It is just this resemblance which inspires doubt. It is too good..."

News of the discovery of the Paris wines captivated authorities at Monticello, and high hopes were held—and still are—

that the bottles could be proven to have belonged to Jefferson. Very extensive research had already been conducted in this facet of his life, as evinced by the first edition of "Jefferson And Wine". Every effort was made to find a relationship in the enormous amount of data that has been studied and re-studied. The result was a detailed report[7] by the Director of Research, Lucia C. Stanton, herself a wine devotee and well-traveled in France. Although no correlation could be found, hope continues that some documentary or archeological evidence will turn up someday. Research will go on.

Optimism will also continue in the minds of all who honor Jefferson and who have a fondness for the moderate beverage as he did, along with respect for the knowledge and integrity of experts in Germany, France and England involved in this fascinating bit of wine history. Perhaps and best way to sum it all up is to say, "the authenticity cannot be proved; but the cynics cannot disprove."

References:

[1]VWGA *Journal*, Fall 1985, pp. 144-147, Winter, pp. 217-223, and Spring 1986, pp. 6-11.

[2]Master of Wine, Director, Wine Department, Christie's, 8 King Street, St. James, London SWIY 6QT.

[3]*Sunday Times*, June 15, 1986, London; *Decanter Magazine*, London, September 1986.

[4]*Decanter*, June 1986.

[5]March 1985, January 1986, and March 1986.

[6]*La Gazette du Palais*, Dec. 1987 (?), 65, Rue de Montmartre, 75002, Paris.

[7]Research Report: Chateau Lafite 1787, with initials "Th. J.". Thomas Jefferson Memorial Foundation, Monticello, Dec. 12, 1985.

JEFFERSON'S DREAM COMES TRUE
Virginia's 41 Farm Wineries and 200 Vineyards

By James E. Mays[1]

> *Wine being among the earliest luxuries in which we indulge ourselves, it is desirable it should be made here and we have every soil, aspect and climate of the best wine countries..."*

Thomas Jefferson was certainly on the right track. It's just that he was ahead of his time.

Now, 212 years after the Declaration of Independence, Jefferson's vision of vine-clad slopes in the Blue Ridge has become a reality. Indeed, from the Piedmont to the Atlantic flatlands, new as well as old varieties of grapes are responding to the advanced viticultural techniques available to this generation, making it possible to predict with confidence the rise of a significant grape and wine industry in the Old Dominion.

Jefferson's objective was to produce high-quality wines, wines in the style and character of the great wines of Europe which he learned early to appreciate and then further sharpened his appreciation during his years in France.

That is precisely the same objective the present-day experimenters have set for themselves. The current effort is shared by people from all walks of life – by amateur and professional viticulturists and enologist alike, by doctors, lawyers, farmers, housewives, investors, you name it.

The point is that when the "grape bug" bites, it bites hard and for keeps. The beginner whose initial goal is to produce some stylish wines for his family and his friends soon finds himself fascinated by the growing of the grapes. Before long he is deeply into such esoteric viticultural considerations as varietal selection and clones, rootstocks and grafting, pest and disease control, head pruning versus cane pruning and the relative merits of Kniffin, Munson, Cordon, Geneva Double Curtain and other trellising systems. He finds there is fascination enough for a lifetime, and the more he learns the more he wants to know.

And why does he think he can succeed where Jefferson failed?

The answer lies in a combination of historical accident and some 20 generations of slow but nevertheless steady progress in viticultural science.

Jefferson's efforts to grow the Vinifera wine grapes (the European species) were foredoomed to failure. It would be some 50 years after his death, however, before the reasons became apparent. That's where the historical accident comes in, but what began as an accident ended in tragedy for the European vineyards.

ROOT LOUSE TRAGEDY

Some American vines were shipped to France for experimental purposes. On their roots they carried some tiny root aphids called *phylloxera*, a vine root pest previously unknown in Europe but which infests all North American soils.

Through centuries of natural adaptation, the wiry, woody roots of the native American species of grapes had developed resistance to *phylloxera* in varying degrees depending upon the species.

For example, the American species known as Vitis Labrusca – the so-called American "fox grapes" – of which the commercially important table and jelly grape variety Concord is perhaps the most famous representative, is moderately but not totally resistant to *phylloxera*. Vitis Riparia – the American "sand bank" or "river bank" grape – also show good resistance, while Vitis Rotundifolia – the Muscadine grape of the South – is totally resistant.

On the other hand, the slightly fleshier, slightly tenderer roots of the European grapes have no resistance at all. Thus, within a few years after the accidental introduction of phylloxera into France the vineyards of that nation were destroyed in what became known as the "great wine panic", one of the worst, if not the very worst agricultural disaster in all recorded history. Many of the great French vignerons fled their country to establish vineyards in Spain, North Africa, Australia, South

America and California, all areas where phylloxera was un-known.

Back in France, government and wine industry leaders frantically searched for an answer. Eventually they hit upon the idea of grafting Vinifera scions onto American grape roots resistant to *phylloxera*. It was expensive, it was troublesome, but it worked. Vineyards that had produced for centuries were uprooted and replanted with grafts, millions upon millions of American roots being imported to France for that purpose.

GRAFTING SOLUTION

But because grafting was troublesome and expensive, the French simultaneously pursued a second avenue that seemed to offer promise. The objective was to develop hybrids that would combine the wine qualities of the classic French varieties and the *phylloxera* resistance of the American grapes.

A word of explanation is in order. Normally, grape varieties are reproduced aesexually, That is, they are reproduced by cuttings. A plant so reproduced is exactly like the plant from which the cutting was taken. Even after generations of such reproduction, the very latest plant so reproduced will be in every way a precise duplicate of the plant from which the very first cutting was taken.

New varieties of grapes come only through fertilizing the flowers of one variety with pollen of another variety, and then planting the seed from the cross-pollinated fruit. The plant that grows from the seed will be a new and different variety, combining in limitless combinations the good and bad qualities of the parent plant.

In the wake of the *phylloxera* problem and the troublesome and expensive solution that grafting presented, the French went to work to develop through hybridization what they called "producteurs direct" (direct producers), i.e., high quality wine grapes that could be grown on their own roots. Millions of crosses, backcrosses, and re-backcrosses, were made and tested. Those that did not measure up in terms of *phylloxera* resis-tance, wine quality and resistance to vine diseases were ruthlessly eliminated. The surviving varieties – about 100 of them – became known as the French-American hybrids, or merely as the French hybrids.

Had Thomas Jefferson only known why his European grapes died, he might have tried grafting them to the roots of the native grapes that grew wild in the woods on the very slopes of Monticello. Gratfing is an ancient practice, and Jefferson's journals reveal that he was thoroughly familiar with it. Apparently it just never occurred to him to try it on grapes, or, he recorded nothing in his records if he did.

Or again, had he known the problem was *phylloxera* he might even have tried hybridizing his European grapes with pollen from the wild native species. There is no evidence that he tried either, but then he was pretty busy indulging in what CBS Newsman Charles Kuralt calls his "passion for liberty".

At any rate, by the time he had retired from the Presidency he had reluctantly concluded that further experiments with Vinifera grapes would not be worth the effort. In 1809, he wrote John Adlum:

"I think it will be well to push the culture of that grape (the American variety called Alexander) without losing time and effort in search of foreign vines, which it will take centuries to adapt to our soil and climate."

Even if Jefferson had tried grafting and hybridizing, he still would have been faced with a formidable array of pests and diseases which plague the vine in the humid climate of eastern North America.

Foremost among these are the fungi diseases – black rot, powdery mildew, downy mildew, dead-arm and anthracnose, all controllable now.

Insect control also would have been a serious problem for both grafted vines and hybrids in Jefferson's time. Control of insects is vital, not only to reduce the physical damage to vine, leaves and fruits, but also for control of virus diseases vectored by insects. Leafhoppers, for example, are known to vector Pierce's Disease, one of the most dangerous, incurable diseases of grapes.

VIRGINIA DEVELOPS IT'S INDUSTRY

The modern-day Virginia premium wine industry *could* have had its beginning in the early 1960's when Dr. George D. Oberle was experimenting with grape varieties and other fruits at the University of Virginia Polytechnic Institute, Blacksburg. A native of Geneva, New York, and with early training there in the state's agricultural experiment station, he observed successful trials with French Hybrid varieties and conducted his own experiments with them and Vinifera also at VPI. He stated the latter were a failure. Details of his cultural practices were not reported, and it was not known if he had used the sophisticated fungi sprays that were coming on to the market for many types of fruits. A VPI report, "Grape Growing in Virginia", February 1972, did not even mention the word *Vinifera*, the species that alone makes the finest table wines. It was therefore the policy of the noted agricultural university for ten years or more to down grade the "first quality" potential that Jefferson so passionately campaigned for.

The next known introduction of experimental Vinifera into Virginia occurred in about 1966, when Eastern Airlines pilot Charles Raney purchased retirement land near Warrenton, and brought down from his home on Long Island, New York, "a handful" of Vinifera vines he had planted. He and his wife went on to plant a vineyard they named "Farfelu", using almost entirely French Hybrid vines.

In 1968, a vineyard was planted at Highbury Farm, between The Plains and Middleburg, in northern Virginia[2]. The proprietor could only find Hybrid vines to plant at the time, but hearing about the success in 1969 of Dr. Konstantin D. Frank's experiments with Vinifera at Hammondsport, New York, the noble Chardonnay, Pinot Noir, Riesling and other Eurpean varietals were planted in 1970, all gifts of the generous refugee from Russian Communism.[3] Using fungicides that protected the fruit in the apple and peach orchards, the Vinifera thrived, their first wine being made in 1972. As the result of this success, the viniculture news spread, and using Highbury as a model experimental vineyard, the non-profit Vinifera Wine Growers Association was organized in 1973.

The volunteers' first task was to teach the planting of vineyards using Vinifera vines. Seminars and courses in wine-growing and winemaking were given in The Plains, Middle-burg, Fairfax, Winchester, and Charlottesville. A twice-yearly *Journal* was started in 1974 (now quarterly and much enlarged) to provide how-to-do-it information and promote the "new" agricultural enterprise. Usually this work is undertaken by the Ag Extension services of the state, but when none was forthcoming from VPI an open letter was addressed to the governor[4] urging him to use his powers to encourage premium wine growing and foster a program to develop the potential. There was no reply, and it was not until about 1976 before VPI began to take some action. Many good years were lost. Mean-while commercial size vineyards (over half acre) began to appear on many Piedmont hillsides, often with wineries. In 1976, year of the Bicentennial anniversary, dedicated volun-teers conducted the first wine festival in Virginia at Middleburg, with the objective of both observing this important Jeffersonian occasion and also to raise funds to enlarge the *Journal* to a quarterly publication. This was successful. While at first almost all members of the Association were from Virginia, word had spread and the membership today is about eighty percent from other states. A national organization for vinicul-ture and enology was born, with its magazine circulating to almost every state and to 14 foreign countries. Some 60 librar-ies and institutions, both in the U.S. and abroad maintain full sets of back issues for current and long term reference.

HIS DREAM COMES TRUE

Over two hundred years after Jefferson planted his grape vines at Monticello, thousands of Vinifera vines, Cabernet Sauvignon, Pinot Noir, Pinot Chardonnay and Riesling began going into the ground on the site of the plantation of his old friend James S. Barbour. (illustration next page)

The stately ruins of the mansion that Jefferson helped design will be restored, and the rolling Piedmont land has seen the addition of thousands of premium wine vines by the Barboursville Vineyard and Winery Corporation. Financed by Italian capital and advised and assisted by the Vinifera Wine Growers Association, this was one of the first large Vinifera investments east of California. Headed by Dr. Gianni Zonin of the respected Zonin Wine Company of Vicenza, Italy, he was tempted to make a multi-million dollar investment in Virginia when he learned that Vinifera could now be grown profitably

Barboursville Vineyard

here. His wines have earned international fame.

One of the next, and most significant in size, of foreign investments, was the planting of Prince Michel Vineyards near Culpeper. Under the capable and friendly direction of Joachim Hollerith, general manager of the VAVIN Company, the largest by far of all Vinifera vineyards in the Commonwealth State (110 acres) was planted and produces award winning vines. He is a member of a winegrowing family in Germany that traces its viniculture connection over three hundred years.

A third foreign winegrowing connection of special note was the arrival at Ingleside Plantation Vineyards, Oak Grove (in the Tidewater country), of Professor Jacques Recht, from Belgium who possessed a European enology reputation. Ingleside, already a very large plantation vineyard, was vaulted into prominence with the arrival of Dr. Recht whose wines began to collect more awards than any other Virginia vineyard.

Outstanding from another point of view was the establishment in coastal Jamestown–site of the first settler's landing–of Williamsburg Vineyard and Winery by the Patrick G. Duffeler family. This was the spot where Captain John Smith exclaimed about the abundance of grapes growing in the trees and incorrectly predicted there would be unlimited winegrowing on the coast of the new continent. The Duffelers were the first after some 375 years to successfully plant the Vinifera and make a quality wine in this heretofore inhospitable climate. They were awarded the Vinifera Association's Grape/Wine Productivity Champagne tray.

The non-profit organization is especially indebted to another premium vineyard, Swedenburg Winery & Vineyard, Middleburg, near Washington, D.C. Considered by many to be the most beautiful and picturesque in the state, its vineyard sloping down to the very old stone house and the Blue Ridge Mountains in the background, this is the site of the premier Virginia wine festival, held every year the last Saturday in August by the Vinifera Association. The proprietors, Mr. and Mrs. Wayne Swedenburg, are a retired Department of State Foreign Service couple who were attracted by the beauty of the grape and taste of the wine, refined by many years in the diplomatic service. After growing Chardonnay and Riesling of the highest quality at five tons to the acre, they built their own winery which is producing wines that Mr. Jefferson would be very proud of.

The third President considered himself first and foremost, a farmer. He would therefore especially applaud one of the most unique vineyard ventures in the country, the Virginia Winery Cooperative, Culpeper, because it was organized and placed in production by about twenty wine farmers who did not choose to build their own wineries. By working together in the true farm cooperative style, they raised about $1.5 million and built a chalet-styled winery on a hill overlooking U.S. Route 29. Surrounded by three and a half acres of its own Vinifera vines, the Co-op under the trade name of Dominion Wine Cellars has won many awards, including Best-of-Show in the Virginia Wine Competition conducted annually by the Vinifera Association.

Yes, Mr. Jefferson's dream has truly come true as visitors enjoy the wines of 40 licensed farm wineries and the graceful sight of over 200 commercial-size vineyards, mainly in the higher Piedmont region just where he predicted they would be one day.

References:

[1]Mr. Mays, Radio and TV, Norfolk, was president, Tidewater Wine & Growers Society, and proprietor of his own Virginia Beach Vineyard, 5320 Gale Drive, VA. Beach, VA. 23464.

[2]By the Editor.

[3]VWGA *Journal,* Fall 1985, "Association Honors Dr. Frank," pp. 194-199.

[4]"The Piedmont Virginian", April 5, 1972, "Governor is Urged to Encourage Wine Industry".

APPENDIX A

To Monsieur le Comte de Neuville

Monticello, December 13, 1818.

I thank your Excellency for the notice with which your letters favor me, of the liberation of France from the occupation of the allied powers. To no one, not a native, will it give more pleasure. In the desolation of Europe, to gratify the atrocious caprices of Bonaparte, France sinned much; but she has suffered more than retaliation. Once relieved from the incubus of her late oppression, she will rise like a giant from her slumbers. Her soil and climate, her arts and eminent sciences, her central position and free Constitution, will soon make her greater than she ever was. And I am a false prophet, if she does not at some future day, remind of her sufferings those who have inflicted them the most eagerly. I hope, however, she will be quiet for the present, and risk no new troubles. Her Constitution, as now amended, gives as much of self-government as perhaps she can yet bear, and will give more, when the habits of order shall have prepared her to receive more. Besides the gratitude which every American owes her, as our sole ally during the War of Independence, I am additionally affectioned by the friendships I contracted there, by the good dispositions I witnessed, and by the courtesies I received.

I rejoice, as a moralist, at the prospect of a reduction of the duties on wine, by our national legislature. It is an error to view a tax on that liquor as merely a tax on the rich. It is a prohibition of its use to the middling class of our citizens, and a condemnation of them to the poison of whiskey, which is desolating their houses. No nation is drunken where wine is cheap; and none sober, where the dearness of wine substitutes ardent spirits as the common beverage. It is, in truth, the only antidote to the bane of whiskey. Fix but the duty at the rate of other merchandise, and we can drink wine here as cheap as we do grog; and who will not prefer it? Its extended use will carry health and comfort to a much enlarged circle. Every one in easy circumstances (as the bulk of our citizens are) will prefer it to the poison to which they are now driven by their government. And the treasury itself will find that a penny apiece from a dozen, is more than a groat from a single one. This reformation, however, will require time. Our merchants know nothing of the infinite variety of cheap and good wines to be had in Europe; and particularly in France, in Italy, and the Grecian islands; as they know little also, of the variety of excellent manufactures and comforts to be had anywhere out of England. Nor will these things be known, nor of course called for here, until he native merchants of those countries, to whom they are known, shall bring them forward, exhibit and vend them at the moderate profits they can afford. This alone will procure them familiarity with us, and the preference they merit in competition with corresponding articles now in use.

Our family renew with pleasure their recollections of your kind visit to Monticello, and join me in tendering sincere assurances of the gratification it afforded us, and of our great esteem and respectful consideration.

Reference:

The Writings of Thomas Jefferson, Vol. XV, p. 177, 1907 edited by Albert E. Bergh, Washington, D.C.

APPENDIX B
CURRENCIES AND MEASURES
[Approximate and Varying]

These are 18th century measures and monetary values that Jefferson listed in his tour notes and other writings, referring to British, French, Portugese, German and United States usage. They often vary in his own calculations. This confusion of systems probably helped to prompt him to prepare studies on coinage. In the winter of 1783-84 he had advocated the adoption of the dollar to be divided into tenths and hundredths. The following were used in the text:

MONETARY

Cent (Br. sterling) – 2 sous (Fr.)

Dollar (U.S.) – 4 ½ shillings (Br.)

Dollar – 20 cents (Br.)

Ecu (Fr.) – 5 francs

Ecu – 1 ½ florin (Ger.)

Franc (Fr.) – 19 cents (U.S.)

Florin – 6 shillings

Gourdes 1 doz. btl. wine @ 2 Gourdes per dozen

Guinea (Br.) – 30 livres (Fr. pounds)

Kreitzer (Ger.) – ⅓ florin

Livre (Fr.) – a pound of 12 ounces

Livre (Fr.) – 20 cents (U.S.)

Livre – 20 sous (Fr.)

Livre –143 reis (Portugal)

Louis (Fr.) – 24 livres

Pound (Br.) – 5 dollars

Pound (Br.) – 2.5 livres

Shilling (Br.) – 22 cents (U.S.)

Sou (Fr.) – 1 cent (U.S.)

Sou – 1/20 livre

Sou – ½ cent (Br.)   Sol (Fr.) – early term for "sou"

MEASURES

Arpent (Fr.) – 1¼ acres	League (Fr.) – 2 ½ miles
Aume (Fr.) – 170 bottles	Liter – 1.05 gallons, (U.S.)
Aume – 42 ½ gallons	Mile (Fr.) – 1 ¼ U.S. mile
Aume – 1/6 foudre	Mile (Fr.) – 1000 toises
Basket (Fr.) – packs 62 bottles	Piece – cask (200 bottles)
Barrique (Fr.) – 215 bottles	Pipe (Fr.) – 110 gallons (U.S.)
Caisse (Fr. case) – 36 bottles	Pipe (Fr.) – 2 hogsheads
Cask (varying) – 168 bottles	Pipe (Fr.) – ½ tun
Demi Piece (Fr.) – ½ cask (Bordeaux)	Toise (Fr.) – 6.4 feet
Feuille (Fr.) – 100 bottles	Tun (Fr.) – 252 gallons (U.S.)
Feuillette (Fr.) – 114 to 136 liters	Tun – 953 liters
Feuillette (Burgundy) – ½ cask	Tun – 8 aumes
Foudre (Fr.) – 6 aumes (255 gals. U.S.)	
Futaille (Fr.) – 124 bottles	
Hogshead – 63 gallons (U.S.)	

Note: The French vineyard worker earned about 20 sous per day, the women half that much or as low as 8 sous per day.

Monetary Equivalents 1784 Through 1789

France	England	Holland	Virginia	United States
24$^\pi$(Louis)	1 pound	10ƒ16	26/8	$4.40
6$^\pi$	5/	2ƒ14	6/8	$1.10
1$^\pi$	10d	9s	1/1⅓	$ .18416

France: 12 deniers = 1 sou; 20 sous = 1 livre tournois; 24 livres = 1 louis d'or.

England: 12 pence = 1 shilling; 20 shillings = 1 pound; 21 shillings = 1 guinea.

Holland: 20 stivers = 1 florin.

d   Penny or denier

s   Shilling, sou or stiver

f and π lovre tounois

†   Florin

£   Pound sterling

/   Shilling

Note: these equivalents, which were subject to fluctuation during the cited period, are approximate and only for the purpose of a more complete understanding of TJ's expenditures.

———————————

APPENDIX C
The Wine Company

The formation of a wine company was the interesting scheme by the fertile brain of Philip Mazzei, who had arrived at Williamsburg from Leghorn, Italy, in Nov. 1773, under the sponsorship of TJ's merchant friend Thomas Adams. He was warmly received in Virginia and was induced by TJ to undertake his experiments in viniculture on a plantation near Monticello which Mazzei named Colle. He appears to have begun them early in 1774, for TJ's Fee Book and Miscellaneous Accounts contain two pages of entries with *The Wine Company* for the period April 6, 1774 to Feb. 11, 1778. The coming of the Revolution prevented the plan from materializing despite it's promising beginnings. (see pp. 19, 23, 29, 176) The projects undertaken seem to refer to wingrowing only. (Boyd, 1774, pp. 156-158)

Plan of Philip Mazzei's Agricultural Company

[1774]

Proposals for forming a Company or Partnership, for the Purpose of raising and making Wine, Oil, agruminous Plants and Silk

1. So much money as may be procured, shall be subscribed in shares of fifty Pounds Sterling each, and in all Proceedings of the Company a Vote shall be allowed for every share; the Subscribers of smaller sums than fifty Pounds, being at liberty to associate in shares, and appoint any one of their Number to vote for such share.

2. Such shares shall not be subject to the Rights of Survivorship; and if any Proprietor shall at any time be disposed to sell out his Part, the Company shall have the Refusal of it, giving for the same, as much as any other person will give: but none to be at liberty to withdraw their Part, until the thirty first day of December 1784.

3. The Monies subscribed shall be paid by the Subscribers, at the City of Williamsburg, to Philip Mazzei Esquire, or any other person to be appointed, as hereafter directed, or in their absence to Robert Carter Nicholas Esquire, in manner following; that is to say, one fourth part shall be paid on or before the first day of November 1774, and one other fourth part at the end of every six Months after, til the whole be paid, which Payments shall be made, either in Sterling, or in other money, at the rate of Exchange then current: and where any Subscribers shall come in after one or more Payments shall have been made, they shall make present Payment of such Proportion of their subscription, as the former Subscribers shall have already paid, and shall pay the residue at the same Times it is payable by the said former Subscribers: and if at any time it shall happen, that any payment shall be one Month in arrear, and unpaid, such Subscriber, so in arrear, shall forfeit his former Payments, and all Interest in the said Partnership, which shall thereon become vested in the residue of the Partners.

4. The said Philip Mazzei is to invest or employ the Monies to be received, as he shall think best for the Purposes aforesaid, and to superintend the said Business, as Factor for the said Company, for which he is to draw from the Proffits, or principal Money paid, five per centum per annum, on the capital sum subscribed, besides being at liberty to use for his Table or Houshold, such necessaries, as may be raised on the Lands of the Company.

5. That any Lands, or other Possessions of the said Philip Mazzei, which he may at this time have, and which are proper for the purposes of the said Partnership, after being valued by three men indifferently chosen by the said Philip Mazzei, and any five of the Partners, shall be taken at such valuation as part of the said Philip Mazzei's subscription, and together with the

Lands, Slaves, Servants, Utensils and other things to be purchased with the monies of the Company, shall become vested in the Subscribers, their Heirs, Executors, Administrators, or assigns, in proportion to the several sums they shall have subscribed.

6. That the expences of carrying on the Business be defrayed out of the Monies subscribed, so that there be no future calls on the Partners, for any other sums of money.

7. That the said Philip Mazzei shall on the last day of December in every year, during the Partnership, make up an Account of all his Buyings, Sellings, Receipts and disbursements whatsoever, made on account of the said Partnership, of which Accounts a Copy shall be lodged in the Hands of Robert Carter Nicholas Esqr. for the free perusal of the Parties interested.

8. That a standing Committee shall be appointed to consist of his Excellency Earl Dunmore, the Honble. John Page of Rosewell Esqr. the Honble. Peyton Randolph Esqr., Robert C. Nicholas, Thomas Nelson Junr., John Blair, Wilson Miles Cary and James McClurg Esqrs. any three of whom may proceed to business. Whose Business it shall be from time to time to give advice to the said Philip Mazzei, or other Factor for the time being, on all matters, relating to the Affairs of the Company, and, whenever they shall think requisite, to call a meeting of the Subscribers, fifteen of whom, possessing or representing not less than fifteen whole shares, may proceed to Business: and such meeting may if a Majority concur in Opinion have power to fill up an Vacancies, which may happen in the standing Committee, to regulate the Salary of the Factor for the time being, to appoint such other person, as they shall think proper, to be Factor, in case of the death, or removal of the said Philip Mazzei, to appoint any other person to be Holder of the Monies belonging to the Company, and to make Dividends of the annual Proffits, if they shall

think that more beneficial to the Company, than adding the same to the Capital would be.

N.B. Subscribers to the Original, or other papers are marked *

*Dunmore, four shares.

*Peyton Randolph,£50. Stel:

*R. C. Nicholas, two shares,

*Thos. Adams, one share.

*James Donald, one share.

*G Mason, one share.

*Go: Washington, one share.

*John Page, one share

*John Page of Rosewell one share

*Joseph Scott, & Ths. Pleasants one share

*Th: Jefferson one share,

*Benja. Harrison, Brandon, one share on condition that he may withdraw his subscription in case, that any slaves should be purchased on account of the Company.

*Thomas M. Randolph, one share.

*James McClurg one share.

*Peter Randolph, one share.

*Thos. Nelson jr., one share

*Richd. & Everard Meade one share

*John Tabb one share

 Chars. Carter Junr. one Share

*Richard Randolph one share

*Mann Page Junr., & Hugh Nelson one share

N.B. It is requested as a favour of those Gentlemen who are

*John Banister one share

*John Blair one share

*Theo: Bland Jr. one share

*John Tayloe one share

*Archbald Cary one share

*Wilson Miles Cary one share

*Jams. Parke Farley one share

John Parke Custis [none?]

*Robert Pleasants, one share

*William Murray one share

*Rayland Randolph one share

*Allen Cocke one share

*Philip Mazzei four shares

*Daniel L. Hilton one share

Kind enough to procure Subscribers, that when any new Subscribers are added to the list, they will transmit their names
to Robt. C. Nicholas Esqr., or the Factor.

———————————

PRINTING ACKNOWLEDGEMENTS

<u>Typesetting</u>:

Canon A-200 EX, HD-20, Desk Top Publishing System. Vinifera Wine Growers Assoc., The Plains, Va.

<u>Printing</u>:

Piedmont Press

Warrenton, Va.

<u>Binding</u>:

Shenandoah Valley Bindery,
New Market, Va.